LAWYERING IMPERIAL ENCOUNTERS

Lawyering Imperial Encounters revisits the relationship between the African continent and global capitalism since the nineteenth-century Scramble. Focused on sites of imperial encounters – in London, Paris, Abidjan, Bujumbura, Kinshasa, Johannesburg or the Hague – it provides an unprecedented account of the correlation between the legacy of legal imperialism and British hegemony, and the uneven and unequal expansion of finance and global justice in the current rush for Africa's 'green' minerals. Tracking the role played by legal intermediaries to negotiate and justify Africa's practical and symbolic subaltern position in the global economy, it demonstrates the interconnectedness between political, legal and economic change in capitalism's cores and its so-called peripheries. Embracing the global turn in sociology, history and legal scholarship, it rubs against the functionalist account of global value chains as engines of development. It also constitutes a powerful post-colonial critique of law's double bind – as both enabler and bulwark against domination.

SARA DEZALAY is a lawyer and political sociologist. She is a professor at the European School of Political and Social Sciences, Université Catholique de Lille, associate researcher at the Institut des Mondes Africains and former adjunct judge at the French national court for asylum seekers.

GLOBAL LAW SERIES

The series provides unique perspectives on the way globalization is radically altering the study, discipline, and practice of law. Featuring innovative books in this growing field, the series explores those bodies of law which are becoming global in their application, and the newly emerging interdependency and interaction of different legal systems. It covers all major branches of the law and includes work on legal theory, history, and the methodology of legal practice and jurisprudence under conditions of globalization. Offering a major platform on global law, these books provide essential reading for students and scholars of comparative, international, and transnational law.

Series Editors

M. E. A. Goodwin
Tilburg University

Randall Lesaffer
KU Leuven & Tilburg University

David Nelken
King's College London

Han Somsen
Tilburg University

Books in the Series

Intimations of Global Law
Neil Walker

Legalized Families in the Era of Bordered Globalization
Daphna Hacker

Transnational Sustainability Laws
Phillip Paiement

The Sociology of Law and the Global Transformation of Democracy
Chris Thornhill

Authority and the Globalisation of Inclusion and Exclusion
Hans Lindahl

Property Law in a Globalizing World
Amnon Lehavi

The Law of the List: UN Counterterrorism Sanctions and the Politics of Global Security Law
Gavin Sullivan

Democratic Crisis and Global Constitutional Law
Christopher Thornhill

The Redress of Law: Globalisation, Constitutionalism and Market Capture
Emilios Christodoulidis

9/11 and the Rise of Global Anti-Terrorism Law
Arianna Vedaschi and Kim L. Scheppele

On Tyranny and the Global Legal Order
Aoife O'Donoghue

Entangled Legalities beyond the State
Nico Krisch

Designing Indicators for a Plural Legal World
Siddharth Peter de Souza

LAWYERING IMPERIAL ENCOUNTERS

Negotiating Africa's Relationship with the World Economy

SARA DEZALAY
Université Catholique de Lille

CAMBRIDGE
UNIVERSITY PRESS

CAMBRIDGE
UNIVERSITY PRESS

Shaftesbury Road, Cambridge CB2 8EA, United Kingdom

One Liberty Plaza, 20th Floor, New York, NY 10006, USA

477 Williamstown Road, Port Melbourne, VIC 3207, Australia

314–321, 3rd Floor, Plot 3, Splendor Forum, Jasola District Centre, New Delhi – 110025, India

103 Penang Road, #05-06/07, Visioncrest Commercial, Singapore 238467

Cambridge University Press is part of Cambridge University Press & Assessment, a department of the University of Cambridge.

We share the University's mission to contribute to society through the pursuit of education, learning and research at the highest international levels of excellence.

www.cambridge.org
Information on this title: www.cambridge.org/9781009493369

DOI: 10.1017/9781009493352

First published 2024

A catalog record for this publication is available from the British Library.

Library of Congress Cataloging-in-Publication Data
Names: Dezalay, Sara, author.
Title: Lawyering imperial encounters : negotiating Africa's relationship with the world economy / Sara Dezalay, Université Catholique de Lille.
Description: Cambridge, United Kingdom ; New York, NY : Cambridge University Press, 2024. | Series: Global law series | Includes bibliographical references and index.
Identifiers: LCCN 2024019495 (print) | LCCN 2024019496 (ebook) | ISBN 9781009493369 (hardback) | ISBN 9781009493277 (paperback) | ISBN 9781009493352 (epub)
Subjects: LCSH: Foreign trade regulation–Africa–History. | Africa–Foreign economic relations–History. | Africa–Economic pollicy–History. | Great Britain–Colonies–Africa–History. | Mining law–Africa. | Africa–Politics and government–History. | International law–Africa. | Lawfare–Africa. | Imperialism. | Capitalism.
Classification: LCC KQC947 .D49 2024 (print) | LCC KQC947 (ebook) | DDC 343.8608–dc23/eng/20240509
LC record available at https://lccn.loc.gov/2024019495
LC ebook record available at https://lccn.loc.gov/2024019496

ISBN 978-1-009-49336-9 Hardback

CONTENTS

Acknowledgements vii
List of Abbreviations x

Introduction 1
I.1 Tracking Symbolic Value between Law, GVCs and Finance 3
I.2 Bringing the Past Back In, in an *Interconnected* Way 11
I.3 'Tracking' *Legal Intermediation* and *Imperial Encounters* 13
I.4 Structure of the Book 16

1 **Imperial Encounters: Localities, Institutions, Structures** 20
1.1 The Politics of Scattered Knowledge 23
1.2 The Legacy of Double-Edged Protection 26
1.3 Big Structures, Local Histories 32
1.4 Zooming In and Out 39
1.5 Lawyering: Critical Junctures and Scales 42

2 **Indirect Rule and Middle Power: 1880s–1950s** 45
2.1 Middle Power *Within* and *Across* European Empires 48
2.2 Gold Coast Juridical Battles 54
2.3 Lawyering the Congo Free State 59
2.4 Pre-independence Military Trials 63
2.5 Conclusion 67

3 **Gatekeeper States and Offshore Capitalism: 1950s–1980s** 72
3.1 France's Post-colonial Block 75
3.2 The Lure of Nationalisation 82
3.3 Revamping the City *as* Middle Power 88
3.4 Competing Legal Ordering Claims 91
3.5 Conclusion 96

4 **The New Scramble, Deregulation, Re-regulation: 1980s–?** 98
4.1 The 'Real' Post-colonial Order 102
4.2 Big Business, Big Law 107
4.3 Middle Power Unshackled 113
4.4 Conclusion 121

5 **Bujumbura: Hyperviolence and Hyperlegality** 125
5.1 Mercenaries, Missionaries and Merchants 128
5.2 Decentralised Despotism 137
5.3 Negotiating Burundi's Transition 143
5.4 Conclusion 148

6 **Abidjan: Lawfare and Accountability Dumping** 154
6.1 Cocoa Gatekeeping Politics 157
6.2 Dismantling the 'Post-colonial Block' 163
6.3 Accountability Dumping 168
6.4 Conclusion 176

7 **Paris: The 'Africa' Corporate Bar – Imperial Revivals and Neoliberalism** 179
7.1 From Françafrique.inc to Public–Private Gatekeeping 181
7.2 Between *Courtroom* and *Corridor* Politics 188
7.3 The Twist of Imperial Redux 193
7.4 Conclusion 198

8 **The Value of Social Class in Global Justice** 204
8.1 Inter/National Justice in Paris 205
8.2 Repeat Players and Inter/National Justice 207
8.3 Professional Cartels and Echo Chambers 211
8.4 The Symbolic Market of Justice 213
8.5 Symbolic Gateways and Institutional Highways 221
8.6 Conclusion 230

Conclusion 232
C.1 The Past Matters, in a Sedimented Way 235
C.2 Tracking Borders of Encounter: A Research *Manifesto* 239

References 243
Index 261

ACKNOWLEDGEMENTS

This book is no exception. It is the result of many encounters.

In many ways, it started as a journey at the 2014 Law and Society Annual Meeting. I had travelled to Minneapolis with a project – coordinating a special issue of the French journal of African politics, *Politique africaine* on lawyers and state transformations in Africa. The project was vague. The topic was surprisingly subversive for political scientists, yet strangely appealing to three big men of the Law and Society who shaped my next decade, as friends and mentors: Rick Abel, Dave Trubek and David Wilkins. It was only as the years went by that I understood what stakes all three had with Africa. I thank you for giving me the first nudge, and Rick for patiently, and generously, supporting my academic journey since between Frankfurt, Cardiff and Lille and foremost for reading through my (very) long (and often obscure) sentences.

It is in Minneapolis, too, that I was introduced to a wonderful young scholar and friend, Swethaa Ballakrishnen, with whom I started a six-year inquiry on the imperial entanglements of Law and Society. Working with Swethaa taught me the empowering strength of collective research. You helped me understand that research networks are also a bulwark against gender, national and disciplinary boundaries.

Thanks to Jan Budniok and Alexander Stroh, who engineered two workshops bringing together scholars from Africa, Europe and North America, I met some of the colleagues who helped me question the puzzling knowledge gap on African lawyers, including Sophie Andreetta, Peter Brett and Jarpa Dawuni. That same year, again, the formidable Ulrike Schultz introduced me to the late and sorely missed Wesley Pue at the International Working Group for Comparative Studies of Legal Professions.

These first encounters built the tracks of what developed into the thread of this book: the relationship between law, globalisation, finance and political power. Thank you, Jonathan Klaaren and Wolf Maier, for espousing the quest for interdisciplinary dialogue across social and earth sciences to consolidate my understanding of the 'new rush' for Africa's 'green' minerals. Thank you, Ole Hammerslev, for your gentle friendship, and Hilary Sommerlad, for your careful reading of what turned into the first iterations of the thread of this book – as two chapters in the monumental volumes you co-coordinated with Rick and Ulrike on *Lawyers in 21st-Century Societies.* Thank you, Christine Deslaurier, for your friendship, for introducing me to the serious business of research ... and that of partying in Burundi. Thank you, too, Sharon Weill, for your unabated intellectual curiosity and telling me to stop rewriting my introductions.

Research would not be possible without mentorship and institutional support. In this I have been blessed with the mentorship of David Boucher at the Cardiff School of Law and Politics, and the friendship of many colleagues along the way, including Romain Bertrand, Philippe Bonditti, Jérôme Bourdieu, Michelle Burgis-Kasthala, Kerstin Carlson, Olivier Corten, Vincent Foucher, Jeremy Gould, Branwen Gruffydd Jones, the regretted Helen Hartnell, Anne Harrington, John Harrington, Jay Krishnan, Stefan Kroll, Anne Lagerwall, Ambreena Manji, Sol Picciotto, Franck Poupeau and Simone Tholens. Thank you, Antoine Vauchez, for believing in my project, to the members of the jury of my Habilitation à diriger des recherches, Marielle Debos, Julian Go, Rainer Maria Kiesow, Sandrine Lefranc and Laurent Willemez, and the book's reviewers, for your generous feedback on my work.

Some of these colleagues were friends and became colleagues. I have kept the notes of my 2019 ramblings about this book with Stefan Donecker. You left this world too early, after a mighty fight. Feel hugged, always. Thank you, Florence Brisset-Foucault and Marie Brossier. Thank you, Isaline Bergamaschi, for your laughter and helping me forget about my damned *problématique.*

Some are friends and keep me running: Pauline Abadie, Hélène Adihou, Estella Bauer, Mélodie Beaujeu, Anne Boigeol, Jean-Yves Caro, Dov Jacobs, Geoffroy Fauquier, Electra Kyriazis, Valérie Raynaud, David Robert, Salvatore Saguès and Nathalie Wade. Thank you for helping me ride through life with my head up.

Some of these colleagues were family from the onset – Ron Levi, Ronit Dinovitzer and, of course, Bryant G. Garth. You have always been a second father to me, and the big brother and sister I always craved.

Writing is a mightily lonely process. It is not when you know you will be read by this one person who will lovingly, yet nonetheless uncompromisingly, nudge you to make it just this little bit better. Thank you,

Yves Dezalay and Berenice Cleeve, for teaching me to believe in the power of words. I hope someday I will also be proud of my own journey as a parent.

Elena, this book is for you.

ABBREVIATIONS

ALSF	African Legal Support Facility
AOF	Afrique-Occidentale française (French West Africa)
ARPS	Aborigines' Rights Protection Society
ASF	Avocats Sans Frontières
AU	African Union
BSAC	British South Africa Company
CAISTAB	Caisse de stabilisation et de soutien des prix des productions agricoles
CAJAC	China-Africa Joint Arbitration Centre
CCFD	Terre solidaire Comité Catholique contre la Faim et pour le Développement
CCJ	Caribbean Court of Justice
CFTC	Commodity Futures Trading Commission
CNDA	Cour nationale du droit d'asile (National Court of Asylum, France)
CNDD-FDD	National Council for the Defense of Democracy – Forces for the Defense of Democracy
DAC	Development Assistance Committee of the OECD
DFC	US International Development Finance Corporation
DRC	Democratic Republic of the Congo, Congo
EACA	East African Court of Appeal
EACJ	East African Court of Justice
EALS	East Africa Law Society
ECCAS	Economic Community of Central African States
ECCHR	European Centre for Constitutional and Human Rights
ECHR	European Court of Human Rights
ECOWAS	Economic Community of West African States
EEC	European Economic Community
EGC	Entreprise Générale du Cobalt
ÉIC	État indépendant du Congo (Congo Free State)
EU	European Union
FCPA	Foreign Corrupt Practices Act
FDI	Foreign Direct Investment

FIDH	Fédération internationale pour les droits humains (International Federation for Human Rights)
FRODEBU	Front pour la démocratie du Burundi (Front for Democracy in Burundi)
GDP	Gross Domestic Product
GTP	Global Traders Programme
GVA	gross value added
GVCs	global value chains
IBC	International Business Company
ICC	International Criminal Court
ICC in Paris	International Court of Arbitration of the Paris International Chamber of Commerce
ICCO	International Cocoa Organization
ICJ	International Court of Justice
ICSID	International Centre for Settlement of Investment Disputes – World Bank Group
ICTR	International Criminal Tribunal for Rwanda
IDI	Institut de droit international (Institute of International Law)
IFIs	international financial institutions
IGLP	Institute for Global Law & Policy – Harvard Law School
IMF	International Monetary Fund
IMTFE	International Military Tribunal for the Far East
INGO	international non-governmental organisation
IO	international organisation
ISDA	International Swaps and Derivatives Association
ISDS	investor-state dispute settlement
JCPC	Judicial Committee of the Privy Council (Privy Council)
LDH	Human Rights League (Ligue des droits de l'Homme et du citoyen)
LID	Living Income Differential
Li-ion battery	Lithium-ion battery
LME	London Metal Exchange
MIFERMA	Mines de fer de la Mauritanie
MPF	Brazilian Ministério Público Federal
MSF	Médecins sans frontières (Doctors Without Borders)
MTLD	Movement for the Triumph of Democratic Liberties
NGO	non-governmental organisation
NIEO	New International Economic Order
ODA	Official Development Assistance
OECD	Organisation for Economic Cooperation and Development
OFPRA	Office Français de Protection des Réfugiés et des Apatrides (French Office for the Protection of Refugees and Stateless Persons)

OHADA	Organisation pour l'harmonisation en Afrique du droit des affaires (Organisation for the Harmonisation of Business Law in Africa)
OPEC	Organization of the Petroleum Exporting Countries
PCA	Permanent Court of Arbitration
PCIJ	Permanent Court of International Justice
PDCI-RDA	Democratic Party of Côte d'Ivoire – African Democratic Rally (Rassemblement Démocratique Africain (Côte d'Ivoire))
SEC	Securities and Exchange Commission (United States)
SFO	Serious Fraud Office (United Kingdom)
TNCs	transnational corporations
TTIP	Transatlantic Trade and Investment Partnership
UNCITRAL	United Nations Commission on International Trade Law
UNCTAD	United Nations Conference on Trade and Development
UNHCR	United Nations High Commissioner for Refugees
UNOC	United Nations Operation in Congo
UPRONA	Union pour le progrès national (Union for National Progress)
USAID	United States Agency for International Development
WACA	West African Court of Appeal
WB	World Bank

Introduction

On 17 July 2012, the Judicial Committee of the Privy Council (JCPC), also known as the Privy Council, one of the apex courts of the British judicial system and former appeals court of the British Empire, gave a decision that shifted the power balance in a long-standing judicial struggle between FG Hemisphere Associates LLC and the Democratic Republic of the Congo (DRC or Congo).[1]

FG Hemisphere is a vulture fund incorporated in the state of Delaware, a tax haven in the United States. Like other vulture funds, it specialises in the purchase of distressed assets (the debt of poor countries or corporations facing bankruptcy) at a cheap rate, and wages multi-front legal wars to recover the debts with an expected 'profit of 3 to 20 times the investment' (Sookun 2010: 8).

The FG Hemisphere case relates to a complex series of post-award legal proceedings over the course of the past twenty years (see Smis et al. 2021). In the 1980s, what was then Zaire (current Congo) entered into a construction agreement with Energoinvest, a then Yugoslav corporation. Energoinvest was to build a hydroelectric facility and high-tension transmission lines. According to the credit agreement, Energoinvest was to finance the project through a Congolese state-owned intermediary, the *Société nationale d'électricité*. When the DRC defaulted, Energoinvest invoked the arbitral clauses included in the agreement and successfully obtained two arbitral awards in 2003, in Switzerland and France respectively, rendered under the aegis of the International Court of Arbitration of the Paris International Chamber of Commerce (ICC in Paris).

FG Hemisphere allegedly paid US$ 3.3 million to redeem the debt. While the original debt totalled around US$ 34 million minus interests, FG Hemisphere claimed over US$ 100 million including interests and the costs of the two ICC in Paris arbitral proceedings. It deployed an

[1] La Générale des Carrières et des Mines (Appellant) *v.* FG Hemisphere Associates LLC (Respondent), Privy Council Appeal No 0061 of 2011 [2012] UKPC 27.

aggressive multi-front legal war to enforce the awards against assets (real estate and bank accounts) owned by the *Générale des Carrières et des Mines*, often called simply Gécamines, the main Congolese metals and mineral trading company. This included proceedings in Jersey, where Gécamines owned shareholdings in a joint venture company called Groupement du Terril du Lubumbashi Ltd that processes the cobalt-rich Lubumbashi tailings, and in Hong Kong, where China Railway Group Ltd, a Chinese state-owned enterprise which had concluded a joint-venture agreement with the Congo, was listed on the Hong Kong Stock Exchange and where its subsidiaries were incorporated.

In the Jersey lawsuit, FG Hemisphere sought to claim Gécamines' shares in the Groupement du Terril de Lumbumbashi and the Groupement's payments to Gécamines for the tailings, worth tens of millions of dollars a year. In Hong Kong, FG Hemisphere was trying to block the second half of a US$ 350 million signing bonus the Chinese investor owed for Sicomines, the large minerals-for-infrastructure project set up as part of the 2007 'deal of the century' between China and the DRC (Carter Centre 2017: 39).

The substantive content of the Privy Council decision is interesting. Contrary to courts in Belgium, Bermuda, South Africa and the United States where FG Hemisphere managed to recover some of the debt, the British court found that Gécamines was an entity distinct from the state, and, as such, FG Hemisphere was unable to enforce DRC debts against Gécamines' assets.

The judicial process that led to the Privy Council as an appeals court is the puzzling part. The Privy Council was seized to appeal a 2011 Jersey Court of Appeal decision which found that Gécamines was an organ of the state. In its rationale, the Privy Council espoused a 2010 decision by the Hong Kong Court of Final Appeal which concluded the opposite.

Both Jersey and Hong Kong are at once part and not part of Britain. Jersey is a self-governing parliamentary democracy under a constitutional monarchy, with its own financial, legal and judicial systems. But Jersey has retained the jurisdiction of the Privy Council in London as its apex court. As part of Hong Kong's 1997 handover to China, the Common Law system continues to be practiced as constitutionally guaranteed, making the city the only Common Law jurisdiction within China. Nevertheless, the Hong Court of Final Appeal was pressured into submitting the matter for constitutional interpretation to the Chinese Central Authorities which found that it related to China's foreign relations, must be interpreted by (mainland) Chinese courts and that absolute immunity of the Congolese state must be upheld.

Thus, a fund incorporated in a tax haven, Delaware, sought to recover assets from a corporation, Gécamines, formally incorporated into a commercial company under private law in 2010 but which is widely known to be a state within the Congolese state (Carter Centre 2017) in a tax haven, Jersey, that is at once part and not part of Britain, and Hong Kong, a former British colony that is at once autonomous and part of the Commonwealth and Mainland China.

I.1 Tracking Symbolic Value between Law, GVCs and Finance

Lawyering Imperial Encounters argues that the example of the *FG Hemisphere* v. *DRC* dispute is *not* an exceptional case. The British Privy Council decision goes well beyond national jurisdictional divides. It harks back in complex ways to the blurry divisions between state/non-state entities and between offshore and onshore capitalism that are shaping divisions between states and societies and capitalism's so-called cores and its peripheries.

The exceptionality of this example, rather, relates to the visibility of the parties involved, and foremost its financial stakes. The *FG Hemisphere* v. *DRC* dispute brings together remote actors, institutions and processes – mineral value chains on the one hand, 'offshore' financial flows on the other – in a way that appears natural only due to the 'reforming common sense' (to use Topalov's (1999) expression) that shapes the understanding of what the Congolese *state* is and how it should be reformed.

If the DRC had not been the target of a myriad of advocacy campaigns and policy moves since the 1990s from the United States, the Organisation for Economic Cooperation and Development (OECD), the European Union (EU) and non-governmental organisations (NGOs) drawing a direct link between the 'digital minerals' of Congo (cobalt, coltan, copper), the exceptional violence of conflicts in the Great Lakes region and the phones and other 'smart' devices of our everyday lives (Vogel 2022), the judicial saga that brought FG Hemisphere to the Privy Council based on two ICC in Paris awards would have remained invisible. Arbitration, by definition, is rendered behind closed doors. Awards are rarely public.

The hyper-visibility of the DRC as both a high-risk site for foreign investors and a magnet of geopolitical rivalries as the main reservoir of one of the critical minerals required for the 'digital' revolution and the post-carbon transition – cobalt – enabled the reconstruction of the FG

Hemisphere judicial saga into a *legal dispute* across jurisdictional divides, to use Felstiner et al.'s (1980–1981) terminology.

It is precisely because this case involves apparently disconnected geographical sites and legal institutions that the FG Hemisphere saga provides a startling starting point to the puzzle that is at the core of *Lawyering Imperial Encounters.*

How can we make sense of the entanglement between the imperial past imprinted in this case (illustrated by the core role played by the Privy Council), the articulation between financial markets, tax havens and states and the roles played by inter/national law and dispute settlement institutions (national courts and international arbitration forums) across the various local nodes of the economic, political and legal components of the dispute?

Lawyering Imperial Encounters argues that *seeing* these links matters. Looking at the raw materials that shape our daily lives – cobalt and rare earths as the critical minerals of the digital revolution and the energy transition, coffee, cocoa and beer, but also the toxic residues generated by the extraction of raw commodities and the 'reverse' value chains leading to their disposal in countries of the African South – *Lawyering Imperial Encounters* revisits the long history of extraction between Africa and the world economy as *a history of the present.*

It does so by tracking *legal and judicial chains* like the FG Hemisphere saga as Petri dishes of the social and professional networks, the norms and the institutions that shape, justify and transform the uneven and unequal relationship between the African South and the world economy.

Identifying the combination of variables (social, professional, normative and institutional) that contribute to the production of the legal categories that shape the relationship between the African South and globalisation provides us with a history of the present because it uncovers how boundaries between what is perceived as *public* (like the state) and *private* (like business interests), *legal* and *illegal*, between the so-called *core(s)* of the world economy and its *peripheries* are transformed, and foremost justified.

Due to the hyper-visibility of the parties and financial stakes involved in the example of the FG Hemisphere judicial saga, law seems to be an apparently obvious entry point to draw this history. It can also be a siren's call due to three sets of *black boxes* that usually characterise the relationship between law, global value chains (GVCs), symbolic power and historical change.

I.1.1 Using Law Not Wisely, but Too Well

In a global economy shaped by GVCs, law is everywhere: from the informal transactions between artisanal miners and the individuals holding the '*comptoirs*' at Kolwezi in the mineral-rich eastern region of the DRC, to the concession agreements negotiated between Gécamines and transnational corporations operating in the country; from the procurement contract between the (primarily) Chinese state-owned companies that manufacture lithium-ion (Li-ion) batteries and the corporate intermediaries in the United States and Europe which assemble them for use in the automobile industry or by tech giants. Law is also a core driver in the financialisation of minerals, including cobalt.

Law is what is going to make a tech giant like Apple cringe if consumers are alerted to the reliance on 'blood minerals' or child labour in the supply chain that produces their smartphones. Law is also the cutting edge of the DRC's relationship with the world economy. Congo has 'historically been constructed in global public imaginaries [as a] type of weak, permeable underbelly of global extraction that is both backwards and in need of civilisation, but also savage and dangerous'.[2] Proceedings against individuals involved as politicians, militiamen and former child soldiers in the Congolese wars of the 1990s have fuelled the docket of the International Criminal Court (ICC) since it became operational in 2003, all the while enabling the contested court to continue existing (Dezalay S 2020a). Just in the past decade, dozens of lawsuits and arbitration disputes involving mining contracts and violence in and around extractive sites in the DRC have been introduced across the world, ranging from a federal action lawsuit in 2019 against Apple, Google and other tech giants in the US filed by the NGO IRAdvocates, a criminal complaint in 2012 by the NGO Avocats sans frontières (ASF) in the DRC against militaries operating at the service of a subsidiary of the Swiss and German timber manufacturer Danzer, to a criminal complaint in 2013 by the European Centre for Constitutional and Human Rights (ECCHR) and Global Witness in Germany, this time against a senior manager of Danzer, to the legal saga pitting FG Hemisphere against the Congolese state.

Global scrutiny over Congo's mineral wealth has also been high on the map of international non-governmental organisations' (INGOs)

[2] E-International Relations, 'Interview – Christoph Vogel' 21 July 2023, www.e-ir.info/2023/07/21/interview-christoph-vogel/ (accessed 22 November 2023).

campaigns, like Global Witness, since the 1990s. The exceptional violence of the Far West-like rush for minerals during that decade, unleashed by the privatisation of state-owned extraction companies fostered by structural adjustment programs, was fuelled by, as much as it exacerbated, what has been dubbed Africa's World War.

But these advocacy campaigns and regulatory initiatives were deployed 'in a game of catch-up where the damage of the initial regulatory gaps has never fully been assessed' (Rosenblum 2016). Ongoing media and judicial battles on the detrimental societal and environmental effects of extractive deals between transnational corporations and resource-rich African states continue to stress the acuteness of contests over the distribution of natural resources and benefits derived from them. They also pinpoint loopholes in the reach of global regulations (Cutler and Dietz 2017) and the difficulty (if not total lack) of judicial remedies available to disenfranchised communities at the national and international levels (Muir Watt et al. 2019).

This framing justifies new forms of regulation aimed at cutting the link between violence, finance and GVCs. Yet law also mediates contradictory geopolitical, social and economic interests when it helps ascertain, depending on the context and shareholders, that the Congolese state is a sound partner for foreign investors, or, on the contrary, a failed state, or that Gécamines is part of the private sphere – that of business – rather than an incarnation of the Congolese state.

Likewise, the financialisation of primary commodities, enabled by future derivatives, can lead to extremely low or high prices for raw materials. Both extremes have proven catastrophic. Here too the role of law could seem obvious: '[w]ith the support of a regulator that requires transparency [...] it is claimed that investors will be in the position to account for the present and future externalities produced by actors in the value chains and make informed sustainable decisions that sanction unsustainable models and will result in a victory for the people and the planet while rewarding virtuous capital' (Ferrando 2020).

However, due to the 'endogenous nature of law in the definition of sustainable and unsustainable practices, and of the notion of sustainability itself', law 'becomes completely irrelevant, and with it the redistributive implications of a system of "sustainable" rent-seeking' (Ferrando 2020).

I.1.2 Symbolic Value: GVCs' Missing Link

The second problem relates to the perception of GVCs. Broadly speaking, GVCs refer to international production sharing, a phenomenon where production is broken into activities and tasks carried out in different countries. Cross-border production is largely seen to have been made possible by the liberalisation of trade and investment, lower transport costs, advances in information and communication technology, and logistical innovations (e.g. containerisation).

GVCs are also usually understood to be driven by the expansion of transnational corporations (TNCs) primarily headquartered in advanced economies, which consolidate their international operations by controlling and coordinating international production networks consisting of multiple firms – including third parties with no equity links to them (what is otherwise known as international outsourcing) headquartered or operating in other national jurisdictions.

According to some estimates, GVCs 'governed' by TNCs account for 80 per cent of world trade each year (UNCTAD 2018). 'The underlying assumption is that because GVCs allow developing countries to focus on individual links in the chain, their firms can integrate with the world economy "on a shoestring" without facing the large risks (and costs) incurred by investing in all the tasks required for producing the finished product or services' (UNCTAD 2018: 50).

Africa remains predominantly integrated to GVCs through what are called *forward* linkages in the sense that resource-rich African countries and/or raw commodity producers supply these commodities as inputs that are used for production in other countries. Emblematically, in 2018, mining contracts between African states and transnational corporations were worth a total of US$ 47 billion[3] – just a little under the total flow of Official Development Assistance (ODA) that same year to sub-Saharan Africa which constitutes – by far – the biggest recipient of ODA (OECD 2018).

For exporting African states, the *value* of minerals and raw commodities, in economic terms, is supposed to be mainly accrued through tax returns – that is, the royalties paid by foreign investors to host states on exported raw commodities and unrefined minerals.

But where does Gécamines – and for that matter, FG Hemisphere – feature in the celebratory pitch about the inclusive growth and shared prosperity fostered by GVCs in an era of hyper-globalisation?

The nickname 'vulture fund' labels FG Hemisphere as a profiteer. Yet, by definition, vulture funds are *risk* investors – the rationale behind the

[3] Investing in African mining Indaba, 'The largest mineral industry in the world' 19 December 2019, www.miningindaba.com/Articles/infographic-the-african-mining-sector-in-numb (accessed 22 November 2023).

risk taken by private investment firms and hedge funds in suing sovereign award-debtors, who, depending on national jurisdictions, may benefit from sovereign immunity and are therefore likely to default, is the high profit margin between the actual investment and the expected returns. In a 2013 Resolution, the UN Human Rights Council 'condemn[ed] the activities of vulture funds for the direct negative effect that the debt repayment to those funds, under predatory conditions, has on the capacity of Governments to fulfil their human rights obligations'.[4] The 'problem' of vulture funds, therefore, harks back to the 'morally outrageous outcome' of their venture (Sookun 2010: 7).

But this moral critique masks the financialisation of sovereign debt. It also overlooks the entanglement between states, GVCs and financial markets. Gécamines constitutes an anomaly for the common understanding of GVCs. One of the largest mining companies on the African continent, the biggest in the DRC, Gécamines is headquartered in Lubumbashi, in the Katanga region, and sits on the world's greatest deposit of cobalt. Transformed into a commercial company in 2010 – with the state as sole shareholder – it formally engages in the exploration, research, exploitation and production of mineral deposits, including copper and cobalt. But, in practice, it does not directly conduct extraction activities.

The adoption of a new mining code in 2003, under the pressure of the World Bank, aimed at liberalising the DRC's mining sector and attracting foreign investors. Yet a subtle transitional clause enabled Gécamines to retain ownership over the exploitation rights of its most valuable concessions. 'Using these provisions, Gécamines conceded some of its titles to fully private companies. More often, however, Gécamines would only partially privatize its titles. In such cases, it would concede one or several titles to a joint venture in which it would get a minority stake' (Carter Centre 2017: 21). Gécamines therefore acts as the de facto gatekeeper to Congo's mineral wealth.

Thus, in the framework of the so-called 2007 'deal of the century' between China and the DRC, Gécamines got into a joint venture with China Railway Group Ltd. Under the joint venture agreement, Congo was to be paid US$ 221 million by the China Railway's subsidiaries, as

[4] Human Rights Council, Resolution 27/30 Effects of foreign debt and other related international financial obligations of States on the full enjoyment of all human rights, particularly economic, social and cultural rights: the activities of vulture funds' United Nations General Assembly, A/HR/RES/27/30, 3 October 2014.

part of the entry fees for a mining project (Smis et al. 2021: 13). On the other hand, Gécamines held shares in the Jersey venture company called *Groupement pour le traitement du Terril de Lumumbashi.*

It is precisely this regulatory framework and financial trail that position Gécamines as a *transnational* corporation with the ability to wage either the 'corporate veil'[5] or state immunity to protect its assets in other jurisdictions. But this significantly complexifies the common understanding of the Li-ion battery value chain from cobalt extraction in the DRC, refining and manufacturing in China, to assembly into final products (be they electric cars or smartphones) in Europe and the United States.

Where and how does the *value-adding* process of the cobalt component of this GVC start? Should it reflect solely, on the one hand, the rate of cobalt on the London Metal Exchange (LME), the world centre for industrial metals trading, and on the other the royalties, bonuses, rents and other contractual fees received by Gécamines in exchange for concession permits?

While this raises the acute problem of accounting, in economic terms, for the value share that *escapes* the cobalt GVC, through bribes, corruption and tax evasion in secrecy jurisdictions and tax havens, it obfuscates the fact that '[a]s the GVC has transformed from business strategy into development strategy, value is regularly invoked in two ways and in two ways at the same time – as an adjective to modify a product that can be measured in price and captured based on one's position in a chain *and* as a social and moral hierarchy' (Cohen 2019).

Capitalism, Pistor (2019) argues, 'is more than just the exchange of goods in a market economy; it is a market economy in which some assets are placed on legal steroids' (11), because they are backed up by the US dollar, and the Common Law system that dominates global trade *and* financial transactions. Capitalism, in other words, is made up of transactions in value, including symbolic value.

Thus, while the UK Privy Council ruled that a state-owned company could only be assimilated to the state in 'quite extreme circumstances',[6] which it found had not been met in the case of Gécamines, it is precisely in the City that the price of refined cobalt is rated: at the LME, based on an expanding array of intermediaries and increasingly sophisticated financial tools. It is also in London's backyard, Jersey, as a tax haven,

5 The 'corporate veil' refers to the limited liability of a corporation's shareholders or directors.

6 Gécamines *v.* FG Hemisphere, 2012: 29.

that part of the value of the cobalt GVC can *at once* escape the formal economy (including as taxes to the DRC state) *and* be converted as legitimate investments in the onshore economy.

Following its two legal victories, before the Privy Council and the Hong Kong Court of Final Appeal, Gécamines chairman Albert Yuma Mulimbi 'announced that Gécamines expected to receive a total of US$ 269 million – US$ 175 million from the Sicomines signing bonus and an initial payment of about US$ 94 million from the Groupement du Terril du Lubumbashi Ltd slag heap payments, both of which had been held in escrow accounts during the course of litigation. This amount is roughly equivalent to Congo's annual health budget' (Carter Centre 2017: 39).

I.1.3 Confronting the Disconnection between Historical Change in the Global North vs the Global South

The third problem hinges on the common understanding of historical change in the Global North compared to the African South. Saying that the past matters is scientifically trendy. Especially since the Brexit and the Russian aggression of Ukraine. But it is a truism: which past and according to what articulation to the present?

Congo continues to loom large in the overwhelming tendency to point to colonial legacies to account for the crumbling of the state in the present. On the sixtieth anniversary of the first wave of independence on the African continent, to the question 'what did independence achieve for African states and societies?' Algerian-French philosopher Seloua Luste Boulbina responded: decolonisation is not over. 'The problem of the present', she pondered, 'is that it inherits, objectively and subjectively, from the past'.[7]

But which past, which present and for that matter, how do we extract the objective from the subjective tracks of this inheritance?

The weakness of the Congolese state induced by the perceived failure of colonial transplants is seen to breed 'loot-seeking' warfare. But the sophistication of the legal and financial tools used by Gécamines also positions the DRC as a Petri dish of capitalism in the present era of hyper-globalisation.

In advanced economies, the 2008 financial crisis spurred growing anxieties over the incapacity of the post-neoliberal turn 'regulatory' state

[7] O Caslin, 'Indépendances africaines – Seloua Luste Boulbina: "le problème du présent c'est qu'il hérite du passé"' *Jeune Afrique* 7 September 2020, my translation from French.

to curb the 'financial curse' (Christensen et al. 2016). Until then, 'tax havens were generally seen as exotic sideshows to the global economy. [The world has since] woken up to two sobering facts: first, the phenomenon is far bigger and more central to the global economy [...]; and second, the biggest havens aren't where we thought they were.'

Most major tax havens are located in advanced economies and their territories: the British Virgin Islands (BVI), Bermuda and the Cayman Islands – all British Overseas Territories – while Switzerland, the United States and the Cayman Islands are the top three jurisdictions for private wealth (Shaxson 2019: 7).

As an old margin of the capitalist system – construed as a foil for arguments about European capitalist history due to the resilience of kinship ties, and the tendency towards personal, anti-entrepreneurial governance (see Cooper 2014) – the DRC is not only emerging as a 'new frontie[r], [a] plac[e] where mobile, globally competitive capital [...] finds minimally regulated zones in which to vest its operations' (Comaroff and Comaroff 2012: 13); it is also part and parcel of the wider trend towards the *onshoring* of offshore capitalism.

I.2 Bringing the Past Back In, in an *Interconnected* Way

Thus, the *FG Hemisphere* v. *DRC* example raises an acute problem for international law – and more generally for the social sciences. The contradictory position of the DRC as at once backwater and vanguard of capitalism pushes against common tropes about historical change as a series of sharp caesuras and breaks – independence, the neoliberal turn or financialisation – when they are understood in isolation. It also underscores that as both a fix and an enabler, law is like a *Möbius ribbon*. Where do we put the cursor of law's *empowering* potential as opposed to its *enabling* role in maintaining the *status quo* of the African South's subsidiary position in the world economy?

That Gécamines, the former jewel of the Belgian Empire, as the successor of the Union Minière du Haut-Katanga, should be involved in judicial battles across the world ultimately arbitrated by the Privy Council is in and of itself a puzzle that rubs against the current historiographic obsession either with the end of formal empires across Africa at the turn of the 1960s, or the expansion of neoliberalism in the 1970s as moments of discontinuities and sharp ruptures.

Overcoming this double obsession does not deny that developing countries are the 'prime losers' from global profit shifting (Albertin et al. 2021: 13). But it underscores that though uneven and unequal, the African South's relationship with global markets is also *reciprocal*.

The central role played by the African continent in the emergence and expansion of contemporary capitalism has been established in a rich body of scholarship in political economy (drawing on Rodney 1972) and anthropological and ethnographic work (see Ellis 2012; Ferguson 2006). These studies have long underscored that successive scrambles over the continent, in the nineteenth century, during the Cold War, through to the ongoing scramble for 'critical' minerals, have produced a symbiotic relationship between the continent and the world economy. This symbiotic relationship has durably entrenched Africa's uneven and unequal relationship with globalisation.

The position of Gécamines as a *transnational* corporation also reflects the relationship between the re-deployment of the state and the financialisation of the economy in the post-neoliberal turn. The reorganisation of the mining industry since the turn of the 2000s fostered by expansive technological transformations (robotisation, geo-exploration, etc.) and the globalisation and financialisation of supply chains is also embedded in wider structural transformations beyond the traditional focus on extractive sites as the nodal points of contact between '*l'Afrique utile*' and global markets. The structuration of GVCs around vastly dispersed networks of logistical infrastructures, transoceanic corridors, financial intermediation and geographies of labour 'cannot be fully elucidated by the *loci classici* of state-centric concepts of political economy, such as resource curse, dependency, imperialism, and so forth' (Arboleda 2010: 5).

Yet '[t]he political authority that underpins the international movement of capital continues to be mediated *nationally*' (Arboleda 2010: 6, emphasis added). As illustrated by the FG Hemisphere judicial saga, the *state* is not simply a handmaiden of global business interests. Sovereignty is both a flexible symbolic device and a territorially entrenched reality.

It is precisely the dual position of Jersey as at once part and not part of Britain that enables the city to be simultaneously part of Britain, yet a de-territorialised global financial capital. What matters, therefore, is the *symbolic mediation* of value – as a price captured based on one's position in a GVC *and* as a social and moral hierarchy that both enables and categorises the international movement of capital *as* offshore or onshore, as illegal or legal, as profit sharing or predatory. Looking at the *structurally* dual role of law, in the *longue durée*, as both an enabler for the expansion of power – through its symbolic function of codification – and as a check on petty arbitrariness, dependent on lawyers' relative success at asserting the autonomy of their professional space (Kantorowicz 1989) is a powerful entry point to track this mediation process.

To escape the trope of determination – law's siren calls – law's relationship to power must be assessed *empirically* and *historically*. The FG Hemisphere saga marshals multiple scales and historical periodisation, from the British imperial realm, to the post-1960s reconversion of the City of London as the world's financial capital and the expansion of the Eurodollar market, and from the globalisation and financialisation of GVCs to the expansion of the geographical, technological and infrastructural landscapes of extraction *beneath* and *beyond* nation states. It brings together, in other words, different localities and time periods, whose *interconnectedness* in the present requires unpacking.

I.3 'Tracking' *Legal Intermediation* and *Imperial Encounters*

Lawyering Imperial Encounters tracks the patterns of symbolic valuation that shape and justify the relationship between the African South and the global economy and, more broadly, relations between law, political power, finance and historical change.

I do so by building on Tilly's analogy between organised crime and war-making/state-making, which he argues are 'quintessential protection rackets with the advantage of legitimacy' (Tilly 1985: 169), by reading it in light of the *global* turn in sociology and history (Go 2009). This turn channels attention towards 'the *relations* between non-Western or southern societies and other spaces' (Go 2013: 39, emphasis added) beyond the unidirectional relationship from cores to peripheries. It also underscores the historical contingency of the modern nation state as a modality for the expansion of power.

I reposition Tilly's nexus between *war-making/state-making* (as the coercive monopolisation of violence internally and in relation to external competitors), *protection* (as the elimination or neutralisation of the competitors of capital accumulating forces within the state) and *extraction* (as the acquisition of the means of carrying out the first three activities) within the context of the successive imperial scrambles over the African continent, from the nineteenth-century Scramble for Africa, the Cold War partition of the continent, through to the ongoing rush for Africa's 'green' minerals.

Lawyering Imperial Encounters tracks *imperial hangovers* in the present (to use Puri's (2021) expression) in Britain, France and the United States; in former British, French and Belgian colonies; in tax havens and secrecy jurisdictions; as well as in the circulation of norms, institutionalisation patterns and the structuration of professional spaces of international and national justice (interstate adjudication, arbitration, international criminal justice, strategic litigation against corporate crimes, asylum justice). The aim is to uncover the *interconnectedness* between these sites as local nodes in the reproduction and justification of the relationship between law, political power, finance and historical change. Espousing an interconnected approach to historical change is a way of shifting from a functionalist understanding of the relationship between law and GVCs towards a sociology of *value* and of *valuation* (Lamont 2012; Levi et al. 2017).

Empirically, *Lawyering Imperial Encounters* focuses on legal intermediation dynamics within spaces of 'imperial encounter' (an expression I borrow from Bertrand 2007) between the African South and the world economy. What I call *imperial encounters* refers to normative, institutional and professional spaces of *real* connections. These spaces offer a vista into histories that are connected due to their reciprocal embeddedness in imperial legacies. They also echo transformations of state power and relations between political power, knowledge, business and finance in the African South and in the Global North.

These spaces are imperial because they reflect processes produced by, as much as they transform, concurrent geographies of power expansion and capital accumulation. Because they take place simultaneously within different scales and in distinct social spaces, imperial encounters also provide us with a history of the present relationship between capitalism's cores and its so-called peripheries, and, more broadly, between states, private interests and societies.

Methodologically, I unpack *legal intermediation* dynamics within and across these sites. Focusing on sites of imperial encounter helps capture the 'exceptional normal' (to use Bertrand and Calafat's (2018: 12) expression, my translation from French) of the conditions of possibility of circulation of norms and individuals, and, with them, of processes of professionalisation and institutionalisation across geographical scales and over time. This involves 'tracking individuals, things, objects, even emotions, outside of a strictly European focus' (Bertrand and Calafat 2018: 12, my translation from French). I track legal intermediation based on the family history, professional trajectory and strategies, and the assets of legal intermediaries – a term which I use to refer to agents, lawyers and non-lawyers, for whom law is a key resource for political access, and social, professional and geographical mobility. This is a way to observe and narrate lived connections and their structural, social and cultural imprint in the present. Foremost, it is a way to track the symbolic valuation processes that enable law's deployment as a Möbius ribbon – at once as an enabler of the consolidation of the *status quo* of Africa's subaltern position in the world economy, and law's empowering potential to disrupt entrenched relations of domination.

Lawyering Imperial Encounters' empirical focus is predominantly on local sites and bundles of relations that were located formally *outside* Britain's imperial realm and the US sphere of military and cultural interests in the context of the Cold War: a former French colony of West Africa (Côte d'Ivoire) and two former Belgian colonies of the Great Lakes region (Burundi and the Congo), which were incorporated within France's areas of political, military and cultural influence during the Cold War.[8]

Lawyering Imperial Encounters is *not* a comparative overview between these African national sites and their uneven and unequal relationship with the world economy. It is a story in which imperial legacies in the present intersect with inter-imperial struggles for hegemony that are also contests over the framing of *global legal orderings*. In their account of Britain's expansion as world hegemon based on the extension of British juridical power *within* and *outside* the British imperial realm, Benton and Ford (2016) 'find active analogies at work between imperial and global order' (193). As they put it, '[n]ot unlike the unstable and merely aspirational dominance of British legal authority in many of the corners of the empire, the contemporary global order takes its shape from largely hidden hierarchies' (Benton and Ford 2016: 194).

Hidden hierarchies were fostered by the circulation of norms, individuals and institutions across empires through to the 1940s. They also shape the institutionalisation of an international legal order since, along with the extraterritorial waging of the City's and New York's law as the law codifying and sanctifying the international movement of capital. Hidden hierarchies therefore connect these sites to some of Britain's former colonial peripheries like Ghana and South Africa, to Paris as a former metropolitan capital and world arbitration centre and The Hague as the global justice capital.

[8] What I refer to as France's '*pré carré*' throughout the book. The metaphor '*pré carré*' refers to the exclusive domain of the public sphere. Applied to French foreign relations, it has been endowed with a negative connotation from the 1980s to underscore the symbiotic ties of the *métropole* with its former African colonies.

Hidden hierarchies can help question and track the dynamics of expansion of China as the world twenty-first century hegemon precisely because, as Benton and Ford (2016) put it, 'focusing anew on the disorganized legal routines that other, aspiring hegemons have deployed in their flawed attempts to project power' can help account for the continuous patchiness, in the present, of the global legal order (181).

Exposing these hidden hierarchies requires confronting ourselves to the 'imperial entanglement' (to use Steinmetz' (2013) expression) of scientific knowledge on legal change, politics and capitalism in former African colonies. I do this by espousing a research strategy that *zooms in and out* across scalar units and analytical lenses (Cooper 2014). Zooming *in* to track legal intermediation at the micro level of individual trajectories, institutions or localities and *out* onto structural geopolitical changes helps to get grips with at least one aspect of the 'grand' narrative of historical *longue durée* by identifying the connections, in the present, between the legacies of formal colonisation and the longer term of trade interests.

Lawyering Imperial Encounters is therefore a plea for what Lonsdale (1981) called 'epistemological impurity' (140). I invite researchers, teachers – readers – to embrace *messiness* to capture the present. *Lawyering Imperial Encounters* is an invitation, in other words, as the historian Marc Lazar puts it so well, for us as researchers and as teachers, to be seismologists,[9] and to convey the curiosity and desire to question boundaries. This, I argue, is a way to respond to the challenge of allowing for the possibility of studying the imperial factor over an extended period.

I.4 Structure of the Book

Chapter 1 lays out the book's research strategy. Deploying a post-colonial critique of the terms of the relationship between the African South and the global economy requires questioning law's *double bind* – as both enabler and bulwark against domination – and confronting ourselves to the imperial entanglement of scholarship (Steinmetz 2013). Building on Tilly's (1985) trilogy of coercion-extraction-protection, the chapter identifies two sets of variables deployed throughout the book to track the articulation between law, politics and capitalist expansion over time: the 'double-edged protection' produced by legal imperialism and the 'middle power' used by the British hegemon and competing imperial *métropoles*

[9] M Semo, 'Marc Lazar: La "peuplecratie" est un défi pour la démocratie libérale et représentative' *Le Monde* 2 May 2019.

to justify colonialism and lessen social disruption and inter-imperial rivalries. Lastly, the chapter explains the book's methodology. Zooming in and out to track imperial encounters at the scale of localities, institutions and global structures exposes pre-existing conflicts and contradictions that help understand ongoing conflicts and contradictions in late capitalism.

Chapter 2 argues that imperial powers (Britain, France and Belgium) deployed a similar strategy of legal imperialism during the nineteenth-century Scramble for Africa. Indirect rule operationalised the contradiction that colonial power was weak in its effective reach, yet strong in the systemic upheavals it engendered. It also fostered legal and capitalist unevenness, what Benton and Ford (2016) call 'lumpiness'. The chapter focuses on three crisis situations that were ostensibly solved through juridical means: 1920s Gold Coast conflicts before the Privy Council; the 1895 Stokes-Lothaire incident before the High Council of the Congo Free State; and pre-independence military trials in French and British colonies. Together, these judicial crises help account for structural commonalities in the articulation of post-independence African states with the world economy: the deployment of merchant law *with* and *without* state sovereignty and *middling* as a durable, though variable, sovereign resource of the post-colonial state.

Chapter 3 revisits the Cold War Scramble for Africa. Throughout the continent, the 'concession model of extraction' – the renting out of land to foreign corporations in exchange for royalties – was based on the early emergence of mining giants in South Africa. The concession model was not dismantled following independence. Gatekeeping politics were consolidated through the alternate paths taken by London and Paris. France incorporated its former colonies within a 'postcolonial block' (Bayart 1993). Britain reconverted as a dual middle power – with London as jurisdictional apex and the City as financial powerhouse. The Cold War sidelining of The Hague justice institutions enabled the deployment of the US Cultural Cold War, based on the formidable sway of the alliance of Wall Street resources – finance, arbitration and corporate law firms – which contributed to the insulation of foreign corporate rights in property in resource-rich African states from national and international oversight.

Chapter 4 examines the ongoing rush for Africa, characterised by the global competition for the critical minerals of the 'energy transition'. I argue that the ongoing Scramble is embedded in previous imperial imprints. The 1980s debt crisis positioned international financial institutions (IFIs) as the vehicles of the neoliberal turn on the continent. But this did not displace gatekeeping politics. Rather, the concurrent *onshoring* of *offshore* capitalism fostered the power of global traders like Glencore or Trafigura as the prime interface between resource-rich African states and global markets and as the core engineers of the transformation of the *geography* of extraction, based on technological and infrastructural innovations and financial deregulation. The onshoring of swashbuckler capitalism is deeply connected to a codification of capital (Pistor 2019) based on Common Law and the law of the state of New York, which is enabled by the globalisation of the 'Wall Street model of the corporate law firm'.

Chapter 5 examines the ongoing rush for Burundi's rare earths twenty-five years after the Arusha agreement that put an end to the violent conflict that tore the country apart from 1993. I argue that Burundi's transition into an origination site leans on the legacy of colonial, post-independence and post-1993 rule of law reforms, which together have fostered what Mamdani (1996) calls 'decentralized despotism'. The conflicting position of legal intermediaries as either representatives of authoritarian power or champions of the rule of law is embedded in a structural *bifurcation* of the Burundian legal field that enables corporate predation, like that of beer giants. According to their political and social resources, lawyers are positioned alternately as gatekeepers of the rent of exported commodities, or vulnerable to another type of extraversion: aid dependency. This bifurcation makes Burundi a Petri dish of the hyper-violence generated by the hyper-legality of late capitalism.

Chapter 6 examines the Probo Koala environmental catastrophe which involved the dumping of toxic oil residue by the global trader Trafigura in the port of Abidjan in 2005. The development of the scandal into transnational litigation strategies in Britain and European capitals exposes the legal lumpiness fostered by the financialisation of GVCs. The 'Ivorian miracle' relied on protected economic integration within the global markets of coffee and cocoa. The dismantling of the 'post-colonial block' fostered a displacement of the terms of Côte d'Ivoire's relationship with global markets. This contributed to reinforcing the prominence of global traders as intermediaries between states, financial markets and corporate power. It also consolidated the symbiotic relationship between the *onshoring* of offshore capitalism and the *offshoring* of *onshore* justice. The case demonstrates that corporate accountability gaps along GVCs are an outcome of the bifurcation of state sovereignty enabled by financial deregulation.

Chapter 7 tracks the transformation of the position of Paris induced by the neoliberal turn. The marketplace of legal intermediaries between resource-rich African states and French businesses has long been derided as an outgrowth of the *Françafrique*, the interpersonal shadow networks linking France to its African '*pré carré*'. The neoliberal turn fostered the prominence of corporate lawyers as key intermediaries between the state and the market. It was also deployed within the *system* of the *Françafrique*. Due to the historical distancing of the Paris Bar from corporate interests, French corporate law pioneers contributed to the expansion of a French corporate bar under the double thrust of the European Common Market and the model of the Wall Street corporate law firm. It is also as intermediaries of US multinational corporate law firms that they entered the former French '*pré carré*' in Africa qua a legal market.

Chapter 8 examines how social hierarchies are reproduced through the operations of justice. I argue that justice institutions, whether national or supranational, are systematically characterised by the structuration of restricted professional markets of 'repeat players' (Galanter 1974) who act as gatekeepers of the relationship with justice users (individuals, corporations or states). The globalisation and financialisation of GVCs is reinforcing rather than weakening the post-Cold War competition between global legal ordering claims. The contrasted development of justice institutions (from the US Supreme Court; asylum justice; interstate adjudication; investment arbitration to international criminal justice) demonstrates that it is fostering the global diffusion of the Wall Street model of the corporate law firm as an engine of legal globalisation and for the reproduction of legal and social hierarchies. This positions justice institutions as practical and symbolic boundary-making sites between capitalism's so-called cores and its peripheries.

1

Imperial Encounters

Localities, Institutions, Structures

The relationship between raw commodities and the expansion of capitalism has been woven into masterfully detailed histories that underscore the interconnectedness between the reorganisation of labour (through slavery in colonised territories to the expansion of a labour class in Europe and the United States from the mid-1850s), the industrialisation of production, the financial and logistical innovations of commodity circulation across the globe through to the capture of a 'consumer class'. On the other hand, the 1990s global advocacy campaigns against 'blood' minerals and the harmful societal and environmental effects of extraction in resource-rich economies in the African South have come along with a global regulatory tide to counter the 'risks' of the poor governance of GVCs.

Law tends to remain a sideshow in these scholarly and policy accounts, 'an institutional backdrop against which the economic and inter-organizational dynamics driving the globalization of production play out' (IGLP 2016: 60) – either because it is not mentioned, at all – or because it is invoked as a *future-oriented* fix to tame the violence of the market or regulate poor governance, foremost in resource-rich economies. Tracking the possibilities shaped by law enables a critique of the distributive effects of commodity chains. This is the objective set out by legal critical scholar David Kennedy for the Institute for Global Law and Policy (IGLP) at Harvard Law School. 'It is by mapping the legal geography of GVCs that we can show what the traditional division of law into discrete subfields misses or conceals, and how domestic and international hard and soft law and private ordering mechanisms intermingle in ways that challenge efforts to maintain clear distinctions between them' (IGLP 2016: 64).

Re-examining the boundaries of law is necessary. Understanding that law itself generates material and symbolic value is essential. But it is not enough. The first issue is a problem of *research scope*. It also harks back to what Steinmetz (2013) calls the *imperial entanglement* of knowledge.

As Beckert (2014) explains in his masterful study of cotton's symbiosis with global capitalism, '[t]his book has been researched on every continent' so as to painstakingly weave back together the scattered archives of cotton production, circulation and consumption over time (445). It also required, quite literally, a battalion of research assistants. For the lone researcher, tracking the various nodes, across territorial scales, of a GVC is not simply materially impossible. It is also an epistemic risk. Cobalt provides an emblematic illustration. A wealth of foremost journalistic and NGO investigations now details the political collusion and capital flight that contribute to the violence of the new rush for the DRC.[1] Their overwhelming focus on sites of extraction, in Eastern Congo, rather than other nodes of the cobalt value chain – including, foremost, the London Metal Exchange (LME) where the price of cobalt is negotiated – questions their status as *primary sources* or as part and parcel of a 'policy pull', a common sense across scholarship that tends to equate the detrimental effects of extraction with the failure of the state in resource-rich economies and the impunity of transnational corporations.

Beyond, the imperial entanglement of scholarly disciplines – including law – means that even while we seek objectivity, our eyes risk remaining wide shut. It is now a truism to say that scholarship is deeply entangled with imperialism and colonisation. Knowledge is also sucked in by finance. To put it bluntly, there is a correlation between the sciences of risk and the price of gold on financial markets – just as there is a relationship of mistrust and reciprocal ignorance between scholarly knowledge and financial actors.

As Peter Munk, the Hungarian-Canadian robber baron–turned philanthropist who contributed to the financialisation of gold through the operations of Barrick Gold as an extractive corporation and financial trader ... and who jump-started the creation of the Munk School of Global Affairs and Public Policy at the University of Toronto in 2010 put it: '[p]olitical uncertainty and political instability increases the demand for gold. That is absolutely natural. The more stability and confidence you have that the status quo will be unperturbed, the less demand there is among retail, even among institutions. [...] There is an almost inverse relationship between uncertainty and the price of gold'.[2]

1 For example, *The Sentry*, 'The Backchannel: state capture and bribery in Congo's deal of the century' November 2021, https://cdn.thesentry.org/wp-content/uploads/2021/11/TheBackchannel-TheSentry-Nov2021.pdf (accessed 4 November 2022).

2 *The Economist*, '"You've got to hedge your bets" An interview with Peter Munk' 29 April 2014.

The questions raised by the example of the *FG Hemisphere* v. *DRC* case in the Introduction – *why* should we see the connections across scales and over time exposed by this judicial saga, *what* do they tell us and foremost *how* do we go about it – therefore expose the issue of *reflexivity* of the researcher herself. To reiterate: the value of the commodities that circulate through GVCs is financial. It depends on power relations along the nodes of GVCs. It is also reflective of social and moral hierarchies that are determined in part by law as a science and by knowledge about law.

Confronting ourselves to law's *double bind* – as both enabler and bulwark against domination – is a condition for a post-colonial critique of the terms of the relationship between the African South and the global economy. To do this, it is essential to go beyond a *functional* deployment of law that risks not just consolidating but enabling the status quo of Africa's subaltern position.

In what follows, I start by exposing the stakes (and limitations) of decolonising legal scholarship. Building on Tilly's (1985) trilogy of coercion-extraction-protection, I then identify variables that can help track the articulation between law, politics and capitalist expansion over time.

These variables are not ideal-typical or systematic; they are structural in the sense that they channel attention to a core feature of power: competition. The prominence of Britain as hegemon, inter-imperial confrontations and local colonial encounters *structurally* built on the double-edged protection enabled by law as justification of brutal domination, the threat or actual use of force *and* as a shield against it. Double-edged protection took many forms according to contexts and over time. But it was deeply imperial, as it enabled the coexistence of instability *and* hegemony.

It is precisely because law fostered the simultaneous deployment of hierarchy and instability that it provides an entry point for a history of the *present*. It underscores that local histories reflect structural changes that produce, due to the circulation of norms, agents, practices, unequal and uneven but also reciprocal effects between the so-called cores of the world economy and its peripheries.

As I suggested in the Introduction, this is a research *agenda* that hails as an invitation to push against knowledge boundaries and re-examine the articulation between power, finance and law in the ongoing phase of capitalism. I then expose what this entails as a research strategy. Zooming in and out involves tracking imperial encounters at the scale of localities, institutions and global structures. Lawyering, in these imperial encounters, in turn, is about looking at the *structurally* dual role of law, in the *longue durée*, as both an enabler for the expansion of power – through its symbolic function of codification – and as a check on petty arbitrariness. It is, in other words, both a *story-telling* strategy and a research method designed to escape the trope of *determination.*

1.1 The Politics of Scattered Knowledge

At summits organised between EU states and the industry on the energy transition, such as the annual European Sustainable Energy Week (EUSEW), two policy moves are broadcast: either industry innovation – like getting rid of the cobalt component of Li-ion batteries, which remains unlikely to happen in the coming decades – or governance, the idea that governance in resource-rich states needs to be reformed, and that extractive value chains must be more transparent and accountable.

Except in the current conjuncture, there are two big issues that make these responses at best inadequate, at worst disastrous. The first is that the heightened global competition for minerals is unfolding in a global economy characterised by the intense globalisation and financialisation of GVCs. Until the oil crises of the 1970s, the 'seven sisters' were vertically integrated companies. This enabled them to control both ends of the oil supply chain: from production and refining through to the negotiation of the price of oil on global markets. The Organization of the Petroleum Exporting Countries (OPEC) cartel changed this power relationship by vindicating the capacity to control the supply end and influence the price of oil. This power struggle also unleashed a legal big bang, that of international arbitration: a type of justice that takes place beyond the boundaries of states – a type of justice that also developed at its own pace, with its own rules and its own societal effects (Dezalay Y and Garth 1996).

Now, when we shift the focus to African sites, the power struggle appears similar but structurally different. Mining giants are still little more than a handful. Dominant players, like Glencore, are global traders who operate vertically integrated supply chains to buy and sell physical commodities. They are also financial traders. The quintessence of an insider's market, global traders are essentially an 'international clearing house for essential goods' (Blas and Farchy 2022: 8). '[Their] power to act as de facto gatekeepers to the market gives large buyers extraordinary advantages over both firms *and* states competing for their favour' (Danielsen and Bair 2019, emphasis in the original). However, for the first time since the city states of Italy, finance is global. But it is uncontrollable. The current scramble is also accompanied by a legal boom. But this legal boom is embedded in distinct patterns of path dependency: the idiosyncratic structuration of global justice institutions as professional markets, and Africa's specifically uneven and unequal relationship with global justice.

The second problem is that there is very little empirical knowledge on the intermediaries who produce and deploy law within GVCs. The issue here is not lack of data per se but what Steinmetz (2013) calls the *imperial entanglement* of scholarship.

Studies of the 'colonial question' have undergone a relative boom in the past fifteen years in Belgium, emulating the rich literature on the British and French Empires. But these studies remain largely entangled in ideologically laden controversies that 'concern the mid-twentieth century "end of empire." [This] is the result of more than just efforts to hide embarrassing pasts. [These controversies] speak to how much the exercise of sovereignty is shaped by post-decolonization concerns' (Shepard 2015: 882).

Legal scholarship and the sociology of the legal profession fall particularly short of this critique. Legal intermediaries in the colonial realms have long remained the suppressed underside of the North. When not marginalised to the point of oblivion, they have predominantly been studied with the lens of the contemporary hegemon, under the purview of the US sociology of legal professions, with two self-opposed images (see Sharafi 2007). They are either construed in heroic terms – whether as missionaries of the rule of law (Halliday et al. 2012), cultural translators (Pue 2016) and in counter-hegemonic readings as freedom fighters (e.g. Pershad et al. 1961); or, they are subsumed under the drive of the market (Abel and Lewis 1988a, 1988b, 1989) – including as mercenaries of neo-colonial interests (see Burgis 2015).

By the same token, the argument of the centrality of law in colonialism has been woven into opposed accounts of legality in colonial realms, reflective of the contradiction between the imperial promise of the rule of law and the total violence of colonial ruling laid out in sets of rules – such as the *Code de l'indigénat*[3] applied throughout French African colonies – which separated colonised populations from Europeans. In these accounts, law is either posited as a fix against the violence of post-colonial repression towards the end goal of political liberalism

[3] The *Code de l'indigénat* ('native code') referred to diverse and fluctuating sets of laws and regulations characterised by arbitrariness which created in practice an inferior legal status for natives of French colonies from 1881 until 1944–1947.

(Halliday et al. 2012), or the violence of day-to-day colonial ruling is considered like a black hole that negates legality (Mann 2009).

This double trope raises an acute problem to track the role of legal intermediation in the *longue durée*. There is some knowledge on the social, economic, political and normative variables at play in building transnational strategic litigation on behalf of disenfranchised communities (see Muir Watt et al. 2019). But this knowledge is by nature post hoc. Legal strategies are studied as if they should fit within the loopholes and strategic opportunities fostered by GVCs. On the other hand, the wealth of (foremost, economic and political economic) scholarship criticising the heuristic limits of the 'resource curse' – the paradox of resource-rich economies entrapped in poverty – documents the predominance of elite bargaining (the *who* wins question) in the post-colonial trajectories of African states (Murrey and Jackson forthcoming). But this scholarship is largely focused on *domestic* rentier politics.

For its part, the expanding scholarship on finance, particularly in political anthropology and sociology, has cut large swaths in showing that financial markets as spaces purportedly dedicated to the pure exercise of market principles are actually the site of an elaborate array of social codes, mutual obligations and reciprocity (see Ho 2009). However, with few exceptions (see Ortiz 2021), studies on the everyday practices of agents working in the financial industry remain by and large disconnected from the global hierarchies produced by financial markets.

These bodies of scholarship channel attention towards the role played by *intermediaries*, be they individuals or institutions, in shaping and transforming the webs of relationships along with the valuation of types of capitals exchanged along GVCs' different nodes. But they do not help explain how law, politics and finance *intersect* in shaping the encounter between Africa and capitalism in the *longue durée* and *across* these different scales.

Unpacking this puzzle requires looking for connections in ways that we are not used to. The dispute between FG Hemisphere and the DRC, for example, exposed some of the nodes of cobalt's GVC through the judicialisation chain constituted by the FG Hemisphere saga. But the relevance of these connections remains limited if studied in isolation. That the British Privy Council should invoke judicial precedents and position itself as umpire of tribunals seated in jurisdictions whose links with London are, if not distended, at least tenuous is certainly a question that can be solved through legal reasoning. After all, legal doctrine reads like a succession of jurisprudential revolutions. Yet the FG Hemisphere judicial saga harks back to imperial legacies in the present. It also refracts dynamics of financialisation, produced at various nodes of cobalt's GVC, through discontinuous junctions and periodisation, by actors categorised, in legal terms, *either* as sovereigns, commodity producers, businesses or financial traders.

The stake, therefore, is also to understand how these actors can be *simultaneously* positioned, depending on contexts, as sovereigns, commodity producers, businesses *and* financial traders to track imperial legacies and their connections with transformations of state power and capitalist expansion over time.

1.2 The Legacy of Double-Edged Protection

Due to the sheer variation of imperial strategies and local specificities – be they characterised as capitalist revolution in South Africa, settler colonialism in Algeria or Kenya, or predatory extraction in Congo – examining the structural effects, over time, of law as a repertoire of power is a delicate exercise. Even more so because legal imperialism was not simply deployed from one core to one periphery.

The stake, however, is not to build a *comparative* overview of Africa's uneven and unequal relationship with the world economy. This would be materially impossible, just like looking at the nodes of GVCs on every continent would be reckless at the level of the individual researcher. But the stake is also to avoid the risk of *reification* – that of objectifying, as *systematic* or *ideal-typical*, relations of domination at the expense of historical and contextual variations.

At first blush, the unprecedented inclusion of sub-Saharan African national case studies in Abel et al.'s (2020) monumental *Lawyers in 21st-Century Societies* – produced as a sequel to Abel and Lewis' (1988a, 1988b, 1989) pioneering comparative studies thirty years earlier – hails as a timely normalisation of the study of Africa's legal professions and their relationship with transformations of state power and globalisation. Just like in other regions of the world, there has been a huge, sometimes staggering, expansion of private legal markets fostered by the expansion of legal education and rights-oriented non-profit sectors.[4] While the

[4] In Burundi, the number of lawyers called to the bar has multiplied forty to fifty times since 1993 (Dezalay S 2020c). In Tunisia, membership in the bar increased roughly twenty-five-fold over the period (from 309 in 1971–1972 to 7,759 in 2011, Gobe 2020). The expansion of the bar in Egypt is even more staggering, with over 700,000 registered lawyers in 2013, compared with 4,433 in 1949 (Bernard-Maugiron and Menna 2020). Zimbabwe, which

norm remains solo or small firm practice, the social and economic divide between large generalist bars and small, exclusive, corporate and political bars follows evolutions found in other regions.

Yet it is striking that the gendered, social (including racial, as in South Africa, see Klaaren 2020)[5] and organisational divisions used to account for the diversification and stratification of the legal profession in these settings are insufficient to explain what is more akin to a *rift* between massive low bars made up of solo practitioners who either provide mostly family legal services or straddle across the legal profession and consultancy for international NGOs or international organisations, and extremely select high bars which combine political clout with access to business and multinational corporate law firms.

For example, in Tunisia, the massive generalist bar that emerged from the 1980s – against the backdrop of the expansion of legal education and the economic crisis – was at the helm of the revolution that toppled Ben Ali's dictatorship in 2011. But the elite bar reaped the benefits of this symbolic revolutionary capital. Free riding on the revolution, this tier not only managed to transform itself from 'bar of the state party' to spokesperson of the revolution but also retained its monopoly of representation of state-owned companies and parastatals (Gobe 2020). Likewise, in Zimbabwe, the revolutionary promise of the 'Africanisation' of the legal profession following independence in 1980 also fostered the enduring political embeddedness in the present of the higher tier of the 'Black bar' that emerged out of the decolonisation struggle built on formal and informal relationships between lawyers and state officials (Karekwaivanane 2020).

What makes these examples striking is that despite the two countries' starkly different colonial and post-colonial trajectories, there appears to be a homology in the relationship between their legal professions, national fields of state power and capitalism. In both situations, the state – be it the colonial state or the post-colonial state in its successive iterations – is ideal-typical of the 'activist state' (Gobe 2013, building on Damaška's (1986) concept), that is a state positioned symbolically as the

became independent in 1980 and whose post-colonial history spans the whole period since Abel and Lewis's seminal studies (Abel and Lewis 1988a, 1988b, 1989), is striking. On the eve of independence, there were only twelve African lawyers (out of 231 attorneys and advocates) compared with 1,200 registered lawyers in 1998 (Karekwaivanane 2020).

5 South Africa is distinctive because it features the oldest domestic corporate legal market. There, this social rift remains racialised despite two decades of Black empowerment policies. In 2017, whites still represented 58 per cent of practising attorneys and 63 per cent of advocates (Klaaren 2020).

sole source of authority and allegiance, and beggaring societal networks and institutions. In both cases, resources drawn from the international (be it the rent of extraction or that of development aid) determine relations within the legal field *and* the field of state power.

But focusing solely on legal elites qua legal professionals provides only partial explanations.

Reducing lawyers' role to either collaborators or rebels obfuscates the *structural* function of law in shaping, justifying and transforming the relationship between these African sites and the global economy. Foremost, commonalities in these two examples urge us to move away from a comparative analysis – which would inevitably, relentlessly, position them as *exceptions*.

Instead, what if we construed these African sites as 'hyper-extensions of the present, harbingers of future history' (Comaroff and Comaroff 2012: 12), where imperial legacies are juxtaposed onto contemporary macro-political and economic transformations – including the competition between the United States, China and other emerging economies for global market shares and influence on the continent, as well as the intensification of the globalisation and financialisation of GVCs? What if, in other words, we sought to position legal professions in Africa as reflecting advanced and sophisticated mutations of globalisation (Ferguson 2006: 41)?

This entails looking 'for the state in places where scholars have not been used to finding it – in the field of law itself' (Vauchez and France 2020: 6). Conversely, this requires looking for law in places where we are not used to finding it: in the field of national state power, and in the legacies of the structural role played by law in the deployment of imperial rule. Foremost, this means that we need to look at the *interconnectedness* between transformations of state power and capitalism across scales.

The term *interconnected*, which I borrow from global history scholarship (Subrahmanyam 2004), is strategically powerful but risky. It is strategically powerful because it is an invitation to re-examine knowledge categories and social spaces constructed in their alterity – be it the distinction between the public sphere and private interests, between capitalism's cores and its peripheries, between the national and the international and even between political revolutions and the structural *longue durée* – as *connected* spaces.

What Benton and Ford describe as the 'vernacular [imperial] constitutionalism' operationalised through the interplay between Britain's position as hegemon, inter-imperial rivalries and the formal colonisation of Africa in the nineteenth century reflected the fact that law was 'a fluid vernacular, articulated by very different groups of people for myriad ends and resolving' (Benton and Ford 2016: 3).

That law could operationalise both hierarchy and difference reflected the interconnectedness between changes in the field of state power in the imperial *métropoles* and that of colonial states and inter-imperial struggles. As the 'cutting edge' of colonialism (Chanock 1985), law was the quintessence of double-edged protection. The 'civilising mission' justified both the deployment of colonial brutality *and* an imperial rule of law. As a fluid vernacular in the expansion of power *horizontally* (between and within metropolitan cores and colonial peripheries) and *vertically* (across and within imperial realms), law was also, by essence, *transnational* and *trans-imperial* as it produced structural effects in the combination between power and capital accumulation that necessarily varied across time and space.

As a result, sovereignty within imperial realms was *layered* as it reflected flows and counterflows (to use Ibhawoh's (2013) expression) between multiple actors (individuals, states, corporations) and different localities of power. Foremost, law enabled the historical coexistence of the consolidation of European nation states, and the expansion of imperialism.

Law also operationalised the contradiction that colonial power was *weak* in its effective reach, yet *strong* in the systemic upheavals it engendered. Despite the contrast often drawn between British indirect rule and French direct rule,[6] a similar pattern of legal imperialism was deployed across all empires as 'colonizing powers could only stray so far from indirect rule without encountering expenses and dangers they did not wish to entertain' (Burbank and Cooper 2010: 316–317). Beyond the local variations of imperial strategies, what arguably distinguishes the European nineteenth-century scramble for Africa is that, as Cooper puts it, rather than being 'modern', the European nineteenth-century Scramble was imperialism 'on the cheap, creating a patchwork of economic exploitation rather than a systematic transformation, ruling

[6] The system of direct colonial rule (associated with the French Empire) implied a direct government over colonies from the *métropole*, through the intermediation of colonial administrators, while indirect rule (associated with the British Empire) referred to the maintenance of traditional structures of power at the local level, under the control of the colonial administration. In practice, however, the maintenance (and at times, creation) of 'traditional' elites throughout empires responded to the very practical and old *imperial* problem of asserting control over huge territories and populations without paying the proportionally large (human, financial, military) costs of colonial administration (see Burbank and Cooper 2010; Mamdani 1996).

through an often-ossified system of "tribal" authority rather than trying to create the docile individual subjects of supposedly modern governmentality' (Cooper 2005: 157).

This meant that the extraction of the commodities that connected the '*Afrique utile*' to the imperial *métropoles* was mediated by intermediaries, at both ends of this encounter, whose characteristics varied across space and time and whose physical and symbolic control over territorial units, peoples and the products of extraction depended on multiple and often contradictory usages of the law.

Middling could be construed as a core imperial repertoire of power of the British hegemon that produced flows and counterflows not only between the Crown and Britain's imperial peripheries but also in dynamics of symbolic and practical boundary-making *outside* the British Empire. As world hegemon until World War II, '[t]he [British] empire itself represented a *middle sort of power*' (Benton and Ford 2016: 10, emphasis added) as its expansion 'consisted in the simultaneous extension of imperial jurisdiction *within* and *without* the empire' with 'such a degree of interplay between "inside" and "outside" law that it bec[ame] at times difficult to separate one from the other' (Benton and Ford 2016: 194, emphasis added).

To put it in simpler terms, the very structure of the British Empire fostered at once capital flight, and the enforcement, beyond the formal boundaries of the empire, of Britain's imperial rule of law. Middling was also a structural feature of colonial empires due to their structuration as spaces of asymmetrical yet reciprocal power relations between *métropoles* and colonies. The field of power of the colonial state was determined by the partial refraction of the field of power in the *métropole*. Conversely, conflicts within the field of state power in the *métropole* – and inter-imperial competition – also affected local colonial politics. This helps explain, for example, that the same colonising power – Germany – could enact dramatically different policies – the brutal slaughter of the Herero people in Southwest Africa; a paternalistic defence of native culture in Samoa; and the alternation between harsh racism and cultural exchange in China (Steinmetz 2007).

Middling, therefore, relates to a *structural* dynamic between law, power and capitalism that must be assessed in the synchrony – at a given point in time – and in the synchrony, in the *longue durée*. Middling, in other words, is what exposes Gécamines' 'structural banality' (to use Vauchez and France's (2020: 156) expression) in the present structure of the international legal, economic and political order, and, over time, as it provides a vista of the structural effects (and their contradictions) of the successive scrambles into the African continent from the second half of the nineteenth century.

It is precisely the contradictory legacies of the 'imperialism on the cheap' deployed by imperial powers that provide a key to deploying Tilly's analogy between organised crime and war-making/state-making as a dynamic of historical change in the present encounter between the African South and the world economy.

What Cooper calls 'gatekeeping' politics to refer to the competition over 'the nodal point where local society meets external economy, dependent on manipulating revenues and patronage deriving from that point, including foreign and commercial deals' (Cooper 2014: 30) is not an exotic feature of African states (Hönke 2018). Competition over the rent – financial and symbolic – derived from controlling the sites connecting a territory with the outside world is one of the features of sovereign power.

While a distinct legacy of the nineteenth-century Scramble is that most resource-rich African states are dependent on *one* node of contact with the world economy, middling also underscores rent seeking as a two-way process: on one hand, the rent derived from international material and symbolic links, deployed domestically for status, political and economic gains; on the other, the uneven resistance to exploitation and adaptability to external economic relations. It also implies that if the viability of gatekeeping politics depends on the extreme asymmetry in economic relations between the African South, advanced economies and financial markets, the stake is conversely to track (vested) interests at the different nodal points of this encounter.

Middling therefore relates to a core capital fostered by the imperial scale: the individual, collective or institutional resource of being positioned *both* inside and outside. Middling is certainly not the monopoly of lawyers. But it *is* law's trademark.

First, because law and, with it, legal intermediaries like multinational corporate law firms constitute one of the main vernaculars of the globalisation and financialisation of GVCs. Second, because law is to international, business, political and social relations what water is to the plumber. Each legal change is based on former legal revolutions, be those explicit, like the reforms undertaken by colonial administrators to insulate European populations from colonised populations, or implicit, like the *Lex mercatoria* – or law of the merchants – that was developed during the Cold War in the shadow of the gunboat diplomacy waged by the United States and former European imperial *métropoles* in the context of the nationalisation of the oil and mineral resources of former colonies upon independence (see Dezalay Y and Garth 1996).

Finally, and mostly, because legal intermediaries are structurally positioned as 'double agents' who juggle contradictory social, political and economic interests. Between the *jurisconsult*[7] at the service of a national diplomacy and the 'law merchant' at the service of transnational corporations, there is a community of situation. The latter is determined by the promotion, under multiple yet converging guises, of a legal type of expertise as a condition to negotiate contradictory social interests. The 'fluidity of the title' (Willemez 1999) held by lawyers opens a capacity, variable according to contexts and periods, to play multiple social and professional roles across different sectors of society – political, administrative, economic (Dezalay S 2015; Dezalay Y and Garth 2002; Vauchez and France 2020).

Lawyers are double agents because they must act as servants of sovereign powers while simultaneously safeguarding the autonomy of the law. This semi-autonomy is a condition for legitimacy (Bourdieu 2012). It is, to build on Tilly's analogy, what distinguishes organised predation from sovereign power.

1.3 Big Structures, Local Histories

As a research strategy, *interconnectedness* is also risky. There is a fine line between global history, micro-histories and totalising history. Field theory can prove particularly effective to avoid this pitfall, as it 'requires us to stop thinking in terms of entities, proper names, concrete individuals, and things and begin grasping all of these as bundles of relations' (Eyal 2013: 158). This approach calls into question the characteristics of the relationship between objectified functions or divisions – such as that of the state, the legal profession, the distinction between public and private spheres, or between capitalism's cores and its peripheries – by tracking the bundles of relations that structure these relationships and their objectification over time.

But it requires considering Steinmetz's (2014) contention that empires 'are more than giant states and are more than the forerunners of modern states' (9). This exposes at once the limitations of methodological

[7] A person authorised to give legal advice to a sovereign.

nationalism, and the need to examine symbolic and physical *boundaries and boundary-making processes* across scales and over time.

The FG Hemisphere judicial saga provides, here too, an emblematic illustration of what this research strategy entails. In 2019, the Congolese state created the *Entreprise Générale du Cobalt* (EGC) as a subsidiary to Gécamines, and entrusted it with the monopoly over the sale and commercialisation of the cobalt extracted by artisanal miners in the DRC. Following the creation of the EGC, Trafigura, the world's second largest metals and oil trader, announced that it would provide funding to create strictly controlled artisanal mining zones in Kolwezi, a mining town in eastern Congo. The installation of ore-purchasing stations ostensibly aims to foster the transparent and traceable delivery of cobalt hydroxide, in compliance with *OECD Due Diligence Guidance for Responsible Supply Chains of Minerals from Conflict-Affected and High-Risk Areas.*

A 2016 *Washington Post* investigation on the 'cobalt pipeline' estimated that about 100,000 cobalt miners in Congo use hand tools to dig hundreds of feet underground with little oversight and few safety measures. 'This informal army is big business, responsible for an estimated 10 to 25 percent of the world's cobalt production and about 17 to 40 percent of production in Congo'.[8] These workers mostly operate in the southeast of the Congo close to Zambia's border, around the city of Kolwezi. They sometimes dig out galleries under their own houses. Or they 'trespass' into concessions owned by industrial miners. Cobalt extracted by artisanal miners is also much cheaper. It is not regulated by health, pension and other labour and human rights-related standards. Foremost, it is carried on both legs and thereby escapes the financial, regulatory, political or reputational costs of *traceability.*

For example, the president of Huayou Cobalt, China Molybdenum's parent company in China, where the cobalt extracted by Molybdenum is refined, declared to the *Washington Post* investigators that they did not really know where the ore sourced by the company originated. Due diligence (just like the company's legal accountability) stops at the gates of its subsidiary.[9] Among Huayou's largest customers are battery cathode makers, like Pulead Technology Industry, which supply battery makers.

[8] TC Frankel, 'The cobalt pipeline. Tracing the path from deadly hand-dug mines in Congo to consumers' phones and laptops' *The Washington Post* 3 September 2016, www.washingtonpost.com/graphics/business/batteries/congo-cobalt-mining-for-lithium-ion-battery/ (accessed 28 October 2022).

[9] Ibid.

Those in turn supply companies like Apple. Apple denied using any cobalt originating from artisanal mining and has since set up internal audits along its supply chain. 'I think the risks can be managed', Pulead chief executive Yuan Gao told the *Washington Post* investigators. '[T]he increased awareness is actually working, as everyone is monitoring everyone else along the supply chain'.[10]

In one fell swoop, therefore, Trafigura positioned itself in such a way as to capture the cobalt produced by artisanal miners that would otherwise enter Chinese commodity chains through unofficial routes lowering the price for global traders, while ostensibly aligning with the OECD's and IFIs' transparency regulations. On the other hand, the move is likely to further reinforce Gécamines' position as gatekeeper for access to Congo's mineral wealth.

Where the move becomes even more interesting is when we zoom in onto the lawyer who coded this arrangement into law: Pascal Agboyibor. The late father of this French-Togolese corporate lawyer, Yawovi Agboyibo, the first corporate lawyer upon Togo's independence, a doctor of law from a university of the former French *métropole*, a political opponent and human rights advocate, was also the first legal counsel of Gécamines at the onset of the *FG Hemisphere* v. *DRC* judicial saga (Dezalay S 2021).

What makes the FG Hemisphere saga an imperial encounter, and, as such, at once a grand narrative and a microhistory, is that it reflects chains of *legal intermediation* that result from *imperial legacies* and *concurrent* transformations that can be tracked at the *individual* level, that of geographical *localities* (within empires, colonial states or nation states) and that of institutions. The biography and professional trajectory of Pascal Agboyibor helps explain the contention that legal intermediation, as an interconnected dynamic, can be tracked across multiple scales and thereby expose connections between big structures and local histories.

Pascal Agboyibor recently set up a multinational corporate law firm, *Asafo & Co*, as 'Africa's law firm' with a '100% Africa focus'.[11] Agboyibor is the only sub-Saharan African corporate lawyer to feature among the top three of the annual 'legal power list' published by the weekly *Jeune Afrique*, and its professionally oriented business letter, *Jeune Afrique Business +*. Until March 2019, Agboyibor headed the Africa department

[10] Ibid.

[11] See the website of the firm https://asafoandco.com (accessed 23 March 2022).

at the Paris office of the US multinational corporate law firm Orrick Herrington & Sutcliffe LLP and was the first African appointed to the board of the firm.

'Our name Asafo', explained Pascal Agboyibor, 'derives its origin from the elite groups of traditional West African warriors of the same name, which were dedicated to the defence of cities and states in the region. The name underlines our commitment to defending our clients' projects in Africa, with military discipline, rapid response, and a high level of coordination'.[12]

The firm's success built in part on the powerful clientele – foremost Gécamines – brought in by Agboyibor, thanks to a lasting relationship with the Congolese businessman Albert Yuma, a close ally of Joseph Kabila and Congo's 'CEO of the CEOs' at the helm of the Federation of Businesses of the DRC (*Fédération des entreprises du Congo*). Controversies over the fees perceived by Agboyibor (an estimated average of US$ 1 million per year between 2012 and 2018) for project financing advice on the colossal hydroelectric dam Inga III, along with his association with Gécamines, certainly lend a sour taste to an 'African victory' materialised by the replacement of the warriors of the Asante Empire with 'commandos in white collars' – to use Lonsdale's (1981: 181) expression – acting as gatekeepers of looting endeavours.

Yet Agboyibor's profile also symbolises a success story – that of a new generation of African business entrepreneurs and corporate lawyers intent on transforming the terms of the continent's relationship with global markets. Agboyibor notably leveraged the intellectual and business club he founded in 1997 in Paris – the Club Kléber – to attract private funding to foster the effective operationalisation of the Organisation for the Harmonisation of Business Law in Africa (OHADA) created in 1993, and reinforce its credibility as an arbitration seat for transnational corporations.[13] Conversely, the tensions raised by Agboyibor's fees in the Inga III project may have also reflected the World Bank's bid at selecting another counsel more inclined to secure a bigger role for the bank.[14]

12 'Asafo & Co. – A Unique Global Alternative Dedicated to Africa' 22 October 2019, www.leadersleague.com/en/news/asafo-co-a-unique-global-alternative-dedicated-to-africa (accessed 21 March 2022).

13 ME Ngisi, 'Pascal Agboyibor, l'avocat qui murmure à l'oreille des grands' *Forbes Afrique* February 2015, p. 36.

14 Jeune Afrique, 'Bras de fer entre Orrick et la Banque mondiale autour d'Inga III' *Jeune Afrique* 6 November 2014.

Against the backdrop of an ongoing backlash of African states against international dispute settlement mechanisms and pressures for 'resource nationalism' (see Dezalay S 2020b), the profile of Agboyibor as an 'African' fits neatly into the narrative of an ideological war of position between a neo-colonial process of capitalism by dispossession (Harvey 2003) and the (rusty) wheels of universalism. Yet looking at Agboyibor simply as a protagonist in this ideological turf battle risks what Bourdieu (1986) called the 'biographical illusion', that is, the trap of correlating an individual story to a linear chain of events and choices. The temptation would be great to construe the prominence taken by Agboyibor as that of an exceptional trailblazer. After all, as Agboyibor declared himself, '[M]y trajectory was accidental. If it's only I, Pascal Agboyibor, in Paris it is not enough'.[15]

The biographical illusion therefore harks back to the risk of construing Agboyibor's trajectory as *ideal-typical* rather than *structurally banal* (to use Vauchez and France's (2020: 156) expression). This is not to deny the exceptional characteristics of his trajectory. Rather, it underscores that tracking legal intermediation dynamics involves tracing the types of social resources that are converted into legal capital, and the legal forms of capital, in turn, that are leveraged as sovereign resources.

Agboyibor was born in 1967 in Togo, in a royal family deposed by the French colonial administration in the 1930s.[16] His introduction into the very select, white and male 'Africa' corporate Bar in Paris[17] grew out of a powerful family and social platform. His father, Yawovi Agboyibo, had also turned to corporate law in the early 1970s by integrating Togo's first local corporate law firm[18] after obtaining a doctorate in law in France. During an era when the newly independent state was massively recruiting into the administration and the judiciary, this choice seemed anomalous. However, investing in corporate law enabled this royal family to convert its resources into connections with the political and economic networks tying the country to the former *métropole* in the framework of what Legendre (1992) calls the French state's 'colonial projection' deployed in its former colonies *after* independence, in the form of

[15] Author's interview with Pascal Agboyibor, co-founder of Asafo & Co, Paris, 22 May 2015. My translation from French.

[16] Through a continuous reinvention of tradition, the family was reinstated as chief of canton by presidential decree under its 'royal' name, Tobgui Messan Agboyibo V, in May 2014.

[17] See Chapter 7.

[18] Founded by the French lawyer Raymond Viale in 1937.

military and judicial cooperation agreements. Conversely, this allowed Yawovi Agboyibo to reconvert these international resources into a political domestic platform, straddling between the position of president of the Lomé Bar, political opponent of Gnassingbé Eyadema and prime minister in the brief transition between the two Gnassingbé regimes (in 2005).

One generation later, Yawovi Agboyibo's political capital and position as corporate legal counsel of powerful clients – foremost Gécamines – helped Pascal Agboyibor integrate Jeantet et Associés in 1993, a French pioneer of corporate law, before joining the Paris branch of the British multinational corporate law firm Watson, Farley and Williams in 2000, which merged with Orrick, Herrington & Sutcliffe LLP in 2002. Agboyibor became a partner at Orrick in 2003. Meanwhile, Agboyibor had expanded his portfolio of African relations during a secondment to the African Development Bank in Abidjan in 1996. When he started his career, Agboyibor strategically invested in securitisation, positioning himself as a legal expert in the financialisation of commodities markets. He reinvested his African portfolio in the wake of the 2008 financial crisis, which prompted multinational corporate law firms to seek new markets in emerging economies, including in Africa. While only 10 per cent of Agboyibor's practice involved business transactions in Africa in 2008, it accounted for 100 per cent of his time ten years later.

Agboyibor's trajectory channels attention to the interlocking between extraction and extraversion (Bayart 2000)[19] as a structuring dynamic – beyond the mining sector – in the expansion of GVCs. Certainly, the predominance now taken by private contracts reflects features specific to the current phase of capitalism: the horizontalisation and financialisation of GVCs, thanks to deregulation; the protection of party autonomy through private mechanisms of dispute settlement (based on arbitration); and the expansion of regulatory governance by contract, through the inclusion of so-called extra-contractual clauses (Cutler and Dietz 2017: 4–5).

But Agboyibor's trajectory also reflects the specific role played by corporate law as a platform of conversion of family and social resources into political capital qua sovereign capital in the pre-colonial through to the post-colonial history of Togo. In Yawovi Agboyibo's case, this involved deflecting and capitalising on two features inherited by the

[19] Using Bayart's expression (Bayart 2000), extraversion refers to the *rent* derived from material and symbolic links with the international and deployed at the domestic level.

'overdeveloped' state of the 1970s: the suppression of all forms of wealth not derived from state access (Lonsdale 1981: 202) and 'straddling' as a dynamic of social reproduction and hierarchy based on the combination of a variety of occupations 'all linked by the use of public wages as private investment funds' (Lonsdale 1981: 195).

Togo – a former German colony entrusted to France as a protectorate after World War I – occupied a central position in France's Cold War 'colonial projection' into the continent. France's financial and military support to Eyadéma – a former French army military who had participated to the *métropole*'s war effort against Algerian independentists – positioned the small country as bulwark against the pan-Africanist project of Ghana's independence ruler, Nkrumah. Phosphate production, which started on the eve of independence and was predominantly earmarked for the French market, fuelled a domestic rent that also consolidated Eyadéma's power. Yawovi Agboyibo's social and family resources positioned him as a credible intermediary between new African rulers in the region and corporations from the former *métropole* precisely because this social capital produced an autonomous platform that deflected both rentier politics at the domestic level, and the stigmata of the *Françafrique.*[20]

One generation later, hailing 'Africa' as the corporate brand of the firm *Asafo & Co.* is even more efficient given that Agboyibor combines the *know-how* of project finance with the *know-who* of political clout. Agboyibor's trajectory underscores the relevance of examining the modalities of reproduction of social capital – as a legal form of capital *and* a sovereign resource – as an interconnected history.

The symbolic strength of the social capital of colonial legal intermediaries – be they *avocats-défenseurs* in the French colonies, Indian barristers in Kenya, *oukils* in Tunisia, merchants, scholars, local chiefs, colonial administrators or Privy Council magistrates – depended on the relative, uneven and evolving capacity to leverage resources (material and symbolic) determined by local hierarchies and transformed by the colonial encounter and inter-imperial confrontations. This means that their social capital can only be understood structurally, and in the *longue durée*, because it is a *sovereign* form of social capital embedded in, and imprinted by, imperial and colonial legal strategies and the post-independence trajectory of African states.

[20] The term '*Françafrique*' refers to France's sphere of influence (or '*pré carré*') over former French and Belgian colonies in sub-Saharan Africa. See Chapters 6 and 7.

Both Agboyibor's trajectory and that of his father illustrate *middling* as a form of capital and its valuation as a sovereign resource. The interstices opened by indirect rule fostered the structural distinction between the mass of what Jacquemot (2012: 17) calls the 'floating' group, those who remain *anchored* in a socially precarious position (usually outside or at the margin of capitalist economic relations), and what we could call the 'straddlers' – individuals and groups benefiting from the uneven and varied capacity to leverage and convert a *middling* capital through access to public positions, external resources, or both.

This *middling* capital also reflects the fact that '[a]s in our own day, the merchant class was transnational. It did not need the state to supervise business' (Lonsdale 1981: 36). Straddling is, in other words, a sovereign form of capital that can be deployed and valued *within* and *without* the state. To boot: the 2012 decision of the Privy Council on the dispute between FG Hemisphere and the DRC does not simply demonstrate that the substance of the new is determined by old forms of legitimacy. It also illustrates the relevance of tracking the structural loopholes *and* ordering fostered by the messiness of middle power.

1.4 Zooming In and Out

To do this, examining the value and valuation of *middling* capital in shaping, justifying and transforming competing boundaries of encounter between African sites and political, legal and economic cores can provide a formidable entry point.

However, looking at the social forms of capital converted into legal capital qua sovereign capital confronts two problems. The role of social capital – including its conversion through legal education – in the diversification of legal professions looms large in contemporary debates of the US sociology of the legal profession. But aggregating national data can obscure the different types of capital that shape social resources and their transformation over time. Agboyibor's social capital can only be understood structurally and in the *longue durée*, because it is a sovereign social capital embedded in, and imprinted by, imperial and colonial legal strategies (Dezalay Y and Garth 2010), the post-independence trajectory of African states and their embeddedness in the financialisation and globalisation of GVCs.

Cooper's contention that it is necessary to zoom in and out (Cooper 2014) to delineate the interconnectedness between individual trajectories, local histories and global structures provides a way out. I have seized upon my own duality as a defrocked lawyer and a sociologist on the job, as an observer, and therefore as a stakeholder, to follow the intermediaries who, like me, contribute to produce (while themselves being embedded in) the symbolic and practical borders between the Global North and the African South, political power, society, economy and finance. I was able to grasp this duality all the better because my own trajectory of internationalisation as a researcher between Paris, Florence, New York, Toronto, Frankfurt, Cardiff and Lille, in institutions like the Munk School of Global Affairs that hail as 'edge' research institutions – as providers of critical knowledge on globalisation – prompted the need to re-examine, each time, my position in relation to my research objects and therefore continuously summon the objectivation process of my research.

Lawyering Imperial Encounters is therefore the product of a reverse problematisation. I bring together a priori disparate research fieldworks not as isolated objects but as interconnected empirical sites. I draw on fifteen years of research on peacebuilding professional markets in Burundi; professional markets of global justice (inter-state adjudication; international arbitration; international criminal justice); international professional markets for peacebuilding and conflict resolution since the end of the Cold War; the Africa corporate Bar in Paris; strategic litigation against transnational corporations; and my own practice as an adjunct judge, appointed by the United Nations High Commissioner for Refugees (UNHCR), at the French National Court of Asylum (CNDA – *Cour nationale du droit d'asile*).

I built these empirical stories by deploying a qualitative approach that combines biographical interviews, prosopography,[21] participant observation, the deployment of international research networks and embedded research. I constructed this approach in many ways *ex post*. My own trajectory, as a student, as an academic, is embedded in the post–Cold War trajectory of scholarly fields, in international relations, political sociology and international law – from the 'new war' thesis of the early 1990s that espoused as much the policy pull of filling the vacuum left by the 'real' post-colonial order (Ellis 1996: 17) as they reflected the anxious, middle-class rekindling of what Lonsdale (1981) described as the 'Committee of Concerned Scholars for a Free Africa' (143). However, in the scholarship I inherited freedom was no longer part of the equation.

[21] Prosopography refers to the social cartography of distinct groups of people or professional fields over time.

These empirical investigations were prompted by the immediate post–Cold War redefinition of the 'problem' of *under*development in the African South and its relationship with the expansion of new forms of knowledge on the state, development and external forms of intervention into the continent. Between 2004 and 2011, I investigated the intermediaries – within state diplomacies, international organisations and NGOs in Europe and the United States – who contributed to this transformation, based on about 100 interviews, visits of archives at the Ford Foundation, the Peace Research Institute of Oslo and that of NGOs,[22] as well as participant observation at what was then the Paris Research Office of the International Secretariat of Amnesty International.[23]

Between 2011 and 2014, I conducted several field trips to Burundi[24] – whose case loomed large in the expansion of non-governmental professional sectors of conflict resolution and peacebuilding, conducting about 100 interviews with diplomats, consultants, agents of local and international NGOs, members of the bar and of the judiciary. In parallel, I investigated the professional networks operating within and around the International Criminal Court (ICC) in The Hague.[25]

From 2014, I built several international and interdisciplinary research networks[26] aimed at questioning the roles played by lawyers in state transformations across the African South; and at building archives, through collective and interdisciplinary knowledge, on law and legal intermediaries in the GVCs connecting resource-rich African states to global markets.

In 2014–2016, I also conducted participant observation at professional conferences (under the aegis of the G7 and the World Bank in particular) to identify the professional networks involved in the negotiation of contracts between transnational corporations and resource-rich African

[22] Based on doctoral funding as a PhD researcher at the European University Institute in 2005–2011.

[23] Based on an internship in 2004.

[24] Based on research funding provided by the French national research agency.

[25] I conducted about twenty interviews and participant observation and built a biographical database of judges and defense lawyers at the ICC, based on research funding provided by the Munk School of Global Affairs, University of Toronto.

[26] Including the Sub-Group 'Lawyers and Legal Imperialism(s)', International Working Group for Comparative Studies of Legal Professions, Research Committee on Sociology of Law, International Sociological Association, which I co-created with the regretted Wesley Pue in 2014, as well as the International Research Collaborative 'Lawyers and state transformations' (Law and Society Association and International Sociological Association) which I co-created with Ole Hammarslev in 2020.

states and conducted over twenty interviews with members of the select Africa corporate Bar in Paris. I complemented this data by building biographical databases (based on interviews and case-law analysis) of the agents involved in international dispute settlement mechanisms (the International Court of Justice (ICJ) and its predecessor, the Permanent Court of International Justice (PCIJ); the Permanent Court of Arbitration (PCA) and the International Centre for Settlement of Investment Disputes of the World Bank Group (ICSID)) since the turn of the twentieth century.[27] Finally, the research draws on my own role as an adjunct judge, appointed by the UNHCR, at the French National Court of Asylum (CNDA) in 2020–2022.

1.5 Lawyering: Critical Junctures and Scales

I redeployed the empirical data I gathered based on these various empirical fieldworks to capture connections between global structures and local histories in instances of empirical encounters. Each story is about modalities of legal deployment – what I call *lawyering* – whose societal, political and economic effects vary according to *historical junctures* and empirical and symbolic *scales*.

In some instances, the interplay between historical juncture and scale seems to lend itself to an obvious understanding of the structural effects of lawyering. In Burundi, for example, the historical juncture of the war that started in 1993 and the multiple international rule of law reforms projects that were deployed in the country through the decade produced effects that can be narrated at the scale of the country – in structural transformations of the legal field and the field of state power.

Major critical junctures like the 1884–1885 Berlin Congress, the two world wars, the 1960s wave of independence, the end of the Cold War, the neoliberal turn and the deregulation of financial markets can also appear straightforward. But in most instances, in the absence of the delicate exercise of going back to original encounters, critical junctures offer limited heuristic value when they do not easily map onto the grid of concurrent changes. It is a truism to say that legal decolonisation did not coincide with the political independence of former African colonies – if only because the trajectories, strategies and choices of the legal

[27] Based on funding provided by the Cluster of Excellence, the Formation of Normative Orders, Goethe Universität.

professionals that served the new states continued to be shaped by the imperial realm for a decade – and much longer in some cases.

Channelling attention to lawyering in *crisis situations* provides an alternative entry. Crises are sometimes objectified through policy and scholarly pulls. They can also be legitimated, *as* crises, through law's objectivation of societal disputes. The Privy Council decision in the *FG Hemisphere* v. *DRC* case emerges as a critical juncture when it consolidates the position of Gécamines as a private–public incarnation of the Congolese state. Crises in all cases 'reactivate the initial conflicts and contradictions that existed at the outset' (Dezalay Y and Garth 2011: 40).

The imperial encounters I narrate in the following stories are selective. They do not intend to capture historical changes in their totality, but rather to expose pre-existing conflicts and contradictions that help understand ongoing conflicts and contradictions.

The time frame of the first imperial encounters (1890s–1950s, 1950s–1980s, 1980s–?) rubs partly against the usual focus on either independence as a break or the neoliberal turn. The concurrent patterns of legal imperialism and capital flight (what I call capitalism's lumpiness, borrowing Benton and Ford's (2016) term) I identify in the first period are imprinted in the patterns of extraverted protection and offshore capitalism of the second, while the legal boom of the third, characterised simultaneously by *deregulation* and *re-regulation*, emerges as a reiteration of the past. The formalisation of indirect rule across sub-Saharan African colonies paralleled the early genesis of institutions of global justice that were themselves reflective of the position of Britain as middle power in world politics.

Independence and the nationalisation of extractive assets did not displace the terms of the relationship between African economies and global markets, due to the combined effect of the Cold War partition of the continent, which reinforced the stakes, for political elites, of holding on to the rent of extraction, the repositioning of the City as the world's financial capital and the expansion of the Euromarket. The new rush for Africa's critical minerals is embedded in these imperial and post-independence tracks, as much as it is reflective of the structural effects of African states' debt crisis and the global thrust of neoliberalism in the early 1980s.

The following stories of imperial encounters build on this broad canvas by focusing on local sites – Abidjan, Bujumbura and Paris – and institutions of global justice – that are at once *imperial in their making* and shaped and transformed by the *interconnectedness of competing local histories*. Each of these selective empirical sites are *partial* refractions of concurrent dynamics of structuration of the global into what I call archipelagos of sedimented imperialism.

The rush for rare earths in Burundi exposes the structural effects of the imperial legacy of double-edged protection. The Probo Koala scandal in Abidjan reveals the connections between the formal end of the exclusive colonial interface between Côte d'Ivoire and the former *métropole* at the turn of the 1990s and the prominence taken by global traders and multinational corporate law firms as the interface between African economies and global markets. Paris' multifaceted position as former imperial core, capital of international arbitration and 'beach-head' for the expansion of US-led corporate legal globalisation from the 1980s tracks the globalisation of the Wall Street model of the multinational corporate law firm as an engine of reproduction of individual, institutional and global hierarchies. The last imperial encounter, focused on global justice institutions, exposes the interconnectedness between global shifts and boundary-making operations in justice institutions as specialised professional remits. Focusing on boundary-making goes beyond the divide between international/national justice institutions. Rather, the prism of social capital – a core characteristic of *middling* – points to the structural position of justice institutions and professional markets as either symbolic gateways or institutional highways in the legal justification of globalised patterns of division between the world's cores and its peripheries.

These imperial encounters reflect global instances of local histories, local iterations of the global. These instances of imperial encounters are not *systematically* connected. To reiterate: the imperialism on the cheap implemented by European powers in the first Scramble produced both hierarchy and instability.

I embrace chaos as a research agenda by tracking processes that can tell us how law, politics and finance *intersect* in shaping the encounter between Africa and capitalism as much as how they intersect with capitalism tout court. In this intersection, it is not only the uneven and unequal relationship between Africa and globalisation that is renegotiated. It is also the symbolic and practical fabric of what is hailed as globalism and the frontiers of sovereignty and state–society relations in globalisation's so-called cores that are being recast.

2

Indirect Rule and Middle Power

1880s–1950s

It is suggestive of law's centrality to the colonial enterprise that victors' histories of independence in the post-colonial world were written by indigenous lawyers: Elias in Nigeria, Nehru in India, Mandela in South Africa. That lawyers could be 'freedom fighters' in the British Empire and to a lesser extent in the French Empire but *not* at all in the Belgian tends to reinforce the common portrayal of Belgian colonialism as *lawless* realm. Recent research on the *État independent du Congo* (ÉIC – Congo Free State) and Belgian Congo is tracing a story much more complex than the common dialectic between the *mission civilisatrice* championed by King Leopold II and the *raubwirtschaft* (plunder economy) deployed in Congo, Burundi and Rwanda (Ngongo et al. 2017; Plasman 2014a, 2014b). Contrary to the image of lawlessness that characterises the Great Lakes region, these studies are demonstrating that just like in the British Empire law played an instrumental role in the colonising process, and the assertion of the Belgian Empire within the European balance of power.

Rather than opposing the British imperial rule of law to Leopold II's predatory imperialism in the Congo – with the French imperial model standing somewhat in the middle of these opposites – this is exposing the structural congruence between military conquest, economic interests and legal imperialism, from the Roman Empire through to the nineteenth-century formal partition of the African continent. As Schmidhauser (1992) puts it,

> legal imperialism universally imposed law where civil stability and order were at stake, where economic penetration – whether land tenure or modern trade and commercial development – was at issue, and, most crucial, where the authority and power of the conqueror might be threatened by invocation of indigenous law. With imposition of conqueror's law inevitably came replacement of indigenous legal and judicial elites by those of the conqueror, at least until a subservient indigenous elite was trained and screened.
>
> (328)

Legal imperialism operationalised through formalised or informal indirect rule was all the more necessary to the nineteenth-century Scramble for Africa that it was imperialism 'on the cheap'. In the *Afrique-Occidentale Française* (AOF, French West Africa), financial transfers from the *métropole* averaged 0.1 per cent of total metropolitan public expenses between 1898 and 1957 (Huillery 2009: 3). There were only ninety-three colonial magistrates deployed in French sub-Saharan African colonies in 1947 (Farcy 2011). The colonial judiciary in the Belgian Congo was perennially understaffed – there were 400 magistrates deployed in the territory between 1908 and independence.

Throughout the African colonies that emerged out of the formal partition of the continent at the 1884–1885 Berlin Congress, the surprisingly limited humane, logistical and financial investment of European powers reflected conflicts in the field of state power in the *métropoles* and inter-imperial confrontations. The contradictory operationalisation of the colonial enterprise was typified by the arrogance of the 'civilising mission' of the Third Republic in France, the unbridled autonomy left to missionaries and generally to European business entrepreneurs, through to the violence and variable success of making 'Africa the object of all sorts of projects to exploit its human and material resources' (Cooper 2004: 11) – ranging from railroads, mines, plantations to transforming the bodies of colonised populations through medical intervention.

Yet it was 'the *non-transformation* of African societies' that was elevated into the 'central claim to the legitimacy of [colonial] rule' (Cooper 2004). Legitimacy claims were part and parcel of inter-imperial rivalries. The ill-named Congo Free State served a general European interest, that of securing free navigation and free trade in the area. The non-transformation of African societies, in turn, involved the contradictory maintenance of the bulk of colonised populations outside capitalist relations *and* the insulation of the extraction of raw commodities harnessed towards global markets from African societies.

The creation of the Indian Raj in 1859 resulted from events in Britain and in India that came together to change the orientation of the empire. Conflicts of interests within the field of state power in the *métropole* – between trade interests, Crown prerogatives and missionary ideals – were displaced on the terrain of the law as a resource of moralisation and 'civilisation'. Court reforms in India and the promotion of an enlightened Indian legal elite served the purpose of promoting India as a 'shining example' of the British Empire. They were also refracted in the British field of power as a laboratory of a rule of law based on legal rationality (see Lardinois 2008).

There was no similar 'shining example' of law's promise to the colonial enterprise in British, French and Belgian African colonies. Law was central to the colonising process, but in a 'curiously ambiguous way' (Merry 1991: 891). With the double purpose of deploying a moral economy of justification and control, the co-optation of local elites fostered the promotion of law and legal arenas as sites of contests and relative emancipation. The intense circulation of agents within each empire, and from the peripheries to the *métropoles*, facilitated the spread of these 'trappings of civilization' (Merry 2003: 576).

But imperialism on the cheap fostered legal and capitalist unevenness, what Benton and Ford call 'lumpiness' of power expansion and legal ordering (Benton and Ford 2016). As Lonsdale synthesises it, 'the opportunities for popular resistance by mobility between and withdrawal from markets [were not] extinguished [by colonial conquest] and may in some parts of Africa even be increasing' (Lonsdale 1981: 167). Rather, 'articulation [. . .] embraced many conflicting social processes, dependent upon the nature of the local food production system, the most readily exploitable export resources, and most of all upon the coalition of dominant interests, capitalist, pre-capitalist, and combinations of the two to which [colonial] governors had to defer if they were to secure profits, peace, and promotion' (Lonsdale 1981: 182).

Articulation also reflected the sway of Britain as world hegemon and inter-imperial confrontations. Resolution of the political crises produced by middle power – be they conflicts in colonies, contests between colonial administrators and the *métropoles* or inter-imperial confrontations – tended to come in the form of sporadic, uneven and scattered jurisdictional responses. These responses served different purposes – from the containment of accusations of tyranny or threats to colonial power, to the avoidance of full-blown military confrontation between imperial contenders. But 'jurisdictional orders under imperial sway were not only difficult to conjure. They were also very unstable' (Benton and Ford 2016: 183–184). The forces of change brought in by imperial law were not systematically designed to foster a radical redistribution of right or authority. They were also 'notoriously difficult to calibrate' (Benton and Ford 2016: 184).

In what follows, I focus on three crisis situations that were ostensibly solved through juridical means. The first concerned conflicts between Gold Coast customary chiefs, European merchants and colonial administrators that were solved by the JCPC, otherwise known as the Privy Council, in the 1920s.

The second instance revisits the well-known 1895 Stokes-Lothaire incident, in which a Belgian administrator summarily executed an Irish missionary-turned-trader. The subsequent crisis between Belgium, Britain and Germany triggered by the incident was arbitrated by the High Council of the Congo (*Conseil supérieur du Congo*).

The third instance contrasts the military trials that were waged against anti-colonial indigenous political elites in French and British African colonies throughout the 1940s and 1950s.

These three instances concern vastly different periods and contexts. Yet, together, they help account for structural commonalities in the articulation of post-independence African states with the world economy – despite widely different post-colonial economic and political trajectories: the deployment of merchant law *with* and *without* state sovereignty and *middling* as a durable though variable sovereign resource of the post-colonial state.

2.1 Middle Power *within* and *across* European Empires

Despite the contrast often drawn between British indirect rule and French direct rule, a similar pattern of indirect rule was deployed across all empires. Lord Lugard's policy of indirect rule, developed for the centralised states of Northern Nigeria in the early twentieth century, was disseminated through the rest of British Africa (whether chiefly or acephalous) as well as the African colonies of France, Belgium, Portugal and Italy (Mamdani 1996: 78–88; Merry 2003: 580).

The expansion of indirect rule (whether formalised in the British Empire or informal, in the French and Belgian cases) generally produced forms of sovereign 'lumpiness' (to use Benton and Ford's (2016) expression). In this age of empire, the natural state of affairs entailed *unevenness* in the actual or claimed penetration of European power. 'Sovereignty was often attenuated, multiplied, and layered, and authority delegated. Local administrations in overseas territories had considerable leeway in drafting company and bank laws or tax codes and accounting standards for these respective entities and sub-entities. Legal and political unevenness greatly benefited tax avoidance, and capital accumulation more generally, on a global scale' (Ogle 2017: 1432).

Generally, 'by the time of the First World War, both French and British officials had learned how difficult it was to implement these projects – to reform Africa or to exploit it. In the vast spaces of the continent, officials had to cooperate with the very leaders who were the object of transformation' (Cooper 2004: 11).

Indeed, 'for all their lack of formal representative institutions, colonial administrations were so feeble in coercive potential, so dependent on the politics of collaboration with African notables' that the dual economies of African colonies 'were in fact faithful registers of local class conflict and expressed within the changing rules of access to colonial government rather than raging outside or against it' (Lonsdale 1981: 191).

Middle power is a general feature of the colonial enterprise and imperialism tout court. Middle power in the nineteenth-century Scramble for Africa also displayed features that were characteristic of this age of empire. Legal lumpiness was a defining feature of the British hegemon. The paradox, certainly 'for a polity that had killed one king and exiled another for their despotism', is that '[w]hether from the centre of the empire or from its peripheries, advocacy for legal reform often turned into calls to extend Crown prerogative in empire' (Benton and Ford 2016: 4). Yet '[t]he recognition of the limits of imperial strategies materialized fitfully, most often in relation to individual crises rather than in connection with a unified ideological position or political program' (Benton and Ford 2016: 183).

Legitimacy contests about the colonial enterprise were arbitrated as *sovereignty* claims among the European nation states that emerged during the period. Legal lumpiness allowed for 'the simultaneous extension of imperial jurisdiction *within* and *without* the empire' (Benton and Ford 2016: 194, emphasis added). This enabled exceptional violence to coexist alongside the expansion and institutionalisation of a British imperial rule of law.

The Privy Council was created in 1833 as the court of last resort with jurisdiction over appeals from the courts of all the colonies and dominions of the British Empire, representing nearly 400 million people. It was the first, and effectively to date the only, *global* court. The Privy Council heard contests over the remits and the legitimacy of middle power in colonies that were also claims about sovereignty. Its case law produced structural effects beyond the borders of the British Empire. Both the French and Belgian *métropoles* emulated this claim to *hierarchy* through juridical ordering.

It is the fear of excesses of uncontrolled delegates of the British Crown, the French or the Belgian *métropoles*, merchants or local chiefs – not revolutions – that 'made humble colonial complaints so powerful in the metropolis' (Benton and Ford 2016: 8). Despots came in many forms, but their common feature was the exercise of arbitrary justice. '[T]his interpretation of petty despotism meant that actions to control their authority became legal interventions' (Benton and Ford 2016: 182) – be it by the British Crown *within* and *at the edges* of Britain's empire or by Paris and Brussels to solve problems of regional disorder, enforce global prohibitions and stave off British economic domination.

That Britain could embark swiftly on the (colonial) business as usual in Mandatory Palestine in the 1920s reflected the intense circulation of imperial repertoires of power and agents throughout the British empires. Indeed, '[t]hey [could] play their pipes as they ha[d] played them in a hundred lands' (Shamir 2000: 20). Tracking these dynamics of circulation is essential as they were also embedded in conflicts that were at once multi-scalar – at the level of *métropoles*, colonial states and between empires – and multi-sectoral, as they involved groups and agents deploying combinations of resources – legal, political, economic, social – that differed according to time and space.

What makes these conflicts so significant for the process of European colonisation of Africa in the later part of the nineteenth century is, precisely, their *messiness*. Struggles over law created new winners and losers, in the peripheries as much as the cores. '[R]eining in petty despotism almost always meant restraining the jurisdiction of some subjects over subordinates and enhancing the jurisdiction of others' (Benton and Ford 2016: 8).

Indirect rule meant that legal change through the reinvention of custom (see Hobsbawm and Ranger 1983) also aimed to limit social disruption. Indigenous law was recognised only when it could no longer offer a true alternative to the power of the colonial state. Law was instrumental in incorporating pre-colonial social formations into the colonial framework and redefining them along new social, political and economic fault lines.

That colonialism created the institutional space for legal professions to emerge across the African continent, whether in the British, French or Belgian Empires, and despite the specificities of local imperial strategies – from the legal fiction of the protectorate in Tunisia to settler colonialism in former Rhodesia – has been amply demonstrated by the large swath cut through scholarship by Chanock's (1985) path-breaking work and the growth since of legal historical scholarship on law and colonialism (see Benton and Ross 2013; Ibhawoh 2013; Merry 1999, 2003).

The colonial enterprise created the *need* for lawyers, whether metropolitan (to protect the personal and economic interests of Europeans) or indigenous (to fill in the political vacuum created when traditional institutions were suppressed or warped to imperial ends) (Oguamanam and Pue 2016: 478).

But *métropoles* as much as colonial administrators generally considered lawyers the 'bête noire' of colonial rule. As Lonsdale (1981: 24) put it, '[i]f the paraphernalia of bureaucracy was understood to be its ritual code, then those who first deciphered it, lawyers and other literati, had obvious claims to be colonialism's most effective usurpers'.

Across sub-Saharan Africa's French colonies, *avocats-défenseurs* were explicitly barred from customary courts, and access to the profession was reserved to Europeans, as well as Africans originating from the *Quatre Communes* in Senegal.[1] The situation of the Algerian colony stood apart – both because it was designed as a settler colony and due to the Ottoman imperial legacy of a pre-existing and socially strong doctrinal and institutional *shari'a* legal system (Christelow 1985). Likewise, the legal imperial strategy deployed by the French *métropole* in what was instituted as the Tunisian protectorate in 1881 reflected the legal fiction of the continuity of the bay's authority. The dual system accommodated on the one hand the pre-existing judicial *shari'a* system populated by *oukils*, and on the other the competition of the French *métropole* with the British and Italian Empires. The cohorts of indigenous lawyers trained at the University of Algiers deployed in Tunisia contributed to incorporating the protectorate within a regional 'North-African' colonial unit. The authorisation granted to Italian and British barristers to appear before the French-styled judicial system was progressively extended to Tunisian lawyers and positioned the latter as at once new notables and nationalist leaders (Gobe 2013).

In sub-Saharan British settler colonies, the dual system of European and 'indigenous' law was complemented by de jure or de facto obstacles to the emergence of indigenous legal elites. It was only in 1953 that the first African lawyer joined the Southern Rhodesian legal profession (current Zimbabwe), over a hundred years after his counterparts in Ghana and Nigeria, which had approximately 120 and 540 indigenous private legal practitioners at independence (Dawuni 2017; Karekwaivanane 2020; Uzebu-Imarhiagbe 2020). In Nigeria, British law

[1] Dakar, Saint-Louis, Gorée and Rufisque.

was 'zoned' to commercial centres, foremost among them Lagos, where a distinct market of indigenous lawyers emerged in the mid-1800s, while English-trained lawyers were barred from the hinterland (Oguamanam and Pue 2016). The restricted legal market in Rhodesia responded to a demand from the mining, agriculture and commercial sectors and mirrored the racial dividing lines that structured the South African legal market, thanks to the mobility of South African lawyers (Karekwaivanane 2020).

South Africa stood in an exceptional position among British colonies in sub-Saharan Africa, having developed a dynamic domestic legal market, though one structured around exclusive racial divisions (Chanock 2001). Like in South Africa, in the British settler colony of Kenya, conflicts between European settlers and the British *métropole* were resolved through a de jure or de facto policy of separation of the population into three groups – Africans, Asians and Europeans. While the coloniser exercised less control over Europeans and Asians, when they had the economic resources to seek education privately, the education of Africans was blocked by denying them bursaries to study law in the *métropole*. The exclusion of lawyers from primary courts and the preservation of a subsistence economy in the rural hinterland were protective devices against the perceived subversion of capitalist expansion.

Despite the wariness of the colonial administration towards European and Asian lawyers, there was also a mutuality of interests. The apathy of European lawyers in the face of colonial violence was traded for monopolies granted by the colonial administrator, which contributed to the structuration of a pre-independence autonomous profession in urban centres – predominantly Nairobi.

Contrary to the West African Court of Appeal (WACA), the East African Court of Appeal (EACA) set up in 1901 to hear appeals from native courts, provincial and district courts, high courts and supreme courts could play a broader inter-territorial political cooperation and legal amalgamation role, as its mandate – exercised by career colonial judicial officers – covered continuous colonial territories.[2] Africans were, however, significantly less involved in appeals to the EACA, due to the greater racial barriers that prevented entry of Africans into the legal profession (Ibhawoh 2013). The legal profession in East Africa was almost entirely non-African until the 1960s. As late as 1962, there were

[2] Kenya, Uganda and Malawi, and following the First World War, Zanzibar and Tanganyika.

only thirteen African attorneys in the whole of Southern Africa. There were no African lawyers in Kenya well into the 1960s, and few in the early years of independence (see Ghai 1981).

'In Kenya [. . .] Africans were concerned that the jurisprudence of the Privy Council reinforced legislation of segregation and the JCPC catered primarily to the immigrant communities who regarded English law as their law' (Ibhawoh 2013: Kindle edition 497). Nonetheless, just as the case law of the Privy Council could flow into East Africa, appeals to the EACA reflected imperial 'counterflows'. For instance, the Indian solicitor M. H. Malik, based in Nairobi, litigated several criminal appeals pro bono for African clients on behalf of humanitarian organisations such as the London-based Howard League for Penal Reform.

The corollary of legal imperial strategies of exclusion/co-optation during the nineteenth-century Scramble for Africa was that the capacity of indigenous (legal) elites to avail themselves of the status granted them by British or French law depended on their embeddedness in local nodes of power (Schmidhauser 1997).

As a strategy for the deployment of power and maintenance of social peace, indirect rule was a pragmatic solution to the sparsity – throughout the empires, and particularly in sub-Saharan Africa – of metropolitan agents deployed in the colonies. It also exposed the fact that

> [c]olonial officials were an external elite, not locally connected [. . .]. They were so distanced from local politics that they suppressed capitalist endeavour as a form of political subversion [. . .]. Colonial rule was therefore self-defeating in the very real sense that what was instrumentally optimal to the *métropoles* was directly antagonistic to their bureaucratic agents, since increasing production necessarily fostered the boisterous politics of local class-formation.
>
> (Lonsdale 1981: 190–191)

The dual legal system of indirect rule could function quite well to the extent that an indigenous elite was screened and trained to be subservient; but it would inevitably be transformed as the local social and political fault lines reshaped through colonialism influenced the imperial judicial system. The weakness of colonial rule opened a vacuum that was filled both by the evolving structure of local hierarchies and the imperial embeddedness of colonial legal fields. Emblematically, the absence of a local hierarchical system of chiefdom in Southeastern Nigeria doomed indirect rule to failure. To be effective, the dual regime providing the foundation of indirect rule in Nigeria required a reduction of the potential threat of indigenous law as an alternative to the power of the colonial state.[3]

2.2 Gold Coast Juridical Battles

The Gold Coast provides an illustration of these conflicts, and the contradictory effects of their judicialisation. Gold Coast lawyers were the most numerous along with Southern Nigeria's indigenous legal elite, across British African colonies, to mobilise the imperial rule of law – through judicial appeals to the Privy Council from the turn of the twentieth century.

In contrast to other British colonial contexts, particularly India, indirect rule also rested on the explicit dominance of state law – with at its apex the Privy Council as the ultimate umpire over 'native' conflicts. As a corollary, indirect rule required the fostering of indigenous legal and judicial elites that would not only be subservient to colonial rule but also be champions of the imperial rule of law. While mostly metropolitan lawyers were involved in appeals to the Privy Council, there were also some indigenous lawyers, mostly from Ghana and Nigeria. All occupied important positions in the colonial judiciary, all became involved in legal politics: fighting within the system by embracing the imperial rule of law is what enabled them to become the 'fighting brigade of the people' (Oguamanam and Pue 2016) by contesting the contradictions of colonialism.

The Gold Coast was the first African coast to be approached by European merchants – first for the European gold trade, and later in the context of the transatlantic slave trade. It was also situated at the edges of an empire, the Asante. Colonisation of the Gold Coast was achieved through expansion into the Asante Empire. The case illustrates the fact that 'save for Egypt and Ethiopia [. . .] Africa was a continent of colonizing societies' (Lonsdale 1981: 34). Yet 'military occupation does not create a political order, but a need to create one' (Lonsdale 1981).

Colonial conquest of the hinterland of the Asante Kingdom – effectively achieved at the turn of the twentieth century – must be read in the context of Asante's imperial strategies towards the coast. Positioned at the crossroad of the trans-Saharan trade in gold and slaves, Asante's core – Kumasi – evolved from capital of a tribal kingdom to financial centre and political capital of a centralised empire over the course of the

[3] This was illustrated by the eradication of the sophisticated ancient Sharia system of legal education in Nigeria's predominantly Muslim North.

eighteenth century, making the provinces of the coast 'pay for their conquest with what the British in India over the same period called "subsidiary alliances"' (Lonsdale 1981: 178).

Nearly all the forest-savannah regions of the Asante Empire had access to alluvial gold, which from the seventeenth century was traded with Europeans and funded conquest wars, along with the trade in slaves centralised at Kumasi. Mining labour was done predominantly within the domestic sphere – either at the scale of conjugal families who mined gold as a complement to subsistence agriculture production, or that of individuals employing slave labour (Arhin 1978: 93). Mined gold attracted a 50 per cent tax owed to the king – the Asantehene – based in Kumasi. 'The King's right to 50 percent of the winnings derived from his paramount or allodial title to land' (Arhin 1978: 93). Taxation and punishments such as confiscations and death 'ensured that the bulk of the gold trade was done by power-holders' (Arhin 1978: 97).

However, '[a]t the heart of resource exchange and control were chiefs and kings who acted as custodians for local resources' (Tsuma 2012: 4). The strength of the empire lay in a system of allegiance to the core based on the administrative institution of the *asomfo*.[4] 'Asante's new officials were very often the sons of the old; the political class was linked by innumerable ties of marriage, descent, and culture [and competed] within a single promotional field' (Lonsdale 1981: 179). At each level of this hierarchical system, Akan rulers were 'elected' following a complex system of consultations with the royal lineage, the Queen mother, Stool Elders as well as the *asafo* groups drawn from non-office-holders' commoners (Addo-Fening 2013: 43–44). Asafo groups (literally 'military companies') stood apart in this hierarchical structure defined by matrilineal kinship ties. Foremost active in the coastal regions of the Asante Empire, these military companies were based on patrilineal membership. They were tasked with warring and policing functions – including that of toppling rulers deemed unfit – and judicial roles of conflict mediation (Datta and Porter 1971: 281).

The proclamation establishing the Gold Coast Colony and Protectorate in 1874 gradually 'enlarge[d] not only European but also African power, if in both cases at the expense of other Africans' (Lonsdale 1981: 184). Trade was at the heart of the political economy of the Asante Empire. The imperial core's control over trade enabled the

[4] Effectively, regional and local stools along the coast and in the savannah.

gradual emergence of a restricted mercantile elite, positioned as intermediary between local and Northern markets, and European trade establishments on the coast. The latter grew in substantial numbers in the colonial period, once British colonial authorities effectively abolished the traditional fiscal constraints on private acquisition of wealth. Asafo companies' numbers expanded with European contact – some, for instance, received payment by Dutch merchants for protection in the early eighteenth century. Until the *Pax Britannica* of colonial rule removed Asafo companies' military functions, British conquest enabled the displacement of their allegiance towards local traders against the Asante imperial core (see Datta and Porter 1971: 285–287).

Anglo-Ashanti wars played a key role in the downfall of the Asante Empire from the 1880s by siphoning state resources into the war effort – leading to the annexation of the Asante Kingdom in 1901 to the Gold Coast Colony after the destruction of Kumasi. This decline also resulted from the loss of the bounties of the slave trade following its abolition by Britain. It moreover reflected the relative disengagement of the imperial core in controlling the gold trade, which allowed official traders to make private deals with Europeans.

Cultivating communities in the savannah resisted to warfare and tributary extraction by turning to traders for protection and leveraging the production of palm oil and rubber, and later cocoa, for external trade. '[T]he intensification of European trade and the onset of colonial rule promoted and benefited from the rise of a newly conscious class, men whose career opportunities had been created first by centralization, then by the increasing power of chiefs over kings, and now, with the growing commodity trade, by the opportunity to put public power to private profit' (Lonsdale 1981: 181).

Conversely, continuous conflicts between the Gold Coast, Kumasi and its Northern neighbours also affected the basis for the expansion of Britain's rule on the ground. Due to the devastating effects of these conflicts on British trade, the British Crown relinquished responsibility for the Gold Coast settlements in 1828 to a committee of London merchants (Reynolds 1975: 99). To broker peace, this committee fostered alliances with local chiefs whose authority – traditionally largely based on profits from war captives – had been shaken by the abolition of the slave trade, by positioning them as brokers with European merchants.

This benefited the emerging class of African traders while enhancing European merchants' position as protectors of coastal communities. The growing trade in cotton and other goods – first imported from India, and progressively from Britain – and export of palm oil and rubber 'led to the rise of a merchant class who began to assume the political and economic power that traditional rulers had formerly yielded' (Lonsdale 1981: 104).

The wealth of this merchant class was fostered by a system of credit backed by European merchants, and the construction of palatial homes – used also for storage – protected by Asafo companies. But the unequal terms of this credit system enabled the gradual domination of European merchants, including as brokers for goods traded with the hinterland. Competition with European traders and British traders' discontent with the lack of protection by the British Crown against Asante invasions in the 1860s spurred a short-lived alliance between local traders and chiefs within the 'Fante confederation' – against British Crown power. This, in turn, paved the way for the formalisation of colonisation in 1874 by Britain 'in order to keep the peace necessary for trade and the protection of British traders' (Reynolds 1975: 116).

The colonial office, under pressure from British mining companies, effectively quashed artisanal mining production with the Mercury Ordinance of 1933 which criminalised the use of mercury by African miners (Tsuma 2012: 5). This, however, also resulted in promoting *land* itself as the staple of trade between chiefs and European merchants. Continuous conflicts between chiefs and pit-miners over the payment of gold-mining surplus 'gave the chiefs the opportunity to rid themselves of the troublesome pit-miners in return for more regular concession payments from the Europeans' (Silver 1981: 525). By 1910, the area of concessions granted by chiefs exceeded the colony's total land area (Luckham 1981: 97).

'Despite the scramble for concession options in the early part of the [twentieth] century [. . .] the direct role of foreign capital in the Gold Coast's economic expansion' was limited (Luckham 1981: 100), as this dynamism was provided by cocoa production for world markets. 'The renewed European interest in the mining of Gold Coast gold was sparked by stories told by officers and soldiers returning from the Asante War of 1873–4 of the vast riches in gold to be found in the Gold Coast' (Silver 1981: 512) – which spurred a speculative financial bubble at the London and Paris stock exchanges and a scramble for land concessions. The boom, however, was short-lived, due to the manipulation of mining company shares and land concessions to produce speculative gains, lack of expertise, managerial and transport shortcomings and foremost the lack of interest of the colonial state in promoting the interests of European mining companies. Both the profits of merchant capital and (indirectly) the colonial government lay in the trade of palm oil, rubber and cocoa based on a peasant-based economy that required little government intervention and expenditure (Silver 1981: 522). Further, the perseverance of resistance of local wageworkers against European mining companies blighted production through the 1940s, and pressured companies to 'provide subsidized housing and electricity, improved medical care, and a variety of sports and recreation facilities' (Breckenridge 2011: 253).

Disputes between local chiefs and traders, European merchants and the colonial state in the Gold Coast trickled to the Privy Council, while contributing to the gradual prominence taken by the Privy Council as a 'veritable clearing house of conflicting legal codes, demands, and disputes, and hence a gateway to both local processes and imperial regulation' (Ibhawoh 2017: 120).

In particular, the lengthy 'Asamankese dispute' between 1919 and 1929 opposed the sub-stools of Asamankese and Akwatia in the Gold Coast to the paramount stool of Akim Abuakwa (Luckham 1981: 94). The former asserted their right to secede from the paramount chief, while the latter demanded recognition of paramount interests in the diamond concessions the sub-stools had negotiated with a British mining corporation, the African Selection Trust. In 1929, legal counsels for both parties agreed to put the matter to arbitration. The arbitrator confirmed the Privy Council ruling – that land ownership lay with the sub-stools – but added that they were politically subordinated to the paramount and therefore had to pay a proportion of their royalties. Further litigation ensued, only to end after the colonial government enacted special legislation to bring Asamankese along with the stool revenues under direct colonial control (Luckham 1981: 94).

As documented by Luckham (1981), the defence of chiefly rights before the Privy Council derived from an ambiguous alliance between metropolitan and indigenous lawyers, local chiefs and local and European merchants against the colonial administration. The preeminence of indigenous lawyers in waging these jurisdictional and political battles rested on the fact that they were drawn from the ranks of the Asante elite who 'took good care to establish what almost amounted to legal dynasties' (Luckham 1981: 109). These disputes also depended on the autonomy of indigenous lawyers, whose market for legal services lay outside the control of the colonial government, thanks to their successful alliance with indigenous traders and local chiefs against the adoption of the public land bill of 1897 which aimed at vesting unutilised land in the control of the colonial government.

The recognition by the Privy Council, in the name of the imperial rule of law, of chiefly rights over land, and therefore to the mineral wealth of the Gold Coast, positioned these lawyers as political champions of the people in the struggle for decolonisation. Indigenous lawyers involved in the Asamankese dispute played a prominent role in nationalist politics. For example, T. Hutton-Mills was the first president of the National Congress of British West Africa. W. E. G. Sekyi, the leading figure in the Aborigines' Rights Protection Society (ARPS) after the mid-1920s, 'was active behind the scenes in coordinating the protests of Asafo Companies – the young men's associations which were later to be a source of grassroots support for Nkrumah – to disrupt the authority of chiefs who cooperated with colonial authorities' (Luckham 1981: 94). These judicial battles in the metropolitan core thereby consolidated the social basis of the Asante elite, while further depleting the authority of chiefs as gatekeepers – positioning, rather, lawyers as gatekeepers of gatekeeping politics.

The conflicts that trickled from the Gold Coast all the way to the Privy Council were ostensibly about the sovereign remit of each contender's authority. But they ended up legitimating modalities of extraction of raw commodities that favoured commercial interests all the while being nested in the assertion of state law supremacy (that of the Crown) over colonial administrators.

2.3 Lawyering the Congo Free State

The exceptional violence of Leopold II's colonial enterprise in the ill-named État indépendant du Congo (ÉIC – Congo Free State) pervades the image of a lawless Belgian colonialism based on the 'colonial trinity' of state, missionary and private company interests (Turner 2007: 28): a 'paternalistic' model implemented by ruthless administrators, awash with rivalries among missionaries and lacking a social vision. Congo's exceptional mineral wealth also loomed large in inter-imperial rivalries. By 1959, a year before independence, Congo was producing about 10 per cent of the world's copper, 50 per cent of its cobalt and 70 per cent of its industrial diamonds. 'It is a well-known paradox that to secure freedom of trade, someone has to be given exclusive rights to enforce it. To deal with the paradox, the powers chose an apparently neutral outsider with philanthropic pretensions' (Koskenniemi 2001: 157).

Justice became a central terrain of conflicts generated by the compromise of building a Congolese 'state' to accommodate the European balance of power. The Stokes-Lothaire incident in 1895, in which a Belgian administrator summarily executed an Irish missionary-turned-trader, symbolised ideological struggles – the right to a fair trial championed by the British, the fight against slavery invoked by the Belgians – while also deflecting direct inter-imperial confrontations. Under pressure of the British, the case ended up being examined by the High Council of the Congo (*Conseil supérieur du Congo*) – set up by Leopold II in 1889.

At the time of the Berlin Congress, Belgium was a young nation, the outcome of European wars. King Leopold II established a colonial legal system in the Congo early on to evade the cost of competition with European merchants in the Congo imposed by Britain's imperialism of the free trade. Leopold II devised a Belgian variant: chartered companies, rule implemented through the military and missionaries, enabling a symbiosis between state and capital, and using custom reinvented as law to achieve social order and present a civilising mission to the international audience. While a pragmatic necessity, justice was also ostensibly promoted to confront the violence of the petty arbitrariness of European merchant justice (including the recourse to harsh physical punishment and the burning of villages as reprisals against unruly labourers) (Plasman 2014b: 135).

In the face of a Belgian population opposed to the colonial enterprise, the handful of magistrates first sent to the Congo Free State originated from 'small' European countries (primarily Italy and Norway). When the ÉIC was returned to the Belgian state in 1908, this colonial judiciary was gradually 'Belgianised', though very poorly staffed with about 400 magistrates sent to the Congo between 1908 and independence.

Ngongo et al.'s (2017) prosopography of these magistrates suggests they constituted a relatively homogeneous milieu, the majority originating from humanist legal networks in Liège. The doctrine they produced reflected the ambiguity of their position. Developing a doctrinal body of customary law, these magistrates sought to position themselves in both the Belgian-style system of justice created for Europeans and the 'customary' judicial system designed for the indigenous population. While the magistrates promoted a model of 'indirect rule' in contrast to the 'direct rule' implemented by Belgian administrators, their flagship journals[5] were funded by Belgian mining companies operating in

[5] Notably the *Bulletin des jurisdictions indigènes et du droit coutumier congolais*, created in 1933 with the collaboration of missionaries to provide guidelines for the hundreds of 'indigenous' jurisdictions established in 1926 in the Congo and Burundi-Rwanda.

Katanga, which considered the codification of customary law indispensable for the management of colonial Congo (Plasman 2014a).

The rubber boom at the turn of the twentieth century profoundly shaped the colony, but the dominant role of the mining industry also contributed to the specificity of the Belgian colonial model (Etemad 2005). Called the 'Empire of the Générale' after the Société Générale, the first European bank established in Brussels in the early 1920s, Belgian colonialism built on the symbiosis between finance, corporate interests and the state, which (a uniquely Belgian feature) directly participated in mining extraction. Osmosis between private capital and the state meant that the colonial state's capital was not in Congo, but in Brussels (Etemad 2005).

However, reducing the ÉIC's trajectory – and that of Belgian colonisation in the Congo – to the economic phases of exploitation is insufficient, as it masks the reciprocal characteristics of Leopold's Congo and Belgium as a 'bicephalous state' (Plasman 2014b) and the embeddedness of the latter in inter-imperial conflicts that played out both in Europe and in the Congo.

The combination between exploitation *and* moralisation deployed by Leopold II was itself embedded in the tension between the national revolution in Belgium as a new nation state in Europe, capitalist expansion and inter-imperial contests. The violence waged by merchants and colonial administrators in the ÉIC stirred up wide media campaigns of denunciation across Europe. But it was viewed with equanimity on the diplomatic front. The public image of the ÉIC as a 'civilising mission' was tailored by a prominent English lawyer, Sir Travers Twiss – a member of the *Institut de droit international* (IDI – Institute of International Law) – employed by Leopold II to rescue 'the mission of empire from its darker, dirtier side' (Mazower 2012: 73). The British consul Pickersgill-Casement concluded his 1898 investigative report by confirming that 'even with the best of intentions, it is impossible to build a pacified *state* in Central Africa without resorting to violence' (Plasman 2014b: 137, my translation from French, emphasis added).

Contrary to the middlemen dispatched across the British Empire as bulwarks against petty arbitrariness (Benton and Ford 2016), the High Council of the Congo (*Conseil supérieur du Congo*) – set up by Leopold II as a supreme court of justice for the ÉIC – was designed ostensibly for the King's international audience as a council of 'eminent lawyers' (Plasman 2014a: 19). As a judicial institution the Council remained quasi-virtual – among its seven cases, the 1895 Lothaire-Stokes incident was the most well-known. The acquittal of Lothaire by the Council discredited the institution. The inter-imperial implications of the incident were resolved by other means, through the payment of a financial compensation to the British and the Germans.

But the profiles of individuals appointed to the Council by Leopold II point to the reciprocal yet ambiguous relationship between colonisation, capitalist expansion and the moralisation of inter-imperial conflicts through judicialisation. The chairs of the Council were predominantly drawn from the Belgian business elite, like Joseph Devolder, vice governor of the Société Générale, and later head of the biggest commercial venture in the Congo Free State, the *Compagnie du Congo pour le Commerce et l'Industrie*. By contrast, the legal experts of the Council were drawn from the *Institut de droit international*, including the Russian professor-diplomat Fyodor Fyodorovich Martens – whose proximity with the tsar Alexander II helped promote arbitration and the codification of the laws of war at The Hague conferences of the last quarter of the nineteenth century. On the Belgian front, the Council featured Gustave Rolin-Jaequemyns, who had begun publishing the world's first international law journals a few years before and had spurred the creation of the *Institut de Droit International* in Ghent in 1873.

Like Martens, Rolin-Jaequemyns was a promoter of the idea of a standard of civilisation that could provide 'a criterion for determining global rank and appropriate diplomatic practice' (Mazower 2012: 71) and legitimate colonial domination over Africans. Combining the promotion of international law and politics of the nation state in the age of revolution was also a family affair. The 'collective biography' of the Rolin-Jaequemyns family reflects the combination between the logics of inheritance/meritocracy and multi-positionality as a structuring dynamic of (inter)national legal fields (see Dezalay Y and Garth 2016). Gustave Rolin-Jaequemyns married into a wealthy family. His wife's father, indicted as an Orangist in favour of the unification of Belgium and the Netherlands, was defended by Gustave Rolin-Jaequemyns' father. Family credentials helped his son and nephew integrate the very select 'invisible college' (Schachter 1977–1978) of international law in the first decades of the twentieth century, while the scholarly affiliations of the latter contributed to the institutionalisation of global justice.

Rolin-Jaequemyns' father, Hippolyte Rolin, a solicitor who had studied law with Savigny and Hegel in Berlin, had played a prominent role in the Belgian Revolution. He was elected to the National Assembly in 1830, the Chamber of People's Representatives in 1848, and held the office of

Minister of Public Works. Gustave Rolin-Jaequemyns himself had a short stint at politics, notably as Minister of Home Affairs in 1878.[6] His son, Édouard Rolin-Jacquemyns, held several public offices, including that of home affairs, and Health Minister in 1925–1926. He was appointed as a judge to the PCA and the PCIJ and elected president of the *Institut de droit international.* Gustave Rolin-Jaequemyns' nephew, Henri Rolin, also involved in national politics, was a prominent member of the Bar of the ICJ in the first two decades of the institution,[7] before his appointment to the European Court of Human Rights (ECHR) in 1958, over which he presided until 1971.[8]

Leopold II's Congo experience built out of the symbolic certification of these international lawyers, who, as guardians of an imperial peace based on the division of the world between civilised and uncivilised populations, also guaranteed the deployment of Belgium as a nation state. The violence of colonial exploitation in the Congo did not produce international law as a gentle civiliser. Contrary to the Privy Council, the High Council was not designed as a court of last resort but as a legitimation powerhouse for Leopold II's operations in the Congo. The High Council hardly ever sat as a court. But its very composition contributed to rationalising the coexistence between hierarchy and instability fostered by middle power and inter-imperial confrontations. The High Council lawyers were architects of the laws of war. They were also, foremost, politicians. Their codification of international law reflected their contradictory position. International law was waged as 'gentler civilizer' (Koskenniemi 2001) to consolidate the European balance of power. But it insulated international law as law of the nations from imperialism.

2.4 Pre-independence Military Trials

The rich scholarship on political trials against anti-colonial leaders across the French and British Empires in the 1940s and 1950s has demonstrated that the stake of the political–judicial battles waged against the *métropoles* was not independence, at least not at first. It was to politicise, through judicial strategies of 'rupture', the hiatus between the rule of law

[6] See his biography by Claudine Moutardier www.sfdi.org/internationalistes/ROLIN-JAEQUEMYNS/ (accessed 7 April 2022).
[7] See Chapter 8.
[8] See his biography by Jean Salmon www.sfdi.org/internationalistes/rolin/ (accessed 7 April 2022).

of the *métropole* and the rule *by* law of colonial administrators. The repressive politics enforced by colonial administrations durably shaped the relationship between the legal field and the field of state power in the post-independence states that emerged out of these battles (see De 2018; Elbaz 2003; Terretta 2015). They also boomeranged back in the legal field of former *métropoles*.

The 'political trials' of political activists in French colonies in the late 1940s through the 1950s in Madagascar, Côte d'Ivoire, French Cameroon (Terretta 2015) and foremost Algeria (Elbaz 2003) exposed the legal crisis that the advent of the Fourth Republic had engendered for colonial administrators. They also promoted the *courtroom* – and with it, political lawyers from the Paris Bar – as an arena for political struggles. Emblematically, the defence team of members of the Algerian independentist party Movement for the Triumph of Democratic Liberties (MTLD) in 1951–1952 included a handful of Parisian lawyers who were all characterised by their anti-colonial Communist leaning.

These left-leaning lawyers from the *métropole* affiliated with the *Résistance* used the tribunals of the AOF as a platform to challenge colonial rule, promote colonial subjects as rights holders and, in so doing, co-opt African politicians as allies of the Communist Party within the French Parliament. The short-lived *Union Française* (French Union)[9] was an attempt at administering, taxing and representing French colonies as parts of France. In applying one standard of justice across the *métropole* and its renamed 'overseas territories', France's Constitution dismantled the boundary separating the metropolitan French justice system from colonial justice (Terretta 2015: 26). The context in which these trials unravelled was therefore not that of the imperial realm – but that of the *empire state* fathomed by the *Union Française* set up in 1946. The failure of this attempt at promoting the primacy of an imperial rule of law was not only due to the fact that these trials were waged before military courts.

In the context of the US Cultural Cold War against Communism, '[t]he political affiliation of these Parisian lawyers reflected [...] the

[9] The *Union Française*, established by the Constitution of the Fourth Republic in France, instituted officially an equal association between the *métropole* and the colonial empire. While short-lived (1946–1958) and riddled from the start with contradictions (with France reaffirming de facto sovereignty over overseas territories), the institutions of the *Union Française* served as incubator for the formation of most of the political elites who served at independence.

marginalization of an anti-colonial cause politically confined to underground political movements and intermittently supported by the PCF' (French Communist Party) (Elbaz 2003: 72, my translation from French).

In the British Empire, military trials against political opponents were predominantly waged in Eastern African colonies, where racial and material barriers de facto prevented the emergence of local legal elites and access to the Privy Council. But the Kenyatta trial in 1952 constitutes a microcosm that also underscores how these battles boomeranged back into the field of state power of the former *métropole* (De 2018).

The Kenyatta trial took place in the shadow of the post–World War II debates about the substance of global justice. It was originally designed as a 'justice of exception' type of proceeding, away from the rule of law of the *métropole* and foremost away from international scrutiny. The Director of Public Prosecutions, A. G. Somerhough, had just returned to Kenya from his stint as a judge at the Nuremberg trials. His argument that Kenyatta was *Führerprincip* of the Mau Mau bore the imprint of that experience. The attempt at trying Kenyatta away from scrutiny quickly failed as a defence team of lawyers assembled, drawn from different parts of the British Empire – from Left-leaning metropolitan lawyers to Indian, Caribbean, Kenyan, Nigerian and Irish ones. Their defence essentially aimed at deploying Justice Radhabinod Pal's dissent at the Tokyo tribunal,[10] which had just been declassified, to contest the legality itself of the trial.

The trajectories of what De (2018) calls these 'mobile' lawyers were produced by the specific legal middling capital fostered by the British imperial realm, which enabled the circulation of laws, legal precedents and lawyers.

Two of the profiles chronicled by De illustrate this. D. N. Pritt, Queen's Council, former Labour MP, and the metropolitan lawyer of the team defending Kenyatta, was the embodiment of the 'mobile' lawyer. Hailing from a family of industrialists and endowed with a cosmopolitan

[10] The panel appointed by General MacArthur, Supreme Commander of Allied Forces in the Far East, was named as International Military Tribunal for the Far East (IMTFE). It constituted of judges from the countries that had signed Japan's instrument of surrender: Australia, Canada, India, China, France, Netherlands, Philippines, USSR, United Kingdom and the United States. In his dissent, Judge Pal referred to the trial as a 'sham employment of legal process for the satisfaction of a thirst for revenge'. See D Kumar Ghatak, 'Radha Binod Pal – The forgotten Indian judge' *The Times of India* 15 December 2021.

education in Switzerland, Pritt had turned to law and Leftist politics in the 1920s. While his sympathies with the Soviet Union hurt his private legal practice, his fluency in French favoured a promising career as council before the Privy Council in appeals trickling from the Canadian dominion and later from different parts of the empire.

In 1931, Pritt represented the Indian Revolutionaries Bhagat Singh, Shivaram Rajguru and Sukhdev Thapar before the Privy Council, arguing that the Ordinance establishing a special tribunal to try them was ultra vires. His first 'international' case – before the Kenyatta trial in 1952 – was as part of the defence team of the peasant rebels in the Telangana region of the semi-autonomous state of Hyderabad in India, in the late 1940s. While positioned against the repressive politics of the newly independent Indian state – and subsequently Jawaharlal Nehru – Pritt worked side by side with a lawyer dispatched by the latter in the Kenyatta trial, Dewan Chaman Lall, who later hailed as an establishment lawyer, as architect of preventive detention laws against suspected Communists in India.

In turn, Sheila Didi nee Sharma had been included in the Kenyatta defence team as an interpreter. Born in Kenya within an Indian lower-middle-class but progressive family, she was one of the first Kenyan Indian female lawyers, and the only one of the 'local' team of three lawyers – comprising two other Kenyans of Indian descent who had both studied law in India – to speak fluent Swahili. After moving to Cardiff to study law, she had joined the Fabian Society and was drawn into a cosmopolitan circle in London where she had her first social interactions with African lawyers at the Inns of Court. In 1956, she moved to India, joined the Communist Party, and spent the next several decades opposing the government in trade union and gender discrimination cases, often at great personal risk.

These two lawyers shared common forms of mobility shaped by the British imperial realm. Didi nee Sharma was part of an imperial diaspora that became a national – and repressed – minority upon Kenya's independence. She had studied with two other female lawyers who also moved from Kenya to India in the 1950s, including Pushpa Kapila Hingorani, who became a leading Supreme Court lawyer and famously filed the first public interest litigation case in 1979 and spearheaded the public interest litigation (PIL) revolution deployed to contest state policies in India. Pritt's legal strategies certainly provided the backbone of public interest litigation while his Soviet Union-leaning politics ran against both Nehru's autocratic style of non-alignment, and Britain's alignment with the US Cultural Cold War against Communism.

Like their French 'mobile' lawyers' counterparts in the political trials that opposed the French *métropole* to political activists in French colonies in the late 1940s through the 1950s, Pritt and his team's strategic anti-imperial litigation was embedded in the Cultural Cold War and the predominance taken by the United States as world hegemon in the aftermath of the World War II.

In both the United Kingdom and in France, this transnational rights movement was redesigned and restructured as part of the US war on communism and the post-independence redefinition of rights 'at home' and in former empires' orbits of influence in the context of the Cold War partition of the African continent (see Madsen 2005). De's mobile lawyers produced genealogies of political opposition through law in India (De 2018). In France, 'lawfare' as a form of political opposition was revived in the post-1968 period (see Israël 2009).[11] Both sets of political trials deeply shaped the political field of the independent states that emerged out of these judicial battles. Generally, African territories under imperial domination became independent once the 'rule of law, promoted by African activists and the cause lawyers who defended them, durably shifted to be circumvented as an instrument of repression, which regimes in power [. . .] waged to eliminate their opponents from the political sphere' (Terretta 2015: 47, my translation from French).

2.5 Conclusion

These three series of crisis situations are not correlated by direct humane, institutional or geographical links. Yet they expose pre-existing conflicts and contradictions that help understand structural conflicts and contradictions in the codification of the articulation between the African South and global markets.

The Gold Coast conflicts between customary chiefs, merchants and colonial administrators that trickled up to the Privy Council helped the court assert its position as the jurisdiction of last resort for the greater part of the British Empire by promoting its role as imperial *umpire*, rather than as part of the colonial political order. The sheer volume of cases examined by the court fed into a 'centripetal jurisprudence of Empire that homogenized law across the British Empire, as judges

[11] See Chapter 7.

smoothed over local differences by applying precedents from colonies, dependencies, and communities across the Empire' (Ibhawoh 2017: 118).

The Gold Coast judicial disputes also contributed to enhancing the power of the British Crown against colonial administrators. They conversely helped consolidate the middling capital of the Asante legal elite, as a legal elite able to navigate between contradictory social interests and across the scale of the empire. Bringing political crises into relief through judicial politics was doubly effective, as it brought into focus the inconsistencies of colonial rule while securing Asante lawyers' own professional interests.

The Gold Coast cases reflected the close relationship between conflicts over legal rights – particularly the status accorded to local chiefs by the colonial administration – and struggles to redefine mechanisms for the distribution of property rights over land and, with them, economic wealth. These conflicts underscore the interplay between cultural forces and political economy in colonial regimes. In particular, the colonial argument of individual property as the quintessential and axiomatic basis of civilised society could easily and pragmatically be turned around in favour of communalism and customary law as more 'naturally' African when the interests of colonial exploitation were at stake.

Interestingly, therefore, the dual legal system of indirect rule could only function in its 'primitive' state. But it was invariably, irrepressibly transformed as soon as the local social and political fault lines reshaped by the colonial encounter were deployed within the imperial judicial system.

The Privy Council was reflective, itself, of the limits of middle power. The alliance between Asante lawyers and European merchants *against* the colonial administration fostered the deployment of merchant law and its authority *with* and *without* the state. The judicial incorporation of conflicts over the rent of extraction under the remit of state's law (that of the Crown) de facto left merchants and merchant law leeway to negotiate the interface between sites of extraction and global markets.

Legal ordering was also part and parcel of legal imperialism in the French and Belgian empires. In both settings, policies of hierarchies and separation between customary and European justice aimed at promoting state law as the apex of an imperial rule of law. Both the Belgian Empire (following the return of the Congo Free State to Belgium in 1908) and the French Empire sought to emulate the legal ordering sponsored by the Privy Council. However, in both instances, the *Cour de cassation* (Court of Cassation) of the Belgian and French *métropoles* played only a marginal role in addressing conflicts in the colonies, as they mostly focused on conflicts between European merchants (who had the means to access metropolitan courts) and the colonial administration (see, for the French case, Fabre 2011). They were never positioned as umpires of an imperial rule of law.

In the French Protectorates, investments in judicial reforms and legal education fostered the emergence of a strong legal elite at independence, with the likes of Habib Bourguiba as the father of the Tunisian nation (Gobe 2013) or in Morocco, where the strong appetence for law among emerging elites in the interwar period 'translated the conscience, among urban elites, of its importance for the appropriation of the state apparatus' and to 'rattle with the weapons of the colonial authorities' (Vermeren 2002: 100, my translation from French).

By contrast, the practice of indirect rule was most thoroughly applied in the interwar period in the Belgian mandates of Burundi and Rwanda. '[T]he juridical framework of intermediation was cast, absorbing the intensely legalistic culture of the Belgian state' (Young 1994: 154). But economic exploitation prevailed over colonial investments in the formation and education of local elites, including lawyers.[12]

The state-centred form of 'legal pluralism' emulated by the French and Belgian Empires was more a common institutional 'fix' than a systematic overhaul through legal ordering (Benton 2002: 4). It was also shaped by Britain's middle power. The High Council of the Congo was short-lived. It was formally dissolved in 1930. From 1924, the bulk of its jurisdictional remit had already been transferred to the Belgian *Cour de cassation* – the apex court of Belgian civil system.

Yet the unique composition of the High Council – which comprised political and legal elites of the new Belgian nation, along with prominent European lawyers – made it a laboratory of *international* adjudication as a modality for the settlement of inter-imperial conflicts. The violence of Leopold II's exploitation of the Congo was certainly ancillary to the promotion of international law as a gentle civiliser. The international law codified by Martens and Rolin-Jacquemyns was *international* to the extent that it sought neither to contradict nor to compete with Britain's legal ordering through middle power. The deployment of adjudication as a locus to administer politics of difference within the imperial rule of law was based on stumbling blocks that were less the beginning of the end of

[12] See Chapter 5.

empire and more 'events that foreclosed certain possibilities of global legal ordering and made other outcomes more likely' (Benton and Ford 2016: 185–186). The offshoring of justice through arbitration and the operations of arbitrators as 'mobile' lawyers in the context of the subsequent Scrambles for Africa built on these earlier tracks.[13]

The interconnected conflicts reflected in the disputes arbitrated by the Privy Council, and the position of the High Council of the Congo as a powerhouse for the legitimation of the colonial enterprise *and* the insulation of international law from imperialism – contributed to coding sovereignty as a symbolic currency that was 'shared out, layered [and] overlapping' (Burbank and Cooper 2010: 17).

These dynamics of trade in symbolic capital produced winners and losers. The capacity of the colonial state in the Gold Coast to certify the types of capital circulating in the legal field at the domestic level was hampered by the autonomy of the Asante legal elite – not only because the modalities of reproduction of the social capital of this elite were based on a strong, local power structure, but also because they were structurally extraverted. It built on merchant capital certified by competing imperial cores (that of the Asante Kingdom and the British Crown), consolidated – in the colonial era and the first decades of independence – by scholarly homologation within the metropolitan core. This middling capital was also weakened, from the onset, by merchant power and merchant law. The leveraging of the Asante Kingdom's warriors as a brand for Pascal Agboyibor's Asafo & Co as 'Africa's' corporate law firm – which I described in Chapter 1 – points to yet another sequel of reproduction of this system of trade in symbolic capital: that of the Wall Street model of the corporate law firm.

Finally, the trials waged in French and British African colonies against individuals seen as spoilers of colonial rule across French and British colonies in the decade before the 1960s wave of independence exacerbated the crisis and subsequent downfall of European empires following World War II. Transformed into anti-colonial platforms, these trials were Petri dishes of imperial contradictions that had long-lasting and structural implications for the gatekeeping states that emerged from colonialism. Great national heroes like Jawaharlal Nehru in India, Jomo Kenyatta in Kenya or Félix Houphouët-Boigny in Côte d'Ivoire saw in civil liberties impediments to achieving social and economic emancipation.

[13] See Chapters 3, 4 and 8.

They used colonial laws and the repressive strategies of the colonial administration to curb political opposition.

But the different scales in which these trials were waged – the *Union Française* on the one hand and the British imperial realm on the other – also underscore the structural effects of the pre-independence imperial legal strategies of the two *métropoles*. 'Whereas Paris's remaining colonies [were] administered, taxed and represented as parts of France, Britain has never attempted to create a coherent framework for its scattered territories' (Bullough 2022: 243). By the early 1960s, 'Britain no longer ha[d] an empire and [was] no longer in the business of stripping resources from the rest of the world so as to enrich itself. But it [was] in the business of using the skills it learned while running an empire in order to help others do what it used to do' (Bullough 2022: 232): trading in speculative capital.

These political trials could therefore be construed as sites of renegotiation of middling capital. In the French case, the middling capital of political and legal elites – whether from the *métropoles* or the new states that emerged out of these battles – was renegotiated as a form of resource certified by the French *and* the post-colonial state within the close-knit interpersonal, institutional and economic gatekeeping politics fostered by the *system* of the *Françafrique*.[14] In the British case, the middling capital of the 'mobile' lawyers described by De (2018) was renegotiated as a capital of middle power determined by the proximity with both state power (that of the Crown or the newly independent states), the legal and political clout of Wall Street corporate lawyers *and* the City as a financial core.

[14] See Chapters 3, 6 and 7.

3

Gatekeeper States and Offshore Capitalism

1950s–1980s

It is usually understood that law and lawyers were a sideshow in the Cold War Scramble for the African continent. Discussions on law, lawyers and political change during the period are often mired by a degree of defensiveness, if not outright suspicion. The threshold question centres on the failure of legal transplants (de Gaudusson 2009) and the twin legacies of brutal colonial experience (Bayart and Bertrand 2006) and post-independence Big Man politics (Vondoepp 2005). In his witty *The Black Bar* (2001: unpaged preface), Kenyan lawyer Paul Mwangi argued that the problem with African lawyers is precisely that they *wanted* to be leaders. Trained by the West as 'agents of development', they shunned the advice of their peers from the developed world to 'ris[e] above the day-to-day politics of their societies and avoid [. . .] the rough and tumble of political agitation', maintaining instead 'that they owe it to their societies to secure freedom and justice for all'. In so doing, they have been entrapped by kinship ties, anti-entrepreneurial governance, corruption and dictatorship.

To be sure, the legal reforms promoted by US foundations across former British colonies in the framework of the Cultural Cold War largely failed to emulate the emergence of legal elites in support of development and as bulwark against the Communist threat. The modernisation paradigm embraced by the first Law and Development movement set out two roles for lawyers: as agents of social change and as rule-of-law brokers. Legal education loomed large in these reform agendas. The aim was ostensibly to respond to the dearth of trained lawyers across the continent. This project was fuelled by Cold War rivalries and the hegemonic ambition of the United States to foster the emergence of a new generation of US-oriented lawyers in the Third World (Krishnan 2012). The Hague Academy of International Law also attracted the support of the Ford Foundation and other US foundations from the 1960s with the intent of 'mak[ing] contact with and influenc[ing] the elites of the newly-decolonizing Third world' (Scott-Smith 2007: 509).

This support waned from the 1970s due to the perceived failure of this institution as a 'beach head' for US interests, and the academy returned to being an 'old world consortium' (Scott-Smith 2007: 509).

In a unique series of studies at the turn of the 1980s focused on former British colonies, Dias et al. (1981: 16ff) noted that the modernisation project's emphasis on the role of 'development lawyers' mirrored the position of their counterparts in the United States. But it hinged on a historical misconception. The legal professions which existed across the African continent were patterned after their European counterparts; yet they enjoyed a very narrow social basis, in terms of recruitment and participation in the economic and political system.

Following the debacle of the deployment of the very first United Nations peace mission in the Congo as an arbiter between the new state and the secession ambitions of the mineral-rich Katanga region, between 1960 and 1970 over twelve military coups were fomented against the political leaders of the newly independent African states.

The imperial promise of the rule of law all but disappeared. Emblematically, the relative invisibility on the international scene of the waves of violence that characterised the post-independence history of Congo, Rwanda and Burundi was compounded by a dearth of research on the Great Lakes region, except for historical studies by Burundian, French or Belgian scholars (see Chrétien and Dupaquier 2007; Deslaurier 2002; Gahama 2001).

Yet this invisibility masks the fact that law was more *sidelined* than a sideshow. Both the colonial and the post-colonial states adopted the idea that exporting minerals and raw commodities could serve as the engine of development. The colonial state played a significant and long-lasting role in allowing subsistence production to continue alongside the production of staples for global markets in the post-colonial trajectories of former African colonies (Iliffe 1983).

Across the African continent '[f]rom the days of the chartered companies to the current oil multinationals, what distinguishes mining investments [...] in Africa [is] the ability unambiguously to identify, commoditize and secure property rights' (Breckenridge 2011: 247). What could be dubbed the concession model of extraction – the renting out of land to foreign corporations in exchange for royalties – that was disseminated throughout colonial Africa was the outcome of the relative disengagement of imperial *métropoles* from the task of surveying and exploiting African colonies' mineral wealth – with the exception of the Congo, where mining extraction was a core component of the construction of the *Belgian* state, based on the symbiosis between finance (through the Société Générale), corporate and state interests.

It was also a *legal transplant* that was based on the early emergence of mining giants in South Africa whose vertical organisation (from mineral exploitation through to financial speculation on the London market) benefited in great part from their monopolistic position in other resource-rich African economies of the British Empire.

The concession model was not dismantled following independence. It was displaced through nationalisation processes that aimed at unambiguously placing the property right over land and its wealth under the sovereign authority of the new states. The failure of the New International Economic Order (NIEO) hailed by independence rulers, like Ghana's Nkrumah, reflected the fact that the nationalisation of the mining sector had to be *negotiated* with former imperial rulers *and* accommodate the social hierarchies produced by the colonial encounter.

That law was sidelined rather than a sideshow is also evidenced in the alternate path taken by London following the independence era. Unlike France, the British Crown did not seek to recast its former and remaining colonies within administrative, military or legal links aimed at representing them as parts of Britain. Rather, the maintenance – through the Privy Council – of jurisdictional links across the overseas territories, former dominions and colonies of the Commonwealth enabled the reconversion of Britain's middle power by repositioning London as a dual capital – that of jurisdictional apex of the Common Law world and financial powerhouse for the expansion of offshore capitalism.

The reconversion of Britain's middle power was *consolidated* rather than weakened by the concurrent jurisdictional aspirations of the new institutions of international justice that emerged in the interwar period and after World War II. It is indeed precisely the Cold War sidelining of The Hague justice institutions that enabled the redeployment of the concession model of extraction, this time backed up by the formidable sway of the alliance of Wall Street resources – finance, corporate law firms and legal tools (contracts and arbitration clauses) aimed at *insulating* foreign corporate rights in property in resource-rich African states from national and international legal orderings.

What follows is the story of concurrent imperial encounters that, too, were triggered by crises – from the crisis triggered by the imperial demise for France and Britain, the acute economic crisis of the new states a mere decade after independence, to the failure of the modernisation paradigm as a Trojan horse to spot and groom US-oriented new legal and political elites in the Third World. These imperial encounters played out in different settings – in Paris, London, The Hague, Johannesburg, New York, the British Virgin Islands and the capitals of newly independent states. It is precisely the messy congruence of their structural effects that helps account for the contradictions and conflicts of the ongoing rush for Africa's mineral wealth.

3.1 France's Post-colonial Block

Ghana's independence in 1957 triggered a wave of violence and precipitated Congo's independence. The *pari congolais* – the Congolese gamble – of the Belgian *métropole* was that 'it would provide Congolese politicians with the trappings of power while purchasing enough goodwill to enable them to continue running the country much as before' (Meredith 2005: 101). The United States had already staked its interests over Congo's mineral wealth. In 1944, secret agreements entrusted the exploitation of Congolese uranium to a military structure under the command of the US Department of State, for a period of ten years, renewed in 1951. In 1958, a Bureau of African Affairs was set up within the US State Department in anticipation of the second Scramble for Africa's mineral wealth which unfolded in the following decade (Guichaoua and Vidal 1997).

The well-trodden story of Patrice Lumumba's demise, as independent Congo's first ruler, is worth recounting, as it symbolically and effectively signalled the start of the Cold War order in sub-Saharan Africa. On 30 June 1960, Lumumba, the new state's first prime minister, delivered a speech before King Baudouin of Belgium, condemning the despoiling of the land by Belgium as the former colonial ruler and denouncing the Congolese 'geological scandal': the scrambling of its mineral-rich soil by foreign corporations.

Panic seized the Union Minière du Haut-Katanga, a Belgian corporation established in the province of Katanga since 1908 to extract copper, gold and uranium. Its straw man Moïse Tshombe proclaimed the independence of the province, claiming secession from chaos while a mutiny in the Congolese army, the *Force publique*, degenerated into scores of acts of violence against the white population. Moïse Tshombe requested the Belgian government's help to set up and train a Katangese army. Belgium sent in troops, ostensibly to protect Belgian citizens in the country – while Patrice Lumumba declared the country officially at war with Belgium. France sent over some military help in the guise of the infamous mercenary Bob Denard.

Within a fortnight of independence, chaos had descended on Congo. What would unravel next would set the ground for the Cold War partition of the African continent. Lumumba appealed to the United Nations to intervene. In a unique bid during the Cold War, the UN Security Council called on the government of Belgium to withdraw from the country and authorised the provision of military assistance to restore 'law and order' and maintain the Congolese territorial unity.[1] Patrice Lumumba's ultimatum, on 19 July 1960, that he would request the help of the Soviet Union if the United Nations did not force Belgian troops out of the country placed the conflict on the map of Cold War rivalry. 'US officials feared the possibility of "another Cuba" – a Communist takeover, similar to Fidel Castro's Cuban revolution in 1959, that would provide the Soviet Union with a base in the heart of Africa' (Meredith 2005: 104).

In September 1960, the army chief of staff of the Congo, Colonel Joseph Mobutu, initiated a coup, actively backed by the Central Intelligence Agency (CIA), and ordered the expulsion of all Soviet Union personnel. But the country remained divided, even after the assassination of Lumumba in January 1961. '[I]n 1964, revolt and rebellion broke out in eastern Congo, Lumumba's former stronghold, on a scale that surpassed anything the Congo had experienced before' (Meredith 2005: 110). Caught in chaos, amidst East and West rivalry over the void of state authority in the country, the UN operation was authorised to use force in order to restore the central government. The cost borne by the United Nations Operation in Congo (UNOC),[2] which at its peak numbered over 20,000 men, was so horrendous as to make it a Cold War exception.

Order was finally restored in 1965, when General Mobutu, stepping forward a second time, seized power over a reunited Congo and renamed it Zaire in 1971. The Cold War order had set on the African continent. The UN Congo operation foremost remained a Cold War exception because of its interference in post-decolonisation violence. The next and only two other UN operations deployed on the continent before the end of the Cold War were respectively in 1978 and 1988, in Namibia and Angola, to accompany the independence of Namibia, the last colony of Africa, and the formal end of the Angola conflict.

[1] UN Security Council, Resolution 143 (1960), 14 July 1960 (S/4387).

[2] Including the death of over 200 Blue Helmets, as well as that of United Nations Secretary General Dag Hammarskjöld in a mysterious plane crash in September 1961.

Between the first waves of independence and the mid-1970s, France and the US completed a series of military assistance and cooperation agreements with African states that effectively divided up the continent into regions of influence. In the 1970s, managing to supplant Belgian influence in the Great Lakes region, France, under the leadership of President Giscard d'Estaing, extended its *pré-carré* through military leadership over Congo-Zaire, Rwanda and Burundi, while military assistance to South Africa was provided by the United States (see Chipman 1989; Luckham 1982).

The Cold War military and cultural partition of the African continent helped maintain the regional partition of the continent inherited from colonisation. Across former French colonies, the 'post-colonial block' fostered a process of ensnared independence that reflected the direct investment of the French state in the negotiation of independence. French interests over the mineral wealth of its former colonies drove independence deals that aimed at once at consolidating reciprocal clientelist relations with the new states' political elites and to secure the position of French state-owned corporations as gatekeepers between resource-rich African states and global markets.

Throughout former French colonies, what Legendre (1992) calls the 'colonial projection' was deployed *after* independence, in the form of military and judicial cooperation agreements that also aimed at securing the material and financial flow of the products of extraction to the former *métropole* – both by ensuring the stability of autocratic rule in resource-rich states and by comforting the position of French corporations. The violence of the decolonisation of oil-rich Algeria evidently stands out. But even while the new Algerian state was opting out of France's 'post-colonial block', it was opting in the only alternative available – the concession model – by relying on US expertise and financial clout.

The French *métropole*'s interest in the mineral wealth of the colonies emerged as a strategic concern in the *métropole* only in the late 1950s. While debates over the 'cost' of colonies were raging in Paris, it is precisely during this period that the French *métropole* deployed an interest in exploring and exploiting the immense mineral deposits of its African colonial territories.

Following the 1929 economic crash, the two main European colonial powers, Britain and France, had sought to protect their respective economies within exclusive economic zones resting on the twin principle of freedom of exchange within the sterling and franc zones, and protectionism outside their imperial frontiers. The partial occupation of France during World War II derailed this arrangement. Trade exchanges between French colonies and other countries expanded, to the detriment of the *métropole*. At the end of the war, the French economy was drained, while that of its colonies was relatively booming.

The creation of the CFA franc in 1946 – as the currency of the Communauté financière africaine (African Financial Community) – helped the *métropole* to regain control over France's colonies in West Africa and relaunch its economy. This was enabled thanks to two characteristics ostensibly designed to foster the development of colonial territories. The overvaluation of the CFA franc offered a comparative advantage to the *métropole* by facilitating the export of metropolitan products to the colonies, while undermining the latter's export capacities to global markets. On the other hand, fixed parity with the French Franc prevented colonies from adjusting their exchange rates (Coquery-Vidrovitch and Deltombe 2021: 84–85).

In parallel, from the end of the 1950s, to contain the pressure for independence, the French *métropole* sought to revamp its colonial pact by demonstrating investment in the development of colonies. The Fonds d'investissements pour le Développement Économique et Social (Investment Fund for Economic and Social Development – FIDES) set up in 1945 did not translate in a break from the previous colonial pact of fiscal self-sufficiency. The 599 billion Francs deployed by the FIDES between 1946 and 1956 were captured either by metropolitan businesses (as profits) or by colonial administrators (as wages). They were disproportionately low compared to the 2,135 billion Francs devoted by the *métropole* to its war effort in Indochina over the same period (Coquery-Vidrovitch and Deltombe 2021: 87). The strategy was foremost coupled with France's investment in the nascent European Economic Community (EEC). The strategy involved transferring part of these financial and symbolic costs to the European Community, in exchange for access to other member states of the Community to French colonial markets.

'We must uncouple ourselves as soon as possible if we want to maintain a certain influence in this country', wrote the French governor of Guinea in 1957, '[u]ncoupling means redeploying or converting colonial administrators, it could also involve their secondment or the secondment of some of them to deploy technical cooperation' (quoted in Meimon 2007: 1, my translation from French). Essentially, former French colonial administrators took the helm in defining the European Commission's development policy towards African states, by reproducing highly personalised, even clientelist relations with the new heads of state. 'Many of the [Development Directorate General of the European Commission]'s neo-patrimonial methods and practices were replicated and merely extended to the new associated countries' (Dimier 2014: 7; see also Meimon 2007).

Foremost, independence generally built out of this political and economic trade-off between Paris and its colonies. The 1956 *Loi-cadre Defferre* transferred some sovereign powers from Paris to elected overseas governments. It also handed over the exploitation of the oil deposits of the Algerian Sahara and Gabon, and that of uranium in Niger and Gabon, to metropolitan state-owned corporations. These endeavours were backed up by public-private funding, foremost by the Rothschild bank, strategically positioned at the heart of capitalist financial flows between France and its former colonies (see Borrel et al. 2021: 328).[3]

Effectively, the resulting *Françafrique* system enabled reciprocal – albeit unequal – processes of legal, political and economic assimilation. The founder of Elf, Pierre Guillaumat, is typical of this generation. Hailing from a military family, Guillaumat graduated from the École des Mines de Paris (Paris school of mining) in 1933. Head of the mining services of the colonial administration in Indochina (1934–1939), he was later sent to Tunisia (1939–1943) where he joined the *Résistance.* Appointed director of the *Bureau de recherche de pétrole* – a governmental agency set up by President de Gaulle in 1945 to explore prospective oil deposits in the Sahara – he was later put at the helm of major French public corporations, including as first president of Elf-Erap in 1966.

The post-colonial block was also embedded in France 'colonial projection', which involved integrating emerging legal elites in the new African states within reciprocal processes of assimilation with the former *métropole.* With Algeria standing in an exceptional position – as France's sole settlement colony – there were fewer than 200 magistrates from the *métropole* deployed in sub-Saharan African colonies until 1946. That number tripled between 1953 and 1961 but remained disproportionally insufficient. Further, across all colonies, independence was accompanied by the brutal repatriation of French magistrates to the *métropole.*

[3] Including the *Societé des pétroles d'Afrique équatoriale française*, SPAEF, the ancestor of Elf-Gabon, and the *Compagnie des mines d'uranium de Franceville*, COMUF, one of the components of the future Cogema.

French magistrates deployed as *coopérants* constituted one-fifth of the judiciary of independent states of the former French Empire ten years after independence (Farcy 2011). The number of indigenous private legal practitioners remained less than or equal to the number of their European counterparts in most African jurisdictions long after independence. On the eve of independence in Mali, for example, there were just twenty *avocats*, all European (Diop 1971). Eight years later there were two Malian lawyers and two Europeans. In Senegal, even in the economically prosperous region of the Cap Vert, there were only twelve Senegalese lawyers compared to twenty Europeans in 1970 (see Diop 1971: Vols 1 and 2, respectively, for Mali and Senegal).

The examples of Algeria and Mali are emblematic, as in both cases post-independence rulers chose (as much as they were imposed) a path of political and economic break with the *métropole* – which contrasted sharply with the *Françafrique* strategy fostered by others to maintain privileged economic relations with France.

The French *métropole* negotiated a technical and cultural cooperation agreement in anticipation of Algeria's independence, in the framework of the Evian agreements of March 1962. Despite the violence of decolonisation, the majority of the 121 *magistrats coopérants* who elected to be seconded as *coopérants* in Algeria had already spent most of their careers in the country, and a number remained well into the 1970s (see Renucci and Réthoré 2014). While Algeria shunned French oil companies in the context of the 1970s oil wars, French lawyers operating within the Brussels offices of US multinational corporate law firms were in charge of negotiating the terms of economic independence over the oil wealth of the new state with the former *métropole*.[4]

Likewise, despite the political and economic socialist path chosen by Mali's first ruler Modibo Keïta and his severance of links with the former *métropole*, the first generations of post-independence legal elites were trained in France (see Dezalay S 2018). Part of the anti-imperial stance adopted by President Keïta during the First Republic in 1960–1968 aimed specifically at decolonising the state's judicial institutions.

But at independence, not only were there very few trained lawyers across the country, but also the judicial institution was still deeply connected to the French legal system. Emblematically, under the short-lived Malian Federation (1960), Senegal and the Soudan Français

[4] See Chapter 7.

(current Mali) concluded judiciary agreements planning for ultimate appeals to be examined by the ordinary chambers of the *Cour de cassation*[5] and the *Conseil d'État* in Paris, until the establishment of the supreme courts of the Federation.[6] Following the break-up of the Federation, the denunciation of the judicial agreements between France and Mali opened a legal vacuum for appeals, as there was only a *Cour d'appel*, created in 1958, and the Supreme Court had to be set up from scratch (see Moulaye et al. 2007: 30–31).

The abrupt denunciation of the judicial agreements with France under Keïta's First Republic therefore triggered a judicial decolonisation that was much more abrupt compared to other former French colonies. Yet this did not sever the path, very much determined by the French former imperial realm, of the emergence of the first legal elites of post-colonial Mali. The trajectory of a prominent Malian lawyer and civil society activist, Demba Diallo, illustrates this.

Born in Koulikoro[7] in 1925, Diallo's profile is characteristic of the ambiguous transition of lawyers from allies of the empire to the 'fighting brigade of the people' described by Oguamanam and Pue (2016). Diallo studied law at the Faculté de Paris in 1948–1955, and graduated from the École des Hautes Études and the École Nationale des Langues Orientales Vivantes, also in Paris. After being sworn in as a barrister before the *Cour d'Appel* of Paris in 1954, he entered the then colonial bench as a judge in Senegal and in Guinea. Director of the *École nationale d'administration* of Conakry, which he set up in 1957, cabinet director of President Sékou Touré in 1957 and member of the Guinean delegation to the United Nations in 1958, he was called back to the Malian Federation in 1960 by President Keïta while in parallel also appointed technical advisor to Patrice Lumumba and member of the drafting commission of the Constitution of Congo-Léopoldville.

After the break-up of the Federation, Diallo played a prominent role in the non-alignment movement's conferences – including as member of Mali's delegation to Bandung in April 1961 and, the same year, at the conference which constituted the non-aligned movement in Belgrade. At the time of the military overthrow of Modibo Keïta in 1968, Diallo

[5] The *Cour de cassation* (Court of cassation) is the apex court with jurisdiction over cases in civil, commercial, social or criminal matters in civil law systems.

[6] The Conseil d'Etat (Council of State) is the highest administrative jurisdiction in France.

[7] A military outpost 60 km south of Bamako.

had gone back to practising as a barrister in Mali, becoming the first historic president of the Bar.

Belgium emulated this process of 'reciprocal assimilation' (Bayart 1989) between Belgian law professors and lawyers in countries of the Great Lakes region. Emblematically, at independence, Burundi's legal framework was officially de-racialised. The 1962 law on the organisation of justice dismantled customary law jurisdictions and universalised the colonial civil law system, previously reserved for Europeans. Since then there has been only one legal system, modelled on the Belgian and regulated by procedural rules inherited from the Germans in 1886. However, legal decolonisation was a slow process. The first codifications were undertaken only in the 1970s by Belgian consultants seconded to the Burundi Ministry of Justice. Belgian professors, judges and barristers continued to practise in Burundi after independence: 'the transition was soft'.[8]

Although nationalised, the post-colonial legal institutions reproduced the urban–rural divide devised by the colonial regime, with professional judges sitting in higher courts in the urban centres and a mostly untrained staff in the lower courts, the *Tribunaux d'instance*, in rural areas. The Université du Burundi was created in 1964 as an extension of the Faculté Notre-Dame de la Paix in Namur, Belgium. The first cohort graduated in 1974. As explained by a law professor at the Université: 'the first generation of Burundian lawyers, it was us in 1969. When I started studying law most of the classes were taught by Belgian professors. [. . .] It was clear that we were there to ensure the succession'.[9] This university, which monopolised legal education until the early 2000s and produced an average of thirty graduates a year, was also quickly affected by ethnic and factionalist politics. From the 1972 massacres until the 2000s, over 90 per cent of law students were Tutsi, according to some reports (Vandeginste 2010: 97).

3.2 The Lure of Nationalisation

The new era of nationalised mining that was ushered in in 1959 when Ghana's ruler Nkrumah bought out six marginal gold mines and set up the State Gold Mining Corporation reflected this process of 'ensnared independence' (Borrel et al. 2021: 182f).

[8] Author's interview with a professor at the Université du Burundi, Bujumbura, 3 May 2013.
[9] ibid.

The development promise of the new states – illustrated by massive infrastructure projects – generally crumbled with the slump in commodity prices and the crisis of the debt at the turn of the 1980s. By 1980, public sector employment accounted for 50 to 55 per cent of all non-agricultural jobs (compared to 24 per cent in OECD states in the same period). In many cases, the expansion of state bureaucracies coincided with the decline of the state's apparent capacities (Young 1994: 6).

In 1969, Zambia had one of the highest Gross Domestic Products (GDPs) on the continent and was officially a middle-income country. From the early 1970s, the industry's substantial revenues were allocated to major social and infrastructure development projects. Lack of investment in the industry resulted in output decline over the next two decades. The oil crises of 1974 and 1979 sent copper prices spiralling downwards. By 1994, Zambia was the twenty-fifth poorest country in the world. Likewise, in 2000, Gécamines, created as successor to the Belgian Union Minière du Haut-Katanga, produced just over a tenth of its copper sales of ten years earlier; zinc production was under 5 per cent of the 1975 total, cobalt went up but fell far short of the 1989 figure.[10]

The idea that exporting minerals and raw commodities could serve as the engine of development not only failed due to the lack of investment of the new states in their mining sector and external economic shocks; it was also because the concession model inherited from colonisation was not dismantled. In the case of former French colonies, it was displaced towards state-owned French corporations. In former British colonies and in the Congo, property rights over extraction sites were placed in joint ventures or state participation in the capital of local mining enterprises incorporated as full subsidiaries of foreign groups (Yachir 1988: 63).

Generally, the nationalisation of the mining sector of the new independent states was based on a *negotiated* trade-off with former *métropoles* and United States and South African mining corporations. It also had to accommodate the social hierarchies generated by conflicts over the rent of extraction inherited from the colonial encounter.

Nationalisation was not imposed. It was negotiated, progressive and conditioned by compensations to metropolitan extractive corporations. In Mauritania, for example, before it was taken over by the government, MIFERMA (*Mines de fer de la Mauritanie*) had made a profit of more than 8 billion CFA francs between 1965 and 1973 and had a foreign debt

[10] J Tilouine, 'RDC: Gécamines, un cadavre minier qui bouge encore' *Le Monde* 4 May 2017.

of 6 billion. But it received compensation of 20 billion CFA francs from the new state. Contrary to what happened in South America, the nationalisation of mines in most African countries was limited in scope and formal in content. 'Nationalization has meant, in fact, Third World governments' partial buying of foreign participation in the local mining companies' capital' (Yachir 1988: 65). Nationalisation nowhere significantly affected the control of foreign capital in the mining sector.

Management was generally left to foreign companies, and unskilled work to local and migrant workers. In the early 1980s in Zaire, 1,000 expatriates received half the total Gécamines wage payments, the other half was distributed among 37,000 African workers. Zambia stood apart as the new state espoused the welfarist slant adopted by colonial *métropoles* in the 1930s and 1940s to defuse workers' protests. The wages of Zimco's 58,000 workers in 1983 varied from 65 to 400 pounds per month; they also received premiums and were housed in townships with low rents, free water and electricity for the poor and free medical care (Yachir 1988: 65).

In countries of the Copperbelt, like Ghana and Zambia, where extraction was dominated by Belgian, South African and US mining giants, 'mining corporations seem not to have offered anything by way of significant resistance' to nationalisation (Breckenridge 2011: 254). By contrast, it was only in 1971 that President Mobutu managed to break the Union Minière du Haut-Katanga's stranglehold on Zairian copper – thanks to the opening of the Tenke Fungurume cobalt and copper mines, with a majority share then held by the US mining giant Phelps Dodge.

'[T]he Western enterprises which saw nationalization as a constraint effected by the world political context quickly understood that it could be very useful to them' (Yachir 1988: 67). Constrained to the position of rentier, the state could not threaten foreign firms' interests. This reduced foreign corporations' financial risks, all the while making recipient states incur colossal debts. It also helped maintain the illusion of the Africanisation of natural resources by 'put[ting] a sort of screen between the foreign enterprises and public opinion' (Yachir 1988).

Retention of capital by foreign corporations also reproduced and strengthened patterns of mining extraction across the continent that were determined by the contradictions of colonisers' policies of separating capitalist from non-capitalist sites of production. It also consolidated the diffusion of a model of extraction shaped by the South African colonial state and its relations with the British Crown.

In South Africa, mining started out as the province of merchants. Between the 1890s and World War I, the boom in mining was siphoned into a speculative financial bubble at the City. '[I]n the same period, enormous capital flows and the special conditions on the Witwatersrand prompted the development of massive vertically integrated industrial corporations; outside of South Africa, these corporations worked with the colonial state in the 1920s to drive the developmental project of a stabilized African proletariat' (Breckenridge 2011: 246).

Following the crucible of the Anglo–Boer War, the British Crown deployed massive investments to develop transportation and policing infrastructures. These financial investments – £220 million between 1899 and 1902 – contrasted starkly with the mere £1 million per year earmarked for the rest of British sub-Saharan African colonies after 1940. By integrating the poor white working class within capitalist relations, these transformations reinforced economic segregation. Deployed to contain Afrikaans nationalism, these imperial policies also reflected the Crown's interest 'in creating a stable white society in South Africa which would also be a loyal link in the strategic chain of Empire' (Lonsdale 1981: 188). 'An internally divided white bourgeoisie as a whole needed [the white working class'] assistance in controlling black workers. A more stable capitalist order was well worth the marginal cost of class bribery' (Lonsdale 1981: 187). By the 1940s and the formalisation of racial segregation, the migrant population of miners was locked in the least organised and skilled jobs, while Apartheid laws entrenched white supremacy and the majority Black population into a poverty trap.

In British colonies outside South Africa, 'the effort to survey, register and secure property was simply beyond the means of imperial administrators' (Breckenridge 2011: 247). At the turn of the 1920s, chartered companies lost their extravagant sovereignty rights over huge territorial chunks in exchange for concession and royalty rights over land and minerals. The well-known story of the British South Africa Company (BSAC) is a case in point (see Slinn 1971). The company received a Royal Charter in 1889 modelled on that of the British East India Company. It resulted from the amalgamation of Cecil Rhodes' Central Search Association and the London-based Exploring Company Ltd, which pulled their economic interests and political clout in London to devise the legal basis of their authority, as private entrepreneurs, on the African continent.

The Charter granted the BSAC powers to administer wide and unspecified territories, subject to negotiating treaties with local rulers.

The BSAC was not involved in mining directly but received mineral royalties and held shares in mining companies which, themselves, were generally involved in financial speculation. A 1918 Privy Council decision asserted that the BSAC had acted as an agent of the Crown in the conquest of Rhodesian territories.[11] Following the termination of the Charter in 1923, the Crown agreed to fund part of the huge deficit incurred by the BSAC but placed the obligation to pay off the rest on Southern Rhodesia itself. The mineral rights of the BSAC over Northern Rhodesia lasted until the independence of Zambia in 1964. The BSAC also created the Rhodesian railway system and owned the railways there until 1947 (see Rönnbäck and Broberg 2019).

The collapse of the speculative bubble at the City at the start of World War I shifted the power to determine the volume and sites of mining investment towards vertically integrated South African and US mining corporations. The De Beers corporation set up a series of monopsonist contracts[12] with the colonial governments of Angola, Congo, Gold Coast, Guinea, Sierra Leone, Tanganyika and Namibia. By the turn of the 1920s, three large corporations – all formed by US engineers with the *know-how* of deep-level mining, along with the support of massive capital input from the City – dominated the mining sector in South Africa: Rand Mines, Consolidated Gold Fields and Anglo-American. From the end of the same decade, the managerial and research expertise of the South African industry shaped mining in the rest of sub-Saharan Africa. By the turn of the 1950s, Anglo-American had consolidated its hold over the Zambian Copperbelt.

As a result of these changes, the colonial state in countries of the Copperbelt took on 'the supervisory role of landlord, banker, and employer. It was in the 1930s that one can see the origins of the over-developed state, but it was scarcely over developed; rather, it was the class-biased solution to crisis' (Lonsdale 1981: 193). Indeed, '[i]n the late 1930s and 1940s, colonial rule chocked on the narrowness of the pathways it had created' (Cooper 2002: 20). Varied forms of social mobilisations – ranging from the urban unrest generated by the deepening poverty of mobile rural dwellers with no other alternative than constituting a cheap 'labour reserve', to the ideological contests of an emerging scholarly elite – combined with the loss of imperial self-confidence in the

[11] Special reference as to the ownership of the *Unalienated Land in Southern Rhodesia (Reasons)* v. *JCPC* [29 July 1918] (JCPC) [1918] UKPC 78 (29 July 1918).

[12] A monopsony is a market condition in which there is only one buyer, the monopsonist.

aftermath of World War II, 'produced a crisis that would lead governments, in something of a panic, to swing the pendulum toward an obtrusively reformist conception of their own role' (Cooper 2002).

Between 1935 and 1950, numerous strikes erupted in ports, mines, railways and commercial centres across Africa. In the British Copperbelt (current Zambia), major mineworkers' strikes in 1935 and 1940 precipitated the deployment of policies of 'stabilisation' engineered by mining companies. Most emblematically in colonial Zambia, vast social investments in 'company towns' – where the stabilisation of workers was secured through the payment of 'family wages', the provision of health care and schooling – generated what Ferguson dubs the 'socially thick mining' (2006) that was emulated by the Zambian state right after independence. Likewise, in the Congo, the Union Minière du Haut-Katanga supported the deployment of invasive medical interventions to foster the 'regeneration' of a stabilised labour force, all the while funding the codification of customary law to foster social peace. Stabilisation foremost meant social and economic separation: the social, geographical and political walling-off of a labour class away from the mass of subsistence agriculture labourers pushed out of capitalist relations.

The independent state's heavy reliance on export and foreign investment consolidated rather than displaced the legal hierarchies inherited from these earlier transformations. In Kenya, the decision that the private legal profession would service the economy (contrasting with Nkrumah's emphasis on the public sector in Ghana) enabled private lawyers to handle public commercial work. Allowing foreign lawyers to continue practicing in the country fostered the stratification of the legal market, with European firms monopolising top-end litigation, Asian law firms servicing the middle commercial sector (itself largely Asian) and Africans practising as generalists in one-two person offices specialised in rural land transactions.

In Kenya, the Africanisation of the profession fostered the emergence of a 'Black bar' which enjoyed a golden period, thanks to the political activism of some members in the struggle for constitutionalism and the rule of law. The maintenance of strong links with the state bureaucracy through co-optation (and repression) also induced the 'fall of the Black bar' described by Mwangi (2001), due to lawyers' dependence on state patronage, corruption and ethnicity politics.

In Ghana too, mineral extraction (foremost gold) and control over land loomed large at independence. The priority of Nkrumah's government was to renegotiate existing mining arrangements and create state enterprises and numerous commodity producer associations to oversee the management of mines and mining operations, including the formation of the State Gold Mining Corporation in 1961. 'Strategically, the post-independence state embraced the colonial mining legislation in which all mineral-rich lands had been vested in the hands of the governor but also had to deal with the threat posed by local chiefs' (Tsuma 2012: 5).

The government's attempt to co-opt chiefs to centralise gold production efforts was weakened by the power vacuum opened by their reduced authority among local communities and the lack of investment and technical expertise. This led to a decline in production that was worsened by the economic recession of the 1970s.

The creation of the first law faculty in sub-Saharan Africa (outside South Africa) in 1958, in Ghana, aimed explicitly at enlarging the market for legal services and responding to the huge demand for personnel required by the rapidly expanding state. However, this strategy failed to break the enduring monopoly of Asante lawyers over the legal market for access to land. While the link between rural wealth and education was disrupted by the provision of governmental scholarships, patterns of recruitment into the private legal market remained unchanged.

Asante lawyers became the 'plumbers of the economy' by brokering the commoditisation of land and consolidating export-oriented capitalist relations after independence, while also serving as the 'masons of politics' (Luckham 1981: 107) through strategies of (re)production of their legal monopoly, strengthened by personal networks 'turned to good account by lawyers [moving] into politics' (Luckham 1981: 178). Foreign investors' preference for direct contact with members of the government and administration, rather than intervention on the legal system, also contributed to organising the market for private legal services around small chambers of one to five lawyers specialising in routine legal work on land matters.

3.3 Revamping the City *as* Middle Power

The position of Britain as the world's financial powerhouse stumbled in the aftermath of the Suez crisis in 1956 which brought the sterling to the brink of collapse. The Bretton Woods system also triggered what Bullough (2022) describes as a trilemma for interstate financial relations, by providing governments with the possibility at any given time to choose only two out of the three options of fixed exchange rates, free capital flow and domestic autonomy. State autonomy ran high as an option in the immediate post–World War II; as did reining in banks seen as the trigger of the economic crisis of the 1930s. So 'productive capital [took] priority over speculative capital' (Bullough 2022: 32).

In 1955, a small British bank, Midland, performed a discrete – though legal – trick to overcome the dilemma of lacking capital to invest – and therefore clients. It borrowed US dollars from Narodny, a Moscow bank, which could not keep its dollars in the United States for fear they would be frozen, to buy pounds sterling. The other part of the trick was that it also circumvented the 1933 US Regulation Q which limited interests commercial banks could earn to just 1 per cent. The move was steadily taken on by other commercial banks, though with a twist: they simply bought US dollars. 'What mattered therefore was not sterling, but the system. [...]. [T]he City had – quite accidentally – invested one of the most consequential financial tools of the twentieth century: the Eurodollar' (Bullough 2022: 44–45).

As simultaneously dollars and not dollars, Eurodollars increased transaction potentials without the restrictions of ordinary dollars, so US banks quickly joined in. 'As one senior banker [said in 1965] "you can't expect people to remain virtuous when the temptation becomes too great"' (Bullough 2022: 52–53). By December 1969, the volume of funds in the market had hit US$ 40 million. The dramatic expansion of Eurobonds – loans issued in dollars on behalf of borrowers seeking investment money – was greatly aided by restrictions in the US against the state's growing balance of payment problems in the 1960s. In spring 1970, President Nixon, infuriated by the inability to control inflation in the United States by limiting the amount of currency in circulation, abandoned the US dollar's peg to gold: '[f]rom then on, the dollar would be worth whatever someone would pay for' (Bullough 2022: 55).

When the Bretton Woods system of fixed exchange rates was dismantled, 'a differentiated global political-legal landscape of avoidance was [...] readily available' (Ogle 2017: 1435). As Bullough (2022) argues, the emergence of the City as powerhouse for the expansion of offshore capitalism was partly accidental. But the repositioning of the City was enabled by the lumpiness of Britain's middle power. 'Decolonization and the end of empires created something of a money panic and a clientele eager to move assets out of the colonial world to havens that would shelter them from the "socialized taxation" [...] at work in the Western world' (Ogle 2017: 1439).

The trajectory of the lawyer Michael Riegels, described by Bullough (2022: 61f), is emblematic. Trained at Oxford and Gray's Inn, Riegels was 'a man of Empire' and returned to Tanganyika, where he was born in 1961. President Nyerere's policy of removing racial barriers in a country where Europeans controlled professions, and Asians trade, forced him to hedge his bets and move back to the United Kingdom in 1971. Disgruntled by the lack of opportunities in the former *métropole*, Riegels shortly after moved to the British Virgin Islands. Constituted as a British overseas territory and located in the Caribbean to the East of Puerto Rico, the British Virgin Islands were extremely poor, as sugar plantations had ceased being viable following the 1833 prohibition of slavery.

A huge change happened when Riegels was contacted by Paul Butler, a partner at the Wall Street corporate law firm Shearman and Sterling, seeking to use the loophole of the double taxation treaty between the United States and the British Virgin Islands to enable his business clientele to bypass US regulatory constraints and taxation.

> Double taxation treaties are foundational to the globalized economy because they ensure that a company that operates in more than one country isn't taxed twice on the same money. There is a flaw in the system, which is that, if one country undercuts the other on tax rates, companies that base themselves in the first can dramatically reduce the amount they pay into government coffers in the second.
>
> (Bullough 2022: 72)

'[A]t a time when natural resources and industrialization were viewed as the sole path to growth and development, small and resource-poor territories had few options for attracting foreign capital other than to turn themselves into tax havens' (Ogle 2017: 1443). The earliest case of tax haven, the Bahamas, was set up with the blessing of the British Crown as a 'development' endeavour (Ogle 2017: 1443). Making use of this rule in the British Virgin Islands was a 'little like the islands had suddenly struck oil, but without all the messy business of having to dig wells or move viscous liquids around' (Bullough 2022: 74).

Within the space of a couple of years, the extent of the rush of US dollars into the British Virgin Islands was so intense that the US initially planned to renegotiate a new double taxation treaty before simply cancelling it in 1982. Butler leaned on existing legislation in Panama and Delaware and, together with Riegels and Lewis Hunte, the British Virgin Islands' recently appointed attorney general, set to work on a bill creating a new kind of corporation. The international business company (IBC) 'was tax free, completely opaque, only ha[d] to keep records "as the directors consider[ed] necessary" [. . .], did not have to tell anyone what it was doing, and could be moved to another jurisdiction at any time, for any reasons' (Bullough 2022: 77).

This legal device took off, thanks to two geopolitical turns at the beginning of the 1980s. The first was the growing tension between the United States and Panama, which until then had been Central America's clearing house for tax evasion through to drug smuggling. The second was the prospect of Hong Kong's return to China, which unleashed 'a wave of funk money as large as anything the world had yet seen' (Bullough 2022: 78). By the end of the 1990s, the British Virgin Islands accounted for almost half of the world's offshore market.

3.4 Competing Legal Ordering Claims

British plans for a West Indies Federal Supreme Court collapsed with the independence of Caribbean states, although most retained the right of appeal to the Privy Council. Like Jersey, the British Virgin Islands are still part of Britain – they both *are* and *are not* British, depending on what suits their clients, as both entities can play the 'autonomy' card of political devolution (Bullough 2022: 238). Foremost, Lewis Hunte was not simply the respondent of Riegels. He was also the epitome of a Caribbean transnational legal elite shaped by the imperial realm. Queen's Council, Hunte was admitted to the Bar of England and Wales in 1965. In addition to his appointment as Attorney General of the British Virgin Islands (1982–1985), he served as a magistrate in Barbados and as Deputy Chief Parliamentary Counsel, a position he held for seven years. Earlier in his career, he served as Deputy Registrar of the Court of Appeal in Jamaica, Deputy Registrar of the Supreme Court of Barbados and completed a one-year secondment at the Federal Department of Justice in Ottawa, Canada. Appointed as one of Her Majesty's Counsel for the British Virgin Islands in 2003, to honour his most notable legal accomplishment as draftsman of the 1984 International Business Act (IBC Act) of the British Virgin Islands, he has also been called upon to act as Judge of the High Court of the Eastern Caribbean Supreme Court.

The reconversion of Britain's middle power was *consolidated* rather than weakened by the post-independence repositioning of the Privy Council as jurisdictional umpire over scattered territories whose sovereignty remained shared out, layered and overlapping. Until the enactment of the Statute of Westminster in 1931, which de facto eliminated the legal obstacles to unilateral abolition of appeals by the dominion parliaments, the Privy Council was the final court of appeal for more than a quarter of the world. Appeals from the courts of the Kingdom of Great Britain and Ireland went to the Judicial Committee of the House of Lords. For its part, the Privy Council had jurisdiction over appeals from the Prize Courts and ecclesiastical courts of the British Isles and appeals from the courts of all the other units of the empire – colonies and dominions.

The Privy Council's operations and case law also reflected the 'uncertain universalism' on which the British Empire was premised (Ibhawoh 2017: 116). The jurisdiction of the Privy Council was a 'very delicate one' as 'even in its quest for judicial uniformity and standardisation, the exigencies of imperial governance made it necessary for Privy Council judges to accommodate divergence and difference' (Ibhawoh 2017: 122).

Foremost, the sheer longevity of this court – which continues to retain jurisdiction over appeals from thirty-two jurisdictions, including eleven independent states – reflects a history of protracted struggles about its *structural* position in relation to the empire. The question of the appellate jurisdiction of the Privy Council was a recurring, if not constant, theme in relations between Britain and the emerging dominions of the 'old' Commonwealth between 1870s and 1930s – even while the court's authority was at its peak, and long before the winding down of the empire (Swinfen 1987).

Emblematically, the judicial outcomes of disputes over land property rights in the Gold Coast reflected less a linear and systematic subservience of peripheries to the imperial core based on the upholding of Common Law principles of property rights than turf battles in the colonial realm between local chiefs, merchants and colonial administrators. Those reverberated in the practical deployment of the Crown's power over other colonies. 'The giving way of the great court of the Empire may [therefore] be examined as a microcosm of the difficulties of creating or maintaining any broad system of international adjudication' (Richard 1988: 244).

The decision to appoint indigenous judges to the Privy Council at the end of the nineteenth century had the paradoxical effect of providing the court with a more representative outlook, while exposing the practical limitations of its approach to judicial universalism. While geographical distance reinforced its position as umpire, limited knowledge of local specificities often 'amounted to applying judicial precedent in such a way that extended the judicial errors of one part of the British Empire to make them law in another' (Ibhawoh 2017: 127).

Conversely, debates to reform the Privy Council from the early twentieth century – be it to revoke appeals from the self-governing dominions or to establish one great Imperial Court of Appeal that would take over the entirety of the jurisdictional remit of the two tribunals of final appeal in the empire – were less about the uneven and unequal principles of 'justice' upheld by the court than its position as arbiter of *political status* in the metropolis, the dominions and the colonies.

That the 'ancient kingly prerogative embodied in appeals to the Judicial Committee is a bond that binds without friction and links without strain' perfectly suited the Canadian and Australian dominions to the extent that – as an American scholar put it in the 1920s – 'the English judge who seeks to drive a coach and four through an Act of Parliament must drive it by the way of interpretation, and not by the route of declaring the Act invalid' (Boutell 1920–1921: 9).

The Canadian dominion retained appeals to the Privy Council against the backdrop of the American Civil War to ensure a strong central government. Appeals to the Privy Council over constitutional matters progressively shifted the balance in favour of the provinces, fostering the court's relevance to oppose both dominion and federal powers. But Canada was the first dominion to start abolishing appeals to the Privy Council, in 1933, when the court invoked its role as guardian of civil liberties to contest the validity of Canadian Acts of Parliament in criminal matters (see Swinfen 1987).

Certainly, the assertion of national sovereignty played a key role in former British colonies in Africa and the general decision of independent states to sever jurisdictional links with the Privy Council. It was also the image of the Privy Council as a 'parochial second-class court' constituted exclusively to adjudicate colonial cases, with no jurisdiction over metropolitan cases, that buried plans to retain appeals to the Privy Council or the establishment of a successor Commonwealth Appeal Court. 'If the JCPC was good enough for colonial subjects, why was it not also considered good enough for British citizens?' (Ibhawoh 2017: 130).

These conflicts provide a fabulous entry point to re-examine the structural triggers of the sidelining of international dispute settlement mechanisms during the Cold War. The ICJ's controversial decisions over the question of self-determination in the early 1950s and 1960s certainly contributed to its shunning by newly independent states in sub-Saharan

Africa.[13] For its part, international commercial arbitration remained largely a sideshow, while the actual resolution of the oil disputes spurred by the post-independence waves of nationalisation were resolved by other means (Dezalay Y and Garth 2012: 2328) – through negotiation and ensnared independence.

The sidelining of the ICJ was also partly linked to the failure of US foundations' investments in the Cultural Cold War. They foremost reflected the legal imperialistic strategies espoused by the United States in the deployment of US business and political interests abroad as an ostensibly 'anti-imperial' hegemon. US legal investments on the international scene at the end of the nineteenth century are emblematic. US settlement in the Philippines – following the cession of the territory by Spain in 1898 – was hailed as a war of 'liberation' from Spanish domination. The co-optation of local elites threaded on previous and parallel tracks of legal imperialism. The highly selective grooming of a co-opted legal and political elite contributed to the symbiotic relationship between conflicts over law and struggles for state power at the local level. This experience also durably restructured the domestic field of state power in the United States, to the benefit of a small elite of corporate lawyers who used the Philippines as a laboratory for the strategies of expansion of a United States 'anti-imperial' moral imperialism in the Cultural Cold War (Dezalay Y and Garth 2008).

The genesis of international justice institutions was structurally linked to these endeavours. In Latin America,

> [t]he United States made a strategic choice for arbitration, imposed by (threats of) force on unfair terms, rather than outright invasion or occupation, to try and oust its European rivals and assert its interests in the region. Arbitration offered the United States a new type of imperialism. It accorded with a widespread US self-understanding as anti-imperialist while, under a guise of legality, allowing for the universalization of the US way of doing things.
>
> (Greenman 2021: 8)

[13] The court's advisory opinions on the *International Status of South West Africa* triggered a protracted crisis with newly independent states. See South West Africa, Second Phase, Judgment, ICJ Reports 1966, p. 6. Arguably, and conversely, its 1952 decision over Iran's nationalisation of the Anglo-Iranian Oil Company also contributed to the sidelining of the court by former colonial powers to protect their interests in decolonisation disputes. See Anglo-Iranian Oil Co. case (jurisdiction), Judgment of 22 July 1952: ICJ reports 1952, p. 93. See also Chapter 8.

International justice institutions in The Hague and Paris – interstate adjudication and commercial arbitration – emerged out of similar strategies and alliances between the domestic interests of a small Wall Street US corporate legal elite with considerable financial resources and political clout, and a select 'international legal community' of European law professors marginalised from state diplomacies and doctrinal hierarchies, as international law was still a nascent and ill-recognised academic discipline (Dezalay Y and Garth 2016; Sacriste and Vauchez 2007).

These alliances led to the creation of the PCA in 1899 and, as a direct offspring, the PCIJ in the aftermath of World War I, with funding provided by the quintessence of the US 'robber barons' turned into architects of US moral imperialism: the Carnegie Endowment for International Peace. Building on similar alliances, the ICC's Court of International Commercial Arbitration in Paris was created in the early twenties in the shadow of the PCIJ by borrowing its public visibility and the academic legitimacy of international law (Dezalay Y and Garth 2016).

The withdrawal of the United States from these alliances in the 1960s exposed the huge disparities of power and status between the United States and European lawyers involved in interwar discussions about international justice. The lack of opportunities for the small cluster of internationalist European professors on the diplomatic and doctrinal scene led them to withdraw into an ivory tower restricted to the institutions of The Hague and shaped by reciprocal assimilation dynamics between European law professors and their counterparts in African states.

Yet the sidelining of The Hague institutions coincided with the appointment of the first judges from newly independent sub-Saharan states to the ICJ. Emblematically, the trajectory of the first African lawyer appointed to the court in 1964, Isaac Forster (see Dezalay S 2017), reflected the interlocking of the meritocratic and elitist channels of mobility enabled by the French imperial realm, along with the former *métropole*'s colonial projection in its African spheres of influence during the Cold War. Hailing from a family of wealthy traders of the *Quatre Communes* in Senegal, Forster completed his secondary schooling in France, and obtained his *Licence* in Law at the Sorbonne in Paris. After pursuing a judicial career as a magistrate across the AOF, he integrated the French presidential cabinet in the *Union Française* in 1952 before being appointed first president of the *Cour Suprême* of independent Senegal in 1960.

Elected to the prestigious Institute of International Law (*Institut de droit international*) before his appointment to the ICJ in 1964, Forster was therefore typical of the 'gentlemen politicians of law' from the Global South described by Sacriste and Vauchez (2007), whose multi-positionality at a time of weak institutionalisation of the international scene simultaneously reflected domestic political and economic interests and deflected them by hailing the doctrine of international law as universalistic. But Forster's state capital was both imperial and national, positioning him structurally as a broker of Senegal's sovereignty within the boundaries of the former French Empire.

3.5 Conclusion

In *Empire*, Hardt and Negri (2000) rekindled the debate on imperialism in world politics by suggesting that (Leftist) opposition had to be rethought in relation to a decentred configuration of empire that had many new, postmodern qualities, making it *total*. The assessment is certainly true when it harks back to the expansion of finance in the past four decades. There is, indeed, a sense of doom in realising that '[t]his pattern – of allowing something, making money from it, then attempting to solve the problems it causes after they've occurred – has repeated itself again and again' (Bullough 2022: 237).

To be sure, both the colonial projection espoused by France and Belgium during the Cold War and the ensnared independence of resource-rich African states contributed to structuring their fields of state power around the stakes of controlling the rent derived from access to international resources, primarily the economic and political boons of extraction. Generally, these characteristics of post-colonial political regimes had a particular impact on the position of legal professions in relation to political power and international resources, be it their capacity of resistance or the ambivalence of their co-optation.

But decolonisation also triggered major global economic and financial transformations. Reopening the history of the period between the 1950s and the 1980s reveals that what Ogle (2017) terms 'archipelago capitalism' commonly understood as referring to tax havens and secrecy jurisdictions is 'by no means a deviation from normal economic practice' (1433). Rather, offshore capitalism emerged as an *outgrowth* of the nation-state system shaped by the New Deal, the European welfare state, decolonisation and modernisation projects in the Third World.

By allowing the offshore world to flourish, and egged on by increasingly assertive businesses communities, these political moves made it impossible not only for the new states but also for the old nation-state–based political economic order to survive after the 1970s.

The competition between international and supranational jurisdictional claims is reflective of the very instability of the middle power that was revived, during the Cold War, by the interconnectedness between these dynamics. Shifting the focus away from the fragmentation of supranational jurisdictional claims towards the structural effects of their competition sheds a whole new light on the structural effects of the interconnectedness of these dynamics. As put bluntly by Bullough (2022) 'regulatory fragmentation works to the benefit of butlering services because a client's activities can be divided up between different jurisdictions, which prevents outsiders from getting a full view of what's happening' (237). This, I argue, produced a global system of archipelagos of *sedimented* imperialism by fostering the blurriness of the boundaries of middle power as a continuous driver in the articulation between politics, capital accumulation and legal change.

4

The New Scramble, Deregulation, Re-regulation

1980s–?

Cobalt, a core component of lithium-ion batteries, is the stuff of our daily lives. It makes our mobiles smart and our computers portable. It is the green gold of the 'energy transition' away from fossil energy that is supposed to help us breathe better and longer. When we use our keyboards, listen to music, fly and take pictures, it is thanks to rare earths elements with magical-sounding names, like neodymium. Those are also core components of the wind turbines and hybrid cars of the green revolution.

The Li-ion supply chain (see Olivetti et al. 2017) illustrates the geopolitical upheaval that is inducing Africa's renewed prominence as the 'global economy's last frontier' (Moghalu 2013). The usual lithium-ion battery types consist of lithium and different amounts of cobalt, nickel, manganese and natural graphite. Of these components, lithium and cobalt are the most critical. Lithium enables Li-ion batteries to be lighter and to pack more energy than conventional lead-acid batteries. Cobalt ensures the batteries' cathodes do not overheat or catch fire.

Extraction of lithium is concentrated in Australia, Chile and Argentina. Cobalt is most often produced as a by-product of copper and nickel mining. Nickel supply is more fragmented, as it can be found in Brazil, Russia, South Africa and Canada. But the ore most suitable for batteries – and foremost the cheapest to extract – is geologically concentrated in Africa's Copperbelt, in one country only: the Congo, whose known deposits contain over 60 per cent of the world's cobalt.

The liberal weekly *The Economist*, often seen as global capitalism's Cassandra, entitled one of its March 2019 issues 'The New Scramble for Africa'.[1] The rush for the minerals of the energy transition, *The Economist* argued, is fostering new opportunities, as it is characterised by the unprecedented extent of foreign diplomatic, strategic and

[1] *The Economist*, 'The New Scramble for Africa' 7 March 2019.

commercial ties of the African continent with China and other emerging economies.

This competition is compounded by the fact that green technologies are 'materials dependent' in that they are 'enabled directly by, or designed around, a particular set of material(s) and are therefore subject to the supply chain issues that accompany those materials' (Olivetti et al. 2017: 229). Cobalt is the most expensive material inside a lithium-ion battery. Refined cobalt is traded on the LME since 2010, the world centre for industrial metals trading. Price per ton is highly volatile. Between 2010 and 2022, it has ranged anywhere between US$ 21,750 and US$ 95,250. Old European imperial cores – and to a lesser extent the United States – are on the consumer end of the 'green' energy supply chain. China dominates the world's lithium-ion market. In 2020 it produced about 77 per cent of all Li-ion batteries that entered the global market in 2020 and controlled 80 per cent of the world's raw material refining, 77 per cent of the world's cell capacity and 60 per cent of the world's component manufacturing.[2]

'If Africa handles the new scramble wisely', *The Economist* argued, 'the main winners will be Africans themselves'.[3] Rising demand for cobalt led to a 300 per cent increase in prices of unrefined cobalt between 2016 and 2018 (UNCTAD 2022: 42). Thanks to its massive geological wealth, the DRC '*could* become the Saudi Arabia of the electric vehicle age'.[4]

To be sure, countries dependent on crude oil exports (like Angola) or with essential societal needs for access to water and electricity now controlled by China as their main creditor (like Zambia) certainly seem unlikely to gain the upper hand. A 2021 International Monetary Fund (IMF) study found that the crisis affecting mineral-rich African countries is foremost related to their dependence on royalties from transnational mining corporations. According to the study, sub-Saharan African states are losing a yearly average of US$ 600 million to US$ 1.5 billion in corporate income tax from transnational corporations – including in economies not defined as 'resource intensive'.[5] For the IMF experts the

[2] See 'BNEF Talk: winning the lithium battery value chain' bnef-summit 18 May 2021, www.bloomberg.com/news/videos/2021-05-18/bnef-talk-winning-the-lithium-battery-value-chain (accessed 31 October 2022).

[3] Ibid.

[4] J Mitchell, 'Kinshasa is already Africa's biggest city – Could cobalt make it the richest?' *Mining Technology* 15 February 2022, www.mining-technology.com/analysis/kinshasa-africa-democratic-republic-congo-cobalt/ (accessed 23 March 2022). Emphasis added.

[5] Resource-intensive economies are defined as states where mining makes a significant contribution to countries' national output, exports and FDI inflows.

solution is that resource-rich states should ramp up their taxation capacities. The *how* question of curbing tax evasion is eluded by dizzyingly chiselled data on the sophistication of corporate profit-shifting strategies – ranging from inbound investment via 'hubs' – third countries that impose light taxation and are used as a conduit to investment elsewhere,[6] to tax treaty shopping. But the report's conclusion reeks the sour smell of rehearsed folklore: the vulnerability of sub-Saharan resource-rich economies to financial shocks and economic booms and busts is conflated with a *crisis of the state.*

Resource-rich African states have loomed large in the 'new conflicts' policy-driven literature that emerged from the break-up of the Cold War. They also feature widely in the concurrent boom of supranational justice institutions that have transformed domestic and global politics into legal and judicial battlefields in the past four decades (see Alter 2014). In both instances, the weakness of the state is seen to breed 'loot-seeking' warfare, while juridical processes deployed in these civil war situations are generally stripped of their geopolitical contexts and described as 'post'-conflict or 'transitional' (Baczko 2021).

The problem, however, is that this inexorable call for law as a *fix* against political predation overlooks the embeddedness of the new rush for Africa in the concurrent transformation of the *geography* of extraction. The increasing spatial separation between extraction/transport and manufacturing is pushing the mining industry towards greater functional integration from technological innovations, to port and shipping industries through to financial speculation (Arboleda 2010).

These technological and organisational changes are fostering the expansion of 'offshore' extraction, thanks to the discovery of offshore oil and gas in West Africa and technological innovations in mining extraction that enable the 'ring-fencing' of the sector. Offshoring, be it geographical or social (higher technologies reducing the need for a local labour force), reinforces reciprocal interests: it limits the social and political cost of extraction for multinationals, fosters wealth capture by political elites and fuels the financialisation of minerals.

The two-step dance between legal *deregulation* and *re-regulation* reinforces the autonomy of financial markets. The 2008 financial crisis triggered growing anxieties over the 'financial curse' (Christensen et al.

[6] Over 60 per cent of FDI flowing into the DRC transit through Mauritius, while between 30 and 50 per cent of FDI flowing into Ghana, South Africa, Tanzania and Botswana transit through the United Kingdom. See Albertin et al. (2021: 19).

2016) – the risk raised by oversized financial sectors for economic growth. To date, the call to Western countries to curb their tax havens remains unchecked. The question of *why* states in advanced economies do not alter the system inevitably stumbles into limited explanations – that states realised too late that financialisation does not enable wealth to trickle down, that they have 'more to gain' because economic growth boosts their tax revenue and allows them to raise debt finance (Pistor 2019: 21) or because collective action, though called on by the IMF and the OECD until then restricted to an 'arm-length approach' to the freedom of markets, is 'like herding squirrels on the trampoline' (Shaxson 2019: 10).

In what follows, I look at concurrent imperial encounters that, together, help explain the re-articulation of resource-rich sub-Saharan African states with global markets. The ongoing rush is in great part embedded in the 'imperial hangover' (Puri 2021) of the Cold War partition of the continent. What Ellis (1996) dubbed the 'real' post-colonial order characterised by the 'policy of abandonment' of former *métropoles*, foremost France, was rather symbolic. The structural adjustment programs imposed on African states to respond to the acute debt crisis that generally plagued them by the turn of the 1980s positioned IFIs as the prime vehicles of the neoliberal turn on the continent. But they did not displace the gatekeeping politics inherited from the colonial state and reinforced by the Cold War partition of the continent. It is, rather, the onshoring of offshore capitalism in the 1980s that contributed to positioning global traders not only as the prime interface between resource-rich economies and global markets but also as the core engineers of the transformation of the *geography* of extraction.

The onshoring of swashbuckler capitalism is tightly linked to the expansion of Big Law. What Pistor (2019) calls the codification of capital based on Common Law and the law of the state of New York is enabled by the globalisation of the model of the Wall Street model of the corporate law firm – as a legal institution that combines the *know-how* of contract negotiation, financialisation and arbitration, through to tax evasion, and the *know-who* of business and political clout. Like the previous Scramble, competitive claims for supranational jurisdictional authority is consolidating rather than weakening this reiteration of middle power, by enabling the United States to deploy extraterritorial jurisdictional power as policeman of the US dollar market while harbouring some of the world's main tax havens. Just like Chapter 3, these imperial encounters are unfolding in different settings – in Paris,

London; The Hague; Washington, DC; New York; along with the capitals and sites of extraction in resource-rich African economies. It is precisely the messy congruence of their structural effects that helps account for the ongoing dynamics of expansion of Chinese business interests into the African continent.

4.1 The 'Real' Post-colonial Order

The Cold War formally ended on the African continent in 1988 with the independence of Namibia, Africa's last colony. The 'policy of abandonment' of the continent by former colonial *métropoles* opened a vacuum that was filled by Bretton Woods institutions to 'articulate most clearly the policy of the industrialized world towards Africa, based on free trade and liberal policy' (Ellis 1996: 20).

'[T]he Bretton Woods institutions, and especially the World Bank [were] left in occupation of the field' (Ellis 1996: 15). The fall of the Berlin Wall coincided almost to the day with the publication of the World Bank report *Sub-Saharan Africa: From Crisis to Sustainable Growth*, which contained the first reference to 'good governance'. Foreign direct investment (FDI) flows in relative terms to sub-Saharan Africa had never been great due to lack of infrastructure, high production costs and the spread of internal conflicts (Duffield 1992). The sharp decrease of ODA flows into the continent (US$ 69 billion in 1991 against US$ 50 billion in 1993) paralleled a wider critique of the United States and other OECD countries of the efficiency of development aid.

By 1998, the World Bank report *Assessing Aid*, which suggested that aid was 'efficient' only in recipient countries with 'good policies' and 'good institutions' consolidated what Duffield (2007) dubs a 'two tier' relationship between developing countries and the world economy: with a first tier characterised by full bilateral relations where partnership with the recipient government has been successfully negotiated and the aid tap is turned on fully, and a second tier of countries deemed *unable* or *unwilling* and subject to a continuum of conditionality ranging from the withholding of assistance to the suspension of bilateral aid.

The Great Lakes region is emblematic of this shift. Until the beginning of the 1990s the colonial Congo-Rwanda-Burundi entity was de facto maintained as the geostrategic lens to manage the political crises of the region. The United States, France and Belgium orchestrated overt and covert military interventions between 1960 and the beginning of the 1990s that focused on maintaining Congo's stability by supporting then

Zaire's president Joseph-Désiré Mobutu (aka Mobutu Sese Seko) – promoted as the region's prime 'big man' until he was supplanted in this role by Uganda's president Museveni in the late 1980s.

While images of the ongoing genocide in Rwanda were hitting the news in the West, the United Nations Assistance Mission for Rwanda (UNAMIR), deployed in the country since October 1993 to foster the implementation of the Arusha Accords signed in August 1993 between the Rwandan Patriotic Front and the Rwandan government, was left understaffed and its mandate reduced. In the United States, the Clinton administration 'began what would be a two-month dance to avoid the G-word' (Power 2007: 7): genocide. In May 1994, following the debacle of the US-led Operation Restore Hope in Somalia, the Clinton administration had adopted Presidential Decision Directive 25 which precluded any future US military intervention in the absence of US interests and disengaged the United States from the United Nations and support to a permanent UN military capacity. The 'New World order'[7] announced by President Bush in 1990 was officially over.

While the UN Security Council adopted Resolution 995 setting up an ad hoc International Criminal Tribunal to prosecute individuals responsible for the genocide in Rwanda, a Mauritanian diplomat, Ahmedou Ould-Abdallah, appointed special representative for Burundi by then UN secretary general Boutros Boutros-Ghali in late 1993, devised a pragmatic plan (channelling funds from the United States Agency for International Development – USAID) that would become the M.O. of the next decades of Western-led 'state-building' interventions (Chandler 2006, 2019; Duffield 2001, 2007): bypassing state authorities to promote peace, reconciliation and the rule of law through (inter)national NGOs. 'This multipolar and private diplomatic practice undoubtedly had its hours of glory in Burundi. In comparative terms, since 1994, this small country has attracted a (disproportionate) volume of activities and international agents specifically oriented towards the resolution of conflicts' (Hara 1997: 80, my translation from French).

What was still in 1994 an ad hoc arrangement in Burundi had become by 1995 a prevailing feature of ODA. The new consensus among state members of the Development Assistance Committee (DAC) of the OECD, the EU Commission and the World Bank was that the developmental state had failed. Foremost, diagnosing *under*development itself as

[7] GHW Bush, 'Toward a New World Order' address to a joint session of Congress and the nation, 11 September 1990.

a security threat in the post-9/11 context further justified circumventing state authorities as recipients of aid moneys. In the space of a couple of years, 'civil society' was promoted as the legitimate vector of *development*, and as bulwark of *protection* against corrupt political elites.

The expansion of the 'extractive frontier' in African contexts in the first decade of the 2000s came at the tail end of these reforms. The timing of the new rush contrasted markedly with the 'new extraction' across Latin America a decade earlier (Bebbington 2009). The mining boom of the previous two decades was most pronounced in Latin America, with a growth of the global share of Latin America in mining investment from 10 to 25 per cent between 2003 and 2012 (Deonandan and Dougherty 2016). In Latin American contexts, the new extraction triggered political and social movements fostering – with varying degrees of success – a radical agenda of 'neo-extractivism'. This included the assertion of indigenous rights of local communities over extractive resources, notably through the increased exercise of the right to free, prior and informed consent institutionalised in various international legal instruments since the 1980s (see Raftopoulos 2017). This agenda 'pictured extractives as carriers of development through strong developmental states, which reinvested extractive rents in social programs and structural transformation' (Greco 2020: 511).

The privatisation policies ushered in by IFIs from the 1980s reinforced what Bayart calls the 'politics of the belly' (Bayart 1993) by consolidating the (political, financial) stakes of access and control over the 'mining rent' for resource-rich African states. Many African governments have experimented with resource nationalism. 'However, contemporary neo-extractivist policies in Africa nowadays are nowhere near as ambitious as those once attempted by African socialist governments' (Greco 2020: 511). Indeed, '[m]ost African countries have moved away from national control over natural resources, towards a more modest agenda aiming at increasing "local content" in extractive policies, not only in mining but also in oil and gas extraction' (Greco 2020: 512).

Across former French African colonies, the death of Côte d'Ivoire president Houphouët-Boigny symbolised the end of the former model. The 'real post-colonial order' in Côte d'Ivoire and other African states belonging to France's *pré carré* in sub-Saharan Africa was confirmed during France's decade of 'post-colonial indolence' in the 1990s, characterised by the former *métropole*'s unprecedented reluctance to provide military support and development aid. The neoliberal turn certainly disrupted the post-colonial block – but privatisation also fostered the repositioning of French business interests.

The *Doctrine d'Abidjan* articulated by French prime minister Balladur in 1993 operated a dramatic shift in French development policy by conditioning French ODA to the implementation of the structural adjustment programs imposed by IFIs. The parallel devaluation of the CFA franc by 50 per cent in 1994 aimed at espousing the liberal doxa and 'by the same token at "normali[sing]" relations between Paris and its former colonies' (Blamangin and Borrel 2021: 735, my translation from French).

The devaluation of the Franc CFA had severe implications for concerned African economies. But the withdrawal of French businesses from Africa over the period remained largely a myth: FDI from French businesses multiplied by twelve between 1995 and 2010. It is rather the wave of corporate restructuration coupled with the deindustrialisation shift and the predominance taken by Asia – specifically China from the early 2000s – as a new economic Eldorado that downgraded the interest – and foremost the capacity – of French extractive giants to continue maintaining control over the entirety of their productive chains.

The aluminium conglomerate Péchiney is a case in point. On the eve of the 1960s wave of independence, the corporation built an aluminium plant leaning back on the Édéa hydroelectric dam in Cameroon. In 1957, the group launched the construction of an aluminium refinery in Fria, Guinea – which was successfully completed despite the violence that characterised the country's independence. The group was severely hit by the 1970s oil shocks. It missed the globalisation turn – which required branching out of the French *pré carré*. Privatised in 1995, the corporation left Guinea in 1997 and was acquired in 2003 by the Alcan Corporation, headquartered in Canada, which was in turn taken over by the British-Australian mining giant Rio Tinto in 2007.

Within the space of fifteen years, most of the state-owned corporate 'jewels' of the *Françafrique* – including Elf – were privatised, restructured or dismantled. But the neoliberal turn also enabled the redeployment of French business interests. The bulk of the French business sphere had initially recoiled at the move to devaluate the CFA franc. For metropolitan businesses, the overvaluation of the CFA de facto subsidised their exports to captive markets in former colonies. But the business sphere quickly adapted to the new deal imposed by the IMF and the World Bank on the governments of the CFA zone. Emblematically, Pierre Castel – the founder of the Castel Group, which rules over the market for beer in

West Africa – benefited from a long-standing friendship with Gabon's Omar Bongo to acquire the Gabonese state-owned sugar company, the Société Sucrière du Haut-Ogouée (SOSUHO).[8]

'These acquisitions [were] even more profitable that these privatizations [were] not necessarily – or not immediately – coupled with the liberalisation of the concerned sectors' (Blamangin and Borrel 2021: 737, my translation from French). Major utilities corporations holding a 'natural monopoly' over the provision of water, electricity, railroads, port or airport infrastructures were ceded to French private businesses: Bouygues (for the distribution of water and electricity in Côte d'Ivoire and water in Senegal, Mali and the Central African Republic); Vivendi (for the distribution of water and electricity in Gabon, Chad and the Comoros and water in Niger) or Bolloré (which until recently[9] controlled the rail network in Cameroun and Côte d'Ivoire and port concessions on the entirety of the African Atlantic coast).

Structural adjustment programs have tended, therefore, to consolidate the rent of extraction – rather than displace it. The example of the Gécamines is emblematic. The corporation has played a key political role in the DRC's post-colonial politics. Mobutu Sese Seko is reported to have frequently tapped the state-owned company's coffers to sustain his vast patronage network. After decades of overproducing and underinvesting the company's factories and mines, Gécamines' production started collapsing from the turn of the 1990s. This ultimately contributed to Mobutu's downfall.

The World Bank–engineered liberalisation reforms from the early 2000s failed to displace the Gécamines' position as gatekeeper of some of the country's most promising mineral deposits, nor did its incorporation into a commercial company under private law in 2010. 'Although its production of copper and cobalt fell, Gécamines maintained its strategic role because it controlled the country's most sought-after mining permits' (Carter Centre 2017: 5). Gécamines started selling permits while war was still raging in the east of the country. The initial deals were signed with relatively junior companies – more risk-inclined than major mining conglomerates. This contributed to the Far West–like looting of the Katanga. 'The fragile context in which these earlier deals

[8] O Blamangin, 'Castel, l'empire qui fait trinquer l'Afrique' *Le Monde diplomatique* October 2018, pp. 1, 8–9.

[9] In March 2022, the Bolloré group ceded its transport and logistics activities in Africa (Bolloré Africa Logistics) to the Italian-Swiss MSC (Mediterranean Shipping Company).

were signed meant that revenues were initially relatively small. Concerns about the lack of revenue going to the DRC state eventually triggered international pressure to review the underlying partnership contracts and negotiate a "fair share for Congo"' (Carter Centre 2017: 6).

From the early 2000s, Joseph Kabila's regime actively retained the Gécamines' role as gatekeeper with foreign investors, while waging the commercial status of the corporation to shield it from governance inquiries such as requests to disclose its contracts, income and deal-making activities. This effectively positioned the company as a state within the state. Thus, the Congolese businessman Albert Yuma, even though he was a close ally of Joseph Kabila, was reappointed by President Tshisekedi as chairman of the board of directors of the corporation, due to his status as 'CEO of the CEOs' in the DRC at the helm of the Federation of Businesses of the Congo (Fédération des entreprises du Congo).

4.2 Big Business, Big Law

The wave of corporate reorganisations, the opening of new markets and the internationalisation and globalisation of deregulated financial markets facilitated the expansion and diffusion of the 'Wall Street' model of the multinational corporate law firm (Dezalay Y 1992; Dezalay Y and Garth 2012). Certainly, as demonstrated by Galanter and Palay (1991) in their seminal study, these 1980s events, particularly financial deregulation and increased transnational corporations' demand for business law, fostered a process of concentration of corporate law in large global law firms, as well as their international expansion (see Flood 2007).

The expansion of US transnational corporations after World War II, first in Europe and then gradually across the globe, was also fostered by the Euromarket and the offshore economy (Ogle 2017: 1447). The Euromarket is an integral part of the offshore world. Roughly 30 per cent of all FDI is invested or at least passes through tax havens. This proportion has remained surprisingly steady since the 1990s (Ogle 2017: 1435). In the United States, corporate profit shifting into tax havens has risen from an estimated 5–10 per cent of gross profits in the 1990s to about 25–30 per cent in 2017 (Albertin et al. 2021: 6).

The deregulatory moves engineered by the United States and the United Kingdom from the turn of the 1980s unleashed the neoliberal Big Bang by introducing certain elements of the deregulation and tax avoidance that were already practised in tax havens within the onshore economy (Bullough 2022: 1452).

Many of the deregulatory shifts of the neoliberal turn were incubated during the 1960s. In 1969, in a context of increased international competition, the US Federal Reserve allowed US banks to set up shell branches in tax havens to tap into the Eurobond market. No taxes accrued until profits were repatriated to the firms' US head office – a strategy that could be indefinitely postponed and allowed for the circumvention of Regulation Q.

The end of the Bretton Woods system of fixed exchange rates in 1971–1973 coincided with the oil shock and the recession of the US economy. 'With demand for loans sluggish in the United States and much of the Western world, Eurodollars were now lent out increasingly to developing countries, where the demand for credit, particularly from non-oil producing deficit countries remained high' (Ogle 2017: 1452).

Foremost, the financialisation of natural resources, starting with oil following the oil shocks of the 1970s, made the movement for a 'new international economic order' and 'its strong claims regarding the economic sovereignty of newly independent postcolonial states rooted in a world of strong territorial nation-states [...] a threatening prospect to advocates of the free market' (Ogle 2017: 1456).

The oil shocks and the financialisation of raw commodities also consolidated the power of traders as business *and* financial actors. Emblematically, Glencore is a vertically integrated natural resource company, meaning that it is involved at every stage of the supply chain of its products, from extraction and processing through to marketing and trading. Its sprawling operations include metals – particularly copper, nickel and cobalt – as well as coal, oil, gas and agricultural products. Glencore extracts and trades a third of the world's supply of cobalt. The company went public in 2011 in the largest ever flotation on the London market.

Since the 1970s, global traders have been conducting their activities in the opaquest corners of the international financial system with remarkable lack of regulation or government scrutiny. Traders are the quintessence of an insider's market dominated by charismatic ties produced within single corporate dynasties. As the world's second-largest oil and metals trader, Trafigura belongs to the same dynasty as the first trader, Marc Rich + Co (now Glencore). It was started by a group of dissatisfied former Marc Rich employees who struck out on their own in 1993. The

'King of Oil', Marc Rich, also epitomises the sulphurous image of the trading industry.[10]

For the most part, commodity traders are privately owned companies, with less obligation to disclose information about their activities than publicly listed transnational corporations. When they hit the news, it is usually due to wrongdoings. Beyond the trope of the scandal, and the seemingly endless two-step dance between swashbuckling and re-regulation, the unique and extremely detailed study of Blas and Farchy (2022) also demonstrates that the *role* taken on by global traders in the global economy is structural, as it leaned on the City's repositioning as financial capital in the 1950s, and the expansion of the Euromarket.

The trading industry took its contemporary form in the aftermath of the Second World War, an era during which 'trading companies became truly global for the first time – and crucially, when oil started to become a tradable commodity' (Blas and Farchy 2022: 16). The decades of global economic growth between the 1950s and the oil crashes of the 1970s spurred massive investments in commodity production around the world. The opening up of markets that had previously been tightly controlled, above all oil, coupled with the financialisation of the global economy and the growth of the banking sector from the turn of the 1970s, further moulded the global economy in commodity traders' favour. '[W]ith the big Western oil and mining companies in retreat, almost no regulatory scrutiny, and with Wall Street banks yet to discover emerging markets, the traders had a free rein' (Blas and Farchy 2022: 84).

Marc Rich (the founder of Marc Rich + Co) developed a portfolio of relations with various dictatorial regimes and embargoed states as a former employee of the commodity trader Philipp Brothers. 'Rich's key insight was that oil – and other raw materials – could be traded with less capital, and fewer assets, than the big oil producers thought, if backed by bank finance. It was this leveraged business model that became the template for modern traders, including Trafigura, Vitol and Glencore'.[11]

The shift in power from large American and European oil and mining companies to governments in what was then dubbed the Third World opened a window of opportunity for the commodity traders 'that they exploited with gusto [. . .]. In the process they became the connection between many newly assertive countries and the global financial system,

[10] A Hill, '"King of oil" who became a target for US' *Financial Times* 26 June 2013.
[11] Ibid.

helping to channel dollars to governments and leaders that had no other source of funding' (Blas and Farchy 2022: 74).

'One of the most profitable disguises of the era was called Cobuco. It involved the world's wealthiest commodity traders disguising themselves as bureaucrats from the poorest nation on the planet' (Blas and Farchy 2022: 91). In the early 1980s, Burundi entered Marc Rich + Co's radar to devise a scheme to circumvent the boycott of oil flows to Apartheid South Africa. 'Monsieur Ndolo' – the pseudonym used by a Marc Rich trader – was operating Cobuco – standing for the *Compagnie Burundaise de Commerce* (Burundi trade corporation) – ostensibly from the company's headquarters in Brussels.

Officially, Cobuco was a trading company buying crude oil in the international market to supply Burundi (which at the time barely needed one tanker of crude to meet its needs for over six years). Cobuco was incorporated as a joint venture between Marc Rich + Co and the Burundian state. 'Monsieur Ndolo' engineered a visit of the then Burundian president Jean-Baptiste Bagaza to Iran to buy crude oil at official OPEC prices under preferential terms. Burundi's status as a non-aligned nation also enabled it to stave off repayment for two years. Officially the oil was transported to Mombasa. But it was diverted into the global market. '[I]n the end, Cobuco did not supply the country with a single barrel of oil, although it helped to line the pockets of a number of Burundian officials' – at 20 cents per barrel (Blas and Farchy 2022: 91).

By the turn of the 1980s, Marc Rich had built considerable financial clout and *know-who* based on the commodification and financialisation of the oil market. This enabled a further consolidation of what would become global traders' M.O.: 'tolling' deals – the exchange of a raw material for a finished product with resource-rich states as a way to fuel the financialisation of raw commodities.

Marc Rich's deals with Jamaica illustrate this shift. With the economic boom that followed World War II, aluminium emerged as 'the world's hottest metal' (Blas and Farchy 2022: 74). This spurred a worldwide scramble for the bauxite found in Guinea, Australia and Jamaica. Until the 1970s, even aluminium from the Eastern bloc was sold by the major producers led by the US Alcoa (and its Canadian sister, Alcan) under a restrictive 'gentlemen's agreement' (Blas and Farchy 2022: 74).

The 1970s wave of resource nationalism in the Caribbean disrupted this arrangement. 'The Cold war was raging, and by the late 1970s, the battle for dominance between Moscow and Washington was playing out in microcosm on the streets of Kingston' (Blas and Farchy 2022: 77).

As President Reagan was hedging his bets to turn the political tide in the region and secure the supply of bauxite to the US market, 'Marc Rich + Co stepped in, paying the Jamaican government in advance for the bauxite it would eventually sell to the US' (Blas and Farchy 2022: 77). The aluminium industry's crisis spurred by the soaring price of the energy needed to produce aluminium coincided with the listing of aluminium conglomerates on the LME.

Marc Rich + Co started offering 'tolling' deals which, in the case of Jamaica, translated in providing cash advance and a market outlet for the country's alumina in exchange for a price calculated as 9.25 per cent of the LME aluminium price. The scheme 'caught on like wildfire [. . .]. The trading house became "like a producer without the problems of owning production"' (Blas and Farchy 2022: 80).

China's spectacular economic growth in the first decade of the twenty-first century further consolidated the power of global traders as gatekeepers between resource-rich sub-Saharan African states and the world economy. The opening of the 'real' post-colonial order coincided with a global slump of commodity prices. By 2001, the size of the economy of sub-Saharan Africa was no larger than it had been in 1981.

In the early 1990s, what had become Glencore (ex-Marc Rich + Co) was still recovering from the financial blow suffered by the company following the 1983 indictment of Marc Rich by the US federal prosecutor for over sixty counts involving fraud, racketeering and tax evasion. Marc Rich was mostly targeted for having rigged an oil pricing scheme during the 1973 oil shock and because he sold oil to Iran during the hostage crisis. In 1994, years before the commodity super-cycle triggered by China's economic growth, Glencore started buying rights over mining concessions on the African continent – to stave off the company's cash crisis and outbid trade competitors.

'The traders also became an important conduit for a new dynamic in the global economy: the rise of trade flows between the emerging market nations that bypassed the West altogether' (Blas and Farchy 2022: 221). In the past ten years, bilateral trade between China and Africa increased by 226 per cent. In the decade of the China-led commodities boom leading up to 2011, the combined profits of the three largest commodity traders were bigger than those of better-known giants of global trade, such as Apple and Coca-Cola (Blas and Farchy 2022: 18). When China entered the 'commodity sweet spot' (Blas and Farchy 2022: 179), Glencore was already pre-positioned in the DRC since 2007 as producer and commodities and financial trader of what would become one of the most coveted resource of the twenty-first century: cobalt.

The power of global traders is deeply connected to what Pistor (2019) calls the 'code of capital': '[A]sset holders do not need to capture the state directly, much less win class struggles or revolutions; all they need is the right lawyers on their side who code their assets in law' (Pistor 2019: 22). Yet the code of capital 'owes its power to law that is backed and enforced by a state' (Pistor 2019: 15). Global capitalism can be sustained by a single domestic legal system provided that other states recognise and enforce its legal code. Most financial assets traded globally are coded in only two legal systems: British Common Law and the laws of the state of New York (Pistor 2019: 143). Conflict-of-law rules have divested the difficulty of harmonising the law by political means enabling, rather, private parties to choose the legal system in which the entity that is issuing their assets is incorporated as the one determining the property law for the assets it issues (Pistor 2019: 134).

The codification of capital under Common Law, backed up by the trade and financial market in US dollars, has fostered the global prominence of a new breed of intermediaries: corporate lawyers. Elite lawyers' real incomes have roughly tripled in the past half century, which is more than ten times the rate of income growth experienced by the median American. This explosion fits into a wider pattern of rising elite labour across the US economy.[12] Of the top global 100 firms by revenue, eighty-one are based in the United States and twelve in the United Kingdom. In the United Kingdom, legal services contributed 1.6 per cent of gross value added (GVA) in 2015. It is considerably less than the financial and insurance services sectors – standing at 7.2 per cent that year. But finance constitutes 40 per cent of the clientele of UK corporate law firms.

The paradox of what Pistor calls the masters of the code's simultaneous dependence on the authority of state law and avoidance of state courts means that 'in the absence of cases that clarify the law, their advice will be sought more frequently. Moreover, as time goes by, private attorneys become the only repeat players in solving disputes over contracts, which they themselves have fashioned, and can therefore position themselves as the only authoritative spokesperson for the law' (Pistor 2019: 181).

[12] See D Marcovits, 'A New Aristocracy' Yale Law School Commencement Address May 2015, https://law.yale.edu/sites/default/files/area/department/studentaffairs/document/markovitscommencementrev.pdf (accessed 29 December 2023).

4.3 Middle Power Unshackled

The code of capital is also connected to the US position as a major tax haven, the US economic market and the role of the US dollar in global trade and financial markets. The targeting of Glencore and the Israeli diamond trader Dan Gertler by US sanctions in 2017 under the 1997 US Foreign Corrupt Practices Act (FCPA) is emblematic. Since the mid-2000s, the FCPA, the US Department of Justice and the US Securities and Exchange Commission (SEC) have launched an average of thirty-six charges per year, predominantly against non-US corporations and individuals. These charges are even more effective that they involve so-called secondary sanctions, including the threat to block access to the US financial system to companies that have done business with sanctioned entities even when these transactions were not conducted in US dollars.

Charges against Glencore related to the payment of an estimated US$ 100 million worth of bribes to secure government contracts in several countries, including Nigeria, Cameroon, Côte d'Ivoire, Equatorial Guinea, Brazil, Venezuela and the Congo, and 'market manipulation conspiracies'. Glencore also had charges brought against it by the UK's Serious Fraud Office (SFO) and reached separate parallel resolutions with the Brazilian Ministério Público Federal (MPF) and the Commodity Futures Trading Commission (CFTC).

At the heart of these charges is Glencore's reliance on intermediaries to access politicians and avoid regulatory constraints. For the trader's operations in the Congo, this role was fulfilled by Dan Gertler, who had struck up an unlikely but long-standing friendship with the country's president. Over the course of more than a decade, before Gertler was targeted by US sanctions in 2017, Glencore and Gertler were involved in at least a dozen transactions, worth over a billion dollars. Glencore bought stakes in mines from Gertler and provided him with hundreds of dollars of loans. In exchange, the trader relied on Gertler to handle relations with the government. In 2017, Gertler was targeted by US sanctions on the charge of having used 'his relationship with the Congolese head of state to act as an intermediary in the sale of mining assets in the DRC, forcing multinational companies to go through Gertler to do business with the Congolese state'.[13]

[13] The Africa Report, 'DRC: Albert Yuma and Dan Gertler in complex Gécamines loan dispute' 7 January 2020, www.theafricareport.com/21839/drc-albert-yuma-and-dan-gertler-in-complex-gecamines-loan-dispute/ (accessed 29 March 2022).

Glencore entered guilty pleas in May 2022, which involved paying US$ 1.1 billion to resolve the charges. In parallel, Glencore Energy, a subsidiary of Glencore incorporated in the United Kingdom, was ordered to pay US$ 314 million by the Southwark Crown Court, based on the 2010 UK Bribery Act. Upon Glencore's agreement to a plea deal, US attorney Williams rejoiced by declaring that 'no one – not even multinational corporations – is above the law'.[14]

The FCPA applies broadly to numerous categories of US and non-US persons and businesses, and in many cases can give rise to liability even where the corrupt act takes place entirely or mostly outside the United States. There is therefore no need for a territorial nexus with the United States. Individuals and corporations doing business in Asia – including China – are not immune to the FCPA reach, although new laws enacted by the Chinese state in 2021 impose government approval for transfer of data stored in China in response to requests from judicial or enforcement agencies outside of China.

This game of catch-up against the regulatory reach of the FCPA is also embedded in an ongoing expansion of the geography of extraction. In 2012, Trafigura redesigned its Singapore-incorporated subsidiary, Trafigura Pte, as the main umbrella for its trading division. The company is now legally registered in Singapore but is owned by Farringford N.V., a firm registered on the island of Curacao, a Caribbean tax haven. Singapore, too, has repositioned itself as an Asian tax haven. Singapore's 2001 Global Trader Programme (GTP) offers traders a tax rate as low as 5 per cent, compared to 10 per cent in the Swiss hubs of Geneva and Zug, and 24 per cent in London. Singapore has been for years a big hub for oil trading, but this is fostering its growing importance as a hub for metals, minerals and agricultural commodities – to the detriment of Geneva as the historical commodities trading hub.

Following the announcement of Glencore's guilty plea on corruption counts in African and Latin American countries, NGOs denounced the failure to date of making the trader accountable for human rights violations. Glencore is reported to have the worst human rights record amongst companies working in green metals extraction and to be linked to the highest number of human rights allegations in Africa and the

[14] US Attorney's Office, Southern District of New York 'Glencore Entered Guilty Pleas to Foreign Bribery and Market Manipulation Conspiracies' Press release 24 May 2022, www.justice.gov/usao-sdny/pr/glencore-entered-guilty-pleas-foreign-bribery-and-market-manipulation-conspiracies (accessed 20 December 2023).

third-highest number of allegations in South America.[15] To be sure, the 2021 US District Court for the District of Columbia in its decision on allegations of wrongdoings by tech giants Apple, Google, Dell, Microsoft and Tesla, *John Doe I, et al.* v. *Apple Inc. et al.*, details allegations of child abuse at Glencore-owned cobalt mines in the Congo. But the case was dismissed for lack of standing because the crime of child labour could not be traced back to the named defendants and because the 2000 Trafficking Victims Protection Act, while potentially applicable to conduct occurring abroad, still required a substantial territorial link with the United States.

In this two-step dance between deregulation and re-regulation, that the corporate veil could be lifted for corrupt conduct but not for human rights violations, harks back to the complex articulation between the transformation of the geography of extraction and the concurrent expansion of the territories of international justice.

In the aftermath of the 2008 financial crisis, the most influential NGO coding the law of derivatives, the International Swaps and Derivatives Association (ISDA), lobbied the United States, Britain and European Union states to set up a Panel of Recognized International Market Experts in Finance (P.R.I.M.E. Finance) located in the capital of international law, The Hague. Its mission 'is to reduce legal uncertainty and systemic risk by ensuring that the requisite expertise is available to anticipate and address any disputes that may arise in the financial markets. Its goal in doing so is to foster financial market stability and confidence in, and a more settled and authoritative body of law for, world finance'.[16] The Panel's core activities revolve around capacity building in developed and developing countries on capital markets and financial contracts; and dispute resolution services, including arbitration.

Thus, '[t]he priests of high finance, who issue their own "private legislation" still like to bask in the aura of legal authority, or so it seems' (Pistor 2019: 146–147). International justice institutions based in The Hague – be they mandated to adjudicate conflicts between sovereign entities or to arbitrate commercial disputes – hardly thrived throughout most of the twentieth century, until their formidable re-emergence in the

[15] See Business & Human Rights Resource Centre, 'Transition Minerals Tracker: 2021 Analysis' May 2022, https://media.business-humanrights.org/media/documents/Transition_Minerals_Tracker_Global_analysis.pdf (accessed 20 December 2023).

[16] Website of P.R.I.M.E. Finance, https://primefinancedisputes.org/page/mission (accessed 13 December 2022).

1980s.[17] Until its revival in the early 2000s, the mother of all international courts – the PCA – froze into Sleeping Beauty from the creation of the PCIJ in 1920, with both institutions competing for the same pool of interstate territorial disputes.

The PCA retreated to being a showcase of international notabilities formally providing a pool of potential candidates to the ICJ bench. With a sole arbitration orchestrated between World War II and 1989, 'by the end of the Cold war, the PCA was a relic of the past' (Romano 2013: 121). Until the boom of international commercial arbitration in the 1980s, international arbitration remained the discrete preserve of the European scholarly architects of the *Lex mercatoria* (Dezalay Y and Garth 1996). The ICJ survived in the shadow of Cold War and decolonisation politics with a meek, at times empty, docket until the second half of the 1980s.

The renewed prominence of The Hague as the world justice 'district' (Marissal 2022) from the 1990s paralleled the wider judicialisation of politics. The multiplication of international dispute settlement mechanisms globally in the past three decades (Klein 2014) has been nowhere more pronounced than on the African continent. After the break-up of the Cold War, there was only one permanent international court in Africa, the inoperative Court of Justice of the Economic Community of Central African States (ECCAS). By 2004, there were nine continental and regional courts – more than any other continent.[18] African states constitute the largest regional bloc in the assembly of state parties of the ICC and were among the first states to ratify the Rome Statute. Domestic and regional politics have also been altered by this judicialisation trend (see Van Doepp 2009). By the early 1990s, all former French colonies on the continent had set up new and formally independent constitutional jurisdictions. In austral Africa – under the impetus of the post-Apartheid South African constitutional court and South African lawyers – judicial review by regional courts is regularly waged as a locus to arbitrate existential national political issues, including the status of certain populations within states of the region (Brett 2015).

Against the backdrop of the surge of international investment arbitration cases involving resource-rich sub-Saharan African states in

[17] As evidenced by sheer volumes alone: 120 new contentious cases introduced before the ICJ from 1984 (against thirty-six in its first forty years of existence) versus 13,000 commercial claims administered by the ICC of Paris from 1976 (against 3,000 between 1923 and 1976).

[18] For a review of this expansion, see Brett and Engbo Gissel (2018, 2020).

the past decade,[19] some of them joined a wider movement of denunciation of the investor-state dispute settlement (ISDS) system. Emblematically, the 2015 South African Promotion and Protection of Investment Bill sought to reroute disputes with foreign investors towards the domestic court system and mediation processes – rather than international arbitration. The parallel conviction of the deposed Chadian dictator Hissène Habré by the Extraordinary African Chambers (EAC) in 2016 in the Senegalese court system, with a mandate of the African Union (AU), seemed an apt response to Ugandan president Museveni's outburst against the ICC's perceived bias against Africa: '[T]his is our continent, not yours!'[20]

These developments could be neatly enfolded within the judicialisation/political backlash narrative that has pervaded media and scholarly discussions on international justice institutions in the past couple of decades. By the entry into effect in 2002 of the Rome Statute establishing the ICC, the tide of international criminal justice had turned on the shores of the US invasion of Iraq (see Dezalay S 2016a). The boom in investor-led disputes following the 2001 Argentina economic crisis and campaigns against the Transatlantic Trade and Investment Partnership (TTIP) agreement between the EU and the United States in 2013–2016 spurred the denunciation of ISDS as an echo chamber of corporate interests wielded against sovereign rights, including access to common goods such as water and electricity (CEO/Friends of the Earth Europe 2015). Likewise, the 'Western monopoly' over the 'international Bar' of the ICJ is seen to be hampering its authority as the 'World Court' (Gaubatz and Macarthur 2001; Kumar and Rose 2014).[21]

The formidable financial stakes of judicial battles involving African states certainly contribute to entrenching these debates in an ideological war of position pitting 'colonial justice [. . .] at the service of the power-

[19] In 2019, African states were involved in a total of 106 known investment treat arbitration claims, which represents 11 per cent of all known investor-state disputes worldwide. Between 2013 and 2018 only, African states received more investor claims than the previous twenty years combined. See Transnational Institute, 'ISDS in numbers. Impacts of investment arbitration against African States' October 2019, www.tni.org/files/publication-downloads/isds_africa_web.pdf (accessed 7 March 2022).

[20] *Der Spiegel*, 'This is our continent, not yours' interview with Ugandan President Museveni 10 June 2016, www.spiegel.de/international/world/interview-with-ugandan-president-yoweri-museveni-a-1096932.html (accessed 1 July 2019).

[21] See Chapter 8.

ful'[22] against universalism. With Burundi to date the only state to have effectively pulled out of the Rome Statute, commentators have asserted that the demurely termed 'fraught' relationship between the AU and the ICC was nurtured by misunderstandings. While some call for a reform of the ICC, starting with the role played by permanent members of the UN Security Council,[23] others continue to underline that there is no working alternative for an 'African' version of global justice as the 2014 Malabo Protocol instituting a criminal chamber within the African Court of Justice and Human Rights is still unlikely to enter into force.[24]

Yet accounting for the re-emergence of international justice institutions as part of a wider post–Cold War turn to legalism provides limited explanations beyond the mere creation of international tribunals. By the same token, examining the uneven and evolving strategic state rent of investing in international justice institutions (Brett and Engbo Gissel 2018) or the availability and variable strength of 'compliance constituencies' at the domestic and international levels (Alter et al. 2016) only partially responds to the 'question of why Africa, to a greater extent than other regions, has made so many commitments to the international legal order that are apparently only "skin-deep"' (Brett and Engbo Gissel 2018: 9).

Rather, the very existence 'on tap' of these institutions points to the interconnectedness between the transformations of the geography of extraction and the competition between multiple jurisdictional claims for supranational legal ordering.

The Caribbean Court of Justice (CCJ) established in 2001 following the abolishment of the right of appeal to the Judicial Committee of the Privy Council provides an illustration that also points to the embeddedness of these shifts in wider, *genealogical*, structural transformations. The CCJ is mandated with a uniquely dual jurisdiction – *original* over Caribbean community law, and *appellate* over civil and criminal matters which until then were retained by the Privy Council.

[22] P Kipré, 'Procès Laurent Gbagbo à la CPI: pour le droit et la justice' *Jeune Afrique* 30 January 2019, www.jeuneafrique.com/723354/societe/tribune-proces-laurent-gbagbo-a-la-cpi-pour-le-droit-et-la-justice/. My translation from French.

[23] See M Kersten, 'How three words could change the ICC-Africa relationship' *Justice in Conflict* 9 May 2017, https://justiceinconflict.org/2017/05/09/how-three-words-could-change-the-icc-africa-relationship/#more-7344 (accessed 1 July 2019).

[24] Fifteen member states need to ratify the protocol. As of 1 July 2019, the fifteenth state had signed it, but there were no ratifications.

The Court's early years reflected conflicting perceptions – between independence claims, and the post-colonial anxiety 'that giving up legal recourse to the JCPC in London might trigger an exodus of foreign investment from the region' (Caserta and Madsen 2016: 90). But the duality of the Court's jurisdiction 'firmly underlines that the Court is by no means a transition from one dimension of integration to the other' (Caserta and Madsen 2016: 91).

The Court's genesis reflected longer and conflicting trends. British plans for a West Indies Federal Supreme Court collapsed with the independence of Caribbean states, although most retained the right of appeal to the Privy Council. The 1993 *Pratt and Morgan* v. *Attorney General Jamaica* ruling of the Privy Council, which resulted in a quasi de facto abolition of the death penalty in the Commonwealth Caribbean, also fostered the unlikely alliance, against the Privy Council, of regional legal elites until then segmented between a 'transnational legal elite' trained in Oxbridge, who combined the political clout of close contacts with London chambers and 'an ability to solve problems with transnational solutions' with a common distrust of local legal talent (Caserta and Madsen 2016: 94), and locally trained self-called 'banana boat lawyers' who 'practiced law by traveling between surrounding islands' (Caserta and Madsen 2016: 96).

The critical juncture for regional economic integration, in turn, originated in a series of external economic shocks, including the Single European Market which 'jeopardized what was left of preferential economic treatment of Caribbean states by the United Kingdom' (Caserta and Madsen 2016: 97). Interestingly, albeit paradoxically, the total number of cases under the CCJ's *original* jurisdiction – that is, those pertaining to the Caribbean as an integrated regional market – remains very limited. Rather, the Court's authority first built out of *appellate* cases which asserted its capacity to diverge from Privy Council precedents – particularly on the death penalty – while the supremacy of Caribbean community law was established only a decade later following a seminal *original* case – *Myrie* v. *Barbados*, in 2012 – which, focused on individual freedoms, promoted the CCJ as the 'Caribbean *peoples*' court' (Caserta and Madsen 2016: 114, emphasis added).

The 'revival' of the East African Court of Justice (EACJ) in the first decade of the 2000s provides an interesting complement to this story. The EACJ was first created as successor to the East African Court of Appeal of the British Empire, dismantled in 1977, and re-established in 2001 with the intent of fostering a common regional market in Eastern

Africa. However, in the past decade, this court has evolved into a jurisdiction that seeks to hold governments accountable for violations of human rights and to promote good governance and the rule of law. This regional jurisdiction is therefore mostly used as a political platform, leveraged by the higher tiers of domestic political bars and the regionally powerful Kenyan law association, and well-connected domestic and international human rights NGOs (Gathii 2013). Business disputes, for their part, are mostly resolved politically (Gathii 2016) or elsewhere, in the framework of *offshore* international commercial or investment arbitration still largely dominated by clusters of white male European and US litigators (Dezalay S 2020b, 2022; Dezalay Y and Dezalay S 2017; Chapter 8).

Certainly, the claim that the CCJ is and is not part of Britain's judicial system and the British Virgin Islands are and are not part of the United Kingdom will depend on what suits clients in proceedings involving transnational trade disputes. By the same token, the EACJ's re-emergence in the 2000s was largely tributary of colonial legacies and their immediate post-independence translation in national rivalries between states of the region. Both courts, therefore, are instances of 'revival', to use Dezalay Y and Garth's (2010) expression, in that they are reflective of *sedimented* imperial tracks in the present.

For example, the formidable investment of INGOs, diplomats and European donors in Burundi from the mid-1990s focused on reforming a justice sector deemed at once a root cause of the 1993 massacres and a potential vector of peace and development. These investments also largely hinged on what a former director of the Belgian section of the NGO *Avocat sans frontières* described as a 'good conjuncture'[25]: the crisis of Belgian development aid triggered by the suspension of Belgium's development programs in the context of the wars in the DRC, Rwanda and Burundi. This was coupled with the desire of then Development Minister Réginald Moreels, former director of the Belgian chapter of Médecins sans frontières, to reengage in the Great Lakes region through informal efforts to implement justice reforms.

These investments largely contributed to restructuring the domestic legal field in Burundi.[26] They also fostered counterflows at the level of the EACJ, where cases waged against the Burundian state loomed large, and

[25] Author's interview with Luc Walleyn, former president of ASF, Brussels, 13 December 2012.

[26] See Chapter 5.

at the level of the ICC, where reliance on pre-positioned NGOs, such as Avocats sans frontières, to marshal evidence for prosecutions is not only the default strategy of a protractedly weak court but also a structural feature of the relationship of the court with domestic fields of national power (Dezalay S 2016a).

4.4 Conclusion

The interconnectedness between the characteristics over time of domestic rentier politics in resource-rich African economies, geopolitical change and capitalist transformations underscores that it is as important to know in what way power is functional to transnational capital as it is to understand how ruling classes in resource-rich African states 'exercise power, how they assemble it and sustain its potential through rewards and punishments' (Lonsdale 1981: 202). Across the African continent, the end of the Cold War and the privatisation of extractive sectors consolidated, rather than displaced, the gatekeeping politics inherited from the Cold War partition of the continent. Privatisation fostered a new iteration of 'nurture capitalism', where substantial parts of the externally oriented economy are controlled by private capitalists, with clientelism and the indigenisation of capital accumulation going hand in hand (Ovadia 2013).

However, the financial and legal Big Bangs of the 1980s structurally altered the articulation of African states with global markets due to the competing middle power exercised by the City, Wall Street and Washington, DC, based on the combination between offshore capitalism and the deployment of US legal imperialism (through the FCPA) outside US sovereign boundaries.

The demise of the 'post-colonial block' linking France to countries of its *pré carré* enabled the expansion of (and competition between) global traders. Global trading is part and parcel of the transformation of the geography of extraction, as it involves strategies of verticalisation of activities (extraction, transport, finance) across scattered territories.

The power of global trading is foremost tied to the codification of capital based on Common Law and the law of the state of New York which is enabled by the globalisation of the Wall Street model of the corporate law firm. The codification of capital involves a transformation of the (social and technical) characteristics of legal intermediation. In *Oligarchy*, Winters (2011) contends that democracy does not displace oligarchy but fuses with it. The rule-of-law problem is a matter of taming the oligarchs. In what he dubs 'civil oligarchies' like the United States, the ultimate test of the strength of a legal system is not its routine or systemic performance, but whether it is stronger than the most powerful actors in society. In the United States, civil oligarchy is characterised by two core elements: the wielding of private wealth to influence political outcomes, and foremost the waging of legal expertise to defend oligarchs' incomes against taxation. What matters politically, therefore, is the threshold of wealth above which actors can afford the costly services and interventions of the 'Income Defence Industry' – that is, armies of fiscal and corporate lawyers. Exerting direct political influence is perilous. But waging material power, by casting the burden on others, is even more efficient when the latter have the *know-how* and the *know-who* to make taxation uncertain.

The game of catch-up between deregulation and regulation is therefore as much about *access* as it is about *competing* legal ordering claims. For global traders without an imperial past, like Glencore and Trafigura, access involves relying on political intermediaries with political clout in resource-rich African economies, and the *know-how* of evading regulatory constraints. For legal intermediaries in resource-rich African economies, access requires political clout and the *know-how* of the Wall Street model of the corporate law firm. The Ghanaian case provides an illustration. As I mentioned before, the Asante legal elite's position in relation to the domestic field of power and global markets built out of sedimented and concurrent imperial histories that enabled it to stave off the independent state's attempt at displacing its position as gatekeeper of Ghana's relationship with the outside economy.

Budniok and Noli (2018) provide an intriguing sequel to this account by looking at the types of capital mobilised by the Asante elite to consolidate their monopoly over legal services. Internal differentiation of the legal profession increased from the 1970s to the 1990s due to the expansion of legal education. The acute economic crisis of the 1990s also devalued the bench as a professional path, along with its poor relations with the military dictatorship (Dawuni 2017). New male judges came from the lower-middle-classes and increasingly from the North, a region historically less connected to international markets, whose law graduates faced high obstacles in entering a corporate legal hemisphere restricted to well-connected men from the Central and Greater Accra provinces of independent Ghana. Yet the increasing numbers of women accessing the judiciary were invariably drawn from upper-middle-class backgrounds and Southern regions because they could increase the social capital of husbands practising as corporate lawyers and the latter's access to international corporate clients.

Family strategies of reproduction of social capital helped consolidate the inherited legal capital of the Asante legal elite – derived from selective meritocratic criteria of access to the legal field (through credentials obtained in the former *métropole*) combined with social and family resources. This enabled them to convert the meritocratic legal capital acquired through legal education in Ghana by male cohorts drawn from the middle classes into a sovereign form of capital: that of access to gatekeeping politics.

However, as mentioned before, the direct role of foreign capital in the Gold Coast's economic expansion was limited (Luckham 1981: 100), as this dynamism was provided by cocoa production for world markets. By independence, much of Ghana's cocoa lands were exhausted. The commercialisation of land increased litigation. 'Land cases became the bread and butter of lawyers, the material base of law practice' (Luckham 1981).

The protracted organisation of the private legal land market into small chambers makes it, furthermore, particularly vulnerable to the external shock induced by the liberalisation of the mining sector in the early 1990s and the gold boom from the 2010s. The predominance of multinational corporate law firms from the United States, United Kingdom and South Africa in representing the interests of foreign corporations (Dawuni 2017) entrenches local lawyers in a subaltern position. Their access to an international clientele is subordinated to referrals by multinational corporate firms.

In turn, the US deployment of the FCPA – and the forum shopping it induces – is 'not unlike the unstable and merely aspirational dominance of British legal authority in many corners of the empire' (Benton and Ford 2016: 194). We could surmise, indeed, that the explosion of supranational dispute resolution mechanisms is reinforcing rather than undermining this reiteration of middle power. Thus, in professional publications, the boom of arbitration centres set up across the African continent in the past decade – eighty as of 2022, with some countries such as Nigeria, Ghana or Sudan hosting several – has been acknowledged as a strategic move to 'Africanise' ISDS. In its comments to the 2018 ICSID Rule Amendment project, the AU raised the issue of representation as a key claim. While nearly a quarter of ICSID cases now involve an African state, the proportion of African arbitrators, conciliators and ad hoc committee members appointed in ICSID cases represented a mere 3 per cent of the overall number of appointments in 2018.[27]

But this move is also derided as undermining 'the development of arbitration as a *credible* dispute resolution mechanism locally'.[28] The China-Africa Joint Arbitration Centre (CAJAC) was created in 2015 as a platform – to be situated in both Shanghai and Johannesburg[29] – designed to manage disputes on the Belt and Road Initiative away from ISDS mechanisms and national courts.[30] While the sheer volume of Chinese state-owned entities investments across the continent[31] is likely to help stock up the docket of the Centre at African seats – rather than the traditional Paris, London or Geneva ones – negotiations stumbled on the demographics of arbitrators. To date, the shared pool of about 2,000 arbitrators at the first operational CAJAC court (at Shanghai) includes a vast majority of inland Chinese lawyers. It also features the usual profiles of the international arbitration community – European and US corporate lawyers based in the United States, Europe, Hong Kong or Singapore – and fewer than twenty Africans, foremost South Africans.[32]

[27] J Sabet, 'Investor-State arbitration meets mediation: Is mediation the future of investor-state dispute settlement in Africa?' 2 October 2020, http://arbitrationblog.kluwerarbitration.com/2020/10/02/investor-state-arbitration-meets-mediation-is-mediation-the-future-of-investor-state-dispute-settlement-in-africa/ (accessed 21 March 2022).

[28] G Travaini, (Herbert Smith Freehills) 'Arbitration centres in Africa: too many cooks?' Kluwer Arbitration Blog 1 October 2019, http://arbitrationblog.kluwerarbitration.com/2019/10/01/arbitration-centres-in-africa-too-many-cooks/ (accessed 7 March 2022). Emphasis added.

[29] Along with other African seats in the coming years in both civil law and Common Law African states.

[30] D Welgemoed, 'CAJAC: a New International Arbitration Centre' 2018, https://droitfrancechine.org/wp-content/uploads/2018/05/DW-CAJAC.pdf (accessed 21 March 2022).

[31] $1.3 billion in 2016. See D Welgemoed, 'CAJAC: a New International Arbitration Centre' 2018, https://droitfrancechine.org/wp-content/uploads/2018/05/DW-CAJAC.pdf (accessed 21 March 2022).

[32] See the website of the CAJAC at: https://shiac.org/pc/SHIAC. See also Chapter 8.

5

Bujumbura

Hyperviolence and Hyperlegality

Frankfurt, February 2014.

There were three Burundians sitting at the table. Burundi's minister of Energy and Mines Côme Manirakiza was daintily sipping a cup of sweet hot milk. The dinner was organised against the backdrop of German-led discussions at the G7 to turn Burundi into a Petri dish of virtuous extraction. The timing was ripe. The mineral wealth of Burundi, in gold, nickel and foremost rare earths – metals indispensable to produce cell phones or wind turbines, but whose supply chain is dominated at 80 per cent by China – had long been known. But these mineral potentials had yet to be exploited at an industrial level.

Germany was heading the 41st G7 Summit, due to take place in June 2015, and planned to invest in Burundi as a test case: one in which mineral extraction could effectively foster development through 'transparency' and 'good governance'. M. Manirakiza's host was a GIZ (Deutsche Gesellschaft für Internationale Zusammenarbeit) consultant. He was organising a series of talks sponsored by the BMZ (German Federal Ministry for Economic Cooperation and Development) to set up the 'Connex initiative' (Strengthening Assistance for Complex Contract Negotiations). Connex aimed to 'level the playing field' between multinationals and resource-rich countries in the Global South by ramping up their capacities for contract negotiation with transnational corporations. The GIZ consultant had also been mandated to discuss the reform of Burundi's mining code.

M. Manirakiza was seemingly unaware of his German host's simmering frustration. Letting his rage explode, the latter finally stood up, knocking off his chair and stormed out of the restaurant. The host was in a difficult position. The GIZ is a service provider. Funding provided by the BMZ directly to the government of Burundi was (in principle) earmarked for his services. Technically, therefore, M. Manirakiza was his employer. But he was refusing to countersign the mission order.

What was remarkable during the fateful 2014 dinner was the profile of the third Burundian sitting at the table, along with M. Manirakiza's secretary. Jean[1] was a lawyer at the Bar of Burundi. He had not invited me to sit at the table as the human rights consultant I had interviewed in Bujumbura in 2011 and who had become an intermediary and friend since, but as M. Manirakiza's mining legal expert.

In 2005, the first general elections organised following the end of the protracted internal war in Burundi had enabled the ascendance of the CNDD-FDD (National Council for the Defense of Democracy – Forces for the Defense of Democracy – a former Hutu-dominated rebel group transformed into a political party). Following President Nkurunziza's re-election for a third mandate in May 2015 and a failed attempted coup, hundreds of people were killed, and over 250,000 Burundians fled to neighbouring countries. In March 2016, the European Commission – Burundi's main development donor – again suspended direct financial support to Burundi. In January of that year, the UN High Commissioner for Human Rights 'warned that a complete breakdown of law and order was just around the corner'.[2]

Yet, that same year, Rainbow Mining Burundi, a subsidiary of Rainbow Rare Earths, a Guernsey-based mining company, acquired a license to develop a trial mining and processing of rare earths in Gakara, a site located 20 kilometres south-southeast of Bujumbura, in western Burundi. With only one other rare earths extraction site (in South Africa) outside of China, Burundi was promising to become one of the new frontiers of the post-carbon transition.

For lovers of John Le Carré, the combination of kleptocratic political elites, the threat of development aid diplomacy – as effective as gunboat diplomacy in this hyper-dependent state – inter-imperial confrontation between the US and China over rare earths, red-neck extraction companies and a poverty-stricken population would be a perfect fit for a sequel to *The Mission Song* – with the additional ironical twist that Nkurunziza's strategies of 'legalised extortion'[3] to expel local communities directly

[1] Pseudonym used to preserve the anonymity of the respondent. Except when their profiles are widely known, I have used pseudonyms for all other respondents. Unless otherwise indicated, I have translated into English all interview quotes.

[2] *The Guardian*, 'EU suspends aid to Burundi's government' 15 March 2016.

[3] E Ndikumana, 'Le pouvoir burundais suspend les activités minières pour renégocier tous les contrats' *RFI* 23 July 2021, www.rfi.fr/fr/afrique/20210722-le-pouvoir-burundais-suspend-les-activités-minières-pour-renégocier-tous-les-contrats (accessed 11 May 2022).

affected by the trial Gakara site were waged while the country's budget was essentially funded by the European Commission.

But looking solely at the economic and financial side of the story would overlook Burundi's position in another revolution as the recipient of dozens of internationally funded rule of law reform projects since the mid-1990s. Certainly, Burundi stands as the epitome of what Comaroff and Comaroff describe as a presumption coupled with a paradox. Post-colonies are more violent, yet many of the same post-colonies seem to make a fetish of the rule of law, of its language and its practices (Comaroff and Comaroff 2006: vi–vii).

Rather than two sides of a paradox, positioning violence and legal extortion as twin modalities of displacement of politics, they ask, *why* has a preoccupation with legalities, and with the legal subject, become to be so salient a dimension of post-colonial dis/order and its mass-mediated representation? How is it related to neoliberalism (Comaroff and Comaroff 2006: 21)?

But is it enough, as they do, to *take exception to exceptionalism* by construing post-colonies as 'hyperextended versions of the history of the contemporary world order running slightly ahead of itself' (Comaroff and Comaroff 2006: 41)?

The ongoing rush for Burundi's rare earths nearly twenty-five years after the Arusha agreement which put an end to the extremely violent conflict that tore the country apart from 1993 provides a Petri dish of the combination between hyperviolence and hyperlegality that is fostering the state's transition from a post-colonial relationship with the world economy determined foremost by aid dependency, to that of origination site of one of the most coveted minerals of the post-carbon transition.

As the fourth guest sitting at that fateful dinner in 2014, Jean was a typical member of the post-2000s generation of Burundian lawyers trained by international NGOs and the UN High Commissioner for Human Rights following the 1993 massacres in the country. His transition from the rule of law reform field to mining, as Manirakiza's legal advisor, was partly due to luck – both had been school friends. It also reflected their respective structural positions. Manirakiza ended up being the longest portfolio holder of the post-independence history of Burundi – not least because he managed to politically and financially gain from Burundi's transformed relationship with global markets.[4] For

[4] La Rédaction, 'Côme Manirakiza, un nom dans l'histoire' *Iwacu* 21 October 2021, www.iwacu-burundi.org/commentaire-come-manirakiza-un-nom-dans-lhistoire/ (accessed 11 May 2022).

his part, Jean was all the better positioned as an intermediary between Manirakiza and the GIZ that he had been trained according to IFIs' good governance conditionalities.

Yet Jean's position is not simply reflective of the dual position of lawyers as representatives of power and champions of the rule of law – it is also embedded in a structural *bifurcation* of the Burundian legal field as lawyers in Burundi are either gatekeepers of the rent of exported commodities or vulnerable to another type of extraversion, that of aid dependency. Burundi's transition into an origination site leans on the legacy of colonial, post-independence and post-1993 rule of law reforms which together have fostered what Mamdani (1996) describes as 'decentralized despotism'. Each post-colonial regime created its own despotism through fluid forms of legal pluralism enabling distinctions of race and/or ethnicity, urban and rural areas, sometimes exacerbated by violence or ossified by post-conflict reforms and subjected to regionalised 'politics of the belly'.[5] It is this bifurcation that makes Burundi a Petri dish of the hyperviolence generated by the hyperlegality of late capitalism.

5.1 Mercenaries, Missionaries and Merchants

On 21 October 1993 – a few months before the start of the genocide in Rwanda on 6 April 1994 – Burundian president Melchior Ndadaye was assassinated by Tutsi military extremists. Waves of violence against the Tutsi population ensued, and the situation quickly degenerated into an outright civil war. The first to be democratically elected a few months earlier, Ndadaye was also the first Hutu to access the Head of a State governed since independence in 1962 by a succession of Tutsi-dominated military dictatorships. Following the assassination of Ndadaye, the beheaded Burundian government turned first to then Rwandan president Habyarimana, requesting that he send in paramilitary troops. Transferred to the French authorities, the demand was rebutted with a refusal. Members of the provisional government of Burundi nonetheless took refuge in the French Embassy where they installed a de facto government. A few weeks later, the French government decided to send

[5] The expression 'politics of the belly', a translation of the French '*politiques du ventre*', refers to a Cameroonian idiom popularised by Bayart (1993) to highlight the significance of idioms of eating and the belly to African conceptions of power and the importance of clientelism and corruption in power relations.

in a contingent of eighteen French policemen to join the twenty military *coopérants* stationed in Bujumbura.

Meanwhile, beer continued to flow. In Burundi, dictators come and go, but Heineken stays (Van Beemen 2019: 119). In 1996, following Major Buyoya's military coup, foreign donors again pulled the plug. With the coffee economy – the country's main export crop – driven to the ground by war and falling market prices, it was left to the Brarudi Brewery (Brasserie et Limonaderie du Burundi) to 'drip-feed the government coffers' – and for that matter, the rebellion – through 'protection taxes' extorted on lorries.[6]

The Brarudi Brewery is 59 per cent owned by Heineken. Its continued activities in the country throughout the war between 1993 and its official end in 2000 created some public outcry in the Netherlands, where the company was accused of helping to perpetuate Tutsi power and the slaughter of Hutu civilians in Burundi while aiding the genocide against the Tutsi in Rwanda. 'The brewery's Belgian manager "went on holiday" the night before the coup, leaving orders forbidding the Burundian staff to talk publicly about the brewery's operations'.[7]

If Primus beer – the most consumed beer produced by Brarudi – ever runs dry, Burundians know that the economy has collapsed. In a country where the inflation rate has fluctuated anywhere between 44.9 per cent and −8.4 per cent in the past ten years, while the local currency has depreciated by 35 per cent since the beginning of 2023, the price of beer is the ultimate litmus test of economic crisis. Since early 2020, for the first time in the post-independence history of the country, after beer prices spiked up by 30 per cent, there is a sporadic penury of beer, fizzy drinks and sugar across the country.

Rumours run wild on this penury. Some commentators point to the greed of local retailers, others to the shortage of foreign currencies since the boycott of the CNDD-FDD's regime – the rebel group turned political party which took over power in 2005 – following Nkurunziza's third presidential bid in 2015.

The issue of beer in Africa – as trivial as it may seem – is a major economic stake for the 'Big 4' which control half of the global beer market: Anheuser-Busch InBev, Heineken, Carlsberg and China Resources Enterprise. Beer consumption in Africa reached around 14.7 million kilolitres in 2019. This was equivalent to roughly 23.3 billion beer

[6] C McGreal, 'Beer, bedrock of Burundi's economy' *Mail & Guardian* 23 August 1996.
[7] Ibid.

bottles of 633 millilitres each. Demand for the alcoholic beverage increased by 5.2 per cent in comparison to the previous year and kept an upward trend. Currently, Africa has a stake of nearly 8 per cent in the global beer consumption market.[8]

The question of beer also harks back to the looting image of the two beer corporations that share the market in Central and West Africa: Castel and Heineken. The Heineken group has been established in the DRC since 1935, when it bought majority shares in the Bralima (Brasseries limonaderies et malterie africaines) created in 1923 by Belgian investors as the Brasserie de Léopoldville with the support of the Société Congolaise de Banque. Following the proclamation of Congo's independence in 1960, to secure the profitability of their operations against nationalist claims over the breweries, Heineken and its Belgian partner, the Lambert Bank, set up a double accounting. Part of the benefits were declared to the local fiscal authorities, while the bulk was transferred to a Swiss holding. Archives examined by Van Beemen (2019) reveal the complexity of this laundering process: investments in new breweries across the region enabled the transformation of 'black Swiss' into 'white Belgian' money, with a Belgian office serving as 'windshield' to protect Heineken against legal risks.

From the turn of the 1970s, President Mobutu started a process of 'Zaireanisation' of the business sphere of the country. He positioned one of his close henchmen at the helm of Bralima, Litho Moboti. Twenty-two years before Mobutu's fall, and despite massive losses incurred following the nationalisation of the brewery, Heineken decided that it was in the firm's best interest to remain in the country, 'until better times, when we will be in a position to expand in as clean a way as possible'.[9]

The firm's slogan, 'Transparency is beautiful when you have nothing to hide', displayed from Sierra Leone to remote villages in Burundi, may speak to local consumers' taste for a colour – light golden rather than the brown of artisanal beer – seen to equate social success. It is certainly ironic when deployed in a country – Sierra Leone – whose population is predominantly Muslim and even more when the bodies of the three Central African presidents killed in the early 1990s – Melchior Ndadaye, Cyprien Ntaryamira and Juvénal Habyarimana, whose deaths

[8] See Statista, 'Annual beer Consumption in Africa from 2015 to 2019' www.statista.com/statistics/1261782/beer-consumption-in-africa/ (accessed 20 May 2024).

[9] O Van Beemen, 'Heineken en RDC: un cocktail frelaté de bière et de politique' *Le Monde* 16 June 2016. My translation from French.

were directly linked to the genocide in Rwanda and the twelve-year war in neighbouring Burundi – were briefly kept in Heineken's local subsidiaries' cold chambers in Bujumbura and Kigali.

In the DRC, from the early 1980s, while Belgian partners withdrew, the majority share and management of Bralima returned to Heineken, on the condition that the group collaborate with a local partner – a powerful businessman close to Mobutu, Jeannot Bemba. The latter bequeathed his shares to his son, Jean-Pierre Bemba, who was later convicted of crimes against humanity and war crimes by the ICC in 2016.

In Burundi, Heineken owns 59 per cent of the capital of Brarudi, with the remainder of the shares controlled by the state. In 2015, following his second tenure, the post-war Constitution required then president Nkurunziza to relinquish power. Failing to attract the required parliamentary majority to amend the Constitution, the president turned to the Burundian Constitutional court, which deemed a third mandate constitutional.[10] Coincidentally, waging the prerogative of the state as a 41 per cent shareholder of Brarudi, Nkurunziza appointed the president of the Constitutional court, Charles Ndagijimana, as president of the administrative council of Brarudi five months later. Formally, therefore, Heineken's subsidiary was controlled by the first justice of the country (Van Beemen 2019: 122).

In a context of spiralling societal violence and repression, with international donors pulling out, fiscal benefits derived from Brarudi – mainly as excise duties – constituted 30 per cent of the state's budget. In other words, excise duties from Primus consumption financed the bulk of the wages of the policemen, soldiers and secret services deployed to implement the regime's repression of political opposition.

'According to the common *cliché*, Western corporations operating in Africa must often adapt to a culture of fraud, corruption and greed, but in the case of Heineken it seems rather that it is the corporation itself that may have contributed to the genesis of such a culture – in a logic of colonial looting'.[11] Yet following the money trail tells only part of the story. Not only because the firm's boasting of local sourcing as a gateway to 'brew a better world'[12] – like the use of sorghum from Sierra Leone or

[10] T Kibangula, 'Burundi: Pierre Nkurunziza peut briguer un troisième mandat, selon la Cour constitutionnelle' *Jeune Afrique* 5 May 2015.

[11] O Van Beemen, 'Heineken en RDC: un cocktail frelaté de bière et de politique' *Le Monde* 12 July 2016. My translation from French.

[12] See Heineken's website, www.theheinekencompany.com/our-global-presence/ameee (accessed 19 April 2022).

Egypt to produce beer in Burundi, with financial backup from bilateral and multilateral donors such as the Netherlands, Germany and the European Commission – has produced doubtful if any development outcomes.[13]

Not even because the 'brewing Yalta' between Castel and Heineken sustains the growth of the two groups, thanks to political collusion and, mostly, the verticalisation of their production chains.[14] But foremost because Bralima's former managing director (between 2004 and 2012) Van Mameren's tirade that Congolese politicians 'are all thieves' (Van Beemen 2019: 167, my translation from French) only goes so far.

The DRC, Rwanda and Burundi feature largely in the 'new conflicts' policy-driven literature (Kaldor 2006) that emerged from the break-up of the Cold War. By the mid-1980s,

> [t]he webs of conflict, social patterns, and governmental dysfunctionalities in many parts of Africa [had made] the state a far less dominating, agenda-setting actor than in the first post-independence decades. The *Bula Matari* [crusher of rocks] personification of the colonial state in the everyday expression of the Congolese subject in Belgian colonial times lived on high Mobutist postcolonial times as a would-be leviathan [. . .], but the shrivelled, dishevelled, and fragmented superstructure of Congo's governance in the Kabila age [bore] only a remote resemblance to its predecessors.
>
> (Young 2004: 24)

Crises in the Great Lakes region have also widely fed into the concurrent boom of institutions, scholarship and policy shifts in international criminal law and transitional justice that have transformed domestic and global politics into a legal and judicial battlefield in the past four decades. The weakness of the state in sub-Saharan Africa is seen to breed 'loot-seeking' warfare, while juridical processes deployed in civil war situations are generally stripped of their geopolitical contexts qua external interventions and embedded in a moral and political economy of conflict management as 'liberal' peacebuilding (see Dezalay S 2011).

Talking about *ethnies* (ethnic groups) is taboo in Bujumbura, where all elites – administrative, legal, political and commercial – are still concentrated. In rural areas, a euphemism is used for the waves of massacres

[13] V Hugeux, 'Les dérives d'Heineken en Afrique sont exemplaires' *L'Express* 11 October 2018.

[14] O Blamangin, 'Castel, l'Empire qui fait trinquer l'Afrique' *Le Monde Diplomatique* October 2018, pp. 8–9.

that have plagued the country since independence – *ikiza* in Kirundi ('great calamity') – a word that also invokes the collective memory of the persistent famines of the Belgian mandate era.

'We were trained to be flexible. A defendant told me that to be assisted by a Tutsi lawyer was like complaining to a python about having been bitten by a viper.'[15] That a Bujumbura lawyer in 2013 should explicitly use the ethnic word to explain his position as a Tutsi lawyer for Hutu defendants was undoubtedly the result of the *juridical* process at play in the country since the mid-1990s. In 1996, the International Commission of Inquiry for Burundi submitted a report to the UN Security Council,[16] officially designating as 'genocides' two mass killings: the 1972 massacres of Hutu by the Tutsi-dominated army, and the 1993 mass killings of both Tutsi and Hutu, perpetrated by the population, the Tutsi-dominated army and Hutu-dominated armed groups. The 1972 events stayed under the radar of Cold War politics, whereas the response to the 1993 massacres was intensely internationalised.

The 1993 crisis in Burundi bulked large in the formidable expansion of international markets for conflict resolution. Burundi became the testing ground for novel forms of external intervention, involving INGOs seeking to promote rule of law reforms 'from the bottom up', sidestepping domestic state authorities and operating outside official diplomatic and military channels (Dezalay S 2016b). But, in 2003, the puzzle for the UN High Commissioner for Human Rights (which established its first local office in Bujumbura that year) and for the dozens of Belgian, French and US NGOs arriving in the country at the turn of the 2000s became how to deal with the thousands of Hutu who had been imprisoned since 1993, given that there were only a dozen lawyers called to the Burundi Bar, including just one Hutu.

A prominent actor in the internationalisation of the post-1993 trials (commonly known as the 'contentieux de 1993'), the Belgian NGO Avocats Sans Frontières (ASF), had been created in 1992 in collaboration with the International League of Human Rights. Its initial objective was to send lawyers – following the *sans frontières* approach of Médecins sans frontières – to observe trials in autocratic contexts, especially in Africa. Following the genocide in Rwanda, ASF shifted focus to criminal defence in the context of the ad hoc International Tribunal for Rwanda and the

[15] Author's interview with Damien, a lawyer at the Burundi Bar, Bujumbura, 7 May 2013.
[16] United Nations, 22 August 1996, pp. 19, 75, S/1996/682.

defence of Hutu defendants tried in the context of the 1993 massacres – what became known as the 'contentieux de 1993' (the 1993 trials).

These endeavours had an enormous impact on the legal field in Burundi. There were only ten lawyers called to the Burundi Bar in 1993. There were over 400 in Bujumbura by 2000–2001 and several hundreds more in the competing Gitega Bar created in the early-2010s. As expressed by a lawyer at the Burundi Bar: 'ultimately, Avocats Sans Frontières created the market for barristers'.[17] The salary international organisations paid to lawyers involved in the 'contentieux de 1993' – 1 million Burundian Franc per month as opposed to roughly 58,000 Burundian Franc for a higher court magistrate – played a large role in making private law practice an attractive market and fostering what one lawyer described as the 'mental gymnastics'[18] necessary to overcome the resistance of Tutsi lawyers to representing Hutu defendants.

The expansion of the pool of private legal practitioners is also attributable to the devaluation of justice institutions. The judiciary and its infrastructure had been relatively unscathed by the 1993 crisis and resulting war, compared to those in Rwanda, but they were deeply discredited by the peace process and the legacy of political subservience and corruption. As encapsulated ironically by a former magistrate called to the Burundi Bar at the end of the 1990s: 'the cow speaks better French than the barrister'.[19]

The political victory of the CNDD-FDD in 2005 signalled the ascendance of 'bush elites' whose symbolic capital is derived mostly from fighting as members of Hutu-dominated rebel groups during the 1993–2003 war. Their prominence in the political field constituted a break with the profile of established elites, including their proximity with the Catholic Church, symbolised by the fact that the previous ruler, Pierre Nkurunziza, was a self-proclaimed 'born again' Christian. This regime change also meant that 'a whole market for training new elites was opened'.[20] The long-standing negotiations between the government and the UN over the transitional justice mechanisms planned by the Arusha agreement (Lima and Dezalay 2015), together with the expansion

[17] Author's interview with Willy, a lawyer at the Burundi Bar, Bujumbura, 3 May 2013.
[18] Author's interview with Damien, a lawyer at the Burundi Bar, Bujumbura, 7 May 2013.
[19] Author's interview with Antoine, a lawyer at the Burundi Bar, Bujumbura, 2 May 2013.
[20] Author's interview with Julien, Thematic Expert, ASF, Brussels, 13 June 2013.

of the market for legal education, also contributed to the legal boom, reflected in the creation of dozens of domestic law-oriented NGOs.

These dynamics fostered the emergence of a new generation of Burundian lawyers who tend to be called to the bar right after graduating, rather than starting their career in the judiciary. However, this legal boom has not been accompanied by an expansion of the private legal services market. This younger generation – embodied by Jean – usually combines solo private practice as barristers with positions as human rights advocates within domestic NGOs and contracts as consultants for INGOs and international organisations. This domestic market therefore suffers from a double bind: it is dependent on and vulnerable to the volatile demand from international donors and organisations while its autonomy is weakened by its position as buffer between international diplomacy and a repressive government.

This contradictory position also affects INGOs within the Burundian market. A former ASF director recalled the 'turf battle'[21] among INGOs competing for the same EU sources of funding and the difficulty of adapting to donors' short-time horizon and changing priorities. Vulnerable to shifting donor demands, INGOs occupy an insecure position in relation to local authorities. To explain the lack of international reaction when the CNDD-FDD abruptly terminated the post-1993 trials and amnestied former Hutu rebel groups, another Belgian ASF employee explained: 'the problem is that political advocacy has been left to NGOs, while donors embrace a technical approach [to development aid] without any political capacity'.[22]

The result of these international rule of law efforts has been a haphazard, decentralised web of small-scale projects, exposed to the volatility of development donors' changing policies and the government's repressive politics vis-à-vis civil society. These rule of law reforms contributed from the onset to a revival of colonial and autocratic politics. International initiatives did not seek to modify the framework of the 'contentieux de 1993', which primarily targeted Hutu defendants. The repressive politics of the CNDD-FDD government from 2005 further accentuated a kind of 'tango dance' among diplomats trying to maintain the appearance of

[21] Author's interview with Luc, Coopération Technique Belge, Bujumbura, 22 April 2014.
[22] Author's interview with Robert, Senior Justice Advisor, ISSAT-DCAF, Brussels, 13 June 2013.

good relations with Burundian authorities in the face of an increasingly violent regime. To bypass a judicial system that remains hard to reform because of political resistance and continuous diffuse interference by the executive, international donors, ironically, are now turning to 'informal' justice, notably by seeking to revive the traditional conflict resolution mechanism, the *bashingantahe* (Deslaurier 2003).

These dynamics are also accentuating the role of the bar and law-oriented NGOs as platforms of political opposition. The current regime is reviving the long tradition of political interference in civil society. The Burundi Bar, considered as a stronghold of the Tutsi elite, has been paired with the Gitega Bar, allegedly infiltrated by the CNDD-FDD. This contest within civil society conceals a professional competition: efforts by the Bar to preserve its monopoly over the very limited domestic market for private legal services and the competitive consultancy market for INGOs and international donors.

Private legal practice in Burundi is still dominated by solo practitioners, including to date only a handful of Burundian corporate lawyers and a couple of local outlets of Tanzanian and South African minor corporate law firms. Willy's firm stands out, as it includes three partners and eleven associates. Willy entered the bar in 2001 and was on the payroll of ASF until 2007. In 2006 he obtained a grant from the Irish government to complete a master's in peace and conflict studies at Trinity College Dublin, where he became proficient in English.

> I did not have enough money for a master in corporate law. I took the risk [. . .]. I was aiming for big money [. . .]. I noticed that investors were using Burundi as a transit country on their way to Kigali. I was not going to compete with Rwandans on their local (private legal) market. But I could build entries at an artisanal level.[23]

Willy enrolled his firm in the network set up by the UK multinational corporate law firm DLA Piper across the African continent. But '[t]he best client is the state'.[24] Yet, as he summed up, 'we deal with transactions that have an impact here but that are negotiated elsewhere'[25]: in the corridors of power.

[23] Author's interview with Willy, a lawyer at the Bar of Burundi, Bujumbura, 3 May 2012.
[24] Ibid.
[25] Ibid.

5.2 Decentralised Despotism

The 2000 Arusha agreement redistributed power in the administrative, political, judicial and military spheres according to ethnic affiliation – a recipe known as 'consociational democracy' (Vandeginste 2010). Ethnic affiliation loomed large in the pre-colonial, colonial and post-colonial history of Burundi. Paired with race in colonial Burundi, ethnicity was used to justify the promotion of certain groups – foremost the princely *Baganwa* and Tutsi elites – as middlemen between the colonial ruler and the population. As in Rwanda, ethnicity has continuously been instrumentalised as a political tool to justify violence through the post-independence period.

Predominantly targeting the Hutu in Burundi,[26] ethnic violence shaped the organisation of the legal system and the distribution of positions within the legal field. The 1972 massacres in Burundi were instrumental in crystallising ethnicity as a vehicle of violence and ethnic discrimination by operationalising it as a defining vector for the allocation of social, political, economic and symbolic power. Hutu elites were eradicated: either killed or forced to flee. These massacres, together with fears of a Hutu uprising fuelled by the military Republics that acceded to power from 1965, contributed to a process of conscientising ethnic divisions through violence. Ethnic violence justified the emergence of each military Republic through a coup d'état and the violent repression each orchestrated by means of military trials and summary executions in 1972, 1988 and 1991.

The new Burundian state had negotiated its independence through Prince Rwagasore, the son of the *mwami* (king), Mwambutsa IV, along with a team of Belgian lawyers, whose nickname, the 'clan of the lawyers', undermines a historiography concerned with constructing Rwagasore as a national hero (Deslaurier 2013). As the son of the *mwami*, Rwagasore embodied a nationalist movement heralding the return of the king at the apex of Burundian society while simultaneously obscuring how the king's position had been reinforced by collaboration with the Belgian administration and weakened by six decades of colonisation.

There is very little information on the Belgian lawyers who assisted his side of the negotiations. These lawyers were decried by the colonial administration as sympathisers of the nationalist cause while being

[26] It targeted the Tutsi minority in neighbouring Rwanda. This is an overly generalised account.

uneasily woven into the nationalist narrative as legal advisors, whose sole role was to assuage the distrust of the colonial administration and the distress of European traders based in Bujumbura (Deslaurier 2002). In any case, their presence sent a clear message to European traders: independence would not greatly affect the operations of indirect rule.

A couple of weeks into these negotiations, Rwagasore was killed by a Greek national and two pro-Belgian Burundians, who were themselves middlemen of the empire as chiefs and princes. This triggered inter-ethnic rivalries among Tutsi and Hutu within the Union for National Progress (UPRONA), a political party created by Rwagasore as an inter-ethnic group, but which dominated political life until 1993 as a Tutsi-dominated party. Rwagasore's murder helped make him a hero of the nation, the personification of a golden age of inter-ethnic harmony despite colonial rule.

Although the Belgian project of creating a 'non-hereditary aristocracy' (Gahama 2001: 247) never succeeded, chiefs were handpicked by the colonial administration for their legitimacy as members of the Baganwa or Tutsi elites (considered racially superior by the Belgian rulers) and their subservience to the colonial administration. The colonial administration had initially resisted the emergence of elites (Gahama 2001: 247). Only in 1959 did the Belgians attempt to reverse this trend. However, efforts to 'Africanise' the bureaucratic cadres abruptly ended with independence.

The elites who competed for power at independence came from two main groups of secondary school graduates: the 'Astridiens' from the École d'Astrida for chiefs and the 'Séminaristes' from the Mugere seminary, originally designed to train local clergy but from which many schoolteachers and public servants also emerged. As a member of the princely elite of the Baganwa, Rwagasore himself was educated at the École d'Astrida, founded by missionaries in the early 1920s with the endorsement of the Belgian administration to (re)create a class of 'chiefs' charged with dispensing 'customary' justice in rural Burundi and Rwanda.

Devolving education to missionaries had already been the norm in colonial Congo. The 1906 agreement between the Vatican and Brussels prioritised Catholic missions, which also held a prominent position in Burundi (while Protestant missions predominated in Rwanda). Conceived as a modality of social control,[27] education in colonial Burundi focused on the formation of the middlemen of the colonial administration.

[27] Based on the model devised for African American pupils in the 1920s by the Phelps-Stokes Foundation in the US.

The dozen university graduates at independence (who did not include any lawyers) had been handpicked by the missions to receive their secondary education at the Collège du Saint Esprit, created in the 1940s for the best primary school graduates in Burundi and Rwanda. This college was conceived as a 'laboratory of inter-racial relations',[28] enrolling sons of Tutsi and Hutu from both Rwanda and Burundi, as well as Europeans. These endeavours contributed to the formation of a small 'bureaucratic-meritocratic elite' of 'semi-diploma' holders, most of whom served in the administration and army, often at high levels (Chrétien and Dupaquier 2007: 24).

The structure of this independence elite also exhibited the colonial administration's divide-and-rule strategy. General Michel Micombero, who took power through a coup d'état in 1966, was part of the small meritocratic elite formed by the Collège du Saint Esprit. Trained as an officer at the Royal Military Academy in Brussels, he was also the product of the Belgians' attempt to create an army from 1958 and pit a Tutsi elite against the princely Baganwa to weaken anti-Belgian factions within the nationalist movement.

In so doing, the colonial administration built on the patrimonial competition among chiefs fostered by coffee production. Promoted as an export crop, coffee culture also relied on chiefs' control over the population, based on their right to extort rent through tributes. The 'Groupe de Bururi', which took power with Micombero and retained it under Colonel Bagaza in 1976 and Major Buyoya in 1987, originated from the Bururi region, which had been sidelined by colonial strategies favouring the Muramvya region of the princely Baganwa.

Belgian colonial policies also extended the power of this small urban elite into the rural sphere. Between 1945 and 1952, colonial administrators introduced several reforms. The chiefs were replaced by elected mayors, while the institution of the *bashingantahe* (literally 'wise men'), which traditionally had played the role of countervailing power in administration and justice, was rendered impotent (Kolhagen 2012).

Throughout the post-colonial history of the country until 1993, this ensured the monopoly of the country's single party, UPRONA, as the sole point of contact between the people and the state (Deslaurier 2003). In Burundi, 'politics provide the opportunity and the means to *eat*' (Chrétien and Dupaquier 2007: 51, my translation from French,

[28] Author's interview with Eric, a lawyer at the Burundi Bar, Bujumbura, 21 December 2011.

emphasis in the original). The state that emerged in the 1970s was intensely bureaucratic, dependent on rents from coffee as the country's primary export crop (Hatungimana 2008) but even more on development aid. Still provided mainly by the former *métropole*, the latter represented 30 per cent of the country's GDP in the early 1970s and ensured a tight Belgo-Burundian operational system in all public sectors. The fluid transition of the colonial administration into 'cooperation' ensured the lasting presence of Belgian *coopérants*, consultants and religious missions.

These dynamics of extraversion, clientelism and exclusion heavily affected the structuration of the legal field, which was segmented between a small elite of law professors and a mass of magistrates distributed according to hierarchies determined by political, economic and ethnic resources. Law professors continue to construct their status by obtaining a PhD at a Belgian faculty. Mostly originating from the same region, Mwaro, they were suspected of bias against students from Bururi, the stronghold of the military elite, creating uneasy relations with the Micombero and Bagaza military juntas. Before the emergence of this academic legal elite, the Micombero regime had appealed to ideologically extremist lawyers, such as Artémon Simbananiye, accused of orchestrating the 1972 purge against the Hutu. It is only from the Third Republic, following the 1987 coup d'état by Major Buyoya and some liberalisation, that law professors were called upon to serve as legal advisors on constitutional reforms.

The intensely bureaucratic nature of the state until the 2000s contributed to the rising demand for lawyers. A former judge, who entered the judiciary in 1998, explained: 'there was work for everybody, there weren't enough law professionals. We were not necessarily assigned where we wanted, but there was work for everybody'.[29] Executive control over the judiciary through a form of 'diffuse interference'[30] (selective promotions and demotions) was facilitated by the absence of an *École nationale de la magistrature* (ENM), which made it easier to remove judges.

The political economy of a country where the bulk of the population depends on subsistence agriculture limited the expansion of a private market for legal services. The repressive politics of the Micombero military regime, reproduced by the Bagaza junta, also made private practice a dangerous form of political opposition. Etienne Ntyiyankundiye was the

[29] Author's interview with Adrien, a lawyer at the Gitega Bar, Bujumbura, 7 May 2013.
[30] Author's interview with Francis, a lawyer at the Burundi Bar, Bujumbura, 24 April 2014.

first Burundian lawyer to be called to the bar in 1966, after graduating from the Université of Namur in Belgium. His trajectory illustrates the bar's relationship to the military juntas until the end of the 1980s. A friend of Micombero, with whom he had attended the Collège du Saint Esprit, Ntyiyankundiye was appointed Minister of Justice in 1969 before being disgraced. He was arrested in 1971 along with his clients – Tutsi militaries from the Muramvya region accused of having fomented a coup.

During the 1970s–1980s, dozens of military trials were conducted to reinforce the military regimes, but defendants were assisted exclusively by foreign lawyers, mostly Belgian. 'The monopoly of foreign lawyers',[31] the Burundi Bar had been founded around 1950, presumably to service European traders based in Bujumbura. Some of the Belgian lawyers associated with the 'clan of the lawyers' who assisted UPRONA in the negotiations for independence – such as Willy Vanderplancken – seem to have represented political defendants in the military trials conducted by the junta in the 1970s. This mobilisation of the bar as a political platform waged by foreign lawyers later became a defining feature. Eric Gillet and Bernard Maingain, of the Brussels Bar, for example, have often represented defendants in Rwanda and Burundi in political cases.

Major Buyoya, who installed himself as president in 1987 after a military coup, embodies the ambiguity of what has commonly been dubbed the 'Third Wave' of global democratisation. A native of the Bururi region like his predecessors, Buyoya continued to deploy the repressive toolkit of previous military juntas, suppressing a 1988 attempted Hutu uprising with extreme violence. But Buyoya also announced an agenda of political liberalisation and better Hutu–Tutsi relations. He justified his coup d'état against Bagaza in the name of civil liberties. At a French-African summit in 1990 in La Baule, French president Mitterrand had announced that aid would flow 'more enthusiastically' to African countries taking steps towards democracy, effectively introducing conditionality in the disbursement of development funds. Belgium did not follow suit. Nonetheless, as Buyoya recalled: 'we were not subjected to the France–Africa summit at La Baule, but we adapted ourselves to the political context'.[32]

[31] Author's interview with Etienne Ntyiyankundiye, a lawyer at the Burundi Bar, Bujumbura, 21 December 2011.

[32] E Ngabire, 'La politique de l'unité nationale, socle de Buyoya 1er' *Iwacu* 23 November 2015.

This liberalisation policy had important domestic effects. The legalisation of opposition parties in 1991 fostered a rapprochement between Hutu and Tutsi. The creation of the Front for Democracy in Burundi (FRODEBU) by Melchior Ndadaye encouraged the return of the Hutu diaspora, who had fled the country after 1972. Exiled in Rwanda, Ndadaye epitomised the new political generation formed by an educated Hutu elite organised into resistance movements. Buyoya also appointed a commission tasked with drafting a new constitution, adopted by referendum in 1992, which called for a non-ethnic government with a president and a parliament.

In practice, the coupling of structural adjustment policies and political liberalisation echoed the contradictory dimensions of the impact of neoliberal globalisation found elsewhere in the world during this period. While opening the possibility of a domestic space for human rights activism attuned to the international market for human rights, liberal reforms in Burundi also reinforced the capacity of the state to shape and neutralise political opposition. The practice of political interference in civil society even bears its own term in Kirundi: 'nyakurisation'. The Ligue Iteka, the country's first human rights organisation, is emblematic of this contradiction. It was created in 1994 as a sister organisation of the International League for Human Rights and became both a platform for political opposition and a site of professionalisation for new generations of human rights activists. But the very year of its creation, a concurrent organisation, the Ligue Sonera, was launched to compete for the same pool of international resources and funding as the preserve of close affiliates of UPRONA and members of the old Tutsi legal elite at the Université du Burundi.

These liberalisation policies had a limited though symbolic impact on the social structure of the legal field. Buyoya's politics of inter-ethnic appeasement sought to transform the ethnic fabric of the judiciary by appointing Hutu judges. But that had little effect on the Burundi Bar, which remained the preserve of a dozen Tutsi lawyers in the early 1990s. Fabien Segatwa, the first Hutu lawyer called to the Burundi Bar in 1993, had lived in exile in the Democratic Republic of the Congo since 1972. He recalled: '[T]o encourage the return of the elite Hutu diaspora, the government and the UN High Commissioner for Refugees organised a visit of Hutu elites to campaign for their return from neighbouring countries'.[33] His own swearing in as a barrister was actively resisted by

[33] Author's interview with Fabien Segatwa, a lawyer at the Burundi Bar, Bujumbura, 16 April 2014.

the bar, which defended its monopoly over the very restricted market for private legal practice.

Democratic elections in June 1993 were won by Melchior Ndadaye, the first Hutu president. But this radical change in Burundi's political landscape was abruptly terminated by his assassination just months later by segments of the Tutsi-dominated army. Ndadaye's murder triggered large-scale massacres and the country's descent into civil war. Following the second coup d'état by Major Buyoya in 1996, judicial proceedings were begun against those suspected of assassinating Ndadaye (before the Judicial Chamber of the Supreme Court) and those suspected of participating in the subsequent massacres (before the Criminal Chambers of the Court of Appeal) (Vandeginste 2010: 87ff). Previous attempted coups and uprisings had been prosecuted before military courts, usually on sedition and rebellion charges. The novelty here was the imprimatur of a genocidal wording in the judicial response to the 1993 crisis. This reflected pressure at the domestic level from victims' associations, including the extremist Tutsi defence organisation AC-Génocide. Thousands of suspects, predominantly Hutu, were arrested in a wartime context immediately after the massacres.

5.3 Negotiating Burundi's Transition

Pierre Nkurunziza died on 8 June 2020, presumably of COVID-19 – though he denied the pandemic had reached Burundian soil. To date, most donors including the EU continue to withhold funding to the country. Against the backdrop of Burundi's high import dependence and the preference of the central bank of using reserves to prop up the currency through continued interventions in the foreign-exchange market, Nkurunziza attempted to boost export earnings (and foreign reserves) by nationalising the coffee sector in late 2019.

The nationalisation plan was a pre-emptive action to monopolise the sector's US dollar earnings (which constitute about 80 per cent of the total).[34] Production has plummeted by nearly 60 per cent since, even though the government announced in 2020 that 93 per cent of earnings had been repatriated. Foremost, the nationalisation process positioned the *Office pour le Développement du Café du Burundi* (Agency for the

[34] Economist Intelligence Unit (EIU) Country Reports Burundi Edition *The Economist Intelligence* 1 November 2019.

development of coffee in Burundi – ODECA) as a state within the state – as both regulator and operator of the coffee sector.[35]

On the other hand, exploitation of Burundi's substantial mineral wealth – in gold, nickel and rare earths – continues to be hampered by the lack of infrastructure. The country is only growingly building up its production of electricity – standing at 304,000 MWh in 2016 when 800,000 MWh are needed to extract nickel. In this landlocked country, the lack of railroads is also preventing the transit of extracted ores towards the main port of the region, at Dar es Salaam in Tanzania.

In March 2013, President Nkurunziza suspended gold extraction across the territory for two months – ostensibly to foster security on the predominantly artisanal sites of extraction and foremost to prevent illegal gold flows to neighbouring countries. In November 2019, Burundi's minister of Energy and Mines Manirakiza again suspended gold trade by local traders, instead requiring artisanal miners to sell their gold to the Banque de la République du Burundi (BRB, the Central Bank) in Burundian Francs. By then the situation had radically changed. Following Nkurunziza's bid for a third presidential term in 2015, Burundi had plunged in a new cycle of violence. Yet, while Nkurunziza's regime was sidelined as a pariah by the diplomatic and development aid community, it was being reinstated as a 'developmental' partner by mining corporations and European states – starting with Germany – intent on fostering the exploitation of Burundi's mineral resources at an industrial scale.

Manirakiza's decree suspending the sale of gold extracted by artisanal miners to local traders did not mention the situation of Tanganyika Gold – a Russian-Burundian corporation – which was granted, through Tanganyika Gold Burundi (with a 15 per cent ownership by the state of Burundi), a twenty-five-year concession in 2013 in the province of Cibitoke at the north-western border with Rwanda.[36] Nor did it apply to other types of ores that were starting to be extracted at an industrial level – including rare earths. As mentioned earlier, in March 2015, President Nkurunziza granted a mining license to Rainbow Mining

[35] F Inyabuntu, 'Deux ans après la nationalisation de la filière café, quel bilan?' *BurundiEco* 23 April 2021, http://burundi-eco.com/deux-ans-apres-nationalisation-filiere-cafe-quel-bilan/#.YoN3vS0RqCQ (accessed 17 May 2022).

[36] M-F Cros, 'L'État burundais se réserve désormais le commerce de l'or. La Banque centrale se réserve désormais le commerce de l'or' *La Libre Belgique* 27 November 2019.

Burundi. Rainbow Rare Earths owns 90 per cent interest in the project, while the remaining 10 per cent is held by the Republic of Burundi.[37]

Burundi's transition as an origination site of mineral boons was steered under President Nkurunziza and the so-called generals of the CNDD-FDD, the term commonly used to refer to the dozen generals drawn from the CNDD-FDD rebel ranks. President Nkurunziza is deemed to have had the final say in decisions to grant licences for mining exploration or exploitation. But companies needed first to 'go through a way of the cross, as [they] had to be "sponsored" by one of the "generals"'[38] and then obtain the authorisation of the mining ministry and that of the head of the presidential party, the CNDD-FDD.

'[E]ach step of the way [they] had to pay'.[39] Investors had to invest in a state budget line entitled 'Support to the President's good initiatives' as well as the 'Ubuntu Foundation' of the First Lady (a title ironically drawn from the context of the South African transition from Apartheid).

Though known for being 'clean', Nkurunziza's successor, Évariste Ndayishimiye, was also drawn from the higher tier of the military ranks of the CNDD-FDD. In a bid to appease development donors, he launched a fight against corruption that is, a priori, doomed to failure. Nkurunziza was elevated to the rank of 'Supreme Guide of Patriotism' while Ndayishimiye claims to be threading on the legacy of the one he calls 'the grandfather of the nation'. Further, the 'generals' all retain shares in extractive companies.[40]

Nonetheless, in April 2021, Ndayishimiye suspended the export of rare earths produced from Rainbow Rare Earths' trial mining and processing at the Gakara site, claiming that the price benchmark was incorrect and that the contract with the mining company should be renegotiated.[41] Three months later, the new minister of Energy and Mines, Ibrahim Uwizeye, suspended the activities of Tanganyika Mining Burundi,

[37] NS Energy, 'Gakara Rare Earth Project', www.nsenergybusiness.com/projects/gakara-rare-earth-project/ (accessed 11 May 2022).

[38] E Ndikumana, 'Le pouvoir burundais suspend les activités minières pour renégocier tous les contrats' RFI 23 July 2021, www.rfi.fr/fr/afrique/20210722-le-pouvoir-burundais-suspend-les-activités-minières-pour-renégocier-tous-les-contrats (accessed 11 May 2022).

[39] Ibid.

[40] D Whitehouse, 'Exclusive: Burundi wants new Rainbow Rare Earths mining convention' *The Africa Report* 23 August 2021.

[41] Ibid.

alleging that the corporation had not delivered on its contractual obligations to duly compensate expropriated communities.[42]

Both Tanganyika Gold and Rainbow Rare Earths are what are called 'junior' mining companies. Junior mining stocks are small, early-stage mining companies that are usually still in the exploration and development phase and have yet to mine any resources. Unlike large-cap companies, junior mining companies often have smaller asset bases. Foremost, they do not have to face the reputational (and legal) costs of publicly listed mining corporations, like Glencore or Trafigura.

Tanganyika Gold is owned by the Burundi-born Lebanese businessman Jean Jbeili, who promised then Energy and Mines minister Manirakiza that the firm would compensate farmers whose fields were destroyed during the exploration phase. To comply with the government's local content rules, the junior company hired a Burundian geologist, Donatien Muyuku, who previously worked for the Russian group Norilsk Nickel before the latter pulled out of the country.

'Tanganyika Gold [won] backing from Russian experts and investors who have been held in high regard in Bujumbura ever since Burundi's central bank and Gazprombank, an affiliate of Gazprom, signed an agreement in June [2016] to promote investment in the country'.[43] The award of a concession to Jbeili 'stirred concern among diplomats from the OECD countries and from NGOs specializing in good governance. To be sure, the deals were struck somewhat secretly, by direct agreement without competitive bidding at a time when several top military chiefs in Burundi and next-door Congo-K [were] suspected of playing a hand in smuggling gold out of Congo'.[44]

For his part, Rainbow Rare Earths' CEO since 2019, South African George Bennett, has a long track record in junior mining.[45] He engineered the public listing of Shanta Gold – a gold company

[42] P Gahama, 'Suspension provisoire des activités de la société Tangnyika Mining Burundi' *Iwacu* 15 July 2021.

[43] Africa Intelligence: Mining, 'Tanganyika Gold's way of winning licenses' *Africa Mining Intelligence* 20 December 2016.

[44] Africa Intelligence: Mining, 'Jbeili the new mining kingpin' *Africa Mining Intelligence* 14 May 2013.

[45] See B Ryan, 'Rainbow Rare Earth pushes ahead with "rapid development" of Phalaborwa project' *Miningmx*, www.miningmx.com/news/battery-minerals/46499-rainbow-pushes-ahead-with-phalaborwa-rare-earths-project/ (accessed 17 May 2022).

operating mainly in Tanzania – on AIM[46] on the London Stock Exchange in 2005 and is best known for founding MDM Engineering, listed in London in 2008, which is a company offering minerals process engineering and project management, and preliminary and final feasibility studies services, as well as plant design, construction and commissioning services. Foremost, with exploration concessions in both Burundi and South Africa, Rainbow Rare Earths could become a globally significant competitor against China.

Rainbow Rare Earths' executive director, J. Peter Pham, the former special envoy of US ex-president Donald Trump for the Great Lakes region, oversaw discussions with Ndayishimiye to lift his moratorium on mining exploration, on the sidelines of the UN General Assembly in September 2021. Foremost, Rainbow Rare Earths is now partly owned by the TechMet Group based in London, which acquires interests in projects related to key metals in energy transition and high-tech sectors (rare earths, nickel, cobalt, lithium, vanadium, tin and tungsten). TechMet Group is headed by the South African tycoon Brian Menell, heir of the family that founded the Anglovaal mining group. Since 2020, one of TechMet's shareholders is the US International Development Finance Corporation (DFC).[47]

'The TechMet founder first cut his teeth in the industry working for South African diamond giant De Beers in 1988. He then took over the helm of the family firm Anglovaal, sold to Patrice Potsepe's African Rainbow Minerals in 2001, a few years after the start of the Black Economic Empowerment programme'.[48] For this 'serial entrepreneur' who created a flurry of 'junior' extractive companies in the past twenty years, the main risk is not reputational or that of transparency – as it is for the publicly listed transnational corporations which eventually buy products extracted through these ventures.

The risk is lack of return. Later in the 2000s, Menell co-created Energem Resources, which he used as a channel to buy assets in fourteen African states, at the time amassing a large portfolio of projects in

[46] AIM is a sub-market of the London Stock Exchange that was launched on 19 June 1995 as a replacement to the previous Unlisted Securities Market that had been in operation since 1980.

[47] Africa Intelligence, 'Will US stake help Rainbow Rare Earths get its mine reopened' *Africa Intelligence* 9 November 2021.

[48] Africa Intelligence, 'Serial entrepreneur Brian Menell bets double on rare earth mining sovereignty' *Africa Intelligence* 14 February 2022.

mining, oil trading – many of which never came to fruition – the agri-food industry, retail and cars. In Angola, he bought shares in Diamond Works created by Tony Buckingham – co-founder of one of the first private military companies, Sandline International, and founder of the oil and gas corporation Heritage Oil.

When Energem was forced to declare bankruptcy in 2011, Menell turned to 'low risk' countries. 'TechMet owes some of its good financial health to the US, China's main rival and a stakeholder in what Menell calls the "cold war" for the control of critical metal supply chains'.[49] Menell's success at obtaining funding from the DFC was in part made possible by the chairman of TechMet's advisory board, Adm. Mike Mullen, who was chairman of the Joint Chiefs of Staff between 2007 and 2011 under US presidents George W. Bush and Barack Obama.

5.4 Conclusion

How are legal intermediaries positioned in relation to apparently two distinct tracks of legal globalisation – one spearheaded by IFIs, bilateral donors and INGOs that builds on the relative currency of the state as a variably willing or unable recipient, the other leaning, on the contrary, on the state's formal *and* substantive sovereignty to protect foreign investments in the country?

To be sure, the shift from *exploration* to *exploitation* of rare earths in Burundi is likely to progressively open legal pressure points along the mineral's global value chain – such as strategic transnational litigation opportunities. But these points of pressure will lean on existing legal stumbling blocks. When Rainbow Rare Earths was granted a mining license by Nkurunziza's government in March 2015, it had already sealed a deal with a global trader: ThyssenKrupp Metallurgical Products, the commodity trading company of the German steel company ThyssenKrupp. According to Gesine Ames of the Ecumenical Network on Central Africa (ÖNZ), an alliance of German church organisations active in the region: '[t]his certainly wasn't the right time for deals with the Burundian government'.[50] Did the contract include human rights

[49] Ibid.

[50] H Fischer, 'Rare earth deal in Burundi criticized amid political turmoil' *DW* 13 May 2015, www.dw.com/en/rare-earth-deal-in-burundi-criticized-amid-political-turmoil/a-18448513 (accessed 18 May 2022).

clauses and the possibility for the German trader to pull out if the environmental and human rights situation called for such an action on the ground? 'Details concerning contracts are confidential, so I'm afraid we can't comment on that', responded ThyssenKrupp spokesperson Stefan Ettwig – adding that the trader relies on its partner Rainbow Rare Earths – 'to assess the situation'.[51]

Rainbow Rare Earths has shown itself open to renegotiating its contract with Burundi 'on a win-win basis'.[52] The implicit message endorsed also by its German trading partner being: '[i]t's definitely better for Burundi if rare earths are extracted and traded by companies that uphold certain values and standards'.[53] The contract between the Burundian government and Rainbow Rare Earths has not been disclosed. But the company's published audit on the Gakara project does specify that it was concluded based on Burundi's mining code which states that the signatory company owns 51 per cent of the project's shares while 39 per cent are detained by other shareholders and 10 per cent by the Burundian state – a distribution of shares which means that Rainbow Rare Earths' partners – foremost TechMet – weigh heavily even though they are *not* sitting at the renegotiation table.

The report also indicates that expropriation and compensation processes are based on Burundian statutory law and that a committee has been created to deal with such issues, comprising, besides members of Rainbow management, 'the President of the Mutambu Communal Council, the Administrator of Mutambu, the Priest of the Gasenyi Catholic mission, a judge from the region and the Chiefs of the zones concerned by the mining activities'.[54] In an agrarian country, where pressure for land is compounded by a 3.1 per cent annual demographic growth and the violent conflicts generated by the return of refugees (along with the complex situation of legal pluralism regarding land ownership where state law coexists and interacts with competing normative systems), the selection of such intermediaries is unlikely to alleviate societal conflicts – and their violence.

51 Ibid.

52 A Yikeze, 'Gitega et Rainbow mining Burundi en terrain miné' *Iwacu* 20 July 2021.

53 H Fischer, 'Rare earth deal in Burundi criticized amid political turmoil' *Deutsche Welle* 13 May 2015, https://www.dw.com/en/rare-earth-deal-in-burundi-criticized-amid-political-turmoil/a-18448513 (accessed 21 May 2024).

54 F Reichhardt, J Witley, and J Hudson (2019) *Rainbow Rare Earths Limited. Gakara REE Project Burundi* (The MSA Group. Specialist Consultants to the Mining Industry, Parkhurst, South Africa) 136.

Yet the leverage of supranational dispute settlement mechanisms – be it by political opponents or by transnational corporations operating in the country – are signalling yet again another legal revolution whose outcome will depend on the sedimented legacies of decentralised despotism and extraverted rule of law in the country. Since the integration of Burundi into the East African Community in 2007, fifty-seven cases concerning the state have been filed to the EACJ – which amounts to 10 per cent of the court's caseload since it was reinstated in 2001. The most highly visible of these cases were those challenging President Nkurunziza's decision to run for a third term in 2015.[55]

In parallel, Burundi has become a repeat player in investment arbitration cases. As of 2019, the ICSID of the World Bank Group – the only international arbitration forum which publishes arbitration awards – stated that sub-Saharan Africa accounted for 15 per cent of the 728 cases registered that year, while the Middle East and North Africa accounted for an additional 12 per cent (Ewelukwa Ofodile 2019: 298). Burundi was a respondent in all four cases introduced before the ICSID.[56]

For international lawyers, the operations of both sets of international dispute settlement mechanisms constitute a paradox rendered especially visible in cases involving Burundi. Though an economic jurisdiction, the EACJ is mostly used as a regional platform for domestic political struggles (see Heinrich 2021). On the other hand, cases involving Burundi before the ICSID raise the question of state responsibility in a context of political turmoil. The first case introduced before the ICSID was in 1999, while the country was at war. It involved a gold trading family, the Goetzs, who claimed that the withdrawal, by Buyoya's government, of the company's certificate of free zone conferring tax and customs exemptions on gold transiting through the country constituted a form of expropriation.

[55] See, e.g., *East African Civil Society Organization Forum vs. The Attorney General of the Republic of Burundi and 2 Others*, EACJ Ref. No. 2 of 2015.

[56] Antoine Goetz & Others v. Republic of Burundi (ICSID Case No. ARB/95/3), Award on agreed terms, 10 February 1999, Belgium-Burundi BIT; Antoine Goetz & Others v. Republic of Burundi (ICSID Case No. ARB/01/2), Award of 21 June 2012, Belgium-Burundi BIT; Joseph Houben v. Republic of Burundi (ICSID Case No. ARB/13/7), Award of 12 January 2016, Belgium-Burundi BIT; Tariq Bashir & SA Interpétrol Burundi v. Republic of Burundi (ICISD Case No. ARB/14/31) registered on 12/12/31, Belgium-Burundi BIT. Discontinued in 2017. In the first Antoine Goetz claim, the ICSID Tribunal considered, and affirmed for the first time, jurisdiction over a counterclaim lodged by a respondent state against the investor.

In other words, in the first case, questions of domestic political governance are adjudicated before a supranational economic court, while in the other the economic order is insulated against war and political change and taken out of the scope of national sovereignty.

Shifting the focus towards applicants against the state of Burundi and legal counsels acting on its behalf helps shed light on the renegotiation and justification of Burundi's relationship with global markets as the country transitions to an origination site of mineral boons. To reiterate and paraphrase Benton and Ford (2016: 185–186), this matters because their strategies as much as their *structural* positions provide an indication of stumbling blocks that are not the beginning of a new order but rather structurally defined legal intermediation roles that foreclose certain possibilities and make other outcomes more likely.

Isidore Rufyikiri, the former president of the Burundi Bar and solo practitioner, introduced five cases before the EACJ against the state of Burundi. He joined forces with members of the East Africa Law Society (EALS), incorporated in 1995 in Arusha, to contest the arrest of lawyers registered at the Burundi Bar. This promoted him as 'an uncompromising champion of the rule of law'.[57] Yet Rufyikiri followed what he described himself as 'an extremely chaotic trajectory'.[58]

Rufyikiri completed a *Licence de droit* (BA of Law) at the Université du Burundi in 1978 and entered the judiciary as deputy prosecutor in the province of Bururi. Close to Jean-Baptiste Bagaza, who seized power after a coup against Michel Micombero in 1976, he was appointed as advisor to the president for legal affairs. Following Major Buyoya's coup, Rufyikiri was sent away as diplomatic envoy in Algiers and Dar es Salaam. In 1994, he contributed to the founding of a political party with Bagaza, the PARENA (Parti pour le Redressement National – Party for National Recovery). Following Buyoya's second military coup, he was detained several times for his alleged involvement in an attempted coup. Released from prison in 2000, he decided to take the bar exam.

In 2010, Rufyikiri was elected president of the Bar of Burundi. After the arrest of François Nyamoya – another lawyer at the Bar of Burundi – Rufyikiri requested that all members of the bar protest. One of them,

57 *Iwacu*, 'L'ordre des avocats du Burundi soutient Me Rufyikiri' 12 November 2013.

58 Author's interview with Isidore Rufyikiri, a lawyer at the Bar of Burundi, Bujumbura, 21 December 2011.

Sixte Sizimwe, left the room, declaring, 'we are not here to do politics'.[59] A sympathiser of the CNDD-FDD, Sizimwe henceforth asked the then Minister of Justice to set up a competing bar in the town of Gitega. Sizimwe is a repeat player in arbitration cases that have involved Burundi: before the ICSID, the ICC in Paris and the PCA, where he appears as the Burundian respondent of the French, US and Belgian corporate law firms that have represented the state of Burundi.

A Hutu, Sizimwe was born in 1968. His family fled to the DRC following the 1972 massacres. He returned to Burundi in 1991 in the context of a UNHCR repatriation scheme. When Ndadaye was assassinated in 1993, Sizimwe was a law student at the Université du Burundi. He fled to the DRC, again, and completed his law degree at the Université Catholique de Bukavu. Following the start of the war in the DRC in 1998, he returned to Burundi. He entered the judiciary as a judge at the *Tribunal de Grande Instance* (Regional court) of Bujumbura by benefiting from the 2000 Arusha agreement's plan for ethnic balance in state institutions.

In parallel, Sizimwe received a grant from the Organisation internationale de la Francophonie (Francophonie – OIF) to complete a master's degree. 'We did not have much choice at the time. It was either human rights or environmental law'. Promoted as Deputy Public Prosecutor before the *Tribunal de Grande Instance* in Bujumbura in 2003 – a promotion again linked to the Arusha agreement – he requested a leave of absence to work as an intern at the International Criminal Tribunal for Rwanda (ICTR), then seated in Arusha. Upon his return in Burundi in 2004, he decided to register with the Bar of Burundi and worked for ASF to represent Hutu defendants in the context of the '*contentieux de 1993*' in 2004–2005.

Both Rufyikiri and Sizimwe's trajectories display the two common core resources that continue to structure the legal field and its relationship to the field of state power in Burundi: ethnicity and extraversion. Both types of capital determine at once these lawyers' relations with power at the domestic level and their incorporation in international legal networks. Both individuals are structurally positioned as respondents – in one case of INGOs and the EALS, in the other of government elites and multinational corporate law firms. Both, in other words, display forms of capital that are homologous to the extent that they are interchangeable:

[59] Author's interview with Sixte Sizimwe, a lawyer at the Bar of Gitega, Bujumbura, 25 April 2014.

according to domestic political changes, their positions may be reversed, along the structural line of bifurcation of Burundi's legal field.

Burundi certainly seems to be a limit case due to its domestic legal field's extreme dependence on external resources and vulnerability to political interference. But it is also an exceptional Petri dish of the violent conflicts and professional battles that are renegotiating the country's relationship with global markets.

6

Abidjan

Lawfare and Accountability Dumping

Since the mid-2000s, Côte d'Ivoire has become a magnet of judicialisation. From petty to grand corruption, electoral fraud to war crimes and crimes against humanity, child labour and uncertified trade to toxic residue dumping, Ivorian politicians, businesses, local victims' associations, international NGOs and global traders have been involved in judicial procedures spanning the whole array of the global justice landscape: be they criminal cases in Paris, Abidjan, New York or The Hague; commercial and investment arbitration cases before the ICSID and the Economic Community of West African States' (ECOWAS) arbitration centre; electoral fraud before the African court on human and people's rights; or tort litigation against global traders in Paris, Amsterdam, Brussels or London.

Apart from their length, as judicial *sagas* these procedures share a common flip-flopping between law and politics. Emblematically, in 2013 the so-called cocoa barons trial in Abidjan – which targeted a couple of dozens of former president Gbagbo's cronies accused of embezzlement of the cocoa boon during the war – delivered prison sentences and fines that are likely to be overturned at appeal due to prescriptions. Yet the most vocal critique of the trial originated from the *defence*. In Blessy Chrisostome's words – the lawyer of Tapé Do, former super baron of the cocoa sector, 'the law has not been enlightened by what endows it with strength: truth'.[1]

Meanwhile, an environmental scandal involving the dumping of coker naphtha, a highly toxic unrefined residue, in the port of Abidjan, by the world's second oil and metals trader, Trafigura, grew into Britain's biggest ever group-action lawsuit, with staggering figures. Representing

[1] Linfodrome.ci, 'Procès café-cacao: Après le verdict, un avocat fait de graves révélations' 8 November 2013, www.linfodrome.com/economie/12854-proces-cafe-cacao-apres-le-ver dict-un-avocat-fait-de-graves-revelations (accessed 27 April 2022). My translation from French.

30,000 victims, the London-based law firm Leigh Day & Co. negotiated an out-of-court settlement in 2009 which secured £30 million for the victims, £105 million in legal costs and a success fee of £40 million.[2]

Nearly twenty years after the Probo Koala disaster, over 100,000 victims have filed complaints against Trafigura. Yet the company has never admitted any liability, arguing systematically that its accountability stopped at the fringe of its 'corporate veil'.[3] The complex corporate structure of Trafigura seems specifically designed to dilute its chain of command across territories, with Trafigura's head office, Trafigura Group Pte Ltd, registered in Singapore, the group's holding company, Trafigura Beheer B.V., incorporated in Amsterdam, and Trafigura Ltd in London, then acting as the coordinating entity for a substantial proportion of the group's oil operations, including those related to the dumping of the waste in Abidjan, which, for its part, was managed by Puma Energy, Trafigura's wholly owned subsidiary in Côte d'Ivoire.

Meanwhile, the bulk of the settlement money was diverted by the self-claimed representative of the victims and the Trafigura saga imploded into several cases in Europe, with a jigsaw of actors: elusive victims with a dozen associations claiming to represent them; another dozen European 'cause lawyers'; the media; NGOs; and a state in the background that is either apparently disempowered or complicit in the face of transnational corporate power in Côte d'Ivoire; or benevolent towards group claims filed by foreign victims, though leaning to the considerable political clout of Trafigura in the UK.

The increasing complexity of corporate restructuration along GVCs has generated a wealth of scholarship, primarily in private international law (see Muir Watt et al. 2019), on the issue of corporate liability, along with strategic litigation aimed at piercing the corporate veil. But opposing the corporate liability of multinationals to what Comaroff and Comaroff (2007) call 'lawfare' – the deployment of the 'rule of law' as a tactic of political repression or extortion – in the Global South does little to understand the entanglement, over time, between GVCs, politics and legal change. To boot: Trafigura continues to thrive on the volatility of

[2] A Hirsh and R Evans, 'Lawyers for claimants in Trafigura case seek £105m in costs' *The Guardian*, 10 May 2010.

[3] The 'corporate veil' is a Common Law doctrine which institutes a separate personality between the corporation and its shareholders. Usually a corporation is treated as a separate legal person, which is solely responsible for the debts it incurs and the sole beneficiary of the credit it is owed. Common Law countries tend to uphold this principle of separate personhood, but in exceptional situations may 'pierce' or 'lift' the corporate veil.

global markets for carbon commodities, advocating a public image neatly orchestrated by the public relations firm Bell Pottinger as a 'decent global citizen' and an agent of development in West Africa. Meanwhile, left largely untreated, the waste continues its environmental and human damage. In Côte d'Ivoire, which transitioned since into one of Africa's booming economic hotspots, business with Trafigura continues to thrive.

Rather, zooming in onto the development of the scandal into a judicial battle, from Abidjan to London and other European jurisdictions, provides a powerful entry point to track the legal lumpiness fostered by the globalisation and financialisation of GVCs – but only at the condition of looking at the role played by *intermediaries* in shaping the relationship over time between law, capitalism and politics (see Dezalay S 2019).

Abidjan constitutes an emblematic case as an *origination* site for cocoa and a *destination* site for waste. The 'Ivorian miracle' had relied on an economic model of protected integration within the global markets of coffee and cocoa. Félix Houphouët-Boigny, Côte d'Ivoire's first president, represented a central component of what Bayart (1993) termed the 'post-colonial block'. The economic crisis triggered by the deregulation of the market of coffee and cocoa in the 1980s[4] had the domino effect of derailing the Ponzi-like 'honeycomb of networks by which the ascendancy of the ruler was maintained' (Young 2004: 35) drawing on patrimonial webs of personalised circuits of distribution reciprocated with clientelist loyalty. It also shook the social, economic, political and institutional ties between the former French *métropole* and the states of its African *pré carré*.

The dismantling of the 'post-colonial block' was symbolically epitomised by the death of Houphouët-Boigny in 1993. But it was foremost fostered by a displacement of the terms of the relationship between Côte d'Ivoire and other raw commodities' exporting states, and global markets towards global traders, financial markets and a legal form of transnational legal coding that leans on the state while operating without it. What the Probo Koala legal saga reveals, indeed, is the need to track the structural effects of the interconnectedness between concurrent processes that unravelled in the post–Cold War period, from the 'judicialization of mega politics' (Hirschl 2008) to the deregulation of financial markets.

[4] Cocoa prices are based on two commodity exchanges: the London Cocoa Futures and the New York Board of Trade. The drop of cocoa prices at the turn of the 1980s was fostered by the double effect of excess supply and large stocks held by consuming countries. During the 1980s, corporations dominating the market for processed cocoa (like Cargill) built up considerable reserves that they used to regulate the market in their favor.

These concurrent dynamics contributed to reinforcing the prominence of global traders like Trafigura as intermediaries between states, financial markets and businesses. They also fostered a symbiotic relationship between the *onshoring* of offshore capitalism and the *offshoring* of *onshore* justice.

6.1 Cocoa Gatekeeping Politics

As an old monarch recalling the exchanges between Louis XV and Madame de Pompadour, Félix Houphouët-Boigny would tell his dinner hosts 'After Us, the Deluge' before concluding with a malicious smile: 'It was not Louis XV's head that was cut off, but his successor's'.[5] To date, two of his political heirs, Laurent Gbagbo and Alassane Ouattara, are still dominating Côte d'Ivoire's political scene. They have alternated between ballot, bush war and lawfare for nearly thirty years, since the death of the *Vieux* ('old man'), Houphouët-Boigny's affectionate nickname, in 1993.

Formerly dubbed a 'miracle' as the economic powerhouse of West Africa, Côte d'Ivoire descended into chaos following a military coup in 1999 and the contested election of Alassane Ouattara in 2010. Between 2002 and 2017, the country was effectively divided between a rebel-held north and a government-controlled south, separated by a French- and UN-secured demilitarised zone, the '*zone de confiance*'.

Until his death in August 2023, Henri Konan Bédié, president of Côte d'Ivoire in 1993–1999, remained at the helm of Houphouët-Boigny's party, the Democratic Party of Côte d'Ivoire – African Democratic Rally (Rassemblement Démocratique Africain (PDCI-RDA)). His manoeuvre to amend the electoral code in 1995 to the effect that presidential candidates were required to have been born of two Ivorian parents and to have resided in the country for five years prior to the election directly targeted his prime opponent, Alassane Ouattara.

The latter had resided in the US since 1990 while serving as deputy managing director of the IMF and his father was rumoured to be Burkinabé. The IMF positioned him as chairman of the Interministerial Committee for Coordination of the Stabilization and Economic Recovery Programme of Côte d'Ivoire in spring 1990 as a condition to steer Côte d'Ivoire out of the abysmal debt that had engulfed the country's economy since the deregulation of cocoa and coffee prices and the fall of the price

[5] C Bensimon, 'D'Houphouët à Ouattara, une tour d'ivoire en héritage' *Le Monde* 18 November 2020. My translation from French.

of the staples on global markets in 1985. As prime minister until Houphouët-Boigny's death, Ouattara implemented the IFIs-led liberalisation of the Ivorian economy.

Bédié's reliance on *ivoirité* ('ivorianness') as the staple of political legitimacy and nationhood also activated the 'identity poison' in this frontier economy, in which 10 to 25 per cent of the population is deemed to originate from neighbouring countries – between so-called *autochthonous* ethnic groups and *allochthonous* (non-nationals) or *allogenous* (Ivorians originating from another locality) – that fuelled a countrywide war from 2002. The conflict effectively ended in 2011 with the swearing in of Alassane Ouattara as president and the transfer of Laurent Gbagbo to the ICC to face charges of crimes against humanity.

Laurent Gbagbo was acquitted by the ICC in January 2019, due to lack of evidence on his direct responsibility over the 2010–2011 post-electoral violence. After nearly nine years in pretrial detention at The Hague and a three-year-long trial, he returned to Côte d'Ivoire in June 2021. Shortly after, he launched a new political party, the African People's Party (Parti des peuples africains – Côte d'Ivoire (PPA – CI)), promising to engage in the political game 'until [his]death'.[6]

Alassane Ouattara, in power since 2010, submitted a new Constitution for referendum ostensibly to dispel the scourge of identity violence and pardoned former political and armed supporters of Gbagbo in 2018, including the latter's wife Simone Gbagbo, as a gesture towards reconciliation. Ouattara was elected for a third mandate in 2020, against the backdrop of an upsurge of violence. 'I am standing for elections against my will, not because I enjoy it. I am insulted even though I could have left with an aura credited in Africa and internationally. I value my aura, but should I abandon my country to those Ivorians who have dilapidated Côte d'Ivoire's wealth for decades?'[7]

Thus, Houphouët-Boigny's prediction proved true.

Yet – between 2012 and 2017, Côte d'Ivoire's insolent growth – an average 8 per cent yearly growth of real GDP coupled with 11 per cent economic growth – has earned the country the World Bank's seal of

[6] N Germain, M Amellal and C Caracena, 'Côte d'Ivoire: Laurent Gbagbo lance son nouveau parti et assure préparer la relève' 18 October 2021, www.france24.com/fr/émissions/journal-de-l-afrique/20211018-nouveau-parti-de-laurent-gbagbo-c-est-une-structure-pour-préparer-mon-retrait (accessed 27 April 2022).

[7] C Bensimon, 'Alassane Ouattara, candidat à un troisième mandat en Côte d'Ivoire: 'Je me présente contre ma volonté, ce n'est pas un plaisir" *Le Monde* 24 October 2020. My translation from French.

approval as one of the ten top reforming countries in the world (Akindès 2017). But Ouattara's 'cocoa OPEC' launched in 2018 to increase Côte d'Ivoire and Ghana's share of the cocoa bounty – which generates US$ 100 billion each year, of which a mere 6 per cent go to producing countries and only 2 per cent to farmers – also bears the ring of permanence.[8] The country's political and societal stability continues to hinge on gatekeeping politics over the rent of cocoa production.

On the 8-kilometre-long Avenue Valéry Giscard d'Estaing – which links Abidjan's business centre, the Plateau, to the city's port in the Treichville neighbourhood, outside of election periods when the avenue morphs into the 'boulevard of death' – in the words of the Ivorian singer Alpha Blondi – one can still enjoy a glass of cold beer or lukewarm red wine on the terrace of the bar-dancing *L'Étoile du Sud*.

Now rather dilapidated, divided in two, just like the country itself, by cinder blocks following a bloody inheritance dispute, the bar was the site of the historical deals that determined Côte d'Ivoire's post-independence relationship with the world economy. From the memory of these political foundational blocks remains a lingering and intoxicating smell: that of the cocoa beans transported on the Avenue to the freight port of Abidjan Terminal to be readied for export.

The bar was founded in 1930 to entertain local elites – the old wealthy families of Treichville – and was strategically facing the Plateau, the European neighbourhood. In 1944, it is at *L'Étoile du Sud* that the *Syndicat agricole africain* (African rural union) was created as the first structure that ostensibly promoted the rights of indigenous cocoa plantation owners against Europeans, with Houphouët-Boigny at its helm.

In 1946, it is also at *L'Étoile du Sud* that the PDCI was created – a party that would rule over Côte d'Ivoire for thirty-nine years. Among the thirty-four founders and eighteen members of the first executive office of the party featured two Corsican men, who as 'notorious Stalinists largely contributed to the drafting of the PDCI's statutes'.[9] With the onset of the Cold War, Houphouët-Boigny, deputy at the French National Assembly between 1945 and 1959 and minister of health under French president Charles de Gaulle, quickly distanced himself from the Communist stance of the RDA.

[8] B Mieu, 'Côte d'Ivoire-Ghana: bras de fer entre 'l'OPEP du cacao' et les négociants' *Jeune Afrique* 30 November 2020.

[9] C Bensimon, 'D'Houphouët à Ouattara, une tour d'ivoire en héritage' *Le Monde* 18 November 2020. My translation from French.

Of the Stalinist model of government, he did keep a pyramidal conception of power. '[T]he post-Independence nomenklatura [. . .] which rarely meets the wider population, except at the cross-roads of urban arteries, must be submitted, at the risk of losing its privileges; those heads that stand above the fray or express their ambitions too ostensibly must be eliminated'.[10] Above all, this conception of communism besuited his understanding of local politics 'where wealth goes to the chief who himself will redistribute it to the community'.[11]

The anti-colonial struggle was very brief in Côte d'Ivoire. Houphouët-Boigny acceded to power with the aura of the nation's father. He had acted as rapporteur and promoter of the 1946 law which abolished forced labour in French colonies. Houphouët-Boigny was trained at the William Ponty School in Gorée as a physician. He was the only Ivorian candidate hailing from a family of chiefs to this school designed for colonial auxiliaries – in a context of wider decay of the authority of traditional chiefdom. By 1936, he was also the wealthiest indigenous plantation owner of the colony.

The conversion of chiefs and colonial auxiliaries to the status of plantation owners was facilitated by the lumpiness of the colonial legislation on land ownership. Land capture benefitted from the progressive erosion of hierarchical relations between chiefs, lineage members and slaves. The boom of cocoa production – which jumped from 1,040 tons in 1913 to 50,000 tons in 1939 – was largely owed to indigenous plantation owners, with European planters accounting for a mere 10 per cent of production.[12]

Cocoa loomed large in Houphouët-Boigny's negotiation of the terms of independence with the former *métropole*. Between 1945 and 1960, the intensification of plantation production towards the west of the country fostered the expansion of migration flows – and with them, tensions between *autochthonous* and *allogenous* populations increasingly expressed through the platforms of the first Ivorian political parties. The aura of Houphouët-Boigny's party, the PDCI, stemmed both from his role in putting an end to forced labour and the party's affiliation to the RDA which held the promise of Pan-Africanism and the rights of African workers.

10 Ibid.

11 Ibid.

12 See Fonds Baulin, www.fonds-baulin.org/ouvrages/la-politique-interieure-d/ (accessed 2 May 2022).

But Houphouët-Boigny's agricultural union represented *big* plantation owners, predominantly from the east of the country – those, precisely, seen to be fostering land capture in the West due to migration flows (Bonnecase 2014). Houphouët-Boigny's symbolic coup lay in imposing the plantation class' rule and a societal stability that hinged on economic, societal and political collaboration with the former *métropole*. Embracing a political and economic strategy of development within the orbit of the former French Empire, Houphouët-Boigny welcomed the massive investment of French businesses and the political domination of cocoa *planteurs*, who rejected the indigenous intellectual elite trained at French universities. The first generation of diploma holders from French universities had to choose between imprisonment and access to high administrative functions (see Simonet 2010).

Politics and anthropological studies have tracked the intensely complex combination of variables that have characterised the conflict in Côte d'Ivoire that followed the death of Houphouët-Boigny as at once a 'second war of Independence' (Banégas and Marshall-Fratani 2003) and the violent expression of the crumbling of the 'enlightened' clientelist system engineered by Houphouët-Boigny, which, beyond funding the country's main infrastructures, involved redistributing the cocoa boon along tacit rules of political, categorial, regional and ethnic balance.[13]

Tensions between northerners and southerners found a particular echo in the west of the country, where most of Côte d'Ivoire's cocoa is cultivated, and degenerated into conflicts at the scale of the village (Chauveau and Bobo 2003). Rather than designating identifiably distinct social and ethnic groups, the categories of *autochthonous* populations as opposed to foreigners were the historical and combined result of colonial expansion and administration, and colonised populations' adaptive responses. *Autochthony* claims operated as discursive devices endowing, in specific historical conjunctures, an additional symbolic 'capital of autochthony' to one group against another, from which differentiated rights over land and access to the state ensued (Bonnecase 2014: 63).

In December 1998, a new legislation restricted land ownership to Ivorians and replaced Houphouët-Boigny's 1967 decree according to which 'the land belongs to he who cultivates it'. While ostensibly clarifying the rules pertaining to land property, the new piece of legislation could be claimed at once by then president Bédié's opponents as a device

[13] A Bednik, 'Tempête sur le cacao de Côte d'ivoire' *Le Monde diplomatique* May 2006.

protecting the regime's 'cocoa barons' or, on the side of the government, as an official recognition of customary rights over land and the authority of traditional chiefs (Chauveau 2000). As such, it reproduced the legal lumpiness foregrounding the French imperial 'frontier' economic strategy in the colony.

Guided by two principles – the colonial administration's monopoly over the delivery of land rights, subject to effective crop production – the French colonial administration's strategy aimed both at developing export crops towards the *métropole* and undermining the status of the populations of the colony's southern forest zones, construed as belligerent and ipso facto unproductive. In parallel, the colonial administration granted concession rights to European planters. Until the 1920s, migration flows into and within the colony originated predominantly from Asante and so-called *dioula* traders from the Muslim North, and Senegalese auxiliaries for the colonial administration. During the interwar period, the colonial administration endeavoured to implement a programme of economic valorisation of its sub-Saharan African colonies. While these plans did not, as such, foster farmers' initiatives, they did accelerate migration flows.

The 1912 forced labour legislation was liberally waged by both colonial administrators and local chiefs to counter migration flows towards the British Gold Coast – where living conditions were deemed better – and for the growth of cocoa plantations in the Southeast and, from the 1930s and 1940s, in the central and western regions of the colony. The colonial administration's shift from a policy of 'assimilation' to one of 'association' of colonised populations was reflected in the reinvention of customary rights to land, through the institution of an 'indigenous land title' in 1925.

Yet the phenomenon of *autochthony* was foremost emulated by the economic capital's elites in Abidjan at the end of the decade. The *Union fraternelle des originaires de Côte d'Ivoire* (Brotherly union of natives of Côte d'Ivoire), created in 1929 by indigenous plantation owners from the eastern part of the country, foregrounded resistance to foreigners on Ivorian soil both to vindicate a stake over the cocoa boon and a claim for access into the colonial administration for Ivorian auxiliaries. In turn, the Syndicat agricole de Côte d'Ivoire (Agricultural union of Côte d'Ivoire) created in 1937 originally joined European and indigenous plantation owners to pressure the colonial administration – in the context of the Popular Front in France and the 1930s economic crisis – to increase the export price of crops. The Syndicat agricole africain (African rural union) was created by Houphouët-Boigny in 1944 as an ostensibly indigenous structure, to promote the rights of indigenous plantation owners, this time against Europeans (see Bonnecase 2014).

6.2 Dismantling the 'Post-colonial Block'

Cocoa beans produced in Côte d'Ivoire are directly sourced at the country's two main ports at Abidjan and San Pedro by two global giants in the food trade – the Swiss-Belgian trader Barry Callebaut and the US firm Cargill. A little over 80 per cent of cocoa beans harvested in Côte d'Ivoire are exported from the country's two biggest ports, at San Pedro and Abidjan, to the main processing centres – the Netherlands and the US – which are also the core destinations for Ivorian cocoa. The remaining 20 per cent of beans are processed in Côte d'Ivoire, before being exported as cocoa liquor, butter and powder.

The successive political crises and violent conflicts in which Côte d'Ivoire was engulfed following Houphouët-Boigny's death – between 2002 and 2007 and in 2011 – did not alter the country's position as the world's largest producer of cocoa since 1960 – accounting for nearly 50 per cent of world production on average. Cocoa exports have constituted around 20 per cent of the country's GDP since Independence; they bring in 40 per cent of its customs revenues, while cocoa production continues to employ two thirds of the country's workforce.

The conflicts did bring to light the alteration of the parameters of the relationship between Côte d'Ivoire and global markets. These transformations, under way since the early 1980s, did not as such sever the political and military links with the former *métropole*. But they fostered a symbolic and practical displacement by granting IFIs and other multilateral donors the power to impose conditionalities in exchange for development aid and foreign investments. The first Lomé Convention, signed in 1975, between what was then the EEC and the Organisation of African, Caribbean and African (ACP) states, aimed in particular at compensating ACP countries for the shortfall in mineral and staples export earnings – such as cocoa – due to fluctuations in the prices of commodities exported or purchased on global markets. It also coincided with the accession of Britain to the EEC – which opened the preferential terms of access to the EEC market to several Commonwealth countries, including Ghana, the then prime exporter of cocoa beans.

Cocoa constituted the cornerstone of the so-called Ivorian 'miracle' which was sustained by high prices until the end of the 1970s. The cocoa boon enabled the state to reap huge benefits and ensure political stability through the CAISTAB (the *Caisse de stabilisation et de soutien des prix des productions agricoles*) which bought cocoa beans at fixed rates from producers, delivered authorisations to export traders and levied taxes. Positioned as the key intermediary between cocoa producers and global markets, the CAISTAB was effectively endowed with the task of maintaining the pyramidal structure of clientelist relations, which, trickling down from political elites to crop producers, secured the stability of societal relations until the turn of the 1980s.

This golden age did not last. Côte d'Ivoire was violently hit by the deregulation of cocoa and coffee markets in the 1980s, the entry into play of global trading conglomerates and emerging Asian competitors (Indonesia and Malaysia). When cocoa prices brutally plunged in 1985, Houphouët-Boigny launched a withholding scheme. He decided to boycott the world market, unless cocoa could be sold at the mandated price he had decreed. In parallel, he also continued paying 'the highest farm price in the world; at 65 cents a pound', which resulted in 'Ivory Coast [drawing] tons of smuggled beans over the border from Ghana and elsewhere'.[14] On the 1988–1989 crop alone, Ivory Coast lost over US$ 520 million. Ivorian banks were drawn to insolvency.

Unable to pay interest on its foreign debt, Ivory Coast arrears soared from US$ 500 million to US$ 2 billion. By 1989 the country's economy had collapsed. Houphouët-Boigny could do nothing but accept the last component of the structural adjustment programme: the liberalisation of the cocoa sector. The liberalisation of the cocoa sector in Côte d'Ivoire was effectively achieved in August 1999, with the dismantling of the CAISTAB, 'the black sheep of international financers'.[15] Coincidentally, four months later, the 'Christmas coup' of 24 December 1999 – the first since Côte d'Ivoire's independence – plunged the country into chaos.

The war only slightly affected cocoa production. 'Of course, the government used the cocoa money to buy weapons. Their only mistake is trying to hide it'.[16] The privatisation policies ushered in by IFIs from the 1980s also reinforced what Bayart (1993) calls the 'politics of the belly' by

[14] MA Hiltzik, '"Old Man" Loses Big: Cocoa Turns Bitter for Ivory Coast' *Los Angeles Times* 12 July 1989.

[15] A Bednik, 'Tempête sur le cacao de Côte d'ivoire' *Le Monde diplomatique* May 2006.

[16] See Global Witness, *Hot Chocolate: How Cocoa Fuelled the Conflict in Côte d'Ivoire* (Washington, DC, Global Witness Publishing Inc, 2007) 4.

consolidating the (political, financial and social) stakes of access and control over the cocoa rent.

The CAISTAB was replaced by a dizzying array of regulatory agencies – ostensibly tasked with the distinct mandates of development, regulation and control. A 2006 audit, funded by the European Commission at the behest of the IMF and the World Bank, to examine the effectiveness of the sector's reform, found that these agencies were not only based on dodgy legal grounds but were each siphoning a slice of the cocoa cake.[17]

The French lawyer co-author of the report was mysteriously kidnapped for three days in November 2004 – by what appeared to be members of Gbagbo's security detail – then in charge of the security of South Africa's president Thabo Mbeki during his bid at negotiating a peace deal between the two warring parties. The judicial information opened in Paris in 2004 – also focused on the disappearance of the French-Canadian journalist Guy-Henri Kieffer in 2006 who was investigating the cocoa sector – led to prison terms and fines against six members of Gbagbo's security detail. However, the trial was conducted in absentia – as all men, except one who died in the meantime, are still well and free in Côte d'Ivoire[18] – an embarrassing fact that may explain the lack of coverage of the sentencing in the French press. The annulment appeal introduced by three French NGOs, including the Fédération internationale pour les droits humains (FIDH) before the Ivorian Supreme Court against Ouattara's 2018 amnesty decree, is also unlikely to yield any results following Gbagbo's return on the Ivorian political scene.

In this 'shadow theatre', lawfare continues to be waged as a 'double discourse' (Dozon 1989), be it by Ivorian authorities, who can pit both economic performance and their powerlessness in the face of global markets; commentators, between the 'miracle' and the 'mirage' of economic growth; or by bilateral and multilateral donors, between deregulation of the cocoa sector and regulatory moves against domestic corruption, and imported deforestation.

[17] S Amiri and X Ghelber, *Étude diagnostic des organisations et des procédures de la filière café-cacao de Côte d'Ivoire* (contrat cadre, AMS/451 NNAGEL – 09ter/2004-ACP-DELCIV, May 2006).

[18] *L'Orient Le Jour*, 'Rapt d'un avocat français à Abidjan en 2004: peines de 2 à 6 ans ferme' 3 March 2017.

The chocolate industry has been under pressure for a few years to make the cocoa sector more sustainable. Several voluntary initiatives have emerged, including third-party voluntary standard certification schemes, companies' own programmes along with multistakeholder initiatives. In 2018, the governments of Côte d'Ivoire and Ghana sought to launch a 'Cocoa OPEC' – saluted by NGOs as the boldest move yet, as it aims at expanding cocoa growers' share of the final product.[19] The share of cocoa producers has reduced over the years as traders, brands and retailers have taken a bigger cut. When cocoa prices were high in the 1970s, cocoa accounted for up to 50 per cent of the value of a chocolate bar. This fell to 16 per cent in the 1980s, and today farmers receive around 6 per cent of the value. Côte d'Ivoire farmers make around US$ 0.78 a day.[20]

Together, Côte d'Ivoire and Ghana produce 70 per cent of the world's cocoa. That is a ratio matched by no petroleum-exporting country in the oil market. As of 2020–2021, the Ivorian Conseil du Café-Cacao (CCC) and the Ghana Cocoa Board (COCOBOD) started charging an extra fee of US$ 400 per ton of cocoa on top of the FOB (Free On Board) price[21] – an amount designed as a 'living income differential' (LID). This was to allow both states to set up a stabilisation fund and guarantee a fixed price of US$ 1820/MT to farmers.[22]

While IFIs were suspicious about the lack of transparency of the planned scheme, by 2021 it was already seen to be failing. To account for this turn, we need to return to Avenue Valéry Giscard d'Estaing in Abidjan, but this time go directly to the Abidjan freight terminal. Houphouët-Boigny's cocoa boycott at the end of the 1980s had left thousands of farmers unable to unload their crop. 'Because they could afford to hold raw beans in their warehouses indefinitely, French, and

[19] See https://fairtrade-advocacy.org/our-work/eu-policies/sustainable-cocoa/ (accessed 2 May 2022).

[20] ME Odijie, 'Why efforts by Côte d'Ivoire and Ghana to help cocoa farmers haven't worked' The Conversation 29 June 2021, https://theconversation.com/why-efforts-by-cote-divoire-and-ghana-to-help-cocoafarmers-havent-worked-162845 (accessed 29 April 2022).

[21] The FOB price (Free On Board price) of exports and imports of goods is the market value of the goods at the point of uniform valuation (the customs frontier of the economy from which they are exported).

[22] 'VOICE Network welcomes historic move to raise cocoa prices, questions remain on implementation', https://voicenetwork.cc/wp-content/uploads/2019/09/190905-VOICE-Position-on-West-African-Cocoa-Floor-Price.pdf (accessed 29 April 2022).

Lebanese traders swarmed into the villages'.[23] While rumours were reaching the capital that some unscrupulous middlemen were being slaughtered after having handed farmers valueless scraps of money for their crop, the boycott not only made global traders richer but also blew apart the economic component of what Houphouët-Boigny demurely called the symbiotic *Françafrique* relationship between Côte d'Ivoire and the former *métropole*.

Houphouët-Boigny's moves in 1988 to prop up the price of cocoa on global markets consolidated a displacement away from the *Françafrique* that was more than symbolic. With the assistance of the French government, Houphouët-Boigny had sought to hold 200,000 tons of cocoa beans off the market indefinitely through the French trading company Sucres et Denrées (Sucden). Financially strapped, Sucden dumped its cocoa on the market, depressing prices further. 'The Ivoirians were so incensed they gave a new sales contract to a Sucden competitor, US-based Phibro, a unit of the Salomon Bros. investment bank'.[24]

This consolidated the shift of the terms of the cocoa export trade between Côte d'Ivoire and world markets towards global traders and financial markets. In the decade to 2011, the world's largest oil, metal and agriculture trading houses – Vitol, Glencore and Cargill – enjoyed a combined net income of US$ 76.4 billion – ten times their profits in the 1990s. As recounted by Blas and Farchy (2022), 'of all the commodity trading houses [. . .] it is the agricultural traders whose business model has traditionally relied the most on speculation' (243). The reason is simple: contrary to oil extraction – concentrated in a handful of regions – food staple production is generated by thousands of producers. In Côte d'Ivoire, cocoa is produced by thousands of smallholders. The power of global traders therefore hinges on access to information on the evolution of *both* demand and supply. Cargill or Barry Callebaut could even more willingly salute the introduction of the LID by the governments of Côte d'Ivoire and Ghana that they could lean on ample studies demonstrating that the main factor in the pricing of cocoa is determined by supply and demand (Blas and Farchy 2022: 253). The US giant Hershey's, for example, which produces Smarties and KitKat on behalf of Nestlé, has

[23] MA Hiltzik, '"Old Man" Loses Big: Cocoa Turns Bitter for Ivory Coast' *Los Angeles Times* 12 July 1989.

[24] Ibid.

historically maintained its margins by reverberating higher costs of commodities on consumers – not producers.[25]

This also reflects global traders' leverage in defining *what* is included in the price of cocoa. The International Cocoa Organization (ICCO) was established as an intergovernmental organisation in 1973 under the auspices of the United Nations and operates, from its Abidjan seat, within the framework of successive International Cocoa Agreements to wager a 'sustainable world cocoa economy'. The organisation continues to critique the fact that cocoa market prices do not reflect the true cost or true price of cocoa production in that it does not include external costs – such as deforestation or the economic infrastructures in zones of production. But beyond claiming that to put an end to the vicious circle of over-supply and downgraded prices, poor, rural smallholders need to stop overproducing,[26] the argument holds little political and legal sway against global traders whose predominance hinges, precisely, on their position as prime *intermediaries* between Côte d'Ivoire cocoa producers and global markets.

6.3 Accountability Dumping

When global traders hit the news, it is more often than not because of some wrongdoing. Since 'the mid-2000s, Africa, in the traders' eyes, ha[s] become a place where the commodities that no one else want[s] [can] be disposed of. It [is] not just the supplier of last resort, but also a *buyer* of last resort. And for the least scrupulous, it [has become] a dumping ground' (Blas and Farchy 2022: 233, emphasis added), notably for toxic residues.

Locals might still recall the repulsive stench of rotten eggs that cloaked the city from the morning of 19 August 2006, when a battalion of trucks dumped 36.2 tons of coker naphtha – a highly toxic unrefined oil residue – in an open-air dump in the neighbourhood of Akouédo, a mere 5 kilometres away as the crow flies from Abidjan's business centre. The coker naphtha had been bought in December 2005 by Trafigura, the world's second-biggest oil and metals trader.

[25] F Goetz, 'La Côte d'Ivoire et le Ghana veulent créer une OPEP du cacao pour soutenir les planteurs' *Les Échos* 14 January 2020.

[26] C Fages, 'Le cacao est trop peu payé pour être durable, selon l'ICCO' *RFI* 26 February 2021.

Subjected to a process called caustic washing on board the *Probo Koala*, a ship registered in Panama, a tax haven, the refining of the fuel generated tons of hazardous waste. In July 2006, Trafigura attempted to deliver the waste in Amsterdam. When the price for treatment was increased upon finding that the waste was highly contaminated, Trafigura ordered it to be reloaded on the Probo Koala. In August 2006, after a failed attempt to unload in Nigeria, Trafigura contracted a local company which dumped the waste in Côte d'Ivoire, without receiving any treatment. A major medical emergency ensued, with tens of thousands of people reporting at local hospitals with headaches, vomiting, skin irritations and breathing problems, and at least sixteen deaths.[27]

What giant oil trader Trafigura demurely calls 'the *Probo Koala* incident' on its internet site – which involved the dumping of 528 m^3 of highly toxic oil residues ('slops') at seventeen or eighteen locations in Abidjan, including municipal dumpsites in 2005 – is described as 'a sad episode in the history of Trafigura', for which the company bears no responsibility. 'Although the dumping of the slops was carried out by a third-party, Trafigura sincerely regrets that it occurred'.[28]

Zooming in onto the development of the scandal into a judicial battle, from Abidjan to London and other European jurisdictions, provides a powerful entry point to trace the legal lumpiness produced by the intersection of outsourced and outlaw economy – but only at the condition of tracking the political, social and legal space carved out by global traders qua intermediaries.

As mentioned before, the history of the companies that have dominated the traded markets in oil, metals and crops over the past seventy-five years channels attention towards single corporate dynasties. As the world's second-largest oil and metals trader, Trafigura was set up by former Marc Rich + Co (now Glencore) employees in 1993.

Trafigura was originally focused on Latin America and Eastern Europe. 'Trafigura's foray into Africa [. . .] coincided with its ascent to the big leagues of commodity trading' (Blas and Farchy 2022: 234). Africa is still, predominantly, 'an "origination" business [as the origin of raw materials to world markets]. But by the mid-2000s, a new business

[27] Ivorian official records variously report fifteen to seventeen deaths; see Greenpeace and Amnesty International (2012: 58), *The Toxic Truth*.

[28] See Trafigura's website, www.trafigura.com/the-probo-koala-incident/ (accessed 2 May 2022).

emerged, a "destination" business' (Blas and Farchy 2022: 232) to dump hazardous waste, thanks to far less strict quality regulations than in the developed world.

After the outbreak of the medical emergency in Abidjan in August 2006, several individuals across Trafigura's hierarchical structure were charged and imprisoned to face proceedings before Ivorian courts for offenses relating to breaches of Ivorian public health and environmental laws, and breach of the 1989 Basel Convention on the Control of Transboundary Movements of Hazardous Wastes and Their Disposal: two Trafigura executives who had travelled to Abidjan to negotiate with the Ivorian authorities, including its president Claude Dauphin, the managing director of the Société Puma; the head of the Compagnie Tommy, the local company contracted to manage the waste; and other customs and ports officials. Ultimately, only these local companies' agents were convicted by the Tribunal de Première Instance d'Abidjan-Plateau.[29]

At the time, Côte d'Ivoire was still in the midst of the protracted civil war that had started in 2002 and had led to the de facto partition of the country in two, with a North controlled by the so-called *Forces nouvelles*, and a South, including Abidjan, held by forces loyal to then president Laurent Gbagbo. While the imprisonment of Dauphin certainly gave Gbagbo and his negotiators the upper hand, the settlement he negotiated with Trafigura in February 2007 granted the multinational substantive and broad-sweeping[30] immunity from prosecution in Côte d'Ivoire in return for a conditional fee agreement (CFA) compensation of 95 billion (€152 million) that, to date, has largely failed to deliver on its intended purpose to compensate the victims and clean up the contaminated zones.[31]

By then the *Probo Koala* disaster had already been built into a scandal through the involvement of other actors: the media, the environmental NGO Greenpeace and a cluster of European lawyers specialising in

[29] Salomon Ugborogbo, the head of *Compagnie Tommy* and Essoin Kouao, a shipping agent from West African International Business Services (WAIBS).

[30] With Trafigura identified under the broad sweeping terms of 'Trafigura Parties' to cover the whole corporate structure of the company.

[31] Including CFA 73 billion to compensate for the harm caused to the state of Côte d'Ivoire, and to the victims, and CFA 22 billion to treat the pollution caused by the waste. See 'Protocole d'accord entre Trafigura et l'État de Côte d'Ivoire' 13 February 2007, https://osibouake.org/?Dechets-toxiques-Trafigura (accessed 2 May 2022).

transnational litigation.[32] The case was sparked first by the activism and media savvy of Greenpeace. In September 2006, Greenpeace activists blockaded the *Probo Koala* at the Estonian port of Paldiski, and the NGO filed a report with the Dutch Public Prosecutor requesting a criminal investigation into the dumping.[33]

Involved early on, the British law firm Leigh Day used the fact that Trafigura's London office then housed the trader's oil trading business to obtain a Group Litigation Order with the High Court of Justice in London in November 2006. This enabled the firm to file a civil claim on behalf of thousands of Ivorian victims (ultimately 30,000) for civil damages for personal injury. To identify victims, Leigh Day mobilised the firm's links with Greenpeace which launched a media campaign in Côte d'Ivoire that same autumn.

The position of Leigh Day in Britain's legal field, and specifically the firm's senior partner Martyn Day, helps explain the opportunity for filing this claim in Britain. Martyn Day, like other transnational litigation lawyers involved in the Trafigura saga,[34] combines a set of resources – legal, political and militant – that have contributed to the growth in Europe of strategic transnational litigation against corporate crimes from the end of the 1990s. These resources enabled Leigh Day to embed politics and media clout in the litigation of the Trafigura case in London.

Described in the press as 'the scourge of the corporations',[35] Day was raised in Zimbabwe before he returned to the UK as a young adult, where he obtained a law degree from Warwick University and qualified as a barrister with Colombotti & Partners in 1981. A former Labour councillor, he helped draft *In Trust for Tomorrow*, the Labour Party's roadmap on the environment in 1994, whose key proposal was to encourage individuals to bring cases against polluting companies by scrapping the traditional 'loser pays' rules, under which an unsuccessful plaintiff had to

32 Greenpeace has been at the forefront of claims filed in Amsterdam, and published a report in 2012, along with Amnesty International, to 'set out the case against Trafigura'. See Greenpeace and Amnesty International (2012).

33 Ibid.

34 For example, William Bourdon, from the Paris Bar, who displays characteristics similar to that of Martyn Day – with a combination of resources across law, politics, economics and militancy. See his portrait in Chapter 7.

35 J Vidal, 'Lawyers Leigh Day: Troublemakers who are a thorn in the side of multinationals' *The Guardian* 1 August 2015.

pay the winner's costs as well as their own.[36] Day has also had a long-standing involvement with Greenpeace, as member of the board of the NGO, director of Greenpeace Environmental Trust and chairman of Greenpeace UK until 2008.

In 1981, Martyn Day first practised in the corporate firm Clifford & Co, before moving to Bindman & Partners, a firm set up in 1974 by a group of lawyers, including Sarah Leigh,[37] that gained prominence as a defender of civil liberties and human rights. Leigh Day, co-founded with Sarah Leigh in 1987 to specialise in international, environmental and product liability claims, pioneered in transnational litigation.

Particularly favourable opportunities within the British legal system – compared to other European jurisdictions – also help explain the development of a professional market for transnational litigation in the UK, notably the possibility to file group claims, and the opening of this jurisdiction for claims made on behalf of foreign victims for wrongdoings in foreign jurisdictions. Leigh Day thus obtained a reversal of the *forum non conveniens* doctrine[38] in the *Cape Gencor lawsuits* (*re-South Africa*).[39]

The British government's proactive public legal aid policy until the early 2000s also played a key role: 'taxpayer cash has helped put [the] firm on the map'.[40] In 1997, Leigh Day received £8.3 million from the Legal Aid Board. This contributed to position the firm as a key player in transnational litigation and to consolidate its strategy of promoting a low profile (defending 'the ordinary guy') in high-profile cases from the end of the 1990s, ranging from the humane and environmental wrongdoings of transnational corporations,[41] political cases involving the British

[36] N Gilbert, 'Profile: Martyn Day: Smoking out the tobacco giants' *The Independent* 10 May 1997.

[37] All then solicitors at Lawfords, a trade union firm in Gray's Inn. Bindman & Partners' original intent was to provide local residents eligible for legal aid with legal services in family law, immigration, personal injuries, housing, social welfare and crime.

[38] The *forum non conveniens* doctrine enabled British courts to decline jurisdiction on the ground that there is a court in another jurisdiction which is clearly a more suitable forum for the trial of the action, in the interests of all the parties and justice of the case.

[39] UK House of Lords: Judgments – Schalk Willem Burger Lubbe (Suing as Administrator of the Estate of Rachel Jacoba Lubbe) and 4 Others and Cape Plc. And Related Appeals, 20 July 2000 [House of Lords decision].

[40] N Gilbert, 'Profile: Martyn Day: Smoking out the tobacco giants' *The Independent* 10 May 1997.

[41] Starting with the first high-profile case against Gallaher & Imperial Tobacco on behalf of lung cancer victims in 1997; or, among other examples of group action claims against

Department of Defence and British troops in wars of decolonisation[42] to Britain's military involvement in Iraq from 2003.[43]

The funding of such claims became an issue with the downsizing of legal aid from the turn of the 2000s. Leigh Day's last application for public funding for a group claim failed in 2005. The firm's strategy to counter this trend, such as in the Trafigura case, has been to bring these claims under a conditional fee basis.[44] However, the amounts claimed by Leigh Day following the settlement of the case in 2009 contributed to prompting governmental plans to implement further cuts to legal aid and to restrict no win no fee agreements[45] – potentially imperilling future opportunities to file group actions against transnational corporations in the UK.

The termination of the judicial proceedings in London with an out-of-court settlement in September 2009 emerged as one of the multiple political and media twists in the development of the case. The settlement agreed between Trafigura and Leigh Day stated that the waste had only caused 'flu-like symptoms' and did not recognise the liability of the company. It also appeared as a last-minute deal, before the case was to be heard before the High Court in London, as parallel political, legal and media battles were unravelling. In May 2009, Trafigura sued (and won) a defamation case against the British Broadcasting Corporation (BBC). In autumn 2009, the Trafigura case also emerged as a test case for the new 'super injunctions' which started being filed in Britain in the 2000s to allow companies and individuals to prevent the publication not just of the substance of allegations involving them, but also of information on the existence of such allegations.

transnational corporations in the 2000s, the settlement secured in 2006 by Leigh Day on behalf of a group of Colombian farmers in a civil group action against BP.

42 For example, the group action against the British government on behalf of 5,228 former insurgents involved in the Mau Mau uprising in Kenya (the firm negotiated a settlement in 2010).

43 Day represented the family of Baha Mousa but faced (and succeeded in) a disciplinary prosecution before the Solicitors Disciplinary Tribunal launched by the defence secretary in 2014, regarding the firm's conduct in the Al-Sweady inquiry. Phil Shiner, one of Day's main competitors in human rights litigation, faced similar charges and his Public Interest Lawyers firm was dismantled in 2016.

44 A Conditional Fee Agreement (CFA) is a funding arrangement between a claimant and their lawyers where the solicitors agree to act on a 'no win, no fee' basis. Under the CFA, the legal counsel can claim a success fee, which is an agreed percentage over and above their normal costs.

45 O Bowcott, 'Impact of cuts to legal aid to come under review' *The Guardian* 31 October 2017.

While the super-injunction granted to Trafigura spurred a public outcry as it was essentially preventing a parliamentary hearing over the case, social media were leaking damning information demonstrating inside knowledge, within Trafigura, about the toxicity of the waste.[46] Yet Trafigura has consistently denied criminal liability for the damage created by the dumping of the waste in Abidjan. In 2010, a Dutch court did confirm the company's liability for the illegal export of waste from Europe, but it did not investigate events in Abidjan, the public prosecutor having decided that it would not be feasible to do so. Criminal charges were brought in Amsterdam against two relatively junior individuals, the tanker's captain and a London-based Trafigura employee. Both were fined and convicted with suspended prison sentences, while the oil trader was fined £1 million for concealing the dangerous nature of the waste when it was initially unloaded in Amsterdam. But the court ruled that the company's chief executive, Claude Dauphin, would not face personal charges; and the prosecution did not cover the events after the tanker left Amsterdam.

Attempts to date to file civil and criminal complaints in other European jurisdictions against Trafigura and its representatives have failed. These include a complaint brought in Amsterdam by Greenpeace in 2009 against the public prosecutor's decision not to prosecute Trafigura Beheer B.V. and Puma Energy, Trafigura chairman Claude Dauphin and other employees of the Trafigura Group for criminal offences related to the dumping in Côte d'Ivoire, as well as, more recently, attempts made by Amnesty International in the UK to get the Crown Prosecution Services and the Environment Agency to open investigations for criminal conspiracy against the company.[47]

In April 2010, two French NGOs, Robin des Bois and William Bourdon's Sherpa filed complaints against Estonia and the Netherlands before the European Commission, so that the cases would be referred to the European Court of Justice. Both complaints failed, the European Commission arguing in the first instance that Estonia did not have all the relevant information about the waste to take action; and in the second, that there were already criminal proceedings under way in

[46] See D Leigh, 'Revealed: Trafigura-commissioned report into dumped toxic waste' *The Guardian* 17 October 2009.

[47] Both public agencies responded that they lacked the expertise and the resources to investigate the oil trader for criminal prosecution: J Ball and H Davies, 'UK authorities "lack resources" to investigate Trafigura over toxic waste' *The Guardian* 23 July 2015.

Amsterdam.[48] An earlier complaint, filed in 2007 by French and Ivorian NGOs acting on behalf of Ivorian victims[49] against the two French Trafigura executives, Claude Dauphin and Jean-Pierre Valentini, before the Paris prosecutor, was also dismissed in 2008, with the prosecutor arguing this time that there was not a sufficient link with France.

The various variables – political, social, economic – at play in the development of the Trafigura case have contributed to shape a legal trail – or 'interlegality' (de Sousa Santos 1987) – across these national scales. Each nudge of the trail followed the structure of Trafigura as a multinational corporation, and opportunities, in each jurisdiction, to define legal entry points for litigation. Meanwhile, the case illustrates the messiness of the legal landscape in which the trader operates, to its benefit, with each national legal system yielding its own characteristic excesses and omissions (Greenhouse and Davis 2019).

Emblematically, Leigh Day was to oversee the distribution of the settlement moneys to the 30,000 victims, but shortly after the settlement was agreed, Martyn Day allegedly received a request to meet representatives of a senior Ivorian figure in Paris to agree to come to an 'arrangement' in 2009. This man, claiming to be the president of the National Coordination of Toxic Waste Victims of Côte d'Ivoire (Coordination Nationale des Victimes de Déchets Toxiques de Côte d'Ivoire (CNVDT-CI)), managed to get the funds frozen in a move backed by the Abidjan state prosecutor. The compensation money was transferred a few days later, to the account of Claude Gohourou, 'one of the dozens of people representing the communities affected by the toxic waste', and henceforth partly disappeared, along with Gohourou.[50]

The controversies sparked by the embezzlement of the bulk of the settlement money secured by Leigh Day also contributed to the implosion of the Trafigura litigation in Amsterdam, with the emergence of a dozen competing organisations claiming to represent Ivorian victims set up with the help of Dutch lawyers from 2009, and a counterclaim in 2011 by yet another victims' organisation against Leigh Day in London to recover the disappeared funds.

[48] Greenpeace and Amnesty International (2012: 168).

[49] The Legal Action Group of the FIDH, the French League for Human Rights, the Ivorian League of Human Rights and the Ivorian Movement for Human Rights (MIDH).

[50] X Rice, 'Fears over £30m payment to toxic waste victims in Trafigura case' *The Guardian* 22 January 2010.

The elusiveness of victims, with accusations of theft identity or 'fake victims' a constant in Trafigura's defence, has also been one of the arguments to disqualify the Ivorian state – both for its role in the *Probo Koala* disaster and as a valid forum to investigate the events. To be sure, 'the vulnerability of Ivory Coast officials to corruption formed part of the background to the original environmental disaster when the waste was dumped'.[51]

6.4 Conclusion

What happens when we shift the question to ask not *why*, but *how* the complex North–South collaboration producing law/lessness at the intersection of onshore and offshore capitalism is shaped and transformed? Certainly, the Trafigura case reads like a bifurcation of sovereignty, with the Ivorian state seemingly a mere shadow, either disqualified due to the inefficiency of local courts and authorities, or their corruption. But this bifurcation of sovereignty also applies to other states involved in the landscape of the case, foremost Britain, where the super-injunctions granted to Trafigura in the London proceedings in 2009 demonstrated the trader's political clout.

This contributes to blurring the connections between Trafigura as a global trader and the state – be it that of Côte d'Ivoire or Britain. Yet the case also constitutes a laboratory of transnational law's meandering in the conceptual and practical spaces left open between borderless capitalism and bordered states, with bifurcated sovereignty enabling both the mobility of capital and the dumping of transnational corporations' accountability across jurisdictions (Seabrooke and Wigan 2017).

Developments in the London side of the Trafigura saga underscored that 'behind Trafigura is a little-known but wealthy group of London oil traders, who have high-level connections in the Conservative party'.[52] Conversely, in Côte d'Ivoire, Trafigura is still conducting a thriving business, nimbly navigating the political transition, from war to peace in 2007, and from the regime of Laurent Gbagbo to that of his successor

[51] D Leigh, 'Corruption fears over Ivory Coast toxic waste victims' £30m Trafigura payout' *The Guardian* 4 November 2009.

[52] D Leigh, 'Inside Trafigura: accusations, sour deals and friends in high places' *The Guardian* 16 September 2009. In particular, Tory peer and former leader of the House of Lords Baron Strathclyde joined Trafigura as a non-executive director in 2013. He had previously stood down from the board of the group's hedge fund arm following the 2009 legal, media and political battles over the *Probo Koala* disaster in London.

Alassane Ouattara since 2010. A nephew of Ouattara, Ahamadou Touré, is now heading the subsidiary of Trafigura in the country, Puma Energy. 'Just like in Angola, where Trafigura holds the monopoly over the oil supply into the country based on close ties with the Presidency, Puma Energy relies in Côte d'Ivoire on ties with the family in power'.[53]

These interpersonal relations illustrate the small world of oil trading in London and Abidjan, and its straddling across business and political interests. However, more than simply pockets of corruptive practices, these ties are at once produced by imperial legacies, and transformed by the onshoring of offshore capitalism.

The 'real' post-colonial order that unfolded in Côte d'Ivoire, the jewel of the *Françafrique*, consolidated a practical and symbolic displacement from the '*ménage à deux*' of the post-colonial block, to a '*ménage à quatre*' involving reciprocal albeit unequal relationships between the state, IFIs, financial markets and global traders. The 'post-colonial block' represented Paris' attempt at creating a coherent political and economic framework between the *métropole* and its former African colonies. By contrast, by the early 1980s, the City's middling position as financial powerhouse for the onshoring of offshore capitalism was all the more efficient that it complemented the US position as middle power.[54]

The Trafigura scandal, though it exploded into a reputational issue for the corporation, did not threaten its existence. But there are signs that the tide may be turning for global traders. Since the 1970s, the French bank, BNP Paribas, has 'been the king of commodity trade finance, the life-blood of the whole industry' (Blas and Farchy 2022: 304). In 2014, the bank decided to stop doing business with Trafigura. Why? Due to an 'aggressive and unpredictable policeman in town: the US government' (Blas and Farchy 2022: 305). BNP Paribas had just admitted liability to violating US sanctions against Cuba, Sudan and Iran and agreed to pay nearly US$ 9 billion to the US government. The bank had made loans to Trafigura to sell oil to Cuba, in US dollars that had to be routed through the US financial system (Blas and Farchy 2022: 306). Washington threatened to block access to the US dollar system to the bank for a year. The problem for Trafigura was that BNP Paribas was not just its largest financier but a 'trendsetter for the mostly European banks that financed the commodity traders' (Blas and Farchy 2022: 307).

[53] J Tilouine, 'Probo Koala: drame écologique et bonnes affaires' *Le Monde* 19 August 2018. My translation from French.

[54] See Chapter 4.

Trafigura managed to keep its other bankers and survived. It also relocated its headquarters in Singapore and its main offices in secrecy jurisdictions and tax havens, Geneva, Houston, Montevideo and Mumbai – away from the sway of the FCPA and the EU regulatory framework. However, the deployment of the FCPA could potentially position every bank around the world as an extension of US law enforcement. The biggest threat to commodity traders – though – comes from China, with Beijing increasingly pushing to build its own commodity trading capability and positioned as the only superpower able to bypass US regulators (Blas and Farchy 2022: 320).

7

Paris

The 'Africa' Corporate Bar: Imperial Revivals and Neoliberalism

How has the neoliberal turn changed gatekeeping politics between Paris and its former African colonies? To respond to this interrogation, Vauchez and France (2020) provide a powerful starting point. Their core thesis is that the neoliberal turn in the 1980s has produced a *blurring* between the private sphere and public interests that is negotiated and sustained by the 'hands-down champions in this new cross-border game: its experts – namely, corporate lawyers' (Vauchez and France 2020: 8). In France, the historical distancing of the bar from business helped position Paris as a 'beachhead' that facilitated the expansion of the Wall Street model of the multinational corporate law firm into continental Europe.

The process of financial deregulation that began in the late 1970s, with the removal of government rules controlling the way that banks and other financial organisations operate, went hand in hand with a legal 'Big Bang' (Dezalay Y 1992).

The wave of corporate reorganisations, the opening of new markets (like the Single Market for Europe) and the internationalisation and globalisation of deregulated financial markets fostered a 'Big Bang' on legal markets in Europe (Dezalay Y 1992). Thirty years ago, Big Law was a US phenomenon. In 2015, just four of the ten largest law firms were US based.

Financial deregulation and the expansion of the Wall Street model of the corporate law firm are both global phenomena, but the second has a distinct US flavour. Financial deregulation induces the competition between legal systems – allowing business actors to 'forum shop' according to regulatory or fiscal advantages. But the financial-legal expertise on futures, swaps, derivatives, options enabling financialisation and forum-shopping is not only law made in the US; it is also reflective of the structural straddling position of Wall Street lawyers across business and politics, and the prominence of the Wall Street model of the corporate law firm – which combines regulatory *know-who* and legal and financial *know-how* – as an engine of deregulation of finance and redeployment of the regulatory state in the neoliberal turn.

Where Vauchez and France's (2020) thesis falls slightly short, however, is in tracking the transformation of the position of *Paris* itself – structurally and symbolically – in these changes: as a former *métropole* and as the beachhead of the globalisation of corporate law into Europe, and now Africa. There have been ample studies on the close articulation between the progressive penetration of new public management and the repositioning of the state as regulator, be it through domestic legislation or externally induced structural adjustment programs. But the role played by corporate lawyers in producing these public–private transactions in the shadow of the regulatory state – be it in France or in its former African colonies – largely remains a blind spot.

The close-knit marketplace of intermediaries negotiating deals between Francophone resource-rich African states and French statesmen and business actors has long been derided as an 'Africa club' made up of 'White marabouts in black robes' (see Péan 2011) – an outgrowth of the *Françafrique*, the interpersonal shadow networks that have reproduced gatekeeping politics between France and its former African colonies following independence.

'It's a White's business',[1] scattily responded a consultant specialising in the economics of extractive contracts when I asked him *how* these negotiations were conducted. Positioned on the fringe of a professional market dominated by corporate lawyers, this informant still described a powerful – albeit symbolical – shift: 'there are the bag (cash) carriers; the incompetent; the competent who know how to carry bags; the competent who know how to manage equity portfolios; and then the competent who combine the *know-who* of relational capital and the *know-how* of contract economics'.[2]

To be sure, this 'Africa club' continues to be dominated by a cluster of predominantly *male*, *white* and *French* lawyers – but with a twist: they generally operate within the Paris offices of US and UK multinational corporate law firms. Though still exclusive, this professional market has

[1] Author's interview with Marc, consultant in contract economics, Paris, 2 July 2015. Unless respondents are public figures, I have used pseudonyms. Unless otherwise indicated, I have translated all interview quotes from French.

[2] Ibid.

enlarged in the past fifteen years to about fifty corporate lawyers, including a cluster who head 'Africa' offices within the Paris branches of UK and US multinational corporate law firms. Foremost, it is now self-defined by the requirements of transparency, corporate social responsibility, prior free, express and informed consent of local populations and development through 'public–private' partnerships.

To put it bluntly: the assertion by corporate lawyers operating within the Paris corporate bar that they are servicing the public good resonates with Vauchez and France's findings – while ringing a sour bell of 'same same, but different'. Is Paris, just like in the 1980s, a 'beachhead' – this time for a US-led corporate legal globalisation thrust into Africa – or is it a symbolic marketplace for the renegotiation of the continent's relationship with global markets? And if so, on what terms? In France, the neoliberal turn certainly fostered the prominence of corporate lawyers as key intermediaries between the state and the market. But it was also deployed by building on the *system* of the *Françafrique* which fostered the reciprocal assimilation of French and post-independence African elites. Due to the historical distancing of the Paris bar from business, French corporate law pioneers contributed to the expansion of a French corporate bar under the double thrust of the European Common Market and the Wall Street model of the corporate law firm. It is also as intermediaries or competitors of US multinational corporate law firms that they entered the former French *pré carré* in Africa qua a legal market.

7.1 From Françafrique.inc to Public–Private Gatekeeping

On 27 September 2007, the Lebanese French lawyer Robert Bourgi was bestowed the Legion of Honour by President Sarkozy in the presence of the representatives and diplomats of West and Central African states known to have covertly funded his greatest political rival – Jacques Chirac.

The ceremony took place two months after Sarkozy's discourse in Dakar during which the French president lamented that 'Africans have not fully entered history [. . .]. They have never really launched themselves into the future'.[3] The son of Mahmoud Bourgi – a wealthy Lebanese trader in Dakar and a close friend of Jacques Foccart, Général

[3] *Le Monde*, 'Le discours de Dakar de Nicolas Sarkozy. L'intégralité du discours du président de la République, prononcé le 26 juillet 2007' *Le Monde* 9 November 2007. My translation from French.

de Gaulle's shadow counsellor and architect of the *Françafrique* – Bourgi was an intimate of Gabon's Omar Bongo (whom he referred to as 'daddy'). Bourgi's 'confessions' in 2011 to the journalist Péan (2011) and before a French court revealed the regular exchange of large quantities of cash between French and African dignitaries (Arfi 2021: 880–881). Abdoulaye Wade, Blaise Compaoré, Laurent Gbagbo, Denis Sassou-Nguesso and Omar Bongo allegedly provided 9.5 million Euros to fund the French 2002 presidential election.[4]

'I know, dear Robert', commended Sarkozy in 2007, 'that I can count on you to serve France's foreign affairs with efficiency and discretion [. . .] and that you will not forget the advice of the man [Jacques Foccart] who once told you to "stay in the shadow to avoid sunburns"' (quoted in Borrel et al. 2021: 639, my translation from French). After studying law in France and completing a doctorate on '[t]he Général de Gaulle and Black Africa', Bourgis wrote to Foccart to find a professional situation. At the time, he was a *coopérant*[5] teaching law in the universities of Cotonou, Nouakchott and Abidjan. At the University of Abidjan, he met Laurent Gbagbo, then a history professor. Foccart introduced Bourgi to France's key political ally in West Africa – Félix Houphouët-Boigny, the inventor of the idea of *Françafrique*, and to Jacques Chirac, who had just founded (in 1976) the *Rassemblement pour la République*.

Upon his death in 1997, Foccart had left no official successor. At his funeral, while Bourgi collapsed in grief over the disappearance of his 'second daddy', then president Chirac hugged him and invited him to 'initiate' his Foreign Affairs minister, de Villepin, to 'Africa'.[6] 'I am not an advisor. Rather, I am a *missus dominicius* ("envoy of the ruler")', specified Bourgi, adding wittingly, '[M]y wife Catherine is the one who handles cases and pleads before the court. I bring her the cases. Besides, I only wore the lawyer's robe once, the day I was sworn in'.[7]

[4] S Abba, 'Grâce à Robert Bourgi, le djembé suscite la vigilance des douaniers français' *Le Monde* 15 December 2016.

[5] The Cooperation Ministry was created in 1959 with the objective of contributing to the development of former colonies through technical aid and military assistance. It was incorporated in the Ministry of Foreign Affairs in 1999. The word '*coopérant*' referred to agents deployed by the ministry and/or individuals voluntarily opting for civilian service in former colonies instead of military service.

[6] R Bacqué, 'Robert Bourgi, vétéran de la Françafrique' *Le Monde* 30 August 2009. My translation.

[7] Ibid.

'Africa has remained for over sixty years – and still is – a playing field for intermediaries, whose shadow has been cast in numerous judicial scandals in France – which hit the headlines' (Arfi 2021: 879, my translation from French) but are usually dismissed by courts – either due to lack of evidence or due to the death of key witnesses. In the past twenty years, the *Françafrique* has continuously been hailed dead albeit embarrassingly present – to use Borrel et al.'s image (2021: 9), like the couple of Ionesco's play *Amédée ou Comment s'en débarrasser* (1954), whose denial of the corpse lying next door renders the latter's presence increasingly invasive.

However, as Borrel et al. (2021: 13–14) also argue, reducing the sulphurous and overbearing legacy of the *Françafrique* to the shadow dealings of Jacques Foccart and his extensive networks within the French political right and France's former African colonies obfuscates the *system* which his intermediation role, just like that of Bourgi, contributed to shape and reproduce. Indeed, no sooner was Alexandre Benalla dismissed as President Macron's shadow advisor over the summer 2018 – following revelations that he had beaten up demonstrators during the 1st of May march – did he travel to London to meet with Ziad Takieddine, the intermediary at the core of the 'Karachi affair'.[8]

The resilience of these interpersonal shadow networks is remarkable given the structural revolution that the neoliberal turn ushered in over the French field of state power and legal field from the beginning of the 1980s.

The French regulatory state that emerged from the 1980s was certainly redeployed as umpire of the market. However, despite its embeddedness in a string of European regulatory constraints, the neoliberal turn also fostered the expansion of an intermediary space across the public sphere and private interests that developed not so much *against* state encroachments, but in symbiosis with the redeployment of the state, through an imbrication and co-dependency between the public sector and private economic actors (Vauchez and France 2020).

The neoliberal turn and financialisation of the global economy contributed to an *aggiornamento* of the legal profession[9] – specifically the corporate bar – that mapped onto both the expansion of a 'private

[8] The Karachi affair was a major military scandal that emerged during the second term of Prime Minister Benazir Bhutto, involving the presidencies of Mitterrand and Chirac in 1992–1997. The scandal involved the payment of massive commissions between France and Pakistan over the negotiations to acquire submarines.

[9] This *aggiornamento* was facilitated by the deregulation of the French legal profession in 1990.

business of public affairs', and the redeployment of the state through the public regulation of business. The figure of the 'corporate lawyer' therefore emerged in the shadow of the state.

Far from a return of the *République des avocats* of the late nineteenth century – when the legal profession and law universities were the main breeding grounds for the emerging Republican elite – this *corporate* bar displays an interest in *producing* the state, but from its position within the legal field, outside formal state institutions. Yet while the "public fabric of private markets' profoundly modified the structure of economic competition [. . .] the major economic and financial operations of corporations [. . .] are now also largely legal battles, conducted simultaneously before a variety of public institutions' (Vauchez and France 2020: 25–26). While the reach of the regulatory state has become a central stake of economic competition, 'the proximity between corporate law firms and political, administrative, and judicial authorities has become a prime field for competition between firms, [which] have developed full-blown strategies to build a reputation of "public-ness"' (Vauchez and France 2020: 34).

More than a circulation enabling proximity with the political field, meanwhile, the symbolic capital of 'publicness' is itself reinvested and renegotiated by the French core bank of symbolic credit: the Conseil d'État. Repositioned as umpire of the competing interests circulating within this public–private sphere, the Conseil d'État itself institutionalises the circulation of civil servants, by homologating their departure into the private sphere not simply as '*pantouflage*',[10] but as a *private* defence of *public* interests.

Yet the reciprocal flow of civil servants and politicians towards the business sphere does not simply serve to leverage access to public regulators. It also builds out of the *system* of the *Françafrique*. This system certainly continues to be partially based on what Weber called charismatic authority – derived from a core resource: relational capital. Emblematically, Michel Roussin, former cabinet director of Jacques Chirac and cooperation minister under the Balladur government was later elected president of the 'Africa committee' of MEDEF International[11] before lending his portfolio of contacts in Africa to the Bolloré group and EDF (Electricité de France), the French transnational

[10] The French equivalent of revolving doors from the public sphere to the private sector.

[11] The international branch of the French business federation, the Mouvement des Entreprises de France (MEDEF).

electric utility company. The close and long-standing links between diplomats, political elites and big businesses contribute to this formidable mix. Meanwhile, 'defectors' from public administrative positions 'switch from one "world" to the other, all the better to maintain the *status quo* within a new context' (Blamangin and Borrel 2021: 742, my translation from French).

But this system is also *structurally* embedded in the political, military, legal and foremost social negotiations of the independence of France's former African colonies, which fostered the reciprocal assimilation of French and post-independence African elites (Bayart 1993).

Characteristically, the OHADA is promoted as a French foreign policy 'success' by the Conseil d'État (Borrel 2021: 744). In a 2001 report, the Conseil d'État acknowledged that 'controlling applicable legal norms is nowadays often the best way to acquire market shares' (quoted by Borell 2021: 745, my translation from French).

The OHADA project was endorsed at the 1992 French African summit in Libreville, which appointed a board of three lawyers to sponsor it. The Senegalese Kéba Mbaye had the impeccable credentials of a 'gentlemen politician of law' (Sacriste and Vauchez 2007) as member of the Institut de Droit International (Institute of International Law), president of the UN International Commission of Jurists (1977–1985), vice president of the International Olympic Committee (1988–1992), vice president of the ICJ (1987–1991) and honorary Chief Justice of the Supreme Court of Senegal from 1964 to 1982. The two other members of this committee, both French lawyers, were Michel Gentot, a member of the Conseil d'État, and Martin Kirsch, Counsellor at the French Cour de Cassation and former advisor on Africa of President d'Estaing (1980–1981).

Certainly, the structural embeddedness of France's legal big bang in the social and political networks linking Paris to its former colonies does not escape the sulphurous image of the *Françafrique*. When I asked the contract economics consultant *who* was sitting at the table of negotiation of extractive contracts between resource-rich former French colonies in sub-Saharan Africa and multinationals, he used the imagery of the Western. 'It's the Good, the Bad and the Ugly. The Good is the World Bank, the Bad is the African civil servant. The Ugly. It's always the same people: the corporate lawyer'.[12] As caustic as it sounded, this depiction also pointed to more than a symbolic shift: the displacement of the

[12] Author's interview with Marc, consultant in contract economics, Paris, 2 July 2015.

Françafrique one-on-one relationship towards a '*ménage à trois*' – between corporations, states (whether resource-rich or clients) and IFIs.

The trajectory of a prominent member of the Bar in Paris illustrates this symbolic shift.

> My specialty now is crisis management. Today, there is not one single country that is immune from the risk of a coup. The risk is not only jurisdictional. It is also reputational. The new generation [of corporate lawyers], they don't really know Africa. They will never be 'real' Africans. This does not mean they don't do good work. But I would like to see them in a crisis situation [. . .]. Crisis management: it starts with me. In 95% of cases, the dispute is solved through settlement, especially in Africa [. . .]. At some point, you need to stand straight, respectfully, and return to the law.[13]

This corporate lawyer started as an associate in 1998 at the Paris office of the UK multinational corporate law firm Herbert Smith Freehills, where he developed the firm's Africa practice, predominantly in the energy and mining sectors from the early 2000s. He was also the mentor of the bulk of a new generation of corporate lawyers specialising in contract negotiations between African states and multinationals, who operate predominantly from the Paris offices of UK and US multinational corporate law firms.

After completing a law degree in France, Antoine left for Vanuatu as a 'conscientious objector',[14] where he was appointed public prosecutor at the country's independence in 1980. He then studied international law in Australia, 'a rare vocation' at the time. After working at the Crédit du Nord for two years in financing, he moved to Gabon, as an associate at Fidafrica, the legal branch of PricewaterhouseCoopers (PwC), where he worked until 1998. It is in this capacity that he became the counsel of Samuel Dossou Aworet – Gabon's 'Mr. Oil'.

> I was asked to negotiate a deal between the Arco company and Gabon's Mr Oil. But I had no knowledge of the law applicable to oil contracts. [Dossou] was present at this first meeting. He could have discredited me, and my career would have been over. Instead, after the meeting he invited me to come see him so that he could explain what an oil contract is about. After that, I never left him.

[13] Author's interview with Antoine, partner, Herbert Smith Freehills, Paris, 4 July 2015. Subsequent quotes are derived from the same interview.

[14] This was the technical alternative to the military service.

The conversion of this 'White African' into a champion of the 'social responsibility of corporations' can be partly explained by external shocks that have contributed to positioning *contracts* – and with them corporate lawyers – as the privileged intermediaries for the codification of the relationship between resource-rich African states and multinationals.

The Enron scandal in 2002[15] exposed the conflicts of interest of accountancy firms like PwC, until then the most widely pre-positioned in former French colonies to provide legal advice to corporations without an imperial past. For their part, French major state corporations, like Elf, leaned on in-house counsels.

For example, Jean, a lawyer who worked for forty years at Cleary Gottlieb Steen & Hamilton, recounted the profile of the lawyers operating on the other side, that of the newly independent Algerian state. He started at the firm in the early 1970s in the context of the nationalisation of Elf's interests in Algeria. A French lawyer operating within the Brussels office of Cleary was tasked with drafting the turnkey contracts demanded by the Algerian government – which rested on the quid pro quo of retaining French interests on the condition that locals be trained as engineers. 'These contracts never worked. It was too early. The political context was too strained [. . .]. Yet they [the Algerian government] specifically wanted a French lawyer'.[16] Jean himself started what he called his 'African history' in Congo-Brazzaville by accident. 'There was an engineers' firm exploring oil deposits at the Pointe noire. Things were going badly. One day they received a document in English that they were unable to read. They contacted our Brussels office and the case landed in my hands'.[17]

Coupled with the liberalisation of the French economy, the structural adjustment programs imposed on resource-rich African states contributed to carving out this professional market. Many lawyers who entered the 'Africa club' in the 1980s got their introduction to the continent by working on sovereign debt restructuring. In turn, the globalisation and financialisation of extractive value chains have increased the technicity and autonomy of the law produced by and for extractive contracts as a *Lex extractiva* – while increasing the financial and reputational risks for

[15] 'Attack of the Bean Counters' *The Economist* 19 March 2015.

[16] Authors' interview with Jean, partner, Cleary Gottlieb Steen & Hamilton, Paris, 29 April 2015.

[17] Ibid.

foreign corporations – be they challenges to extractive contracts, such as national fiscal policies of 'upwards adjustments' (so-called 'resource nationalism') or jurisdictional contests.

As external shocks, these changes have certainly contributed to the dominance of multinational corporate law firms, which thanks to their collective *know-how*, are better positioned than solo practitioners to provide the whole gamut of legal services and adapt to market changes, from negotiation to arbitration.

These external shocks also fostered generational changes. Regulatory endeavours to 'level the playing field' between foreign corporations and African states, such as the G7 'Connex initiative' and the African Legal Support Facility – established in 2010 in Abidjan under the joint sponsorship of the INGO Transparency International, the African Development Bank and the World Bank – ostensibly aim to reinforce the legal expertise of resource-rich African states. Just like the first generation of post–World War II traders – like Marc Rich[18] – who leaned on extensive interpersonal networks to access information and evade regulatory constraints, the first generation of extractive contract negotiators mobilised their social capital to – as Antoine summed it – deal with any situation like 'emergency doctors'.[19] As another French lawyer, Jean, explained:

> [t]he Congo Brazzaville became my history. My name has been linked to that country's history for forty years. I did everything for them. Nationalisations. Privatisations. I was traveling to the Congo once a month. [. . .] But there has been a diversification of legal services from the 1980s [. . .]. Then came the requests for proposals, via the World Bank [which opened a tender's market]. The position of the legal advisor has changed. We have become a *commodity*.[20]

7.2 Between *Courtroom* and *Corridor* Politics

Yet it is impossible to understand the conversion of Antoine the 'White African' or what Jean described as a demotion – from the *know-who* of interpersonal networks to a highly competitive market of tenders – without considering two other connected dynamics: the structuration

[18] See Chapter 4.
[19] Author's interview with Antoine, partner, Herbert Smith Freehills, Paris, 4 July 2015.
[20] Authors' interview with Jean, partner, Cleary Gottlieb Steen & Hamilton, Paris, 29 April 2015. Emphasis added.

of the corporate Bar in Paris, and the (social, political, economic) threads of relations between France and its former African colonies.

The profile of William Bourdon provides an emblematic entry point – albeit as a limit case that exposes the segmentation of the French legal field across three poles – a massive low bar of generalist solo practitioners, a small political bar of tenors who endorse political causes – be they victims of white-collar crimes or a political clientele – and the corporate bar described by Vauchez and France (2020) as an 'interstitial space' sitting astride the regulatory state and the corporate sphere.

The former head of the NGO Sherpa created in Paris in 2001 to 'protect and defend victims of economic crimes',[21] Bourdon is a prominent advocate of the criminalisation of white-collar crimes. He became known for the amicable settlement he negotiated in 2005 on behalf of eight Burmese who had filed a complaint against the French firm Total for forced labour. More recently, he endorsed the cause of whistleblowers as the lawyer of Antoine Deltour, the alleged source of part of the Lux Leaks scandal, Edward Snowden, Hervé Falciani (ex-HSBC) and Stéphanie Gibaud (ex-UBS).

Bourdon was also vice secretary general (1994–1995) and secretary general (1995–2000) of the French human rights NGO International Federation for Human Rights (FIDH). In this capacity, he was one of the vocal proponents of the campaign for the ICC throughout the 1990s. He initiated, on behalf of the FIDH, the complaint for crimes against humanity filed against Chad former dictator Hissène Habré in Senegal in 2000, which triggered a wave of universal jurisdiction complaints against former African heads of state (Seroussi 2008). He was also one of the drivers of several complaints before French courts against sitting and former African heads of state for their 'ill-gotten wealth' ('*biens mal acquis*').

But Bourdon is also the counsel of private corporations – even though his prominence as a human rights advocate drove some of his corporate clientele away. 'I think they are wrong in thinking that being a cause lawyer prevents me from having a cynical and manipulative side. I can be as cynical as they are'.[22] On the contrary, he described his legal practice as 'a constant juxtaposition'.

[21] See the website of Sherpa, www.asso-sherpa.org/accueil (accessed 22 May 2024).

[22] Author's interview with William Bourdon, a lawyer at the Bar of Paris, Paris, 12 December 2012.

> My associate once scowled at me. Birman refugees had fallen asleep in the waiting room in the lotus position while we were expecting a CAC 40[23] client. We quickly moved them to the office of another collaborator. It did not look quite right with a guy coming in in an Armani suit. It's always been like that, this juxtaposition, this medley between the powerful and the wretched of the earth. But all this is very fluid.[24]

Bourdon's capacity of circulation leans on his own background and trajectory as the grandson of the engineer in chief at Michelin, and the great-grandson of one of the founders of the corporation, which grew as a tyre giant out of rubber plantations in the French colony of Cochinchine (current Vietnam). Originally aiming for a diplomatic career, Bourdon ended up studying law. He was called to the Paris Bar in 1980. He started his career by interning with two tenors of the Paris Bar: Philippe Lemaire, a criminal lawyer and one of the proponents of the abolition of the death penalty in the 1970s, and Marc Barbé. The latter had founded one of the first French corporate law firms in Paris in the early 1970s, BCTG et Associés, with a portfolio of powerful corporate clients built up by Barbé while at Stephenson Harwood in London (Nike, Cadbury, etc.). Bourdon then set up his own law firms in the mid-1980s.

This juxtaposition certainly also reflects a capacity to accommodate diverging interests. As Bourdon noted, 'the posture of denunciation and indignation is not a competency in and of itself [...]. You need a qualitative *plus* to gain credibility [with corporate actors]'. But it is also exceptional in a French legal field structured around a sustained hiatus between *courtroom* and *corridor* politics that largely reflects colonial legacies.

As I noted in Chapter 3, the 'political trials' waged against political activists in French colonies in the late 1940s through the 1950s in Madagascar, Côte d'Ivoire, French Cameroon (Terretta 2015) and foremost Algeria (Elbaz 2003) promoted the *courtroom* – and with it, political lawyers from the Paris Bar – as an arena for political struggles.

These trials initiated judicial 'disruption' ('*stratégie de rupture*') as a political strategy deployed domestically by French NGOs to mobilise the 'tribunal of public opinion' against the state. The Algerian War fostered the reawakening of the French 'old lady' (Madsen 2004: 101) of human rights organisations, the Ligue des droits de l'Homme et du citoyen

[23] The benchmark French stock market index.

[24] Author's interview with William Bourdon, a lawyer at the Bar of Paris, Paris, 12 December 2012.

(Human Rights League – LDH) through its international branch, the FIDH. The practices of the FIDH were embedded in a wider process of building Paris as a 'bar without borders' (Madsen 2004: 101) by leaning on professional legal expertise and a moral platform largely derived from colonial missionary ideals.

Though including the word 'international' in its logo, the FIDH has remained largely Franco-French; likewise, the Comité Catholique contre la Faim et pour le Développement (CCFD-Terre Solidaire), one of the drivers of the complaints for the 'ill-gotten wealth' ('*biens mal acquis*') against African heads of state built out of French missionary colonial networks on the African continent. Relying on the principle of 'horizontal catholicity' (*catholicité horizontale*), the organisation fostered a conception of '*Tiers-mondism*' based on the idea of a social debt of the French *métropole* in relation to its former African colonies *and* support for wars of liberation (Mabille 2001).

On the other side of this ideological Cold War divide, the human rights NGO Amnesty International had devised a non-aligned type of engagement of the 'tribunal of public opinion' by defending simultaneously political opponents from the East, the West and the South. Nonetheless, the Paris Office of the International Secretariat of Amnesty International was set up in 1978 precisely to accommodate the enduring links between Francophone African political elites and the former *métropole*, and the position of the French capital as a harbour for political opponents. Amnesty was therefore de facto involved in dynamics of 'reciprocal assimilations of elites' (Bayart 1993) whereby West African political elites would be, in turn, defended as opponents or denounced, once in power, for their human rights violations by the organisation (Dezalay S 2007).

These developments promoted lawyers as 'heirs to a quasi-aristocratic conception of their role emphasizing disinterested detachment and noble vocation' (Vauchez and France 2020: 18) though in a confined setting, that of the *courtroom*. Following World War II, the creation of the *École nationale d'administration* (ENA) along with other *grands corps* designed to build a modernist state elite had signed the demise of the '*République des avocats*' (Willemez 1999).

'In this context, the little group of practitioners who in the 1960s popularized the notion of *avocats d'affaires*, that is the most internationalized segments of the Paris bar [. . .] were in many ways heretical figures' (Vauchez and France 2020: 18). In the 1950s, there were only a handful of corporate law firms. The growth of a corporate legal market in France, foremost in Paris, followed the drive of these pioneers, in the context of the emergence of the European economic market.

One of these pioneers was Jeantet. This corporate law firm was founded in 1922 by Pierre Lepaulle, the first Frenchman to obtain the *Scientiae Juridicae Doctoris* at Harvard. Lepaul was joined by Fernand-Charles Jeantet after World War II, himself a law professor at Harvard and a specialist of competition law. In the framework of the Marshall Plan, the firm played an instrumental role to foster the implantation of US corporate law firms in Europe and to develop European community law by leaning on the characteristic double-hatting of partners at Jeantet as both practitioners and law professors.

Similarly, one of the founders of Gide Loyrette Nouel, Pierre Gide, was called to the bars of Paris and London in 1920 and continued practising in Paris during the occupation of France by Nazi Germany. 'US authorities had decided not to interfere in the Vichy government's affairs. They were looking for intermediaries in France. [Gide] worked on different cases at their behest not only to foster US interests, like those of Coca-Cola and Gillette, but also to defend French individuals tried by German authorities'.[25] Gide was also appointed vice president of the Paris American Chamber of Commerce created in 1894 to 'bridge the gap between [French businesses' and authorities'] fear of the US economic and business might and attempts to contain US powerful drive into French industry on one side, and admiration of US technology' on the other (Higbee 2008: 411).

These ties with major US corporations helped Gide

> follow these companies on the European road that was just opening up [with the launch of the European Common Market]. [. . .] The firm was one of the first to take advantage of a 1954 decree that permitted lawyers to create groups of associated partners [. . .]. Up until the late 1980s, Gide was the 'national champion' and the only firm (with a couple of smaller ones such as Jeantet and Rambaud Martel, also present in Brussels very early on, or Bredin Prat) that could compete with large American and British law firms.
>
> (Vauchez and France 2020: 19)

[25] Atlantico.fr, 'Pierre Gide: le quotidien difficile d'un avocat sous l'Occupation' 31 October 2020, https://atlantico.fr/article/decryptage/pierre-gide–le-quotidien-difficile-d-un-avocat-sous-l-occupation-second-guerre-mondiale-biographie-histoire-justice-michel-guenaire (accessed 25 May 2022).

7.3 The Twist of Imperial Redux

These French pioneers contributed to the expansion of a French corporate bar under the double thrust of the European Common Market and the model of the Wall Street corporate law firm. It is also as intermediaries or competitors of US multinational corporate law firms that they entered the former French *pré carré* in Africa qua a legal market. The trajectory of a lawyer hailed as the 'godfather' of the Africa Bar and that of one of his protégés, are emblematic.

Julien received me in his spacious office: a room with softened light, strewn with African masks, fabrics, a picture on the wall showing the basketball team of Zaire in the 1970s and featuring a young version of himself. This lawyer, now well into his eighties, explained that he entered the field 'by accident'[26]: 'My trajectory is unusual. I obtained a scholarship from the US Officers' Wives Club after World War II to go study in the US'. After completing a Juris Doctor degree, he entered the US corporate law firm Duncan Allen & Mitchell in New York and was dispatched as the local respondent of the firm in 1974 in Kinshasa, the capital of then Zaire.

The firm wanted to set up a local office. The context was also that of the 'white elephants' infrastructure projects in Zaire (Verhaegen 1985).

> Mobil, Texaco, First National Citibank: business was booming. But [t]he firm's associate there was an American 'with big boots', the son of an infrastructure entrepreneur. He did not have the sensitivity to work with Africans. At first, I was not interested, but I decided to stay. At the time [in New York] there was hardly any international work, I never saw clients. There I could combine the two.

Julien returned to Paris at the end of the 1970s as an associate of the US corporate law firm Coudert Brothers. 'A month later, I was contacted by Air Zaïre, to be the advisor of the [Congolese] presidency'. As counsel to the presidency, he undertook the reform of the pharmaceutical sector, and was also in charge of military contracts along with the negotiation of bank loans. 'When I came back to Paris I was inevitably branded with an "African" label. Due to my Zairean background, I have always practised in mining law. But I became a generalist "African."'

Julien developed Coudert's Africa practice – with, and that was exceptional at the time, a team of African lawyers. 'At the time, Coudert was

[26] Author's interview with Julien, partner, McDermott Will & Emery, Paris, 5 May 2015.

the only firm to do international law. If you worked at the Paris office of a US or UK corporate law firm, as a Frenchman it was automatically to practise international law' due to the strategic position of Paris as an offshore site to settle transnational commercial disputes – thanks to the creation of the arbitration chamber of the International Chamber of Commerce (ICC in Paris) in the early 1920s.

Admitted to the Paris Bar in 1991, Pierre was one of Julien's protégés at Coudert, before he started his career at Jeantet & Associés in 1992. As an associate and chair of the energy, mines and infrastructures department of the firm, Pierre is also an academic specialised in international and comparative energy law – a field of practice he has contributed to carve out as a *doctrinal* space. Before entering Jeantet, Pierre had worked for five years at Total. Once at Jeantet, Pierre set up the firm's energy and mining department in 1993, which, a novelty at the time, also included arbitration services. 'It was the only one, focused on energy and natural resources, to offer the whole gamut of services: contract negotiation all the way through to arbitration. We have a single team that can deal with both. If the market shifts, one of the poles can compensate for the other'.[27]

Both Julien and Pierre's trajectories display a core resource that has durably structured this professional market: social capital. As Pierre summed it up, '[c]ontracts, project finance cases have a snowball effect. Reputation is difficult to establish, but once it's there, it's there'.[28] But it is also a space characterised by charismatic mentor–pupil relations. Emblematically, after the disbanding of Coudert in 2006, Julien switched to the Paris office of the US firm Dewey and LeBoeuf, and later that of the Canadian firm Fasken Martineau. While the later part of his career reflected the increasing pace of transformation of the market for corporate law (characterised by mergers and lateral flows of associates), each time he brought along his team to reconstitute a collective *know-how* on extractive contracts with resource-rich African states.

Dominique, for example, entered the Paris bar one generation later, as an associate at the Paris office of Herbert Smith Freehills – as a protégé of Antoine – between 2001 and 2010. 'I did not turn to Herbert Smith Freehills by accident. At the time, it was the only corporate law firm which provided legal services to both states and corporations in Africa. I have a background in public law. Administrative law is an ancillary

[27] Author's interview with Pierre, partner at Jeantet & Associés, Paris, 28 April 2015.
[28] Author's interview with Julien, partner, McDermott Will & Emery, Paris, 5 May 2015.

science in France. I did not want to be a "support" lawyer. I wanted to do transactions'.[29]

This younger generation, just like their mentors, combines an experience in the extractive business sector (foremost at Total) and/or within the audit sector (at PwC) increasingly with stints at multilateral banks – just as, in the case of Dominique, the European Investment Bank. As Julien explained, '[B]anks orient dealings in Africa, mainly US and UK banks. The French have always done business in Africa. Though they rarely invest. For Anglo-Saxon law firms [having an Africa department] is certainly a marketing strategy'.[30] An American partner at the Paris office of Clifford Chance explained: '[i]f you look at law firms' expansion, it is through project finance, and generally development and financing. Now, almost 100 per cent of my time is focused on Africa [. . .]. We turned to Africa in the context of the [2008] crisis. I am not sure [US and UK corporate law firms] will stay after the market picks up because it is certainly a lot easier to do business in New York.'[31]

Since 2014, the professionally oriented website *The Lawyer* chronicles transformations of the corporate legal landscape in Anglophone sub-Saharan Africa to flag out opportunities for the expansion of US and UK multinational corporate law firms into the continent. Since 2016, the French weekly *Jeune Afrique* and its business-oriented bulletin *Africa Business +* also publish a widely circulated yearly ranking of the most prominent corporate lawyers involved in corporate dealings, predominantly in Francophone Africa.[32]

White & Case was the first US multinational corporate law firm to set up an office on the African continent in 1995, in South Africa, followed in 2008 by Eversheds, and over two dozen other firms, including Allen & Overy in 2014, a member of the UK 'magic circle'.[33] Yet 'an Africa office is no magic door to deals'.[34] Emblematically, after a widely publicised move to open an 'African' office in Conakry in 2012, the UK

[29] Author's interview with Dominique, associate at Jones Day, Paris, 9 April 2015.

[30] Author's interview with Julien, partner, McDermott Will & Emery, Paris, 5 May 2015.

[31] Author's interview with Fabrice, partner, Clifford Chance, Paris, 5 May 2015.

[32] In the extractive sector, as well as in telecommunications, infrastructure and international arbitration.

[33] The Magic Circle is an informal term describing the five most prestigious London-headquartered multinational law firms (Allen & Overy, Clifford Chance, Freshfields Bruckhaus Deringer, Linklaters, Slaughter and May). The term has also been used to describe the most prestigious barristers' chambers in London.

[34] M Taylor, 'An Africa office is no magic door to deals' *The Lawyer* 21 March 2016.

multinational corporate law firm Herbert Smith Freehills, which systematically features in the top three firms of the *Jeune Afrique* and *Africa Business* + ranking for energy and infrastructure projects, cancelled these plans a year later, asserting that it would 'continue to service client needs in Francophone Africa, including Guinea, on the same basis as we do now'[35]: from Paris. Likewise, Nicolas Jean, an associate at the French law firm Gide Loyrette Nouel, who was awarded the golden medal of *Jeune Afrique*'s 2021 '100 Legal Powerlist' notably for his services to the Ivorian state oil company Petroci,[36] operates from Paris.

The structure of Asafo & Co, the firm created by the Togolese-French Pascal Agboyibor in spring 2019,[37] certainly – at least partly – echoes the perception of a demand for business law fostered by multinationals and the financialisation of GVCs. As an integrated firm with no ostensible headquarters, but offices in Abidjan, Casablanca, Johannesburg, Mombasa, Nairobi, Paris, London and Washington, DC, Asafo & Co. hails as a 'law firm that combines sophisticated local advice with international experience'.[38] But these market and symbolic markers do not help explain how this very new firm managed within the space of a few months to have 'the "magic circle" of law firms quaking in their boots, scooping up deals previously reserved for them'.[39]

Rather, two shifts are transforming, through contracts, the relationship between former resource-rich French colonies in sub-Saharan Africa with global markets. As Pierre reminisced, 'when I started [at Jeantet] I was derided. Everybody was criticizing the endeavour [. . .]. We were the only law firm with a local office in Africa, from the colonial era, then in Algiers, because Jeantet was from there. I innovated, I brought in an African to the office [it was Pascal Agboyibor]'.[40] Agboyibor himself recalled the symbolic violence he experienced, as a Black African, during his first years at Jeantet. 'It was the old argument at the time, they wanted an African [sitting at the table of negotiations]'.[41]

[35] A Reynolds, 'Herbert Smith Freehills calls off planned Guinea office launch' *Law.com* 4 September 2013.

[36] P-O Rouaud, '"100 Legal Powerlist": les poids lourds' *Jeune Afrique* 13 September 2021.

[37] See Chapter 1.

[38] See Asafo & Co's website, https://asafoandco.com/vision/ (accessed 23 May 2022).

[39] T Ayeni, E Conroy, A Culliford, N Norbrook and H Banda, *Top 50 Disruptors* (The Africa Report, 1 June 2020) 8.

[40] Author's interview with Pierre, partner at Jeantet & Associés, Paris, 28 April 2015.

[41] Author's interview with Pascal Agboyibor, co-founder of Asafo & Co., Paris, 22 May 2015.

Structural adjustment programs and the liberalisation of extractive economies in resource-rich African states contributed to transforming the symbolic terms of this relationship, by enabling the introduction of corporations without an imperial past in former French colonies. As my respondent at Jones Day explained, '[w]hen you look at the corporate side, you find a lot more firms. It is the same for everything else: you do one transaction and then you become a specialist [in mining, oil, infrastructure]. But when you look at the government side it's completely different'.[42] As Julien, the 'godfather' of the Paris Africa Bar concurred:

> [w]e still work a lot for states, but it is mostly private practice. The practice of counselling to states has evolved. It is more transparent, more open. Now it works a lot based on tenders. Before it was by chance encounters. Presidents and political advisors would meet their counsels in restaurants. Now – except for counsels to Presidents, where it is different – it is all based on tenders.[43]

Indeed, as the partner at Clifford Chance summed it up, 'business in Africa is not the most lucrative. But we want to be a blue-chip firm that corporations look to'.[44]

Tenders position the World Bank as an invisible yet overwhelming partner at the negotiating table. Not only because all mining codes, just like 'public–private partnerships', are modelled out of similar templates designed by World Bank experts. But because initiatives like Connex or the African Legal Facility tend to embed the negotiation of contracts within the parameters of relationships between development donors and resource-rich African states qua recipients. Certainly, these initiatives have contributed to chipping the charismatic structure of the Africa Bar in Paris, by allowing multinational corporate law firms lacking the social resource of imperial relations to lean on the Trojan horse strategy of using pro bono or tenders to enter the market of legal services to states. It is also contributing to reinforce the legal expertise at the service of African states and to stave off the risk of contractual renegotiations and arbitration.

Yet – as a partner at Jones Day explained:

> [y]ou cannot make a career working solely on deals in Africa. 'Africa' work is either for corporations or governments. For corporations it is

[42] Author's telephonic interview with Louis, partner, Jones Day, 1 April 2015.

[43] Author's interview with Julien, partner, McDermott Will & Emery, Paris, 5 May 2015.

[44] Author's interview with Fabrice, partner, Clifford Chance, Paris, 5 May 2015.

> primarily energy, project finance. You can do that full time. But you cannot do government work full time. It does not pay. There is no way you can make billable hours working for a government. It is a different way of doing business. If I have a corporate client, they will call me and ask me for the costs, then they will call back, and they will say, 'let's move'. Governments, they never pay. There is always an international organisation that pays. They always have a tender process that takes months, a technical proposal, a financial proposal that will take forty hours. And this, you cannot bill it. My credentials are well known. For instance, when GIZ [the German development agency] call, they know me, but still, it takes months.[45]

As the contract economics expert explained:

> African states look for the best bidder. It is only when there is a crisis, when the dispute goes to arbitration that they call in the big shots. The law then is dealt with at the highest levels. Connex: it is a smart initiative. But the sticking point was that the Germans [just as other development partners] wanted services to states to be *pro bono*. Why ask law firms to do *pro bono* work? It's beautiful, but it's neo-colonial. If you want to restructure the market, you need to do it right.[46]

7.4 Conclusion

Is Paris, just like in the 1980s, a 'beachhead' – this time for a US-led corporate legal globalisation thrust into Africa, or does it remain a symbolic marketplace for the renegotiation of the continent's relationship with global markets? At the 2015 round of Connex talks, a panel member introduced himself as one of the 'bad guys' – as a member of the board of a major oil company – and apologised that he had not managed to secure the presence of CEOs of the extractive industry.

In any case, discussions did not focus on them. Multinational corporate law firms were the elephant in the room. They were not in attendance either. In the words of the then senior legal counsel of the African Legal Support Facility, the problem was not simply that there was a lack of domestic legal expertise on extractive contracts in resource-rich states or that, when such expertise existed, it was politically collusive.

It was not either that that expertise – when provided by the African Legal Support Facility – was funded through development aid, and

45 Author's telephonic interview with Louis, partner, Jones Day, 1 April 2015.
46 Author's interview with Marc, consultant in contract economics, Paris, 2 July 2015.

therefore integrated in an uncomfortable *ménage à trois* between governments, transnational corporations and donors. It was foremost that getting lawyers themselves to abide by an externally imposed code of conduct was doomed to failure. In any case, he argued: 'nobody wants to know what gets into sausages'.[47]

Still – the Connex initiative was reflective of a turning tide. For the first time, the 2020 edition of the *Jeune Afrique* and *Africa Business* + ranking included a rating of the ten best 'African' firms headquartered in French-speaking African states. While the emergence of 'African' corporate law firms has been hailed as reflecting the *Zeitgeist*, professionals – including Pascal Agboyibor himself – have been quick to assert that it is also related to economic downturns: 'when profit margins are limited, the client [chooses] the most attractive offer'.[48]

After all, as the godfather of the Africa Bar in Paris exclaimed: '[w]e do not do *offshore* law. But we do not need to work with local lawyers. Anyway, if clients contact us, we can do the work, we do not need to go through local lawyers'.[49] Certainly, indeed, for the time being the competition with local firms is limited, as it is restricted to legal services provided to states – for which the glass ceiling of access to political actors remains a deciding factor – and medium-sized corporations.[50]

The profile of Pascal Agboyibor, who combines the *know-how* of project finance and the capacity to speak to heads of state, points, albeit ambiguously, to the enduring structure of the Africa Bar – as offshore, yet deeply embedded in a social capital moulded by imperial legacies. Pro bono initiatives or legal services financed through development aid have contributed to a slight displacement of the interpersonal relations between the elite of the Africa Bar in Paris and their political counterparts towards the framework of development assistance. But this still reinforces the stronghold of agents with capacities of access built out of a portfolio of political, economic, social and legal resources, such as Agboyibor. Yet, when at Orrick, the latter initially failed at opening a local branch of the firm in Abidjan, due to the opposition of the Abidjan bar.[51] But the

[47] My conference notes. G7 CONNEX Consultative Conference, Berlin, 9–10 March 2015.

[48] E Maussion, 'Avocats africains, avocats internationaux: la guerre est finie?' *Jeune Afrique* 8 September 2021.

[49] Author's interview with Julien, partner, McDermott Will & Emery, Paris, 5 May 2015.

[50] E Maussion, 'Avocats africains, avocats internationaux: la guerre est finie?' *Jeune Afrique* 8 September 2021.

[51] F Maury, 'Le barreau de Côte d'Ivoire fustige l'arrivée d'Orrick' *Jeune Afrique* 31 October 2014.

endeavour succeeded once he set up Asafo & Co, which includes an Abidjan office that now directly competes with Orrick and other multinational corporate legal players.[52]

Herein, perhaps, lies an imperial twist. The expansion of a corporate bar in Paris, fostered by the European Single Market, benefited from the continuation of the economic, political, legal and social links between the *métropole* and its former colonies, favoured by the *system* of the *Françafrique*. At the same time, it was also embedded in the globalisation of the model of the Wall Street corporate law firm fostered by the Big Bang of the market for corporate law at the turn of the 1980s. The transformation of the Africa Bar in Paris from a market of insiders shaped by charismatic and interpersonal relationships towards an enlarged market self-regulated by the principles of transparency and corporate social responsibility is reflective of connected histories that are imprinted by the position of Paris as 'beachhead' for the deployment of US and UK corporate law firms in Europe – and as a historic capital for international commercial arbitration.

As the godfather of the Africa Bar explained: 'multinational corporate law firms are scared to be outpaced by local lawyers'.[53] But the profile of the Guinean Salimatou Diallo, whose firm was ranked 'firm of the year' in 2020,[54] underscores that these 'locals' have honed their skills within the Paris offices of multinational corporate law firms.

Salimatou Diallo's corporate law firm SD Avocats was ranked first in the new ranking of 'best corporate law firm in Africa' established by the French weekly *Jeune Afrique/Business +* in 2020 to celebrate the emergence of competitive corporate lawyers in West Africa. Diallo obtained a law degree at the Sorbonne in Paris, which she complemented with an LLM (Master of Laws) in the US. She was recruited as an associate in the Parisian office of Lovells in 2005, before joining Herbert Smith Freehills, where she specialised in project finance. After the failure of Herbert Smith Freehills to establish a local office in Conakry, she set up her own firm, calling herself a '*repat*' (repatriate).

[52] *Africa Business +*, '"Nous sommes en négociation avec trois cabinets pour des partenariats en Afrique" Yves Lepage, Orrick' 17 May 2019.

[53] Author's interview with Julien, partner, McDermott Will & Emery, Paris, 5 May 2015.

[54] *Jeune Afrique*, 'Avocats d'affaires: Salimatou Diallo plébiscitée par ses pairs' 11 August 2020, www.jeuneafrique.com/mag/1025322/economie/avocats-daffaires-la-guineenne-salimatou-diallo-plebiscitee-par-ses-pairs/ (accessed 25 May 2022).

'I was bilingual, I had worked for major multinational corporate law firms and was therefore highly competitive on the local market'.[55] Diallo's success builds out of a combination of resources – social, familial and educational – that has been shown to have befitted the US multinational corporate law firms' strategies of expansion into the French corporate legal market (Dezalay Y 1992) and that have consolidated the model of the Wall Street corporate law firm as an engine of both legal globalisation and reproduction of legal hierarchies at the domestic level. Diallo's success, however, will be tested by her capacity to convert this international and institutional legal capital into a *state* capital, which requires interconnected resources to navigate a decisive glass ceiling: gatekeeping politics in Guinea.

The profile of these competitors reflects the dynamic at the core of the expansion of the international corporate legal market – and, with it, the Wall Street model of the corporate law firm: the combination of a *know-how* collectively detained by these firms as transnational corporations, and the *know-who* of lawyers who know the better how to navigate local gatepolitics when they, themselves, hail from a strong social, political and family platform. For example, one of the 'Big 5' corporate law firms in Senegal – Géni & Kébé – is now positioned as a regional group with clients all over West Africa – as well as Anglo-Saxon corporate clients through the framework of the OHADA. This firm built its reputation in London by establishing a specialisation in the granting of exploitation permits. This reputation foremost hones on the profile of the founder of the firm who studied law in both Senegal and Britain and that of the firm's collaborators who are required to have completed an LLM in the US, Canada or Australia – or a master's degree in finance.[56]

It is not therefore so much the structure of the Africa Bar in Paris that is changing – and for that matter the terms of the relationship between resource-rich African states and transnational corporations – but the structural position of Paris itself as a symbolic marketplace for the negotiation and justification of the uneven and unequal relationship between the former *métropole* and African states.

The position of the Sciences Po Law School in Paris – one of France's *grandes écoles*[57] – illustrates this ongoing shift. The creation of the law

[55] A Couder, 'Les avocats à l'assaut d'une Afrique nouvelle' *La lettre des juristes d'affaires* 24 November 2015.

[56] Holzbauer, 'L'âge d'or des cabinets d'affaires africains' *African Banker* 10 February 2016.

[57] The *grandes écoles* are specialised elite higher education schools.

school in 2009 spurred a violent controversy with French law universities. The law school aimed at expanding the legal education market in France by offering a post-grad LLM in corporate law modelled on the US system that would enable students with no prior background in law to directly access the Paris Bar after two years while building their portfolio of contacts with major UK and US multinational corporate law firms based in Paris. Symbolically, the first director of the school was shunned by Parisian law universities – he was not invited to sit on doctoral vivas for several years. But all of them, since, have followed suit, starting with the Université Panthéon-Assas which now delivers an LLM in International Business Law. When I asked the current director of the school whether he considered – nearly fifteen years on – that Sciences Po's strategy had succeeded, he responded: 'our objective is to contribute to fighting against social inequalities'.[58]

'Diversity' in higher education (and education tout court) has loomed large in French political debates in the past twenty years: as both an obsession with the failure of the universalistic model of Republican education and the ongoing battles surrounding the liberalisation of the sector heralded by President Macron. Certainly, the French students who enrol at the school benefit from fees – ranging from 0 to nearly 19,000 Euros calculated based on their parents' revenues – that are extremely competitive compared to higher education fees in the US, or even in the UK. But the language of 'diversity' is also *demand*-driven, as it echoes the position of the multinational corporate law firms partnering with the school: 'they want to invest in diversity'.[59] The structure of the curriculum mirrors this market demand, by combining a specialisation in arbitration with a model of clinical education that leans on the pro bono input of partnering firms. But most of these students are French – with only a minority originating from outside the European Union – foremost Latin America, India and Singapore.

Bruno, a partner at the UK corporate law firm Eversheds Sutherland where he heads the 'Africa Group' of the firm's office in Paris, provided a complementary explanation of the competitive market in which Sciences Po Paris' law school is positioned. In 2007, Bruno launched an 'Africa Law Institute', a network designed to enable members of the firm's thirty-eight partners (in both Francophone and Anglophone Africa) to access

[58] Informal interview with Sébastien Pimont, director of the Sciences Po Law School, Paris, 9 February 2022.
[59] Ibid.

legal training. With now eight local offices on the continent – in Casablanca, Johannesburg, Mauritius, Morocco, Tangier and Tunis – the firm has also been at the forefront of the development of the OHADA system in West Africa, including through an OHADA law diploma delivered to Francophone (French and African) students by the Universities Panthéon-Assas and Paris 13 since 2014.[60]

At a conference organised by the Sciences Po Law School on arbitration in Africa in 2015, the consensus was that it was 'time for Africa'[61] in the context of a boom of investment arbitration involving African states – and foremost the expansion of arbitration centres set up ostensibly to compete with the ICC in Paris, such as the CAJAC created in 2015.

Tunde Ogunseitan, a British-Nigerian and former head of the Secretariat of the ICC in Paris where he acted as counsel for Common Law jurisdictions, including the UK, Ireland, the Caribbean, Anglophone African states and states in the Indian Subcontinent in 2013–2020, was asked whether the ICC in Paris felt threatened by the competition. 'We are not in competition', he responded. '[W]e get parties the seat that is closest to them'. In any case, he added that 'the ICC in Paris is the Rolls-Royce of arbitration. Maybe you need a Skoda that will get you from A to B'. The 'Skoda' referred to African lawyers, still largely absent from an international market of arbitration dominated by a cluster of male European and US corporate lawyers.

The issue, then, as another panellist responded, was rather 'how do you share space, how does the Rolls Royce influence the Skoda, so that ultimately the Skoda can aspire to get there?' In other words, she implied, how do you maintain the position of *Paris* itself as a symbolic marketplace for the renegotiation of the relationship between resource-rich African states and the global economy?

[60] Author's interview with Bruno, partner, Eversheds, in Paris, 8 April 2015.

[61] Arbitration in Africa, conference organised by Sciences Po Law School and Queen Mary University of London, Paris, 9 December 2015. Author's conference notes.

8

The Value of Social Class in Global Justice

When the first international justice institutions were created, at the turn of the twentieth century, international law explicitly fostered racism. Racism is now understood as existing at the local, national level, but not in the international realm (Anghie 2006: 110).

How do national courts and international dispute settlement mechanisms contribute to the 'transmission and reproduction of deeply embedded social hierarchies and prejudices rooted in a past characterized by territorial concepts of belonging and notions of civilization that both generated and were generated by racial inequalities' (Thomas and Kamari Clarke 2013: 306)?

This chapter opens with two judicial decisions concerning the Guinean state delivered in Paris, respectively by an arbitral chamber set up under the aegis of the ICSID – the World Bank's arbitration and conciliation arm, and by the French National Court of Asylum (Cour nationale du droit d'asile – CNDA) in 2021–2022.

So-called *offshore* justice, in the form of arbitration which is rendered in seats (predominantly in the Global North) with no territorial link to the parties in given disputes, is never studied in comparison with national 'routine' justice, that is, justice delivered by domestic tribunals. Beyond their common geographical seat (Paris), the position of Guinea as a state of origin (at the CNDA) and a respondent (at the ICSID), and the unique characteristic of the CNDA – which comprises since inception judges appointed by an international organisation (the UNHCR) – the CNDA and the ICSID are a priori instances of distinct patterns of legal globalisation. As an *onshore* national court of justice, the CNDA defines the status of individuals as included/excluded, citizens/aliens of the French state. As an *offshore* supranational dispute settlement mechanism, the ICSID arbitrates on the distribution of capital between states and markets.

Yet both institutions are instances of globalisation as 'highly selective economic, social and political macroprocesses of mobilization in time and space' (Thomas and Kamari Clarke 2013: 306). As such, they are also instances of encounter between the world's core and its peripheries in that they codify, through law, movements of people and capital that occur across political boundaries, and over time.

Looking at the operations of justice allows, therefore, as Mbembe put it, an examination of the 'interlocking of presents, pasts, and futures that retain their depths of other presents, past, and futures, each age bearing, altering, and maintaining the previous ones' (Mbembe 2001: 16). In other words, law enables the symbolic authority of justice precisely because it negates social, racial or national boundaries. Yet it is also through the operations of justice that these social, racial and national boundaries are transformed and justified.

To explore this paradox, it is useful to build on Bourdieu's (1971) analogy of religion as a market of 'symbolic' goods. Justice gains authority when it is not only seen but also believed to be impartial – that is, rendered beyond social, racial or political distinctions. But this symbolic operation of justice is produced, itself, through social hierarchies, between those who produce justice because they are positioned as repeat players – to use Galanter's term (1974) – and users of justice institutions. Exploring the boundary-making operations of justice institutions is therefore an invitation to examine their position *as* boundary-making institutions. To do this, I examine the similar pattern of social hierarchisation that characterises dispute settlement mechanisms, be they national or supranational, to then channel attention to the characteristics of what I call the gatekeepers of the relationship between users and producers of justice. This is a way, in turn, to understand how inter/national justice institutions contribute to the reproduction of social hierarchies beyond the state – in the structuration of the position of the world's cores *as* cores, and its peripheries *as* peripheries.

8.1 Inter/National Justice in Paris

4 June 2021, Montreuil.

We are sitting as judges at the French National Court of Asylum (CNDA) in Montreuil, a suburb on the outskirts of Paris. Ms D. enters with her lawyer. The hearing room is windowless and stifling. In the context of the COVID-19 pandemic, we are all wearing masks. Ms D. features among the 68,243 individuals who appealed the rejection of their asylum claim by the office for the protection of refugees and stateless persons (OFPRA) in 2021. Her country of origin, Guinea, is also the second top country of origin – after Bangladesh – of asylum seekers that year in France. Like most female Guinean applicants, Ms D.'s claim is founded on persecutions based on membership to the social group of women seeking to escape forced marriage. According to her file, she is barely twenty. Orphaned at a young age, she was wedded as fourth wife to a wealthy elderly trader at the age of twelve after being raped by a cousin. After several attempts, she managed to flee and take the well-trodden and perilous exile route towards France through Mauritania and Morocco. Raped in Spain, she gave birth to a little boy once in France.

I wildly search the eyes of the applicant, to no avail. Ms D. keeps her head down, her petite body visibly shaking with fear. The president of the court insistently questions Ms D. about dates, speaking through the interpreter. *What year was she married? Does this mean she left her husband's compound six years later? Why after so many years of marriage? How did she know about the exile route to France? How did she pay for the journey*? Ms D.'s whispered responses, translated from Soussou, barely filter through her tears. She does not know dates. She has never been to school. Her lawyer argues that she suffers from psychiatric collapse due to the multiple instances of sexual violence she has experienced in Guinea and during her exile journey.

Comparative studies on national asylum regimes have underscored the central importance of luck in creating or alleviating the socio-legal conditions of precarity faced by asylum seekers (see Burridge and Gill 2017; Gill and Good 2019). Ms D. is lucky. In the end, Ms D.'s acute vulnerability trumps other considerations. She is granted asylum.

18 May 2022, Paris. An arbitral chamber set up under the aegis of the ICSID – the World Bank's arbitration and conciliation arm – closes a long-running dispute between the Guinean government and the mining firm BSG Resources (BSGR).[1] The case concerned a project in the Simandou mountains, which are believed to contain the second-largest iron ore reserves in the world. The backstory of the Simandou exploitation 'has been Chinese industrialization which has driven up worldwide iron ore demand and prices, especially during the 2000s' commodities super cycle' (Kalm 2021). BSGR, part of the business empire of Israeli minerals magnate Beny Steinmetz, obtained mining rights in the Southern blocs of Simandou during late Lansana Conte's military rule.

[1] Intellinews, 'World Bank arbitrator supports Guinea over Simandou iron-ore project' 1 June 2022.

In the context of the multiple coups d'état that followed Conte's death in 2008, the mining corporation secured half of the Anglo-Australian Rio Tinto's mining rights over the Northern blocs of Simandou. In April 2010, BSGR sold a 51 per cent share of its Guinean operation to the Brazilian mining giant Vale for US$ 2.5 billion. 'BSGR had up until then spent less than US$ 50m on mineral exploration and according to documents revealed in the different proceedings a little over US$ 50m for various local consultants and bribes' (Kalm 2021). In 2018, BSGR was put into administration against the backdrop of several court cases and investigations targeting Steinmetz in Switzerland, Romania, Israel, the UK and the US. Ruling in favour of Guinea, the ICSID verdict of 24 May 2022 confirmed that 'BSGR must have acquired its license through a vast system of corruption'.[2]

Shortly after the decision, the Guinean government issued a communique announcing that the project had been taken over by the mysterious-sounding SMB (Société manière de Boké)-Winning Consortium, which consists of the Singaporean shipping company Winning International Group, the Guinea-based integrated logistics company United Mining Supply (UMS) and two Chinese corporations – aluminium producer China Hongqiao Group and the Yantai Port Group.

Our perception of Ms D. at the CNDA hearing was informed by the court's research unit's depiction of Guinean state institutions as endemically corrupted: 'all [official] acts are bankable [. . .] from the community leader to the magistrate, there is a real informal value chain' said to capture 80 per cent of the country's economy.[3] By contrast, the BSGR decision espoused a constant approach taken by the ICSID and other arbitral tribunals since the 1991 *AAPL* v. *Sri Lanka* award (Greenman 2021: 1): that of the continuity of the state, despite and beyond political turmoil, to protect foreign investments. The BSGR verdict construed corruption as *external* to the state. A rare occurrence, it therefore leaned *against* the corporate claimant.

8.2 Repeat Players and Inter/National Justice

In policy and scholarly accounts, the expanding role of justice institutions in domestic and global politics, be they operating within

[2] Intellinews, 'World Bank arbitrator supports Guinea over Simandou iron-ore project' 1 June 2022.

[3] OFPRA, *Rapport de mission en Guinée du 7 au 18 novembre 2017* (Paris, OFPRA/CNDA, 2018), 77. My translation from French.

international dispute settlement mechanisms (see Nollkaemper et al. 2017; Terris et al. 2007) or national tribunals ruling over transnational phenomena, such as terrorism (see Weill 2020) and asylum (see Gill and Good 2019), has spurred a growing interest for the role played by the lawyers (judges or counsels) operating these institutions.

Emblematically, the boom of investment arbitration from the early 2000s fuelled a grey literature that criticises the professional market of international arbitrators as a 'mafia' or 'inner mafia', where the position of prominent members as partners at multinational corporate law firms is seen as a sign of bias of international dispute mechanisms in favour of corporate interests. Bias is seen to be fostered by lawyers' perceived conflicts of interest as predominantly white and male along with their 'double-hatting' position – whether as partners within multinational corporate law firms (Eberhardt and Olivet 2012) or as 'moonlighting' judges of the ICJ (Bernasconi-Osterwalder and Dietrich Brauch 2017).

Likewise, bias loomed large in my perception qua an adjunct judge appointed by the UNHCR at the CNDA. During the hearing of the 4 June 2021, bias – my own, and what I perceived to be my colleagues' – were predicated on geographical and symbolical assumptions: that Ms D.'s characteristics as a social agent were overshadowed – if not totally erased – by her contested status as either a victim of oppression or a 'fake' asylum seeker. Her social status, within and across social fields, was thereby reduced to *physical* mobility – migration across national borders – and chromatic remoteness in a room filled with white agents.

Much of the response to the perceived bias of justice institutions is focused on their (lack of) *representativeness* – from a social, gender or national point of view. However, *representativeness* is not enough to understand *who* operates justice institutions, *how* they gain their professional status and whether this impacts *how* they interpret the law and deliver justice.

In his classic distinction between '*repeat players*' and '*one-shotters*', Galanter (1974) suggested that the consolidation of judicial processes – in terms of practices and outcomes – was correlated to the existence and operations of repeat players. To put it simply: the routinisation of tribunals qua institutions is a function of the rate of their use. Users with dominant forms of resources – particularly institutional players (insurance companies, major corporations or prosecutors in criminal cases) – tend to feature among repeat players, while individuals – be it a divorced woman filing for alimony, or Ms D. as an asylum applicant – are one-shotters.

But the asymmetrical relationship between these two types of actors and the judicial system is not so much determined by their pre-existing endowment in socially dominant forms of capital than their very status as repeat players. In other words, repeat players are dominant actors before courts precisely because they are repeat players.

Indeed, the relationship between repeat players and judicial institutions is also *structurally dynamic*. It reflects the relationship between *users* of judicial institutions and the *producers* of the symbolic authority of these institutions. The exclusiveness of the 'transnational arbitral community' (Garth 2018) is constructed by insiders themselves as a condition of their credibility (Gaillard 2015). Likewise, the remarkable resilience of the profiles over time of international judges since the 1920s – as national elites with a multi-positioned background across the higher tiers of their judicial systems, selective legal education in Oxbridge or Ivy League universities, prestigious academic positions and appointments as *jurisconsultes* at the national and international levels – points to the correlation between *elite status* and the authority of international dispute settlement mechanisms (Terris et al. 2007).

Out of the three arbitrators of the BSGR case, two featured among the 'elite 15' of the 'movers and shakers of investment-treaty arbitration' (Eberhardt and Olivet 2012: 38). Appointed as president of the tribunal by the two other arbitrators, the Swiss Gabrielle Kaufmann-Kohler is, with Brigitte Stern, one of the two women of this elite group. Co-founding partner of the firm Lévy Kaufmann-Kohler, created in 2007 with a focus on investment arbitration, she predominantly operates as president of arbitral tribunals and on the side of investors. Kaufmann-Kohler is also an academic (now professor *emerita* at the University of Geneva) and has published extensively on international arbitration. Appointed by the claimant (BSGR), the Dutch Albert Jan Van den Berg similarly combines the dual platform of practice and academia. The firm he co-founded in 2001 also specialises in investment arbitration. Its practice grew in the context of the Argentina crisis during which he was appointed in five cases by corporations in investment treaty disputes.

As an adjunct judge appointed to the CNDA by the UNHCR, my own profile as an academic with a background in international law fit with that of about half of my colleagues. The other adjunct judges appointed by the UNHCR are all practitioners – foremost employees of INGOs, international organisations or French civil society organisations providing services to migrants/asylum seekers. The other adjunct judge sitting with me at the hearing of the 4th June 2021 was appointed by the Conseil d'État and was, like most of his colleagues, a former French diplomat. Other adjunct judges appointed by the Conseil d'État are generally public agents within the Ministry of the Interior, and a minority are now international law scholars. For his part, the president of our judicial formation was, like most of his peers, a judge at the Cour des Comptes (Court of Auditors). Collectively, we reflected a combination of resources similar to the judges of ICSID tribunals – across practice and academia – and 'clear signs of path dependence to [the] ancestors [of international justice institutions, like the Permanent Court of International Justice, PCIJ]) and their socio-professional constellations' (Madsen 2014: 333).

However, 'holding several positions at the same time is only possible for agents with particular accumulation of capital' (Christensen 2021: 789). The social ascendency of repeat players operating international dispute settlement mechanisms conditions the routinisation of these mechanisms as institutions. But their social mobility is also determined by specific patterns of production, reproduction and accumulation of capital across symbolic, institutional and geographic boundaries.

For example, the third arbitrator, appointed by the state of Guinea in the ICSID–BSGR dispute, Pierre Mayer, combines core characteristics of the main players of the Africa corporate Bar in Paris[4] with key resources of the international arbitration community. Now an emeritus professor at the Université Panthéon-Sorbonne in Paris, elected to the Institut de droit international (Institute of International Law) in 2007, he has written extensively on private international law, particularly to build the institutional design and legal operations of the OHADA. He also practised as an associate at the Paris offices of Coudert Brothers and Clifford Chance before contributing to the international arbitration practice of Dechert from 2015 and co-founding a boutique arbitration firm, Mayer Greenberg, in 2021 to 'focus on his arbitration practice and avoid conflicts of interests'.[5] Likewise, as a judge at the Cour des Comptes, the president of the 4th June 2021 hearing at the CNDA pursued the typical trajectory of the French political-bureaucratic elite as he accessed this position through the '*botte de l'École nationale d'administration*' – as part of the fifteen top students of his cohort at the French national school of administration.

[4] See Chapter 7.

[5] Le Monde du droit, 'Création du caibnet Mayer Greenberg' 29 March 2021, www.lemondedudroit.fr/vie-des-cabinets/74676-creation-cabinet-mayer-greenberg.html (accessed 29 December 2023).

The characteristics of repeat players along with their *structural* relationship with users of justice institutions helps explain how 'an institution, without a priori being corrupted or oriented towards predetermined outcomes, will tend to favour certain types of actors, or, in other words, deliver a form of justice that cannot claim impartiality as it most often arbitrates in favour of certain categories of users' (Israël 2013: 544, my translation from French). This does not negate the individual qualities of judges and counsels – or, conversely, their bias. Rather, it points to the structural dynamics that position justice institutions as *boundary-making* institutions that will favour, depending on contexts and periods, specific social, political or economic interests over others. This structural inclination of justice institutions is therefore paramount to understand boundary-making processes between capitalism's cores *as* cores, and its peripheries *as* peripheries.

8.3 Professional Cartels and Echo Chambers

The US Supreme Court provides an interesting entry point for this investigation, as this court has the power to decide itself which petitions to examine. Biskupic et al.'s (2014) study underscores the direct correlation between the selection patterns of successful petitions and the status of petitioners as repeat players. Of the 10,300 petitions filed to the court between 2004 and 2012, judges agreed to hear just 5 per cent – 528 – of those appeals. Only sixty-six attorneys, less than 1 per cent of the total number of lawyers who petitioned the court filed at least one petition a year from 2004 to 2012, and each had at least three petitions that were granted in that period.

At the time of Biskupic et al.'s (2014) study, the Supreme Court was the most diverse it had ever been – three of the nine justices were women and two hailed from minorities – but this 'elite bar is strikingly homogeneous: of the 66 top lawyers, 63 are white. Only eight are women' (Biskupic et al. 2014).

In 2014, Neal Katyal was a relative newcomer into this elite bar. He fit all the self-replicating characteristics of this group – except for his Hindu origin. He clerked for a Supreme Court justice. He also worked in a top position in the US Office of the Solicitor General, whose lawyers represent the federal government before the Court. Katyal patterned his career after one of the most successful members of the Court's elite bar: John G. Roberts. 'Before becoming chief justice in 2005, Roberts served in the solicitor general's office and then built a thriving Supreme Court practice at the law firm where Katyal now works. From 1989 through 2003, Roberts appeared thirty-nine times before the court' (Biskupic et al. 2014).

'[T]he involvement of attorneys recognized for their Supreme Court experience can influence whether a case simply makes it before the court, a prerequisite to a decision affecting the law of the land' (Biskupic et al. 2014). The great majority of this elite bar also works at law firms that primarily represent businesses and are increasingly specialised in Supreme Court litigation. 'Business can pay for the best counsel money can buy. The average citizen cannot', [one of the Court's most liberal justices, Ruth Bader Ginsburg] said. 'That's just a reality' (Biskupic et al. 2014).

This specialty bar emerged against the backdrop of structural changes within the US field of state power in the mid-1980s. The rise of the first star of this market of insiders, Rex Lee, coincided with 'a demand for lawyers who could help roll back workplace, environmental and consumer regulations that had roots in the late 1960s and early 1970s' (Biskupic et al. 2014). After a stint as President Reagan's first solicitor general, Lee moved to the firm Sidley Austin and launched a high court practice focused on business clients.

In the post-2008 financial crisis, the Court's role in domestic politics increased against the backdrop of the Congress' political gridlocking and corporations turning to the court to weigh in on state and federal regulations. Conversely, the financial capacity of corporations to wage legal battles all the way from circuit courts through to the Supreme Court reinforces the latter's pro-business leaning. Individuals challenging large companies must seek counsel from a pool of attorneys that is not only smaller – as they work for the most part for legal clinics or based on pro bono for large corporate law firms – but collectively less successful. The result, Biskupic et al. (2014) argue, is

> a decided advantage for corporate America, and a growing insularity of the court. [The] reliance on a small cluster of specialists, most working on behalf of businesses, has turned the Supreme Court into an *echo chamber* – a place where an elite group of jurists embraces an elite group of lawyers who reinforce narrow views of how the law should be construed.
>
> (Emphasis added)

Certainly, the Supreme Court offers quite a unique vista into the social patterns that contribute to what Hirschl calls the 'judicialization of mega politics' (Hirschl 2008) precisely because due to its wide discretion in selecting petitions, the Court has a direct bearing on its market of users. It is an ideal-typical illustration of the importance of understanding the dynamic relationship between markets of users and producers of justice. The professional cartel of counsels appearing before the Supreme Court also channels attention to the role played by *gatekeepers of this relationship* in the valuation of the forms of capital marshalled through tribunals qua boundary-making institutions.

8.4 The Symbolic Market of Justice

International dispute settlement mechanisms – be they globally oriented national courts like the CNDA or offshore mechanisms like the ICSID – tend to operate in what criminal justice scholars identify as 'atypical political environments', that is, 'highly contentious environments in which surrounding political conditions lead to a departure from routinized [. . .] justice, so that courts must develop organizational models to cope with, mobilize, and at times deflect, the political landscape in which they operate' (Levi et al. 2016: 91).

Exposure to external shocks can at once transform and consolidate patterns of path dependency within inter/national dispute settlements mechanisms. But the social characteristics and professional strategies of the gatekeepers of the relationship between their users and producers can also provide an insight into the structural position of inter/national justice institutions as echo chambers. To put it simply: the competition between diverse dispute settlement mechanisms certainly generates the possibility of forum shopping for users of justice. But it also leads justice forums to have to 'shop' for users.

The contrasted dynamics of expansion of the CNDA and the ICSID are interesting in this regard. Though a national court, and since 2009 a component of the administrative judicial branch in France, the legal operations of the CNDA are regulated by the complex interplay between the 1951 Geneva Convention, national law, EU directives (see Fleury Graff and Marie 2019) – and, importantly, an in-house research organ which establishes factsheets about the Court's case law and political, economic, legal and social developments in countries of origin.

The recent history of the CNDA has been characterised – in the terms used by the Court itself – by 'protracted embolism'[6] due in great part to

[6] See the website of the CNDA, www.cnda.fr/La-CNDA/Histoire-de-la-Cour-nationale-du-droit-d-asile#mutation (accessed 23 May 2024).

external shocks: the explosion of asylum claims[7] and the prominence taken by immigration as a 'moral panic' blinker (Cohen 1972) within the French political field since the 1980s. So far, most scholarship on the CNDA – and more generally asylum justice – has been driven by anthropological and social geography studies of the post-1980s period.[8]

Akoka's (2020) institutional biography of the OFPRA since inception in 1952 as the administrative agency operating as the first tier for asylum applications draws an interesting hypothesis that connects the boom of the demand for asylum at the turn of the 1980s, the sharp decline of recognition rates for asylum seekers and the demographics of the agents of the OFPRA.

Recognition of asylum status reflects, she argues, not only macro-political factors but also the recruitment patterns of OFPRA agents. The first generations of OFPRA officers until the 1980s were themselves refugees or the offspring of former diplomats who represented their countries of origin in France before the Soviet invasions of the 1920s (in Ukraine and Georgia); the Communist political takeovers in 1947–1949 in Hungary, Yugoslavia, Czechoslovakia, Poland and Romania; or anti-Franco political opponents in the case of Spanish agents. There was, therefore, a social homology between the demand and supply side of asylum that was directly correlated to France's diplomatic interests in the Cold War.

'The OFPRA constitute[d] a form of consulate for toppled regimes and invaded countries [. . .]. Between the different actors at play (the state, the agents [of the OFPRA] and exiles, there [was] a convergence of interests and usages of the category of refugee' (Akoka 2020: 347 *Kindle* edition, my translation from French). The OFPRA was therefore positioned as an echo chamber reflecting the reciprocal relationship between the producers of asylum as a legal regime and their users. This relationship was reinforced by the common social capital of agents qua refugees and asylum seekers as their social homologues.

By the time I was appointed as an adjunct judge by the UNHCR in 2020, the institutional features – as much as the geopolitical landscape –

[7] Asylum claims in France exploded at the end of the 1980s, jumping from 30,000 in 1988 to 61,422 in 1989 and 60,000 in average since 2013. See www.ofpra.gouv.fr/fr/l-ofpra/l-ofpra-en-chiffres/evolutions-historiques-en-chiffres (accessed 2 July 2022).

[8] These studies tend to focus either on the demand side (asylum seekers and their experience, see Burridge and Gill 2017) or on the perceptions of asylum judges (be it their 'inner belief' or the moral economy of their practice, see Gill and Good 2019).

of the CNDA had radically changed. In 2010, what became the CNDA was institutionally recast as an administrative jurisdiction, under the Conseil d'État, France's apex administrative appellate court. The OFPRA was placed under the authority of the Ministry of Internal Affairs, rather than the Foreign Affairs Ministry as was previously the case. This changed geopolitical context was compounded by the rate of legislative reforms – with new laws and regulations on asylum procedures and migration adopted each year since the 2015 'migration crisis'.

As an institution, the CNDA has grown exponentially and now comprises twenty-three judicial chambers along with an internal research service, and the registry which allocates admissible claims to the chambers. Interestingly, the institution reflects the offshore characteristics of international dispute settlement mechanisms. While chamber presidents are professional judges, for the most part they intervene sporadically at the CNDA, while adjunct judges operate as 'consultants' selected for an expertise that is ambiguously defined as international legal expertise and/or geopolitical expertise. On the other hand, 95 per cent of the 1,150 lawyers representing asylum applicants operate based on jurisdictional aid, with individual cases referred to them by the registrar.

Collectively the repeat players operating at the court display resources that are drawn from their multi-positionality. But their position in relation to the Court is also 'uberised' – that is, their mobility into the Court and their status are structurally (including financially) determined by the state as regulator and their position within the French field of state power. Surprisingly, however, the rate of successful applications – 25 per cent in average – has not only remained constant since the 1980s but also reflects the rate of successful applications in other European Union countries despite the idiosyncrasies of their respective national asylum processes (see Gill and Good 2019: 8).

The research I carried out in parallel on professional patterns within the ICC (Dezalay S 2016a) suggests a hypothesis to account for this apparent paradox. The analogy can be drawn from the fact that the ICC constitutes the core institutional feature of a 'common sense' over global crimes even though the criminalisation of certain types of conduct internationally remains contested, uneven and deeply fragmented. One may recall that the ICC has jurisdiction over the most egregious crimes under international law (genocide, crimes against humanity, crimes of war and aggression). But it does not cover crimes committed by corporate actors.

The un-tapping of the Nuremberg legacy from the 1980s benefited from the alignment of great power political interests and the expansion of the international human rights movement. In turn, the break-up of these coalitions, following the North Atlantic Treaty Organization (NATO) intervention in Kosovo in 1999 (see Dezalay Y and Garth 2006) and foremost the 9/11 attacks and US-led military intervention in Iraq, help explain the less-than-favourable early years of development of the ICC and its protracted 'African bias' (Bosco 2014). This has contributed to position the ICC as a kind of hollow core in a 'weak field' of international criminal justice. The concept of the 'weak field' refers to a 'field that is completely immerged into other fields that are mapped out and constituted more firmly' (Topalov 1999: 469, my translation from French). This is reflected – and reinforced – in the collective characteristics of the repeat players who operate the ICC.

The professional profiles of the agents invested in the ICC display complementary, though structurally and institutionally segmented, sets of social and professional characteristics. On the one hand, 'high judges', or lawyers-diplomats, predominantly among the elected members of the Court,[9] overwhelmingly possess a combination of strong social and symbolic resources and are multi-positioned across national and international justice and political spheres.

By contrast, legal counsels operating in chambers typically have an academic background and have built their professional career within and around international criminal tribunals from the mid-1990s. This induces generational and institutional effects. Compared to the relative autonomy of the legal counsels that were assigned to chambers at the ad hoc international criminal tribunals for the former Yugoslavia and Rwanda, legal counsels at the ICC are placed in an institutionally dominated position as their access to, and mobility within and from, the court tends to be determined by political constraints (the election of given judges by the Assembly of state parties) and interpersonal relations. The judiciary form of capital they collectively develop contributes to the routinisation of the operations of the court as much as its insulation, as the doctrine of the ICC tends to be produced in an exclusive network of academic institutions clustered around The Hague.

For their part, the bulk of the hundreds of lawyers registered as potential defence counsels are unlikely to appear before the court. Repeat players within this highly competitive market are a handful of individuals, increasingly operating from boutique law firms specialised in

[9] There are eighteen elected judges, who, along with the prosecutor and vice prosecutor of the Court as well as the registrar, represent the elected authorities of the ICC.

transnational criminal litigation within two hubs – London and Amsterdam. The scarcity of cases before the ICC is compounded by their length. These agents, funded through jurisdictional aid provided by the court, consolidate their position as repeat players through activities that are 'often either related to commercializing their expertise, or sometimes in parallel, strengthening their positions vis-à-vis (actual or potential) victim communities' (Christensen 2021: 800).

Contrasting these patterns of professionalisation and institutionalisation to the ICSID opens interesting avenues, as the trajectory of this institution was also largely determined by external shocks. The ICSID was set up in 1967 as an independent entity of the World Bank Group with the specific aim of providing a forum for the settlement of disputes between foreign investors and host states away from the uncomfortable '*ménage à trois*' generated by the diplomatic protection of foreign corporations by home states against host states (Alshner 2014).

In the 1960s–1970s, the ICSID was shunned in the context of the NIEO debates that dominated the UN General Assembly – illustrated by the fierce opposition of Latin American states against international arbitration.[10] The ICSID's second Secretary General, Ibrahim Shihata, appointed in 1983 and a proponent of the NIEO, contributed to easing this ideological divide. According to doctrinal accounts, the revival of the ICSID was also fostered by the jurisprudential 'revolution' of the *AAPL* v. *Sri Lanka* verdict which recognised the capacity for foreign investors to introduce claims based on treaties, notwithstanding the specificities of their contracts with host states.

The explosion of bilateral and multilateral investment agreements[11] further spurred the growth of investment treaty arbitration, along with the Argentina debt crisis at the end of the 1990s, and the Greek economic crisis from 2012. From the early 2000s, the threat of challenges by corporations against governmental policies in advanced economies to regulate the health or environment sector[12] fuelled a debated 'backlash' against this form of derivative justice criticised as befitted to the

[10] The Calvo doctrine prevented foreign nationals from invoking diplomatic protection to settle international disputes with Latin American states.

[11] Totalling over 3,000 worldwide, up from just a few hundred in the late 1980s.

[12] In an emblematic case, tobacco giant Philipp Morris responded to Uruguay and Australia's anti-smoking laws by introducing claims before different international settlement dispute mechanisms, respectively the ICSID in 2010 and the PCA in 2012, under UNCITRAL Rules.

expectations of private businesses to the detriment of sovereign powers (Waibel et al. 2010).

Yet the ICSID, along with the PCA, emerged at the turn of the 2000s as the 'two major players' (Gaillard 2015: 7–8)[13] of the thriving market for investment arbitration. Both institutions had remained dormant for decades.[14] In their pioneering study, Dezalay Y and Garth (1996) recall that the expansion of international commercial arbitration from the 1980s itself had been linked to external shocks and wider transformations in the global economy. The oil crises of the 1970s and the move towards North–South economic relations fostered the demand by transnational corporations for flexible forms of conflict resolution, away from national courts in the Global South. They also underscore the key role played in this boom by battles among key groups of legal elites over the definition of commercial arbitration as a new arena of professional practice.

Contests over the stakes and remit of commercial arbitration reflected the relative positions of agents within the field according to the portfolio of capitals they could muster and 'capitalise' to consolidate or contest existing professional hierarchies (Dezalay Y and Madsen 2012). Key to the growth of commercial arbitration was the entry into play of a new generation of contenders: US multinational corporate law firms which combined considerable resources, including their proximity with political power and businesses.

The alliance between US corporate lawyers with European professors, the 'grand old men' and architects of the principles of the *Lex mercatoria*, contributed to legitimating this form of justice by granting a legally principled manner to treat multinational agreements with sovereign states in the Middle East and Africa as if they were private contracts. The alliance and complementarity of positions between these professors and practitioners (King's Counsels (KCs), high judges, senior partners of multinational law firms) gradually converged towards a small cosmopolitan network of professors and practitioners – the 'transnational arbitral community' – who collectively embody the symbolic authority of this form of justice (see Dezalay Y and Garth 2016): what some commen-

[13] The ICSID attracts about thirty new claims per year, while the PCA has officiated as an umbrella for 150 new arbitration cases in the past fifteen years.

[14] The ICSID barely survived with a mere thirty-seven disputes registered between its creation in 1967 and the end of the 1990s while the PCA dwindled to a one-man Secretariat at The Hague Peace Palace.

tators refer to as the 'super arbitrators', who are 'not just the mafia, but a smaller, inner mafia' (Barker 2012).

The transition from contract-based to investment treaty-based arbitration opened the potential for 'a new market for public international lawyers'[15] by making public international law applicable. But it 'took place without any significant ruptures in the professionals dealing with such arbitration' (Schill 2011: 883). Indeed, 'the professionals who later became active in the then emerging field came from the same type of law firms that had dealt with the earlier contract-based ICSID arbitrations and other international commercial arbitration between private parties. They were commercial arbitration specialists' (Schill 2011).

The Argentina cases and the legitimacy crisis they triggered fuelled a symbolic displacement in the profile of arbitrators, with the entry into play of agents associated with the symbolic authority of the ICJ. For example, the appointment of Georges Abi-Saab as 'an advocate for the periphery' (Terris et al. 2007: 137) as much as a guardian of the legitimacy of public international justice in the Argentina cases played a symbolic role to signal that the ICSID had 'become more responsive to sovereign concerns' (Alvarez and Topalian 2012: 532).

This also contributed to moving 'the centre of gravity increasingly [...] toward the commercial arbitration bar' (Schill 2011: 888). The ICJ judges and counsels are pulled into treaty investment arbitration through multinational corporate law firms acting as gatekeepers. Charles Brower, one of the 'elite 15' of investment treaty arbitrators as a partner with White & Case and now 20 Essex Street Chambers (Eberhardt and Olivet 2012: 39), noted somewhat scathingly that '[w]hile lack of familiarity with public international law may be a barrier to commercial arbitration practitioners entering the field of investment treaty arbitration, it is a barrier that can be overcome with relative ease [...]. The [...] lack of familiarity with litigation techniques and commercial transactions [...] is less easily remedied. [...] It must be "soaked up" through extended exposure' (Brower 2008: 191–192). As confirmed by a prominent member of the bar of the ICJ: 'they [corporations] have to research five names in 24 hours, and then you come out with a label' – as more or less state- or investors-oriented.

[15] Author's interview (with Yves Dezalay) with Pierre-Marie Dupuy, counsel at the ICJ and arbitrator, Paris, 20 May 2014. My translation from French.

By contrast, 'multinational corporate law firms have the capacity to play it both ways'.[16]

The growth of the ICSID – and more largely the expansion of the field of investment arbitration – largely built out of the social complementarity of position between European professors and US practitioners that fostered the expansion of the field of commercial arbitration. The alliance between European professors and US practitioners allowed the latter to gain some scholarly credibility and the former to get closer to business interests. In turn, high barriers of entry – LLMs from North American law schools and positions within top-tier multinational corporate law firms – enabled the consolidation of this marketplace as an exclusive professional space.

The contrasted trajectories of the marketplaces constituted around the CNDA and the ICC on the one hand and the Supreme Court and the ICSID on the other display a common driver in the judicialisation of corporate and political interests: the dynamic relationship between producers of institutional and normative forms of codification of social disputes, and users of these mechanisms. All four examples underscore the key role played by the *gatekeepers* of this relationship.

Both the CNDA and the ICC could be construed as *hollow core* institutions, that is, institutions whose demographic composition and internal stratification reflect the structural fragmentation of the atypical political environments in which they operate but whose boundary-making effects on these geopolitical contexts are neither linear nor homogeneous. In other words: gatekeeping positions between producers and users of these forms of justice are contested and structurally determined by the relative value of the resources (be they social, financial or political) they bring into these institutions from other fields.

By contrast the dynamic of expansion of the market of users of Supreme Court litigation and commercial/investment arbitration reflect the instrumental gatekeeping role of a specific type of institution: the model of the Wall Street corporate law firm as a provider of legal services *and* an engine of reproduction of social status within these professional markets. This begs the question: how does social mobility, *towards* as much as *from*, international dispute settlement mechanisms (re)produce

[16] Ibid. For example, the two main firms involved in treaty investment arbitration, Freshfields and White & Case, represent both investors and states (though mainly corporations) (Eberhardt and Olivet 2012: 20).

structural 'dynamics of racialised power' (Anghie 2006: 112) between African states and individuals as users of inter/national justice?

8.5 Symbolic Gateways and Institutional Highways

The ICJ provides a good entry point for this inquiry. The Court gained prominence as the 'world' court only following the *Nicaragua* decisions of 1984–1986 and the *Frontier Dispute* between Burkina Faso and Mali in 1986, which according to doctrinal accounts brokered the 'reconciliation of the ICJ with the Third World' (Pellet 2013: 277). Certainly, this symbolic position contrasts markedly with the parallel boom of international arbitration.[17]

But our study of the profiles, over time, of judges and counsels operating the ICJ (and its predecessor, the PCIJ since the 1920s (Dezalay S and Dezalay Y 2017)) underscores the remarkable resilience of the characteristics of the 'invisible college' of international lawyers (Schachter 1977–1978). Confirming other studies on the profiles of international judges (Terris et al. 2007), we found that international judges continue to be multi-positioned. However, we identified a stark contrast between judges from Europe and the US, and judges from the Global South. Typically judges from Europe and the US are no longer defined by a scholarly form of capital. They primarily, if not essentially, start their careers within the legal services of foreign affairs ministries, as *jurisconsultes.*

By contrast, judges from the Global South – particularly from former African colonies – generally continue to display the characteristics of what Sacriste and Vauchez (2007) dub 'gentlemen politicians of law'. They tend to hold the triple heading of political elites, high magistrates in their respective countries and law professors – with international credentials gained at core European universities and institutions, foremost the Institut de droit international (Institute of International Law), as well as the UN International Law Commission.

Our study also underscores that the symbolic revival of the ICJ from the 1980s coincided with the monopolisation of the professional market of interstate adjudication by a cluster of predominantly male counsels from continental Europe, Britain and the US. While counsels at earlier

[17] With fewer than 130 new contentious cases introduced before the ICJ from 1984 compared to the over 13,000 commercial and investment claims administered by the ICC in Paris from 1976.

periods also originated from core European countries, they shared the characteristics of judges. From the 1980s, we identified thirty-nine repeat players,[18] including a more restricted group of fifteen counsels who have appeared in seven cases or more. Two individuals – Alain Pellet and James Crawford – appeared in over forty cases before the ICJ. The defining characteristic of these repeat players is that they are essentially scholars. This suggests that, compared to their earlier counterparts, access to this small marketplace is no longer defined by resources drawn from outside the field. Yet, like Kumar and Rose (2014), we also found a growing number of solo practitioners and lawyers from law firms, suggesting that these counsels increasingly – like in other judicial fora (see Romano 2003) – tend to appear not just qua academics but also as attorneys or partners within law firms.

Looking back to the position of the ICJ in the Cold War helps understand these changes in the diachrony – by channelling attention to the dynamic relationship between this two-tiered structure of the ICJ as a social space, and state users of interstate adjudication. The shunning of the ICJ by newly independent states in the Global South after controversial decisions taken by the court in the 1960s meant that interstate adjudication became a sideshow in Cold War politics.

The sidelining of the ICJ consolidated contradictions that were present from the stage of the genesis, in the early efforts to promote international justice institutions – notably the unequal relationship between European law professors then relatively marginalised from doctrinal hierarchies and state diplomacies, and US corporate lawyers close to US business and political interests (Dezalay Y and Garth 2016). The shunning of the ICJ throughout the Cold War – illustrated by an at times empty docket – fostered the insulation of the small marketplace of interstate adjudication around drivers of reproduction defined by charismatic authority, mentor–pupil relations and at times family legacies at a cluster of European academic centres.[19]

As noted by a then young recruit into this small milieu, 'any caste must organise the conditions of its own survival'[20] – a rule of the game

[18] Who appeared as lead counsels in four cases or more.

[19] Like the Chichele Chair of Public International Law at Oxford, which, along with the Whewell Chair at Cambridge, are incubators of international litigators from the UK, or the Université de droit of Paris-Ouest Nanterre around Alain Pellet in France.

[20] Authors' interview (with Yves Dezalay) with a junior member of the bar of the ICJ, Geneva, 4 April 2014. My translation from French.

confirmed by a senior member of the ICJ Bar: 'to enter this universe, it is preferable but not essential to be good; what matters is to belong to the small circle of renown [counsels]'.[21] In our study (Dezalay S and Dezalay Y 2017) we hypothesised that the two-tiered social structure of the market for interstate adjudication makes it more vulnerable to external shocks – including the pressure growingly exercised by multinational corporate law firms as contenders. This could indicate that the dynamics that spurred the expansion of the field of international arbitration from the 1980s are now encroaching into the professional market of interstate adjudication.

Emblematically, the US multinational corporate law firm Foley Hoag branched out into interstate adjudication through an intensive political marketing vis-à-vis Latin American states, which remain prominent users of this side of international justice, by leaning on the symbolic aura of Paul Reichler who was part of the team representing Nicaragua in the 1984 decision. It is also a prominent member of the 'club' of private arbitrators, Jan Paulsson, who played an instrumental role in introducing the multinational corporate law firm Freshfields to ICJ adjudication, through his appointment as counsel for Bahrain in 2001. His profile is emblematic of the generational shift that characterised the market for international commercial arbitration from a type of informal justice dominated by law professors – the 'grand old men' of international law – to a form of 'offshore' justice dominated by US litigators predominantly operating from multinational corporate law firms (Dezalay Y and Garth 1996).

'In a recent speech marking its 75th anniversary, the President of the ICJ noted the "unsatisfactory situation" that "very few of the counsels [appearing before the ICJ] are from developing countries."'[22] Certainly the self-replicating features of the bar of the ICJ are durably entrenched. But the most striking transformation illustrated by the evolution of the social space of professionals operating as counsels at the ICJ is arguably the relative devaluation of scholarly capital as a channel of (re)production of hierarchy within this marketplace.

The vulnerability of this professional market to external shocks may also affect their position as *gatekeepers* of the relationship with users of

[21] Authors' interview (Yves Dezalay) with Pierre-Marie Dupuy, counsel at the ICJ and arbitrator, Paris, 20 August 2014. My translation from French.

[22] See the website of the ICJ, www.icj-cij.org/public/files/press-releases/0/000-20210419-PRE-01-00-EN.pdf (accessed 20 June 2022).

this form of international justice. ICJ judges – just like all international judges – are elected through highly political processes. The 2017 elections provide an emblematic example. The ICJ is composed of fifteen judges elected to nine-year terms by the UN General Assembly and the UN Security Council. In 2017, five new judges needed to be elected. The race for the last mandate involved weeks of diplomatic lobbying between the British candidate, Sir Christopher Greenwood, and the Indian candidate, Dalveer Bhandari. Just minutes before the eleventh round of votes, Greenwood admitted defeat. For the first time in the seventy-five-year history of the ICJ, Britain therefore did not have a judge on the bench of the ICJ. Certainly, the context of Brexit (and India's position as a trading partner for Britain), attacks against Greenwood's role in advising then prime minister Blair to participate in the 2003 invasion of Iraq and, more generally, 'residual international resentment in the UN General Assembly of the dominance and privileges of the permanent five members of the Security Council – the US, Britain, France, China and Russia'[23] – played a role in this outcome.

But Bhandari's profile also suggests another, symbolic, displacement. Nominations of candidates for election to the ICJ are made by a group consisting of the members of the PCA, designated by each state. Members of the PCA act in 'national groups'.[24] In the case of UN member states not represented in the PCA, the state in question may select up to four individuals to be its 'national group' for the purpose of nominating candidates to the ICJ. The list of arbitrators of the PCA is symbolic. When the PCA operates as an arbitration forum, parties – be they states, corporations or international organisations – can select arbitrators outside of this pool. But in their capacity of endorsement of nominees to the ICJ bench, PCA members constitute a *who's who* of national legal elites. Their profiles therefore reflect states' preferences. They conversely point to the types of resources valued for access to the ICJ.

Just like the three other Indian lawyers elected as judges to the ICJ since India's independence, Bhandari accessed the ICJ bench in 2012 from the higher tier of the Indian judiciary, as member of the Supreme Court. Unlike his predecessors, however, he is not a typical 'gentleman politician of law' in that he predominantly built his

[23] O Bowcott, 'No British judge on world court for first time in its 71-year history' *The Guardian* 20 November 2017.

[24] That is, all the PCA members from any individual state.

professional credentials from a judicial national platform, combined with scholarly credentials acquired in India and the US – not in Oxbridge, and not in the usual incubators of international legal elites from former colonies – The Hague Academy, the Institute of International Law and the UN International Law Commission.

Though in broad strokes, in our study (Dezalay S and Dezalay Y 2017) we found concurrent symbolic displacements by comparing the 1999 and the 2013 PCA list of arbitrators. The 1999 list still reflected a universe of national elites of international law very similar to the profiles of the lawyers involved in international justice institutions at the time of the genesis. The 213 members of the PCA from outside Europe/the US combined multi-positionality with strong national political resources[25] reinforced by diplomatic appointments in key postings (New York, Geneva or The Hague). Significantly, among the 1999 cohort of notables of international law, very few mentioned an experience in arbitration or any proximity with corporate legal practice.

By contrast, the 2013 list suggested a diversification towards profiles much closer to international arbitration and specifically corporate legal practice. In the 1999 list, 3 per cent of arbitrators mentioned an expertise in corporate law, compared to 22 per cent in the 2013 list. Conversely, in the 2013 list, less than one third were identified as law professors-*jurisconsultes*. These shifts are more evident for states that could be qualified as the periphery or new contenders within the international markets for international justice, particularly new or more recent contracting states of the PCA, typically from the former USSR block and Asia. The radical transformation of the profiles of the Singapore group between 1999 and 2013 provides a case in point. The 1999 group included one professor-*jurisconsulte* and two solicitors. By contrast, all four arbitrators appointed in 2013 had an expertise and a professional trajectory connected to corporate law.

This shift is certainly biased due to the multi-positionality that still characterises international lawyers from the Global South at the national and international levels, in that practice within a corporate law firm can often be combined with multiple positions. But this shift could indicate strategies of repositioning that are at once political *and* professional.

[25] About a quarter had been appointed to high governmental positions, most often as foreign affairs ministers, as well as prime ministers, presidents of the Parliament, even heads of state.

Singapore's arbitrators could reflect this state's strategic positioning as a new hub for commercial arbitration in Asia.

More generally the profiles of the arbitrators of recent member states of the PCA all underscore their skills and positions in corporate law. With a tendency to be less multi-positioned, they more often hail from legal practice rather than academia, and fewer have held high judicial or governmental functions at the domestic level. Rather, they tend to mention their arbitration experience at the national level, notably within chambers of commerce, and especially at the international level within diverse arbitration forums: the ICC in Paris for a third of them, and for another third the ICSID, the Southern Common Market (MERCOSUR) and World Trade Organization (WTO) panels. This could indicate that these newcomers vie to access the marketplaces for international justice more from a professional platform in international (corporate) law than as 'gentlemen politicians of law'. This seems to be corroborated by their academic credentials, with an important proportion now holding an LLM in corporate law from US law schools.

Although there are currently seventeen states from the African continent that are members of the PCA, only Uganda has nominated four arbitrators, all displaying the typical features of 'gentlemen politicians of law'.[26] Zooming in onto the profiles of the African lawyers elected to the ICJ bench over time can help connect these wider shifts to the transformation of the ICJ Bar. Four African lawyers had been elected to the ICJ bench before the turning point of the *Nicaragua* decisions of 1984–1986 and the *Frontier Dispute* between Burkina Faso and Mali in 1986: two hailing from former West African French colonies, and two from a former British colony, Nigeria.

The first African to be elected to the ICJ was the Senegalese Isaac Forster, in 1964. As I recalled in Chapter 3, Forster was successively a member of the indigenous legal elite within the French Empire and then the French colonial nation state after World War II (the *Union française*) before becoming one of the most prominent architects of independent Senegal, whose close political, military and judicial links with the former *métropole* embraced France's 'colonial projection' during the Cold War. His endorsement as a member of the international legal elite was consolidated by his election to the Institute of International Law. The second African elected to the Court from a former French colony, in 1970, the

[26] See the current list of members of the Court on the website of the PCA, https://pca-cpa.org/en/about/structure/members-of-the-court/ (accessed 16 September 2022).

Beninese Louis Ignacio-Pinto, displayed similar characteristics (see Dezalay S 2017b). Hailing from a family of wealthy coastal traders, Ignacio-Pinto was sent to France for his secondary-level studies and returned to what was then Dahomey after completing a doctorate in law. He was elected to the ICJ from a triple platform – as a trader, *avocat-défenseur* and member of Parliament in France in the context of the *Union française* – and diplomatic credentials as representative of Dahomey in Washington, DC and the UN.

The first Nigerian judge at the ICJ, Charles D. Onyeama, was elected in 1967 after the series of unpopular judgments of the court in 1966,[27] which prompted African countries to demand greater representation amongst its judges. The Australian judge filling the seat dedicated to the Commonwealth was replaced with Onyeama, raising the number of African judges on the ICJ bench to two. While Onyeama acceded to the court from a high judicial platform – as member of the Nigerian Supreme Court – his successor to the seat, Taslim Olawale Elias, elected in 1976, combined both meritocratic credentials from the former colonial *métropole* and a strong social and political platform. Vice president and then president of the ICJ between 1979 and 1985, Elias was the first African to earn a PhD from the University of London in 1949. He was then appointed governor of the School of Oriental and African Studies (SOAS) and played an instrumental role in drafting Nigeria's independence Constitution. Thereafter, he combined top governmental and academic positions at the domestic level – as Attorney General, Minister of Justice, Chief Justice of the Supreme Court and dean of the Faculty of Law – with key international positions, including as member of the International Law Commission, before being appointed to the ICJ after the 1975 military coup in Nigeria.

During the two first decades after the 1960s wave of independence, the profiles of these four judges complemented that of their European and US counterparts who, like their predecessors at the PCIJ, were typically *jurisconsultes*. Counsels representing states tended to share a similar profile. Sir Henri Beckett, one of the repeat international litigators before the PCIJ, is a case in point. Called to the Bar of the Inner Temple in 1922, he joined the UK Foreign Office in 1925 as legal advisor. His final years at the Foreign Office coincided with a period of heavy litigation involving the UK, which he represented in five cases. He contributed to the

[27] In its advisory opinions on the *international status of South West Africa*, the ICJ refused to pronounce itself on the right to self-determination.

institutionalisation of a legal department within the British Foreign Service after 1945, before his appointment to the International Law Commission, the nascent European Commission of Human Rights and to the ICJ, which he chaired from 1979.

By contrast, the generation of counsels that emerged between 1960 and the 1986 *Nicaragua* and *Frontier Dispute* decisions gained their position as repeat players before the ICJ primarily as scholars. For example, Sir Claud Humphrey Meredith Waldock, a repeat player during the first thirty years of the ICJ (between 1948 and the early 1980s, with a dozen cases), combined legal practice at the Gray's Inn bar in 1928 with the Chichele Chair at Oxford from 1947 and acted as counsel to the UK, as well as to India, Spain and Denmark between 1949 and 1970.

The monopolisation of the 'international bar' of the ICJ by a scholarly elite can be related to a twofold process: the constitution of this small marketplace around scholarly meritocratic and personal (mentor–pupil) rules of access; and its gradual insulation from politics and state diplomacies. The retreat into a doctrinal ivory tower reflected the shunning of the court by newly independent countries from the mid-1960s. Contrary to the multi-positioning that characterised the generation of the genesis, since the 1980s these repeat players are primarily characterised by the combination of meritocratic scholarly credentials and mentor–pupil relations.

With an aura gained as main counsel for Nicaragua in 1984, Ian Brownlie monopolised more than half of the ICJ docket from this case until his death in 2010. Hailing from modest origins, he won a scholarship to read law at Hertford College, Oxford, and completed his Oxford DPhil in 1961 under the supervision of Waldock at the Chichele Chair of Public International Law. Brownlie also typified a UK model in this small scholarly milieu, that of a learned barrister, which contrasts with the continental model of professor-practitioner, in France or Germany. Nonetheless, it is as a member of his team in the *Nicaragua* case that Alain Pellet – currently the most prominent member of the ICJ Bar – acceded to this select professional market.

Now, zooming in further into the social microcosm constituted by the *Nicaragua* and *Frontier Dispute* decisions provides a fascinating vista into the relationship members of this learned meritocratic elite entertained with the generation of African judges appointed to the Court at the turn of the 1980s. The *Frontier Dispute* decision was chaired by Mohammed Bedjaoui, elected to the bench in 1981 (and president of the Court in 1994–1997) – and third judge appointed to the ICJ from a former French colony. An Algerian diplomat and lawyer, Bedjaoui completed his PhD in France before cumulating high academic, political and diplomatic positions in Algeria: as dean of the Faculty of Law at the University of Algiers, ambassador to France, president of Algeria's Constitutional Council, foreign minister in 2005–2007. With many publications calling for a NIEO in the 1970s, he lectured in The Hague Academy in 1970 and 1976 and was elected to the Institute of International Law in 1976 (Dezalay Y and Garth 1996: 25).

Like the other African judges elected to the court since then,[28] the profile of Georges Abi-Saab, ad hoc judge in the *Frontier Dispute* decision, also illustrates the links with the scholarly elite of the international bar of the ICJ. Born into a French-speaking family of Cairo, a professor at the Geneva Graduate Institute of International Studies from 1963, he became an occasional member of the international bar of the ICJ from the *Tunisia* v. *Libya* case in 1978 through his acquaintance 'with many of the well-known players in international justice' (Terris et al. 2007: 134) as a former pupil of Sir Robert Jennings, the president of the Institute of International Law from 1983 and the successor of Sir Hersch Lauterpacht at the Whewell Chair of International Law at Cambridge from 1955.

But Bedjaoui is also one of the few well-known commercial arbitrators from former colonies and more generally the Global South, along with Professor Ahmed El-Kosheri from Cairo, and another former judge of the ICJ, Eduardo Jiménez de Arechaga from Uruguay. Like them, his profile is

> very much like those of the 'grand old men' [of arbitration] – with one crucial difference [. . .]. The difference is that an arbitrator from the Third world must find a way to gain access to and credibility with the centre. National stature is probably not enough without close connections to Paris, London or elsewhere in the legal centre. Indeed, one of the characteristics of the successful third-world arbitrator is that they get pulled to the centre, spending much of their time residing in places like Paris.
>
> (Dezalay Y and Garth 1996: 25)

These profiles underscore a break in the patterns of access to the status of international legal elite for lawyers hailing from former African colonies from the 1980s, with channels of co-optation no longer defined

[28] The Senegalese Kéba Mbaye was elected to the Court in 1981, the Nigerian Bola Ajibola in 1991, the Sierra-Leonese Abdul Koroma in 1994, the Somali Abdulqawi Ahmed Yusuf in 2009 and the Ugandan Julia Sebuntinde in 2012.

solely by meritocratic credentials (combined with strong social resources) within the imperial realm (legal education in the *métropole* and endorsement by the Institute of International Law). From the 1980s, mentor–pupil relations with the repeat players of the bar of the ICJ play an instrumental, yet ambiguous, role of endorsement into the international legal elite[29]: while the charismatic rules of the game of the ICJ Bar foster the domination of a happy few (or a happy two), resources acquired through these relations by the 'grand old men' of arbitration from the South now tend to be capitalised elsewhere: in commercial and investment arbitration.

8.6 Conclusion

How do justice institutions – be they supranational or national tribunals ruling over global matters – reproduce structural 'dynamics of racialised power' (Anghie 2006: 112) between African states, individuals and corporations as users of inter/national justice? Discussions on the 'corporate bias' of investment arbitration or the 'neo-colonialism' reflected by global justice institutions are emblematic of the symbolic politics at play not only in the judicialisation of disputes but also in the social and symbolic construction of 'Africa' and its relationship to the world. These symbolic politics underscore that the authority itself of global justice is contested. They are also a reminder that global justice is a symbolic market, that is, to use Bourdieu's reflections (1971), a space in which the belief in global justice as a symbolic good is a condition for the authority of global justice institutions.

As such, therefore, the judicialisation of politics is shaped by the dynamic relationship between restricted markets of producers and wider markets of users of inter/national dispute settlement mechanisms. But focusing solely on the symbolism of appointing an 'African' as international judge or, for that matter, my own position as a French white woman at the CNDA obfuscates the 'entangled' social hierarchies at play in the operations of national and international dispute settlement mechanisms – as institutions and as professional markets.

[29] With one exception: as the first African female judge at the ICJ, Julia Sebuntinde combines a strong national portfolio of resources (as former high court judge and *jurisconsulte*) and international credentials drawn from the field of international criminal justice, as judge at the Special Court for Sierra Leone between 2007 and 2012.

The social and professional characteristics of professionals involved in inter/national justice institutions are far from anecdotal. They help identify the professional drivers – rules of the game and competition – that define justice institutions as professional markets. They also point to the structural drivers that sustain these mechanisms over time. The operational context of these institutions matters. It impacts their capacity to produce a symbolically effective codification of social relations. It also shapes their authority in the conversion of forms of capital (social, political, economic) and their validation in other fields. In other words, it impacts their structural position as either gateways or highways in the reproduction of symbolic capital – including that of 'Africanness'.

Beyond their diversity, what is striking when we channel attention to the *parallel* trajectories of the marketplaces of the US Supreme Court, the CNDA, the ICSID, the ICC and the ICJ is that they reflect a common driver of judicialisation over time: the cartelisation of the professional markets of producers of justice. They also underscore the relevance of looking at the structurally dynamic position of the *gatekeepers* of the relationship between producers and users of justice institutions. While the CNDA and the ICC could be construed as hollow core institutions, which reflect conflicting forms of capital brought in from other fields, the ICJ illustrates a complex process of *hollowing out*. The institution is still a channel of access to the international realm for legal elites from the African South. But it is no longer an *institutional highway* for the accumulation and conversion of resources at the national and the international levels.

Rather, it reflects the growing role played by the Wall Street model of the corporate law firm in the restructuration of the international justice landscape, and as a symbolic driver of reproduction of professional hierarchies – that is, as a driver at once in the ongoing transformation of professional marketplaces for international justice, and in the symbolic and practical redefinition of the relationship between the African South and the global economy.

Conclusion

Souleymane[1] hails from Burkina Faso – the state whose name 'the home of honest people' ('*la patrie des gens intègres*') was coined by Thomas Sankara, the military-turned-Communist revolutionary, who promised to bring this former French colony onto the path of national emancipation, economic development and women's empowerment before he was murdered in 1987.

Souleymane arrived in Paris over two decades ago, following on the trails of two of his half-brothers. He is the eldest son of his mother. His father, well into his eighties, sired a couple of dozen children. Souleymane's father experienced colonial rule, the painfully short glimmers of independence, dictatorships, now a simmering jihadist war that has plagued the northern region of the country since 2015, and the doom of extraverted hope: sons and daughters scattered across Europe, in the quest of a better future.

Souleymane has a relentless dream. He wants to position himself as a trader operating directly between Burkinabe small-scale producers of sesame and other seeds and the organic retail industry in continental Europe. Souleymane's dream is relentlessly crushed. When his fret is not stolen or packed with stones, the seeds arrive in Europe rotten after months at sea, blocked by the COVID-19 crisis, or simply because the wrong hand was greased with the wrong amount at the freight port. Souleymane is keenly aware that he lacks the social capital and the financial clout that would enable his loads to transit swiftly from his landlocked birth country to Europe; that would position him as intermediary between the women farmers of his native village and global markets.

What I do not know is why there is no other alternative, for him, between success as a trader and the brutal work he has finally accepted to

[1] Souleymane is a pseudonym. He is a friend. I thank him for lending me his story.

take on as a security guard – like his half-brothers. In the preface to the twenty volumes of his monumental family saga, *Les Rougon-Macquart*, the French writer Zola explained the project in these words:

> [I] want to account for the behaviour of a family, a small group of individuals, within society, which expands to give birth to ten, twenty persons who appear, at first glance, deeply different, but who turn out [when analysed in their collective biography] intimately linked to one another. [. . .] And once I will hold all the threads, once I will grasp this social group in its entirety, I will show this group as a living body, as the actor of an historic era.
>
> (Zola 2019 [1871]: 12, my translation from French)

As Zola points out in 1871, the romantic epic is also a *scientific* fresco. The first episode, *The Fortune of the Rougons*, is also entitled by its scientific title, *The Origins* (Zola 2019 [1871]: 13). For Zola, there is an adequacy, otherwise symptomatic of the naturalist literary current which characterised the nineteenth century as an era of political, social and economic turmoil,

> between the nervous and bloody accidents which declare themselves in a race following 'a first organic lesion' and the 'fall of the Bonapartes', which, specifies the author, 'I needed as an artist, and which I always inevitably found at the end of the drama, without daring to hope for it so soon, came to give me the terrible and necessary denouement of my work. It is, as of today, complete; it moves in a finite circle; it becomes the story of a dead reign, of a strange era of madness and shame'.
>
> (Zola 2019 [1871]: 12, my translation from French)

Lawyering Imperial Encounters does not hail as a totalising history. First because it cannot dare to recount in their entirety the collective biographical encounters of symbolic intermediation between the African South and global markets. In her magisterial Ted talk, 'The danger of a single story',[2] the Nigerian-American writer Chimamanda Ngozi Adichie recalled the warning of the Palestinian poet Mourid Barghouti that 'if you want to dispossess a people, the simplest way to do it is to tell their story, and to start with, 'secondly''.[3] Start Souleymane's story with his physical removal from his birth country, and not with the French colonisation of

[2] CN Adichie, 'The danger of a single story' TEDGlobal July 2009, www.ted.com/talks/chimamanda_ngozi_adichie_the_danger_of_a_single_story?language=en (accessed 29 December 2023).

[3] Ibid.

the Haute-Volta, and you have an entirely different story. Start Souleymane's story with the necessity of converting to brutal labour in Europe despite his university degrees, and not his relentless dream, and you have an entirely different story.

As Adichie argues, '[p]ower is the ability not just to tell the story of another person, but to make it the definitive story of that person'.[4] And perhaps, indeed, there is no other way than fiction to escape the problem with stereotypes. The fact that they are not untrue, but incomplete. Perhaps, thus, the best venture into the past to make sense of the present as a kaleidoscope rather than a single black line is to read Okonkwo's story – Chinua Achebe's (1990 [1958]) *Things Fall Apart*'s hero – as a sequel, and not just a prequel, to Adichie's (2016) *Americanah*. Perhaps there is no other way to understand how an Igbo warrior could end up committing the tabooest gesture of his people, suicide, than to follow Ifemelu's return to Igboland, from the US, back to her first love, Obinze, who never 'made it' in Europe but who met the right people at the right time in present Nigeria. And in so doing lost a little bit of himself.

Thus, it is also, and foremost, because *Lawyering Imperial Encounters* tells the story of the protracted hangover of the past in the present. Ask any student and they will all agree that allowing *us*, in the so-called North, to breathe better, while Africa continues to suffocate, is horrifying. Ask any student, and they will all have stories to tell about colonialism, stories that often hark back to their family genealogies. Certainly, not all of them are imperial *cadets*. But all of them eat sugar. And we know, thanks to Mintz' magnificent *Sweetness and Power* (Mintz 1986), that the palatability of sugar is not just an acquired taste. It is eminently imperial.

Students will all respond with indignation to the one-sided and partial storytelling about the past recounted in their history books. But the past cannot be erased, or rewritten. Nor can it be reduced to a 'hangover' (Puri 2021). The past matters to the present because it can help track future paths. But for this, we need to ask, like Mitra argues in her superb study of 'deviant female sexuality' in colonial India (Mitra 2020: 206): what if 'the thousands of pages of social scientific description' that reinforce the position of law and legal professions as the 'cutting edge' of colonialism and post-colonial development 'could not claim the mantle of objectivity from their form alone'?

[4] Ibid.

C.1 The Past Matters, in a Sedimented Way

Law remains the vernacular of Africa's uneven and unequal relationship with the world economy. It is through law that forms of financial and symbol capital are negotiated *as* sovereign resources – be it that of a state, an empire or a corporation. Using law as an entry point can help switch from those questions that ask '*either-or*' to answers that assess '*both-and*'. Looking at the *structurally* dual role of law, in the *longue durée*, as both an enabler for the expansion of power – through its symbolic function of codification – and as a check on petty arbitrariness, can help escape the trope of *determination.*

Field theory can prove particularly effective to avoid the siren call of law's unyielding promise to respond to an increasing array of problems, from social and political unrest to the climate crisis, *and* law's inexorable failure. Espousing the global turn in sociology and history prompts us to depart from the current historiographic obsession with either imperial legacies or the 1980s' neoliberal turn. But this requires that we look for the state in places we are not used to finding it, law and finance, and for law in the articulation, over time, between political change and capitalist accumulation.

The exceptionality of the trajectory of the Great Lakes region since the 1884–1885 Berlin Congress provides a formidable illustration of the stakes of this research agenda. Not only as the epitome of the imperial entanglement of scholarship. Not simply as a region that has been at the heart of the three Scrambles for Africa, from the nineteenth century, the Cold War partition of the continent to the ongoing rush for Africa's 'green' minerals. But because looking at the intermediaries – be they lawyers, *jurisconsultes*, merchants, local chiefs, transnational corporations, national and international NGOs, global traders, militaries, diplomats, international financial institutions or simply individual entrepreneurs trying their luck – that are renegotiating the region's articulation with capitalism underscores that the past matters, in a messy, haphazard way. And attending to the imprints of past relationships on the nexus between politics, GVCs and finance is the only way out: to enable *us* to breathe better, *without* suffocating what has become the lung of the global economy.

As I mentioned in the Introduction and Chapter 1, the empirical vignettes I tracked throughout the book between Abidjan, Bujumbura, Ghana, The Hague, Johannesburg, Kinshasa, London, New York, Paris or Washington, D.C. are selective. Each endeavoured to *systematically* track the connections (humane, professional, normative or institutional) at play in the justification of the borders of encounter between the African continent and the world economy. These borders are physical and symbolic. Each of these vignettes of localities of imperial encounters foremost underscores that the relationship between law, politics and capital accumulation is at once intensely local, as it is determined by local struggles, and intensely global as it refracts the flows and counterflows of conflicts playing out in other localities.

Just like past scrambles, the ongoing rush for Africa's 'green' minerals reads like a complex plot, mixing grand corruption, warlords, missionaries and innocent victims – as a sequel, in other words, of the 'Great Game', this time between the US, China and emerging economic powers. Certainly, the present encounter between resource-rich African states and global markets has been deeply impacted by the global economic and political upheavals of the past forty years. Financial deregulation combined with technological and logistical innovations have dramatically transformed the *geography* of extraction by empowering global traders as producers, traders and financial actors. The onshoring of swashbuckler capitalism is also deeply connected to a codification of capital (Pistor 2019) based on Common Law and the law of the State of New York which is enabled by the globalisation of the Wall Street model of the corporate law firm.

These structural changes heighten the risk induced by a functionalist and economicist understanding of GVCs. To be sure, as Bullough (2022: 237) argues, financial deregulation and the subsequent globalisation of finance – outside sovereign remit and democratic oversight – were in part a political choice. And there is a sense of doom in realising that allowing the 'financial curse' to occur, only to pay lip service, over and over, to solving it is a pattern that is likely to continue.

But the past also matters because it is *sedimented* in the present. Taming *messiness* is not part of the solution. Thinking so would precisely mean falling into the trap of law's siren call. Messiness is a structural component of the relationship between political power, capital accumulation and law. The frescos I drew of the successive Scrambles for Africa in Chapters 2, 3 and 4 demonstrate that each built on the tracks of the previous ones, albeit with at times major transformations. Most often these displacements were symbolic. The pattern of middle power unshackled by the simultaneous onshoring of offshore capitalism in the 1980s and the expansion of US power *without* formal imperialism – based on the extraterritorial waging of US law, backed up by the power of the US dollar – means that the lack of a global legal ordering is not reflective of the *problem* of the globalisation of finance. It is an *outgrowth* of it.

The competition between claims for legal ordering – illustrated by the dramatic judicialisation of global and domestic politics since the 1980s – *and* the blurriness enabled by the instability of middle power are a core driver in the competition between the US, China and old imperial European cores. Competitive claims for legal ordering are also a core driver in the uneven, unequal and messy justification of the practical and symbolic boundaries between sovereign and private interests, and capitalism's cores and its so-called peripheries.

The patterns of legal imperialism deployed during the nineteenth-century Scramble for Africa operationalised the paradox that this colonial encounter was weak in its effective reach but strong in the upheavals it engendered. Both the nation states that emerged or consolidated during the period in Europe and the US *and* the colonial states that were fitfully created on the African continent reflected law's structural role in operating the symbolic distinction between organised crime and war making/state making, which Tilly argues are both 'quintessential protection rackets with the advantage of legitimacy' (Tilly 1985: 169). In the former US colony, in Britain, in London, in the Congo Free State, Belgium, the Gold Coast or Southern Rhodesia, the nineteenth century was a period of major upheavals in the political, social, geographical and legal parameters of power expansion.

Tilly does underline that the trilogy between *coercion* (for the monopolisation of violence internally and in relation to external competitors), *protection* (as the elimination or neutralisation of the competitors of capital accumulating forces within the state) and *extraction* (as the acquisition of the means of carrying out the first three activities) are *processual*, not ideal-typical. The middle power exerted by Britain by deploying law's double-edged protection *within* and *outside* its imperial remits, and by competing imperial powers through indirect rule, also meant that these patterns of power expansion were deeply impacted by the nineteenth-century colonial encounter itself, in both the global economy's cores *and* its peripheries.

The conflicts over land of the Gold Coast that trickled up to the Privy Council, Belgian King Leopold II's attempt at justifying the looting of Congo's humane and mineral wealth *through* the codification of international law, or the pre-independence trials waged against political opponents in the French and British colonies were interconnected precisely because they reflected flows and counterflows *across* and *between* imperial realms. These conflicts contributed to coding sovereignty as a symbolic currency that was 'shared out, layered [and] overlapping' (Burbank and Cooper 2010: 17).

These dynamics of trade in symbolic capital produced winners and losers. They at once consolidated the British Crown's sway over African colonies, and restricted it by empowering financial and merchant power. They at once fostered international law as a device to manage imperial confrontations and insulated its codification remit to the relationship between *national* sovereign entities. They at once confirmed the contradictions of legal imperialism and consolidated gatekeeping and middling – the struggle over the rent of extraction and the ability to benefit from it locally and internationally – as structural features of the nation states that emerged out of colonisation. Thus, that post-colonies should be deemed more violent even though they are seen to be making a fetish of the rule of law is not a paradox. It is part and parcel of the structural dynamic of legal imperialism tout court.

What consolidated the structural banality of Gécamines' position, though, rather than its characteristics as an emblematic paradox, as I surmised in the Introduction, as at once vanguard and backwater of capitalism, is the symbolic displacement of the legal imperialism of the nineteenth-century Scramble during the Cold War partition of the African continent. To be sure, both the colonial projection espoused by France and Belgium during the Cold War and the ensnared independence of resource-rich African states contributed to exacerbating the stakes – and the violence – of gatekeeping politics within the nation states that emerged out of formal colonialism.

But the geographical scattering of offshore capitalism – within the archipelagos of Britain's informal empire – *and* its legal codification, through devices like the international business company – also enabled the redeployment of Britain's middle power, through the dual position of London as both jurisdictional *and* financial apex. This dual position too reflected and produced flows and counterflows. The competing jurisdictional claims for legal ordering fostered by the expansion of inter/national justice institutions in the 1980s simultaneously allow sovereignty to remain layered, shared out and overlapping *or* bifurcated. And it is precisely in these tracks that the expansion of the US hegemon can be delineated. The Cold War sidelining of The Hague justice institutions enabled the redeployment of the concession model of extraction, backed up by the formidable sway of the alliance of Wall Street resources – finance, corporate law firms and legal tools (contracts and arbitration clauses) – aimed at *insulating* foreign corporate rights in property in resource-rich African states from national oversight.

Law remains the vernacular of Africa's relationship with the world economy, but it is a vernacular that is at once *vernacularised*, in the sense that it reflects the social fault lines that are marshalled and transformed through law, and *selective*. To reiterate, capitalism, as Pistor argues, 'is more than just the exchange of goods in a market economy; it is a market economy in which some assets are placed on legal steroids' (Pistor 2019: 11). The codification of capital based on Common Law and the law of the state of New York enables a redefinition of legal hierarchies as *sovereign* and *social*, through the globalisation of the Wall Street model of the corporate law firm. But these selective hierarchies remain entrenched in the hidden hierarchies produced by the sedimentation of past imperial encounters.

This selective codification is not imperilled by the position of Ivory Coast, the Congo or Burundi as 'new frontiers, places where mobile, globally competitive capital [. . .] finds minimally regulated zones in which to vest its operations' (Comaroff and Comaroff 2012: 13). Rather, the hyperviolence of the ongoing rush is enabled by the competition between legal ordering claims.

C.2 Tracking Borders of Encounter: A Research *Manifesto*

This is precisely why the two policy moves generally broadcasted to tame the violence of climate change and that of the rush for 'green' minerals – either industry innovation, like getting rid of the cobalt component of Li-ion batteries, or governance, the idea that governance in resource-rich states needs to be reformed, and that extractive value chains need to be made more transparent and accountable – are at best inadequate, at worst disastrous. This is not only because law means different things according to contexts, and foremost according to the political and economic power marshalled through it. To boot, *sustainability*, as a legal concept, will not easily mean the same for a risk entrepreneur, like FG Hemisphere, and a disenfranchised community. But it is precisely the blurriness of the concept that makes its social and political deployment – what I call *lawyering* – all the more effective due to the conceptual and practical spaces left open between borderless capitalism and bordered states, with sovereignty, whether layered, shared out, overlapped or bifurcated, enabling both the mobility of capital and the dumping of transnational corporations' accountability across jurisdictions.

It is foremost, therefore, because waging law to tame the violence of the market will irrepressibly morph into *lawfare* if the sedimentation of past imperial encounters is not taken into consideration. This is perhaps most acutely and violently illustrated by the transition of Burundi as a boon for rare earths. In Burundi, the contradictory, yet concurrent, legacies of colonialism – that of the Cold War Scramble, the post-1990s re-enchantment of civil society as bulwark against state violence and the developmental state as interface with global markets – have positioned lawyers in a structurally schizophrenic position. They are positioned alternately as gatekeepers of the rent of exported commodities, or vulnerable to another type of extraversion, aid dependency.

It is this structural *bifurcation* of sovereignty – rather than the malleability of layered sovereignty in other settings – that makes Burundi a Petri dish of the hyperviolence generated by the hyperlegality of late capitalism.

But the structuration of concurrent professional markets of international justice – clustered around the repeat players operating the ICJ, investment arbitration mechanisms or the ICC – demonstrates that the competition for access and status within these markets, too, is about gatekeeping politics. Looking at justice as a market for the valuation of symbolic goods, beyond the distinction between *national* and *international* justice institutions, demonstrates that the institutionalisation of justice is at once embedded in dynamics of *boundary making* to define the remits of sovereignty – between the international, the national, the public sphere and private interests – and in concurrent politics of middle power.

This exposes the structural community of situation, beyond historical eras, institutions and geographical contexts, between the Rolin Jacquemyns and the Asante lawyers' dynasties, the meritocratic aristocracy of the international bar of the ICJ, that of the investment arbitration 'mafia' or that of the 'Africa' Bar in Paris. This community of situation is as much about middling as it is about the revival of middle power. Each of these lawyers' professional status hinges on their intermediation capital – middling – based on the uneven and unequal capacity to promote the value of certain forms of capital (social, political, financial). The explosion of supranational institutions that paralleled the advent of the 'real' post-colonial order was fostered, precisely, by their capacity to promote competing forms of capital *as* sovereign resources. Conversely, it is that very competition that sustains both middle power as a structural dynamic in the justification of politics of difference *and* its instability.

The conclusion, therefore, harks back to that of Benton and Ford's *Rage for Order* (2016). The boom of adjudication in the past forty years as a locus to administer politics of difference in the name of a 'global' rule of law is based on stumbling blocks that are less the beginning of the end of a previous era and more 'events that foreclosed certain possibilities of global legal ordering and made other outcomes more likely' (Benton and Ford 2016: 185–186).

Congo's example underscores that China's investments in Africa are threading on the trail of global traders. The twist is that despite the fact that they cannot benefit from the sociopolitical and cultural threads of an imperial past on the continent, Chinese mining corporations can evade the cost of relying on fixers, like Gertler, thanks to the 2007 'deal of the century' with Congo which enabled the expansion of state-owned Chinese corporations while essentially positioning the Chinese state as Congo's prime market outlet *and* creditor.

The competition between China and the US also reflects the imprint of past imperial encounters. The US debt has exploded since the start of the twenty-first century, sitting at nearly US$ 30.6 trillion in the second quarter of 2022. China, which owns an estimated US$ 972 billion in US Treasuries is the US number two investor among foreign governments. China has a vested interest in buying Treasuries to help depress the value of its currency, the yuan. A cheaper yuan makes the country's exports less expensive for foreign buyers.[5]

China's stakes as world hegemon follow on the tracks of sedimented patterns of imperialism. Chinese expansion in Africa, and particularly in the Congo, relies on the selective legal codification enabled by the US dollar. China's moves to evade the regulatory sway of the US FCPA illustrates that the game of catch-up between deregulation and re-regulation is therefore as much about *access* as it is about *competing* legal ordering claims.

But Chinese legal ordering claims also remain vested in old imperial tracks. The position of Hong Kong is a case in point. 'While most other global spaces of Chinese law are still in the making, such as the new legal hubs along the [Belt and Road Initiative] map and frontier markets for Chinese investments in Africa or Southeast Asia, Hong Kong has already played a dominant role for the export of Chinese capital and legal

[5] T Kenny, 'How much US debt does China own' The Balance 21 October 2022, www.thebalancemoney.com/how-much-u-s-debt-does-china-own-417016#citation-1 (accessed 24 December 2022).

institutions in the past two decades' (Liu and Au 2020: 311). Zooming in onto professional flows across corporate law firms, Liu and Au (2020) and Liu et al. (2022) track Hong Kong's economic transformation since the 1990s, following Hong Kong's handover to China in 1997 and the 2008 global financial crisis. The unique position of Hong Kong as at once a Common Law jurisdiction and part of continental China is reflected in the exceptional internationalisation of its legal market.

While elite law firms, namely the Magic Circle and Wall Street firms, continue to dominate this market, their power has been increasingly shaken since the turn of the 2010s by lateral moves towards Chinese firms' offices in the city. In other words, while Hong Kong was until the 2008 financial crisis foremost a *gateway* for the expansion of US and UK corporations into continental China, it is now increasingly a key financial gateway for the expansion of Chinese business interests abroad. The emperor, thus, may be wearing new clothes. But they are woven in an old fabric: the engine of the Wall Street model of the corporate law firm.

REFERENCES

Abel, RL, Hammerslev, O, Sommerlad, H and Schultz, U (eds) (2020) *Lawyers in 21st Century Societies: Vol. I: National Reports* (Oxford, Hart Publishing)

Abel, RL and Lewis, PSC (eds) (1988a) *Lawyers in Society: The Civil Law World* (Berkeley, University of California Press)

(1988b) *Lawyers in Society: The Common Law World* (Berkeley, University of California Press)

(1989) *Lawyers in Society: Comparative Theories* (Berkeley, University of California Press)

Achebe, C (1990 [1958]) *Things Fall Apart* (London, Penguin Classics)

Addo-Fening, R (2013) 'Ghana Under Colonial Rule: An Outline of the Early Period and the Interwar Years' 15 *Transactions of the Historical Society of Ghana* 39–70

Adichie, CN (2016) *Americanah* (London, Harper Collins)

Akindès, F (2017) '"On ne mange pas les ponts et le goudron": les sentiers sinueux d'une sortie de crise en Côte d'Ivoire' 148 *Politique africaine* 5–26

Akoka, K (2020) *L'asile et l'exil: Une histoire de la distinction réfugiés/migrants* (Paris, La Découverte)

Albertin, G, Yontcheva, B and Devlin, D (eds) (2021) *Tax Avoidance in Sub-Saharan Africa's Mining Sector* (Washington, DC, African and Fiscal Affairs Departments, International Monetary Fund)

Alschner, W (2014) 'The Return of the Home State and the Rise of "Embedded" Investor-State Arbitration' in Lalani, S and Polanco, R (eds) *The Role of the State in Investor-State Arbitration* (Leiden and Boston, Martinus Nijhoff/Brill) 192–218

Alter, K (2014) *The New Terrain of International Law: Courts, Politics, Rights* (Princeton, Princeton University Press)

Alter, KJ, Gathii, JT and Helfer, LR (2016) 'Backlash against International Courts in West, East and Southern Africa: Causes and Consequences' 27(2) *The European Journal of International Law* 293–328

Alvarez, JE and Topalian, G (2012) 'The Paradoxical Argentina Cases' 6(3) *World Arbitration & Mediation Review* 491–544

Anghie, A (2006) 'Decolonizing the Concept of "Good Governance"' in Gruffydd Jones, B (ed) *Decolonizing International Relations* (Lanham, Rowman & Littlefield Publishers, Inc) 109–130

Arboleda, M (2010) *Planetary Mine: Territories of Extraction under Late Capitalism* (London, Verso)

Arfi, F (2021) 'De Takieddine à Benally: la République des intermédiaires' in Borrel, T, Boukary-Yabara, A, Collombat, B and Deltombe, T (eds) *L'Empire qui ne veut pas mourir: Une histoire de la Françafrique* (Paris, Seuil) 779–890

Arhin, K (1978) 'Gold-mining and trading among the Ashanti of Ghana' 48(1) *Journal des Africanistes* 89–100

Baczko, A (2021) *La guerre par le droit: Les tribunaux Taliban en Afghanistan* (Paris, CNRS Éditions)

Banégas, R and Marshall-Fratani, R (2003) 'Côte d'Ivoire, un conflit régional?' 89 (1) *Politique africaine* 5–11

Barker, A (2012) 'Taking on the "inner mafia"' 7(6) *Global Arbitration Review*

Bayart, J-F (1989) *L'Etat en Afrique. La politique du ventre* (Paris, Fayard)

(1993) *The State in Africa: The Politics of the Belly* (London, Longman)

(2000) 'Africa in the World: A History of Extraversion' 99 *African Affairs* 217–267

Bayart, J-F and Bertrand, R (2006) 'De quel legs colonial parle-t-on?' 12 *Esprit* 134–160

Bebbington, A (2009) 'The New Extraction: Rewriting the Political Ecology of the Andes?' 42(5) *NACLA Report on the Americas* 12–20

Beckert, S (2014) *Empire of Cotton: A New History of Global Capitalism* (London, Penguin Books)

Benton, L (2002) *Law and Colonial Cultures: Legal Regimes in World History, 1400–1900* (Cambridge, Cambridge University Press)

Benton, L and Ford, L (2016) *Rage for Order: The British Empire and the Origins of International Law, 1800–1850* (Cambridge, Harvard University Press)

Benton, L and Ross, RJ (eds) (2013) *Legal Pluralism and Empires, 1500–1850* (New York, NYU Press)

Bernard-Maugiron, N and Omar, M (2020) 'Egypt: The Long Decline of the Legal Profession' in Abel, RL, Hammerslev, O, Sommerlad, H and Schultz, U (eds) *Lawyers in 21st Century Societies: Vol. I: National Reports* (Oxford, Hart Publishing) 565–580

Bernasconi-Osterwalder, N and Dietrich Brauch, M (2017) 'Is "Moonlighting" a Problem? The Role of ICJ Judges in ISDS' *International Institute for Sustainable Development* [online] www.iisd.org/system/files/publications/icj-judges-isds-commentary.pdf

Bertrand, R (2007) 'Rencontres impériales: L'histoire connectée et les relations euro-asiatiques' 54(4) *Revue d'histoire moderne & contemporaine* 69–89

Bertrand, R and Calafat, G (2018) 'La microhistoire globale: affaire(s) à suivre' 73(1) *Annales. Histoire, Sciences Sociales* 1–18

Biskupic, J, Roberts, J and Shiffman, J (2014) 'At America's Court of Last Resort, a Handful of Lawyers Now Dominate the Docket' *Reuters* [online] www.reuters.com/article/us-scotus-elites-special-report-idUSKBN0JM0ZX20141208

Blamangin, O and Borrel, T (2021) 'La Françafrique prend la vague libérale' in Borrel, T, Boukary-Yabara, A, Collombat, B and Deltombe, T (eds) *L'Empire qui ne veut pas mourir: Une histoire de la Françafrique* (Paris, Le Seuil) 735–744

Blas, J and Farchy, J (2022) *The World for Sale: Money, Power, and the Traders Who Barter the Earth's Resources* (London, Penguin Books)

Bonnecase, V (2014) 'L'État, les étrangers et la terre en Côte d'Ivoire sous la colonisation: la construction d'une autochtonie à échelle variable' in Tolan, J, El Annabi, H, Lebdai, B, Laurent, F and Krause, G (eds) *Enjeux identitaires en mutation* (Paris, Peter Lang) 61–96

Borrel, T (2021) 'Le droit au service de la France: l'OHADA, une "réussite africaine" très parisienne' in Borrel, T, Boukary-Yabara, A, Collombat, B and Deltombe, T (eds) *L'Empire qui ne veut pas mourir: Une histoire de la Françafrique* (Paris, Seuil) 744–745

Borrel, T, Boukary-Yabara, A, Collombat, B and Deltombe, T (eds) (2021) *L'Empire qui ne veut pas mourir: Une histoire de la Françafrique* (Paris, Seuil)

Bosco, D (2014) *Rough Justice: The International Criminal Court in a World of Power Politics* (New York, Oxford University Press)

Bourdieu, P (1971) 'Le marché des biens symboliques' 22 *L'année sociologique* 49–126

(1986) 'L'illusion biographique' 62–63 *Actes de la recherche en sciences sociales* 69–72

(2012) *Sur l'État: Cours au Collège de France (1989–1992)* (Paris, Le Seuil)

Boutell, HS (1920–1921) 'Judicial Committee of the Privy Council' 9 *Georgetown Law Journal* 2–11

Breckenridge, K (2011) 'Special Rights in Property, Why Modern African Economies Are Dependent on Mineral Resources' in Bayly, CA, Rao, V, Szreter, S and Woolcock, M (eds) *History, Historians and Development Policy: A Necessary Dialogue* (Manchester, Manchester University Press) 243–260

Brett, P (2015) '*Cause Lawyers* sans frontières: juristes sud-africains et judiciarisation du politique en Afrique australe' 138 *Politique africaine* 93–113

Brett, P and Engbo Gissel, L (2018) 'Explaining African Participation in International Courts' 117(467) *African Affairs* 195–216

(2020) *Africa and the Backlash Against International Courts* (London, Zed Books)

Brower, CN (2008) 'W(h)ither International Commercial Arbitration?' 24(2) *Arbitration International* 181–198

Budniok, J and Noli, A (2018) 'The Ghanaian Middle Class, Social Stratification, and Long-Term Dynamics of Upward and Downward Mobility of Lawyers and Teachers' in Kroeker, L, O'Kane, D and Scharrer, T (eds) *Middle Classes in Africa: Frontiers of Globalization* (London, Palgrave) 109–134

Bullough, O (2022) *Butler to the World: How Britain Became the Servant of Tycoons, Tax Dodgers, Kleptocrats and Criminals* (London, Profile Books)

Burbank, J and Cooper, F (2010) *Empires in World History: Power and the Politics of Difference* (Princeton, Princeton University Press)

Burgis, T (2015) *The Looting Machine: Warlords, Tycoons, Smugglers and the Systematic Theft of Africa's Wealth* (London, William Collins)

Burridge, A and Gill, N (2017) 'Conveyor-Belt Justice: Precarity, Access to Justice and Uneven Geographies of Legal Aid in UK Asylum Appeals' 49(1) *Antipode* 23–42

Carter Centre (2017) *A State's Affair: Privatizing Congo's Copper Sector* (Atlanta, The Carter Centre)

Caserta, S and Madsen, MR (2016) 'Between Community Law and Common Law: The Rise of the Caribbean Court of Justice at the Intersection of Regional Integration and Post-colonial Legacies' 79 *Law and Contemporary Problems* 79–115

CEO/Friends of the Earth Europe (2015) *Lawyers Subverting the Public Interest: Lobby Group EFILA's Stake in Investment Arbitration* (Briefing) https://corporateeurope.org/sites/default/files/efila_report-web.pdf

Chandler, D (2006) *Empire in Denial: The Politics of Statebuilding* (London, Pluto)

(2019) 'Intervention and Statebuilding Beyond the Human' in Lemay-Hébert, N (ed) *Handbook on Intervention and Statebuilding* (Cheltenham, Edward Elgar) 10–18

Chanock, M (1985) *Law, Custom, and Social Order: The Colonial Experience in Malawi and Zambia* (Cambridge, Cambridge University Press)

(2001) *The Making of South African Legal Culture, 1902–1936: Fear, Favour and Prejudice* (Cambridge, Cambridge University Press)

Chauveau, JP (2000) 'Question foncière et construction nationale en Côte d'Ivoire: Les enjeux silencieux d'un coup d'État' 78 *Politique africaine* 94–125

Chauveau, JP and Bobo, KS (2003) 'La situation de guerre dans l'arène villageoise: Un exemple dans le Centre-Ouest ivoirien' 89(1) *Politique africaine* 12–32

Chipman, J (1989) *French Power in Africa* (Oxford and Cambridge, Basil Blackwell)

Chrétien, J-P and Dupaquier, J-F (2007) *Burundi 1972: Au bord des génocides* (Paris, Karthala)

Christelow, A (1985) *Muslim Law Courts and the French Colonial State in Algeria* (Princeton, Princeton University Press)

Christensen, J, Shaxson, N and Wigan, D (2016) 'The Finance Curse: Britain and the World Economy' 18(1) *The British Journal of Politics and International Relations* 255–269

Christensen, MJ (2021) 'The Professional Market of International Criminal Justice: Divisions of Labour and Patterns of Elite Reproduction' 19 *Journal of International Criminal Justice* 783–802

Cohen, A (2019) 'On Law and Value' *LPE Project* [online] https://lpeproject.org/blog/on-law-and-value/

Cohen, S (1972) *Folk Devils and Moral Panics* (London, Routledge)
Comaroff, J and Comaroff, JL (ed) (2006) *Law and Disorder in the Postcolony* (Chicago, University of Chigaco press)
Comaroff, J and Comaroff, JL (2007) 'Law and Disorder in the Postcolony' 15 *Social Anthropology/Anthropologie Sociale* 133–152
(2012) *Theory from the South: Or, How Euro-America Is Evolving toward Africa* (Boulder, Paradigm Publishers)
Cooper, F (2002) *Africa Since 1940: The Past of the Present* (Cambridge, Cambridge University Press)
(2004) 'Development, Modernization, and the Social Sciences in the Era of Decolonization: The Examples of British and French Africa' 10(1) *Revue d'Histoire des Sciences Humaines* 9–38
(2005) *Colonialism in Question: Theory, Knowledge, History* (Berkeley, University of California Press)
(2014) *Africa in the World: Capitalism, Empire, Nation-State* (Cambridge, Harvard University Press)
Coquery-Vidrovitch, C and Deltombe, T (2021) 'Les habits neufs du capitalisme impérial' in Borrel, T, Boukary-Yabara, A, Collombat, B and Deltombe, T (eds) *L'Empire qui ne veut pas mourir: Une histoire de la Françafrique* (Paris, Seuil) 83–92
Cutler, AC and Dietz, T (eds) (2017) *The Politics of Private Transnational Governance by Contract* (Abingdon and Oxon, Routledge)
Damaška, MR (1986) *The Faces of Justice and State Authority: A Comparative Approach to the Legal Process* (New Haven and London, Yale University Press)
Danielsen, D and Bair, J (2019) 'The Role of Law in Global Value Chains: A Window Into Law and Global Political Economy' [online] https://lpeproject.org/blog/the-role-of-lawinglobalvalue-chains-a-window-into-law-and-global-political-economy/
Datta, AK and Porter, R (1971) 'The Asafo System in Historical Perspective: An Inquiry into the Origin and Development of a Ghanaian Institution' 12(2) *Journal of African History* 279–297
Dawuni, JJ (2017) 'Lawyers in Ghana' Presented at the International Meeting on Law and Society, Mexico City
De, R (2018) 'The Kenyatta Trial and Mobile Lawyer: Decolonization, Diasporas and a Global History of Rebellious Lawyering' Presentation at Harvard Law School, 5 April
de Gaudusson, JB (2009) 'Le mimétisme postcolonial, et après?' 129 *Pouvoirs* 45–55
Deonandan, K and Dougherty ML (2016) *Mining in Latin America: Critical Approaches to the New Extraction* (Abingdon and Oxon, Routledge)
Deslaurier, C (2002) 'Un monde politique en mutation: le Burundi à la veille de l'indépendance (circa 1956–1961)' PhD thesis in History (Université Paris I, unpublished)

(2003) 'Le "bushingantahe" peut-il réconcilier le Burundi?' 92 *Politique africaine* 76–96

(2013) 'Rwagasore for ever: Des usages contemporains d'un héros consensuel au Burundi' 118 *Vingtième Siècle. Revue d'histoire* 15–30

de Sousa Santos, B (1987) 'Law: A Map of Misreading – Toward a Postmodern Conception of Law' 14 *Journal of Law and Society* 279–302

Dezalay, S (2007) 'Gérer un conflit armé comme une cause judiciaire: l'exemple d'Amnesty International en Côte d'Ivoire' 36(3) *Critique internationale* 55–70

(2011) 'Revamping Law by Circumventing the State. Non-Governmental Organizations in the International Management of Social Violence on the African Continent' PhD of Laws (Florence, European University Institute)

(2016a) 'Weakness as Routine in the Operations of the International Criminal Court' 17 *International Criminal Law Review* 1–21

(2016b) 'Répondre aux crises? Dynamiques de "gestion des crises" par l'instrument: de la Commission européenne aux réformes de la justice au Burundi' 5(2) *Gouvernement & action publique* 31–50

(2017a) 'Isaac Forster' *Galerie des internationalistes* Société Française pour le droit international [online] www.sfdi.org/internationalistes/forster/

(2017b) 'Louis Ignacio-Pinto' *Galerie des internationalistes* Société Française pour le droit international [online] www.sfdi.org/internationalistes/ignacio-pinto/

(2018) 'Fatoumata Dembélé Diarra: Trajectory of a Malian Magistrate and Civil Society Advocate to the International Criminal Court' in Dawuni, JJ and Kuenyehia, A (eds) *International Courts and the African Woman Judges: Unveiled Narratives* (London, Routledge) 77–97

(2019) 'Building an Environmental and Human Disaster into a Transnational Case: A Socio-Political Perspective' in Muir Watt, H, Fernandez Arroyo, D, Bizikova, L and Brandao de Oliveira, A (eds) *Adjudicating without Frontiers: The Global Turn in Private International Law* (Cheltenham, Edward, Elgar Publishing) 93–102

(2020a) 'Africa against Global Justice? Stakes for Building a Political Sociology on the Futures of International Criminal Justice' in Weill, S, Thuy Seelinger, K and Carlson, KB (eds) *Prosecuting the President: The Trial of Hissen Habré* (Oxford, Oxford University Press) 219–232

(2020b) 'Le "barreau africain" de Paris: entre *Big Bang* sur le marché du droit des affaires et sillons d'Empire' 119–120 *Cultures & Conflits* 67–93

(2020c) 'Burundi: Middlemen and Opponents in the Shadow of the Ethno-State' in Abel, RL, Hammerslev, O, Sommerlad, H and Schultz, U (eds) *Lawyers in 21st Century Societies: Vol. I: National Reports* (Oxford, Hart Publishing) 473–493

(2021) 'Le Barreau africain de Paris: entre "Big Bang" sur le marché du droit des affaires et sillons d'Empire' 119(12) *Cultures & Conflits* 71–97

(2022) 'Africa's Lawyers: From Imperial Agents to Legal Brokers on Global Markets' in Abel, RL, Hammarslev, O, Sommerlad, H and Schultz, U (eds) *Lawyers in 21st Century Societies: Vol. II: Comparisons and Theories* (Oxford, Hart Publishing) 51–72

Dezalay, S (with the contribution of Dezalay, Y) (2017) 'Professionals of International Justice: From the Shadow of State Diplomacy to the Pull of the Market of Arbitration' in Nollkaemper, A, d'Aspremont, J, Wouter, W and Gazzini, T (eds) *International Law as a Profession* (Cambridge, Cambridge University Press) 287–310

Dezalay, Y (1992) *Marchands de droit: La restructuration de l'ordre juridique international par les multinationales du droit* (Paris, Fayard)

Dezalay, Y and Garth, BG (1996) *Dealing in Virtue: International Commercial Arbitration and the Construction of a Transnational Legal Order* (Chicago, University of Chicago Press)

(2002) *The Internationalization of Palace Wars: Lawyers, Economists, and the Contest to Transform Latin American States* (Chicago, University of Chicago Press)

(2006) 'From the Cold War to Kosovo: The Rise and Renewal of the Field of International Human Rights' 2 *Annual Review of Law and Social Science* 231–255

(2008) 'L'impérialisme moral: Les juristes et l'impérialisme américain (Philippines, Indonésie)' 171–172 *Actes de la recherche en sciences sociales* 40–55

(2010) *Asian Legal Revivals: Lawyers in the Shadow of Empire* (Chicago, University of Chicago Press)

(2011) 'State Politics and Legal Markets' 10 *Comparative Sociology* 38–66

(2012) 'Corporate Law Firms, NGOs and Issues of Legitimacy for a Global Legal Order' 80(6) *Fordham Law Review* 2329

(2016) 'Constructing a Transatlantic Marketplace of Disputes on the Symbolic Foundations of International Justice' in Mallard, G and Sgard, J (eds) *Contractual Knowledge: One Hundred Years of Legal Experimentation in Global Markets* (New York, Cambridge University Press) 185–215

Dezalay, Y and Madsen, MR (2012) 'The Force of Law and Lawyers: Pierre Bourdieu and the Reflexive Sociology of Law' 8 *Annual Review of Law and Social Sciences* 433–452

Dias, CJ, Luckham, R, Lynch, DO and Paul, JCN (eds) (1981) *Lawyers in the Third World: Comparative and Developmental Perspectives* (Uppsala, Scandinavian Institute of African Studies and New York, International Center for Law in Development)

Dimier, V (2014) *The Invention of a European Development Aid Bureaucracy* (Basingstoke, Palgrave Macmillan)

Diop, M (1971) *Histoire des classes sociales dans l'Afrique de l'Ouest*, 2 vols (Paris, L'Harmattan)

Dozon, J-P (1989) 'L'invention de la Côte-d'Ivoire' 20(2) *Le Genre humain* 135–162
Duffield, MR (1992) 'The Emergence of Two-Tier Welfare in Africa: Marginalization or an Opportunity for Reform?' 12 *Public Administration and Development* 139–154
(2007) *Development, Security and Unending War: Governing the World of Peoples* (Cambridge, Polity)
Eberhardt, P and Olivet, C (2012) *Profiting from Injustice: How Law Firms, Arbitrators and Financiers Are Fuelling an Investment Arbitration Boom* (Brussels and Amsterdam, Corporate Europe Observatory and the Transnational Institute)
Elbaz, S (2003) 'L'avocat et sa cause en milieu colonial: La défense politique dans le procès de l'Organisation spéciale du Mouvement pour le triomphe des libertés en Algérie (1950–1952)' 62 *Politix* 65–91
Ellis, S (1996) 'Africa after the Cold War: New Patterns of Government and Politics' 27 *Development and Change* 1–28
(2012) *Season of Rains: Africa in the World* (Chicago, The University of Chicago Press)
Etemad, B (2005) *De l'utilité des Empires: colonisation et prospérité de l'Europe* (Paris, Armand Collin)
Ewelukwa Ofodile, U (2019) 'African States, Investor-State Arbitration and the ICSID Dispute Resolution System: Continuities, Changes and Challenges' 34 (2) *ICSID Review* 296–364
Eyal, G (2013) 'Spaces between Fields' in Gorski, PS (ed) *Bourdieu and Historical Analysis* (Durham, NC, Duke University Press) 158–182
Fabre, M (2011) 'La place de la Cour de cassation dans la construction d'un droit aux colonies' *Clio@Themis* [online] https://journals.openedition.org/cliothemis/1385
Farcy, J-C (2011) 'Quelques données statistiques sur la magistrature coloniale française (1837–1987)' *Clio@Themis* [online] https://journals.openedition.org/cliothemis/1367
Felstiner, WLF, Abel, R and Sarat, A (1980–1980) 'The Emergence and Transformation of Disputes: Naming, Blaming, Claiming…' 15(3–4) *Law & Society Review*, 631–654
Ferguson, J (2006) *Global Shadows: Africa in the Neoliberal World Order* (Durham, NC, Duke University Press)
Ferrando, T (2019) 'How Finance Structures Global Value Chains' *LPE Project* [online] https://lpeproject.org/blog/how-finance-structures-global-value-chains/
Fleury Graff, T and Marie, A (2019) *Droit de l'asile* (Paris, PUF)
Flood, J (2007) 'Lawyers as Sanctifiers: The Role of Elite Law Firms in International Business Transactions' 14(1) *Indiana Journal of Global Legal Studies* 35–66
Gahama, J (2001) *Le Burundi sous administration belge*, 2nd edn (Paris, Karthala)
Gaillard, E (2015) 'Sociology of International Arbitration' 31 *Arbitration International* 1–17

Galanter, M (1974) 'Why the "Haves" Come Out Ahead: Speculations on the Limits of Legal Change' 9(1) *Law and Society Review* 95–160

Galanter, M and Palay, T (1991) *Tournament of Lawyers: The Transformation of the Big Law Firm* (Chicago, The University of Chicago Press)

Garth, BG (2018) 'The Transnational Arbitral Community' Max Planck Encyclopedia of International Procedural Law [online] https://opil.ouplaw.com/browse?access=all&ct=d11f54ab-124c-4ae6-a6c9-fdfd9b8f0ee9&level=all&pageSize=20&sort=title&sb_0=61d99aea-8e37–46ed-a315--2be169904e5c&sb_1=421d1388-fc0b-4ec2–8cc6–8507d147c805

Gathii, JT (2013) 'Mission Creep or a Search for Relevance: The East African Court of Justice's Human Rights Strategy' 24 *Duke Journal of Comparative & International Law* 249–296

(2016) 'Variation in the Use of Subregional Integration Courts between Business and Human Rights Actors: The Case of the East African Court of Justice' 79 *Law and Contemporary Problems* 7–62

Gaubatz, KT and MacArthur, M (2001) 'How International is "International" Law?' 22(2) *Michigan Journal of International Law* 238–282

Ghai, YP (1981) 'Law and Lawyers in Kenya and Tanzania: Some Political Economy Considerations' in Dias, CJ, Luckham, R, Lynch, DO and Paul, JCN (eds) *Lawyers in the Third World: Comparative and Developmental Perspectives* (Uppsala, Scandinavian Institute of African Studies and New York, International Center for Law in Development) 144–173

Gill, N and Good, A (eds) (2019) *Asylum Determination in Europe: Ethnographic Perspectives* (Bristol, Palgrave Socio-Legal Studies)

Go, J (2009) 'The "New" Sociology of Empire and Colonialism' 3(5) *Sociology Compass* 775–788

(2013) 'For a Postcolonial Sociology' 42 *Theory and Society* 25–55

Gobe, E (2013) *Les avocats en Tunisie de la colonisation à la révolution (1883–2011): Sociohistoire d'une profession politique* (Paris, Karthala)

(2020) 'Tunisia: A Political Profession?' in Abel, RL, Hammerslev, O, Sommerlad, H and Schultz, U (eds) *Lawyers in 21st Century Societies: Vol. I: National Reports* (Oxford, Hart Publishing) 657–674

Greco, E (2020) 'Africa, Extractivism and the Crisis This Time' 47(166) *Review of African Political Economy* 511–521

Greenhouse, C and Davis, C (eds) (2019) *Landscapes of Law: Practicing Sovereignty in Transnational Terrain* (Philadelphia, University of Pennsylvania Press)

Greenman, K (2021) *State Responsibility and Rebels: The History and Legacy of Protecting Investment Against Revolution* (Cambridge, Cambridge University Press)

Greenpeace and Amnesty International (2012) *The Toxic Truth* (Greenpeace Netherlands and Amnesty International) www.greenpeace.org/static/planet4-international-stateless/2012/09/9161d5e8-the-toxic-truth.pdf

Guichaoua, A and Vidal, C (1997) 'Les politiques internationales dans la région des Grands Lacs africains' 68, *Politique africaine* 3–22

Halliday, TC, Karpik, L and Feeley, MM (eds) (2012) *Fates of Political Liberalism in the British Post-Colony: The Politics of the Legal Complex* (Cambridge, Cambridge University Press)

Hara, F (1997) 'La diplomatie parallèle ou la politique de la non-indifférence: le cas du Burundi' 68 *Politique africaine* 78–92

Hardt, M and Negri, A (2000) *Empire* (Cambridge, MA, Harvard University Press)

Harvey, D (2003) *The New Imperialism* (Oxford, Oxford University Press)

Hatungimana, A (2008) 'Le café et les pouvoirs au Burundi' 243 *Les Cahiers d'Outre-Mer* 263–284

Heinrich, A (2021) 'Sub-regional Courts as Transitional Justice Mechanisms: The Case of the East-African Court of Justice in Burundi' in Gathii JT (ed) *The Performance of Africa's International CourtsL Using Litigation for Political, Legal, and Social Change* (Oxford, Oxford University Press) 88–105

Higbee, A (2008) 'The History of the Paris American Chamber of Commerce (1894–1994)' in Bonin, H (ed) *American Firms in Europe (1880–1980): Strategy, Identity, Perception and Performance* (Paris, Dalloz) 411–433

Hirschl, R (2008) 'The Judicialization of Mega-Politics and the Rise of Political Courts' 11(1) *Annual Review of Political Science* 93–118

Ho, K (2009) *Liquidated: An Ethnography of Wall Street* (Durham, NC, Duke University Press)

Hobsbawm, E and Ranger, T (eds) (1983) *The Invention of Tradition* (Cambridge, Cambridge University Press)

Hönke, J (2018) 'Beyond the Gatekeeper State: African Infrastructure Hubs as Sites of Experimentation' 3(3) *Third World Thematics: A TWQ Journal* 347–363

Huillery, E (2009) 'History Matters: The Long-Term Impact of Colonial Public Investments in French West Africa' 1(2) *American Economic Journal: Applied Economics* 176–215

Ibhawoh, B (2013) *Imperial Justice: Africans in Empire's Courts* (Oxford, Oxford University Press)

(2017) 'Confronting Colonial Otherness: The Judicial Committee of the Privy Council and the Limits of Imperial Legal Universalism' in Hendrix, B and Baumgold, D (eds) *Colonial Exchanges: Political Theory and the Agency of the Colonized* (Manchester, Manchester University Press) 116–132

IGLP Law and Global Production Working Group (2016) 'The Role of Law in Global Value Chains: A Research Manifesto' 4(1) *London Review of International Law* 57–79

Iliffe, J (1983) *The Emergence of African Capitalism* (London, MacMillan)

Israël, L (2009) 'Un droit de gauche? Rénovation des pratiques professionnelles et nouvelles formes de militantisme des juristes engagés dans les années 1970' 73(1) *Sociétés contemporaines* 47–71

(2013) 'Les joueurs répétés ont-ils plus de chance de gagner? Débats sur le sens de la justice: Présentation du dossier' 85 *Droit et Société* 543–557

Jacquemot, P (2012) 'Africa's "Middle Class": Realities, Issues, and Perspectives' 244 *Afrique contemporaine* 17–31

Kaldor, M (2006) *New and Old Wars: Organised Violence in a Global Era*, 2nd edn (Cambridge, Polity Press)

Kalm, G (2021) 'Who Owns the Mountain? Contesting Property over the Simandou Mountain Chain and Its Iron Ore Reserves' Presentation, Law and Society Annual Meeting (online, 25 May)

Kantorowicz, E (1989) *Les deux corps du Roi* (Paris, Gallimard)

Karekwaivanane, GH (2020) 'Zimbabwe: Legal Practitioners, Politics and Transformation since 1980' in Abel, RL, Hammerslev, O, Sommerlad, H and Schultz, U (eds) *Lawyers in 21st Century Societies: Vol. I: National Reports* (Oxford, Hart Publishing) 547–564

Klaaren, J (2020) 'South Africa: A Profession in Transformation' in Abel, RL, Hammerslev, O, Sommerlad, H and Schultz, U (eds) *Lawyers in 21st Century Societies: Vol. I: National Reports* (Oxford, Hart Publishing) 535–546

Klein, N (ed) (2014) *Litigating International Law Disputes: Weighing the Options* (Cambridge, Cambridge University Press)

Kolhagen, D (2012) 'Oser une refondation de la Justice en Afrique: Attentes citoyennes et alternatives au Burundi' in Eberhard, C (ed) *Le courage des alternatives* (Paris, Karthala, Cahiers d'anthropologie du droit, Hors-série) 177–195

Koskenniemi, M (2001) *The Gentle Civilizer of Nations: The Rise and Fall of International Law 1870–1960* (Cambridge, Cambridge University Press)

Krishnan, J (2012) 'Academic SAILERS: The Ford Foundation and the Efforts to Shape Legal Education in Africa, 1957–1977' 52 *American Journal of Legal History* 261–324

Kumar, SP and Rose, C (2014) 'A Study of Lawyers Appearing before the International Court of Justice, 1999–2012' Grotius Centre Working Paper 018-PIL

Lamont, M (2012) 'Toward a Comparative Sociology of Valuation and Evaluation' 38(1) *Annual Review of Sociology* 201–221

Lardinois, R (2008) 'Entre monopole, marché et religion: L'émergence de l'État colonial en Inde, années 1760–1810' 171–172 *Actes de la recherche en sciences sociales* 90–103

Legendre, P (1992) *Trésor historique de l'État en France: L'administration Classique* (Paris, Fayard)

Levi, R, Dezalay, S and Amiraslani, M (2017) 'Prosecutorial Strategies and Opening Statements: Justifying International Prosecutions from the International Military Tribunal at Nuremberg through to the International Criminal

Court' 26 *Comparativ: Journal for Global History and Comparative Social Science* 58–72

Levi, R, Hagan, J and Dezalay, S (2016) 'International Courts in Atypical Political Environments: The Interplay of Prosecutorial Strategy, Evidence, and Court Authority in International Criminal Law' 78(4) *Law and Contemporary Problems* 289–314

Lima, J and Dezalay, S (2015) 'La "cause" de la justice de transition dans le Burundi de l'après-conflit' 67 *Critique internationale* 51–66

Liu, S and Au, A (2020) 'The Gateway to Global China: Hong Kong and the Future of Chinese Law Firms' 37(2) *Wisconsin International Law Journal* 309–349

Liu, S, Blocq, D, Honari, A and Au, A (2022) 'Professional Flows: Lateral Moves and Law Firm Partners in Hong Kong, 1994–2018' 9(1) *Journal of Professions and Organization* 1–19

Lonsdale, J (1981) 'States and Social Processes in Africa: A Historiographical Survey' 24 *African Studies Review* 139–226

Luckham, R (1981) 'Imperialism, Law and Structural Dependence: The Ghana Legal Profession' in Dias, CJ, Luckham, R, Lynch, DO and Paul, JCN (eds) *Lawyers in the Third World: Comparative and Developmental Perspectives* (Uppsala, Scandinavian Institute of African Studies and New York, International Center for Law in Development) 90–122

(1982) 'Le militarisme français en Afrique' 5 *Politique africaine* 95–110

Mabille, F (2001) 'La catholicité horizontale ou l'action humanitaire au sein de l'Église catholique: L'exemple du CCFD' Presentation at the conference 'ONG et action humanitaire: entre militantisme transnational et action publique' La Rochelle 12–13 April

Madsen, MR (2004) '"Make law, not war": Les "sociétés impériales" confrontées à l'institutionnalisation internationale des droits de l'homme' 151–152 *Actes de la recherche en sciences sociales* 96–106

(2005) '"La Cour qui venait du froid": Les droits de l'homme dans la genèse de l'Europe d'après-guerre' 26(1) *Critique internationale* 133–146

(2014) 'The International Judiciary as Transnational Power Elite' 8(3) *International Political Sociology* 332–334

Mamdani, M (1996) *Citizen and Subject: Contemporary Africa and the Legacy of Late Colonialism* (Princeton, Princeton University Press)

Mann, G (2009) 'What Was the Indigénat? The "Empire of Law" in French West Africa' 50(3) *The Journal of African History* 331–353

Marissal, A (2022) *Faire carrière au rythme des procès? Structuration et restructuration du marché du travail des juristes pénaux internationaux à La Haye PhD in Sociology* (Institut d'études Politiques de Paris)

Mazower, M (2012) *Governing the World: The History of an Idea* (New York, Allen Lane)

Mbembe, A (2001) *On the Postcolony* (Berkeley, University of California Press)

Meimon, J (2007) 'L'invention de l'aide au développement: Discours, instruments et pratiques d'une dynamique hégémonique' 21 Research in Question, CERI
Meredith, M (2005) *The Fate of Africa: From the Hopes of Freedom to the Heart of Despair* (New York, Public Affairs)
Merry, SE (1991) 'Law and Colonialism' 25 *Law & Society Review* 889–922
(2003) 'From Law and Colonialism to Law and Globalization' 28 *Law & Social Inquiry* 569–590
Mintz, S (1986) *Sweetness and Power: The Place of Sugar in Modern History* (New York, Elisabeth Sifton Books, Penguin Books)
Mitra, D (2020) *Indian Sex Life: Sexuality and the Colonial Origins of Modern Social Thought* (Princeton, Princeton University Press)
Moghalu, C (2013) *Emerging Africa: How the Global Economy's "Last Frontier" Can Prosper and Matter* (London, Penguin)
Moulaye, Z, Diabaté, A and Doumbia, Y (2007) *Gouvernance de la justice au Mali* (Berlin, Friedrich Ebert Stiftung)
Muir Watt, H, Bizikova, L, Brandao de Oliveira, A and Fernández Arroyo, DP (eds) (2019) *Global Private International Law: Adjudication without Frontiers* (Cheltenham, Edward Elgar)
Murrey, A and Jackson, N (forthcoming) 'Africa and the Resource Curse Idea' in Falola, T and Mbah, E (eds) *Routledge Encyclopaedia of African Studies* (London, Routledge)
Mwangi, P (2001) *The Black Bar: Corruption and Political Intrigue within Kenya's Legal Fraternity* (Nairobi, Oakland Media Services Ltd)
Ngongo, E, Piret, B, Montel, L and le Polain de Waroux, P (2017) 'Prosopographie et biographie: regards croisés sur la magistrature coloniale belge' 40 *C@hiers du CRHIDI* [online] https://popups.uliege.be/1370-2262/index.php?id=356
Nollkaemper, A, d'Aspremont, J, Wouter, W and Gazzini, T (eds) (2017) *International Law as a Profession* (Cambridge, Cambridge University Press)
OECD (2018) '2. Africa' in *Development Aid at a Glance: Statistics by Region*, 2018 edn [online] www.oecd.org/dac/financing-sustainable-development/development-finance-data/africa-Development-Aid-at-a-Glance-2018.pdf
Ogle, V (2017) 'Archipelago Capitalism: Tax Havens, Offshore Money, and the State, 1950s–1970s' 122(5) *American Historical Review* 1431–1458
Oguamanam, C and Pue, W (2016) 'Lawyers' Professionalism, Colonialism, State Formation and National Life in Nigeria, 1900–1960: "The Fighting Brigade of the People"' in Pue, W (ed) *Lawyers' Empire: Legal Professions and Cultural Authority, 1780–1950* (Vancouver, UBC Press) 465–483
Olivetti, EA, Ceder, G, Gaustad, GG and Fu, X (2017) 'Lithium-Ion Battery Supply Chain Considerations: Analysis of Potential Bottlenecks in Critical Metals' 1 *Joule* 229–243

Ortiz, H (2021) 'A Political Anthropology of Finance: Studying the Distribution of Money in the Financial Industry as a Political Process' 21(1) *Anthropological Theory* 3–27

Ovadia, JS (2013) 'The Reinvention of Elite Accumulation in the Angolan Oil Sector: Emergent Capitalism in a Rentier Economy' 25 *Cadernos de Estudos Africanos* 33–63

Péan, P (2011) *La république des mallettes* (Paris, Fayard)

Pershad, A, Jain, AP and Suri, P (1961) *Motilal Nehru: A Short Political Biography* (Delhi, S. Chand and Co.)

Pellet, A (2013) 'Remarques cursives sur les contentieux "africains" devant la CIJ' in Kamga, M and Mbengue, M (eds) *Liber amicorum en l'honneur de Raymond Ranjeva: L'Afrique et le droit international: variations sur l'organisation internationale* (Paris, Pedone) 277–295

Pistor, K (2019) *The Code of Capital: How the Law Creates Wealth and Inequality* (Princeton and Oxford, Princeton University Press)

Plasman, P-L (2014a) 'Un État de non-droit? L'établissement du pouvoir judiciaire au Congo léopoldien 1885–1889' in Braillon, C, Montel, L, Piret, B and Plasman, PL (eds) *Droit et justice en Afrique coloniale: tradition, production et réformes* (Brussels, Université Saint-Louis) 27–49

(2014b) 'Le gouvernement bicéphale de l'État indépendant du Congo et le *red rubber*' in Van Schuylenbergh, P, Lanneau, C and Plasman, P-L (eds) *L'Afrique belge aux XIXè et XXè sicèles: Nouvelles recherches et perspectives en histoire coloniale* (Brussels, Peter Lang) 131–143

Power, S (2007) *'A Problem from Hell': America and the Age of Genocide* (New York City, Harper Perennial)

Pue, W (2016) *Lawyers' Empire: Legal Professions and Cultural Authority, 1780–1950* (Vancouver, UBC Press)

Puri, S (2021) *The Shadows of Empire: How Imperial History Shapes Our World* (Oakland, CA, Pegasus Books)

Raftopoulos, M (2017) 'Contemporary Debates on Social-Environmental Conflicts, Extractivism and Human Rights in Latin America' 21(4) *The International Journal of Human Rights* 387–404

Renucci, F and Rhétoré, T (2014) 'Juristes en coopération: Magistrats et professeurs de droit en Algérie des années 1960 au début des années 1980' 2 *Outre-Mers. Revue d'histoire* 187–210

Reynolds, E (1975) 'Economic Imperialism: The Case of the Gold Coast' 35(1) *The Journal of Economic History* 94–116

Richard, K (1988) 'Review, Imperial Appeal: The Debate on the Appeal to the Privy Council, 1833–1986' 4 *Connecticut Journal of International Law* 239–250

Rodney, W (1972) *How Europe Underdeveloped Africa* (London, Bogle-L'Ouverture Publications)

Romano, CPR (2003) 'The Americanization of International Litigation' 19(1) *Ohio State Journal on Dispute Resolution* 89–120

(2013) 'Trial and Error in International Judicialization' in Romano, C, Alter, K and Shany, Y (eds) *The Oxford Handbook on International Adjudication* (Oxford, Oxford University Press) 111–134

Rönnbäck, K and Broberg, O (2019) *Capital and Colonialism: The Return on British Investments in Africa 1869–1969* (London, Palgrave Macmillan)

Rosenblum, P (2016) 'Out of Storage: Law and Minerals in the African Oil Boom' Presentation at the Law and Society Annual conference, New Orleans, June 2–5

Sacriste, G and Vauchez, A (2007) 'The Force of International Law: Lawyers' Diplomacy on the International Scene in the 1920s' 32 *Law & Social Inquiry* 83–107

Schachter, O (1977–1978) 'The Invisible College of International Lawyers' 72(2) *Northwestern University Law Review* 217–226

Schill, S (2011) 'W(h)ither Fragmentation? On the Literature and Sociology of International Investment Law' 22(3) *The European Journal of International Law* 875–908

Schmidhauser, JR (1992) 'Legal Imperialism: Its Enduring Impact on Colonial and Post-Colonial Judicial System' 13(3) *International Political Science Review/Revue international de science politique* 321–334

(1997) 'The European Origins of Legal Imperialism and Its Legacy in Legal Education in Former Colonial Regions' 18 *International Political Science Review* 337–351

Scott-Smith, G (2007) 'Attempting to Secure an "Orderly Evolution": American Foundations, The Hague Academy of International Law and the Third World' 41 *Journal of American Studies* 509–532

Seabrooke, L and Wigan, D (2017) 'The Governance of Global Wealth Chains' 24 (1) *Review of International Political Economy* 1–29

Seroussi, J (2008) 'La cause de la compétence universelle: Note de recherche sur l'implosion d'une mobilisation internationale' 173 *Actes de la recherche en sciences sociales* 98–109

Shamir, R (2000) *The Colonies of Law: Colonialism, Zionism and Law in Early Mandate Palestine* (New York, Cambridge University Press)

Sharafi, M (2007) 'A New History of Colonial Lawyering: Likhovski and Legal Identities in the British Empire' 32(4) *Law and Social Inquiry* 1059–1094

Shaxson, N (2019) 'Tackling Tax Havens' *Finance & Development* 6–10 [online] www.imf.org/external/pubs/ft/fandd/2019/09/pdf/tackling-global-tax-havens-shaxon.pdf

Shepard, T (2015) '"Of Sovereignty": Disputed Archives, "Wholly Modern" Archives, and the Post-decolonization French and Algerian Republics, 1962–2012' 120(3) *American Historical Review* 869–883

Silver, J (1981) 'The Failure of European Mining Companies in the Nineteenth-Century Gold Coast' 22(4) *The Journal of African History* 511–529

Simonet, T (2010) 'Les composantes du pouvoir de Félix Houphouët-Boigny en Côte d'Ivoire (1958–1965)' 368–369 *Outre-Mers. Revue d'histoire* 403–420

Slinn, P (1971) 'Commercial Concessions and Politics during the Colonial Period: The Role of the British South Africa Company in Northern Rodhesia 1890–1964' 70(281) *African Affairs* 365–384

Smis, S, Kashironge, DN and Mushagalusa Rwabashi, JP (2021) 'The FG Hemisphere Case: Congo's Resistance to Investor-State Arbitration or Just a Malaise with Vulture Funds' 18(3) *Transnational Dispute Management* [online] www.transnational-dispute-management.com

Sookun, D (2010) *Stop Vulture Fund Lawsuits: A Handbook* (London, Commonwealth Secretariat)

Steinmetz, G (2007) *The Devil's Handwriting: Precoloniality and the German Colonial State in Qingdao, Samoa, and Southwest Africa* (Chicago, University of Chicago Press)

(2013) *Sociology and Empire: The Imperial Entanglements of a Discipline* (Durham, NC, Duke University Press)

(2014) 'Book Review "Focus on Pierre Bourdieu": Pierre Bourdieu, On the State: Lectures at the Collège de France 1989–1992, Cambridge Polity, 2014' 2014 *Sociologica* 3

Subrahmanyam, S (2004) *From Tagus to the Ganges: Explorations in Connected History* (New Delhi, Oxford University Press)

Swinfen, DB (1987) *Imperial Appeal: The Debate on the Appeal of the Privy Council, 1833–1986* (Manchester, Manchester University Press)

Terretta, M (2015) '*Cause lawyering* et anticolonialisme: activisme politique et État de droit dans l'Afrique française, 1946–1960' 138 *Politique africaine* 25–48

Terris, D, Romano, CPR and Swigart, L (2007) *The International Judge: An Introduction to the Men and Women Who Decide the World's Cases* (Oxford, Oxford University Press)

Thomas, DA and Kamari Clarke, M (2013) 'Globalization and Race: Structures of Inequality, New Sovereignties, and Citizenship in a Neoliberal Era' 42 *Annual Review of Anthropology* 305–325

Tilly, C (1985) 'War Making and State Making as Organized Crime' in Evans, P, Rueschemeyer, D and Skocpol, T (eds) *Bringing the State Back In* (Cambridge, Cambridge University Press) 169–191

Topalov, C (ed) (1999) *Laboratoires du nouveau siècle: La nébuleuse réformatrice et ses réseaux en France (1880–1914)* (Paris, Éditions de l'EHESS)

Tsuma, W (2012) 'Mining Sector Reforms in Ghana: Institutionalizing and Legitimizing Large-Scale Land Deals and Acquisitions in Rural Communities of Western Ghana' Presentation at African Studies Centre Leiden, 9 July

Turner, T (2007) *The Congo Wars: Conflict, Myth, and Reality*, 2nd edn (London, Zed Books)

UNCTAD (2018) *Trade and Development Report 2018* (New York and Geneva, United Nations)

(2022) *World Investment Report 2022: Investing in Sustainable Recovery* (New York and Geneva, United Nations)

Uzebu-Imarhiagbe, E (2020) 'Nigeria: An Account of Adaptation' in Abel, RL, Hammerslev, O, Sommerlad, H and Schultz, U (eds) *Lawyers in 21st Century Societies: Vol. I: National Reports* (Oxford, Hart Publishing) 515–534

Van Beemen, O (2019) *Heineken en Afrique: une multinationale décomplexée* (Brussels, Éditions Rue de l'échiquier)

Vandeginste, S (2010) *Stones Left Unturned: Law and Transitional Justice in Burundi* (Antwerp, Intersentia)

Van Doepp P (2009) *Judicial Politics in New Democracies: Cases from Southern Africa* (Boulder, Lynne Rienner)

Vauchez, A and France, P (2020) *The Neoliberal Republic: Corporate Lawyers, Statecraft, and the Making of Public-Private France* (Ithaca, NY, Cornell University Press)

Verhaegen, B (1985) *Les Safaris Technologiques au Zaïre* 18 *Politique africaine* 71–87

Vermeren, P (2002) *Ecole, élite et pouvoir au Maroc et en Tunisie au XXème siècle* (Rabat, Editions Alizée)

Vogel, CN (2022) *Conflict Minerals, Inc. War, Profit and White Saviourism in Eastern Congo* (London, Hurst)

Vondoepp, P (2005) 'The Problem of Judicial Control in Africa's Neopatrimonial Democracies: Malawi and Zambia' 120(2) *Political Science Quarterly* 275–301

Waibel, M, Kaushal, A, Chung, L and Balchin, C (eds) (2010) *The Backlash against Investment Arbitration: Perceptions and Reality* (London, Kluwer Law International)

Weill, S (2020) 'Transnational Jihadism and the Role of Criminal Judges: An Ethnography of French Courts' 47(S1) *Journal of Law and Society* 30–53

Willemez, L (1999) 'La "République des avocats": 1848: le mythe, le modèle et son endossement' in Offerlé, M (ed) *Profession politique XIXè-XXè siècle* (Paris, Belin) 201–229

Winters, J (2011) *Oligarchy* (Cambridge, Cambridge University Press)

World Bank (1989) *Sub-Saharan Africa: From Crisis to Sustainable Growth* (Washington, DC, World Bank)

(1998) *Assessing Aid: What Works, What Doesn't and Why* (Washington, DC, World Bank)

Yachir, F (1988) *Mining in Africa Today: Strategies and Prospects* (London, Zed Books, The United Nations University and The Third World Forum)

Young, C (1994) *The African Colonial State in Comparative Perspective* (New Haven and London, Yale University Press)

(2004) 'The End of the Post-colonial State in Africa? Reflections on Changing African Political Dynamics' 103 *African Affairs* 23–49

Zola, E (2019 [1871–1893]) Les Rougon-Macquart (Série intégrale) e-artnow (online edition)

INDEX

Abel, R, 4, 24, 26
Abi Saab, G, 219, 229
Achebe, C, 234
Adichie, CN, 233
African Legal Support Facility, 188, 198
African Union, 117, 124
Afrique Occidentale française, 46, 64
Agboyibor, P, 34–35, 37, 39, 196, 199
  Asafo & Co, 70, 196
Algeria, 26, 64, 77, 79, 187, 190, 229
Aluminium, 105, 110
Amnesty International, 41, 174, 191
Angola, 76, 99, 148, 177
AOF *See Afrique-Occidentale française*
arbitration, 101
  commercial arbitration, 116, 200, 218, 220, 223
  gunboat diplomacy, 94
  investment arbitration, 116, 197, 203–204, 206, 208–209, 217–219, 240
  mafia, 208, 219, 240
  professional market, 120, 194, 203, 209–210, 225, 230
archipelago capitalism, 96
articulation with capitalism, 4, 10, 16–17, 22, 47–48, 67, 97, 101, 115, 121, 180, 235
asylum seekers, 40, 42, 204, 206, 209, 214
AU *See African Union*
Avocats Sans Frontières, 5, 121, 152

Bayart, JF, 72, 82, 104, 156, 164, 185, 191
Beckett, H, 227
Bédié, HK, 157, 161
beer, 4, 105, 129–130, 132, 159
Belgium
  colonial projection, 82
  colonial question, 24
  Coopérants, 140
  crisis of development aid, 120
  legal imperialism, 68
Benton, L and Ford, L, 15, 28, 30, 43, 47–50, 70, 123, 151, 241
Berlin Congress, 42, 46, 60, 235
Bertrand, R, 14, 72
Bhandari, D, 224
Big Man politics, 72
Blas, J and Farchy, J, 23, 109–111, 167–169, 177
Bongo, O, 106, 182
Borrel, T, 79, 82, 105–106, 182–183, 185
Bourdieu, P, 32, 36, 205, 230
Bourdon, W, 174, 189–190
Bourgi, R, 181–182
Bourguiba, H, 69
Boutros-Ghali, B., 103
Breckenridge, K, 58, 73, 84–85
Bretton Woods system, 88–89, 108
British Virgin Islands, 11, 75, 90–91, 120
Brower, C, 219
Bullough, O, 71, 88-91, 96-97, 108
Burbank, J and Cooper, F, 29, 70, 238
Burkina Faso, 232
Burundi
  1993 war, 133
  Bar of Burundi, 126, 136, 142
  CNDD-FDD, 126
  Contentieux de 1993, 133, 135, 152
  decentralised despotism, 18, 128
  East African Court of Justice, 150

Burundi (cont.)
ethnicity, 87, 128, 132, 137, 152
ethnic violence, 137
European lawyers, 141
European traders, 138
legal professions, 134, 152
rule of law reforms, 42, 103, 120, 127
rush for rare earths, 18, 44, 126–127, 146, 240
Tanganyika Mining Burundi, 145
Buyoya, P, 129, 139, 141–143, 150–151

Caribbean Court of Justice, 118–119
CCJ *See Caribbean Court of Justice*
China
deal of the century, 2, 8
domination of green supply chain, 99, 126
economic take-off, 105
FCPA, 114, 241
Huayou Cobalt, 33
investment in Africa, 111, 241
investment in arbitration, 203
molybdenum, 33
city, 9, 12–13, 15, 43, 71, 85–86, 89, 109, 121, 177
Clinton, B., 103
CNDA *See Cour nationale du droit d'asile*
cobalt, 2–3, 5, 8–9, 21, 23, 25, 33–34, 59, 83–84, 98–99, 106, 108, 112, 115, 147, 239
cocoa, 4, 18, 56–58, 123, 154, 156–157, 159–167
code of capital, 112–113, 239
coffee, 4, 18, 129, 139–140, 143, 156–157, 164
Comaroff, J and Comaroff, J, 11, 28, 127, 155, 239
Comité Catholique contre la Faim, 191
Congo
artisanal mining, 33
colonial judiciary, 46, 60
Comptoirs, 5
Congo Free State, 45–46, 59, 68
deal of the century, 2, 8, 241
FG Hemisphere v DRC dispute, 1–3, 22, 25, 34, 39
Gécamines, 2, 6–12, 30, 33–34, 37, 43, 83–84, 106
High Council of the Congo, 17, 48, 60–61, 63, 69
new rush, 21, 107
postcolonial violence, 73, 75
Société générale, 62, 74
Stokes-Lothaire dispute, 17, 48, 60
Union Minière du Haut-Katanga, 11, 75, 83–84, 87
connex initiative, 125, 188, 199
Cooper, F, 16, 39
copper, 3, 8, 59, 75, 83–84, 98, 106, 108
Copperbelt *See Zambia*
corporate veil, 9, 115, 155
Côte d'Ivoire
civil war, 161, 163, 170
Cocoa OPEP, 166
economic growth, 158
Françafrique, 167
independence, 160
Ivoirité, 158
liberalisation of cocoa sector, 164
pre-independence political trials, 190
Probo Koala judicial saga, 156
Probo Koala scandal, 44, 169–170
Cour nationale du droit d'asile, 40, 42, 204–205, 207–208, 210, 213, 215, 220, 230
courtroom politics, 64, 190–191
Crawford, J, 222
critical minerals, 3–4, 13, 43, 98–99, 114, 235–236, 239
Cultural Cold War, 64, 66, 72, 94
cutting edge, 5, 29, 234

deregulation, 42–43, 100, 107, 115, 122, 156–157, 159, 164, 179, 241
Dezalay Y and Garth, BG, 23, 32, 43, 94, 107, 120, 216, 218, 222–223, 229
Diallo, D, 81, 200
Diallo, S, 200–201
Didi nee Sharma, S, 66
digital minerals *See Critical minerals*
digital revolution, 3–4
Dossou Aworet, S, 186
double agents, 32

double-edged protection, 16, *See legal imperialism*
DRC *See Congo*
Duffield, 102, 103

EACJ *See East African Court of Justice*
East African Court of Justice, 119–120, 150–151
Economic Community of West African States, 154
Elf, 79, 105, 187
Elias, TO, 45, 227
Ellis, S, 12, 40, 101–102
energy transition, 4, 17, 23, 98, 147
Enron scandal, 187
Eurodollars, 89, 108
Euromarket, 107, 109
European Union, 3, 23, 115, 202, 215
extraction
  concession model, 17, 73–74, 77, 83, 238
  geography of extraction, 18, 100–101, 115, 118, 121
  new extraction, 104
  predatory, 8, 12, 18, 26, 32, 45, 100, 126
  rent of extraction, 28, 43, 68, 83, 96, 238
extraversion, 18, 37, 128, 140, 152, 240

FCPA *See Foreign Corrupt Practices Act*
Fédération internationale pour les droits humains, 189
Ferguson, J, 12, 28, 87
FG Hemisphere, 1, 3-4, 7, 12–13, 33
FIDH *See Fédération internationale pour les droits humains*
field theory, 32, 235
financial curse, 11, 100, 236
financialisation, 5–6, 8, 11–13, 18, 21, 23, 26, 28, 31, 37, 39, 101, 108–110, 156, 179, 183, 187, 196
Foreign Corrupt Practices Act, 113–114, 121, 123
Forster, I, 95, 226
France
  colonial projection, 36, 38, 77, 79, 95, 226
  Conseil d'État, 81, 184–185, 210, 215
  Coopérants, 80
  devaluation of CFA franc, 105
  Doctrine d'Abidjan, 105
  Françafrique, 19, 38, 71, 79–80, 105, 167, 177, 180–182, 184–185, 200
  military and judicial cooperation, 129
    National Court of Asylum *See CNDA*
  neoliberal turn, 105
  postcolonial block, 77, 79, 105, 156, 177
  Pré carré, 19, 77, 104–105, 121, 156, 181, 193
  Union Française, 64, 71, 95, 227

Gabon, 79, 106, 182
Galanter, M, 107, 205, 208
gatekeeping politics, 17–18, 31, 59, 70, 101, 121, 123, 159, 179–180, 220, 238
Gbagbo, L, 118, 154, 157–158, 165, 170, 176, 182
genesis of international justice institutions, 62, 95
gentlemen politicians of law, 96, 221, 226
Gertler, D, 113, 241
Ghana
  African traders, 56
  Asafo, 55, 57
  Asante Empire, 35, 54, 56
  Asante lawyers, 68, 88, 240
  cocoa OPEC, 166
  European merchants, 56
  Gold Coast, 17, 47, 54, 56–59, 70, 92, 162
  Gold Coast Colony and Protectorate, 55
  legal profession, 123
  Privy Council disputes, 58–59, 67
  scramble for concessions, 57
Gide Loyrette Nouel, 192, 196
Gide, P, 192, 196
Glencore, 23, 108–109, 111, 113–114, 122, 146, 167, 169
global traders, 148, 176, 241
global turn, epistemic, 13, 235
global value chains, 4, 6–8, 12–14, 20, 22–23, 25–26, 28, 31, 37, 39, 41, 155–156, 196, 235

Gobe, E, 27, 51, 69
gold, 21, 54, 56–57, 75, 82, 87–89, 123, 125, 144, 146, 150
Gold Coast *See Ghana*
good governance, 102, 120, 125, 128, 146
Great Lakes region, 3, 45, 73, 77, 82, 102, 120, 132, 235
Greenpeace, 170, 172, 174
Guillaumat, P, 79
Guinea, 78, 201, 204–207, 210

Heineken, 129–131
Herbert Smith Freehills, 186, 194, 196, 200
hollow core, 216, 220, 231
Hong Kong, 2, 124, 241
  Common Law, 242
  handover to China, 2
  Hong Kong Stock Exchange, 2
Houphouët-Boigny, F, 70, 104, 156–161, 163–164, 166, 182
Hunte, L, 75, 91

Ibhawoh, B, 29, 50, 52, 58, 68, 92–93
ICC *See International Criminal Court*
ICC in Paris, 1, 194, 203, 226
ICJ *See International Court of Justice*
ICSID, 42, 123, 150, 152, 154, 204, 207, 210, 213, 217–220, 226, 231
IFIs *See international financial institutions*
Ignacio-Pinto, L, 227
imperial entanglement, 16, 20–21, 24, 235
imperialism of the free trade, 60
imperialism on the cheap, 29, 31, 44, 46–47
Institut de droit international, 61–63, 96, 185
interconnectedness, 20, 28, 32
international business company, 91, 238
International Centre for Settlement of Investment Disputes of the World Bank Group *See ICSID*
International Court of Arbitration of the Paris International Chamber of Commerce *See ICC in Paris*
International Court of Justice, 42, 63, 93, 95, 116, 185, 208, 219, 221–224, 226–227, 229–231, 240
  international bar of the ICJ, 117, 219, 223, 228, 240
International Criminal Court, 3, 5, 41, 95, 116–118, 121, 131, 152, 158, 189, 203, 215–216, 220, 231, 240
international financial institutions, 17, 34, 101, 104, 128, 158, 163–164, 166, 186, 235
International Law Commission, 221, 225, 227
International Monetary Fund, 99, 157
investor-state dispute settlement, 117, 123
invisible college of international law, 62, 221
Israël, L, 67, 211

JCPC *See Privy Council*
Jeantet, 37, 192, 194, 196
Jersey, 2–3, 9, 12, 91
Judicial Committee of the Privy Council *See Privy Council*
judicialisation, 25, 54, 62, 116, 154, 156, 212, 220, 230–231, 237
Jurisconsult, 32, 209, 221, 225, 227, 235

Kabila, J, 35, 107, 132
Katanga, 8, 60, 106
Keïta, M, 80–81
Kenya, 26, 38, 52–53, 66, 87
Kenyatta, J, 65–66, 70
Klaaren, J, 27
Kolwezi, 33

lawfare, 155, 157, 165, 240
lawyering, 42, 239
legal imperialism, 16, 26, 43, 46, 51, 54, 68, 121
  co-optation of legal elites, 47, 53, 94, 96, 229
  double-edged protection, 22, 29, 44, 237
  indirect rule, 29, 39, 43, 48, 53, 60, 68, 138, 237
  institutional and legal revival, 116, 119–120, 135, 217, 221

legal intermediation, 14, 25, 34, 36, 121, 151
legal lumpiness, 18, 43, 48–49, 89, 156, 160, 162, 169
legal ordering, 15, 68–69, 118, 122, 237, 239, 241
  boundary making, 19, 30, 33, 44, 205, 211, 213, 240
  jurisdictional authority, 101
  jurisdictional claims, 97
legal transplants, 72
Legendre, P, 36, 77
Leigh Day, 155, 171, 175
Leopold II, 45, 59–63, 69
Lepaulle, P, 192
Levi, R, 14, 213
Lex extractiva, 187
Lex mercatoria, 31, 116, 218
Ligue des droits de l'homme et du citoyen, 190
LME *See London Metal Exchange*
London Metal Exchange, 9, 21, 99, 111
Lonsdale, J, 16, 35, 38–40, 47, 49, 51, 53–55, 57, 85–86, 121
Luckham, R, 57–59, 77, 88, 123
Lumumba, P, 75–76, 81

Mali, 80, 221, 226
Manirakiza, C, 125–127, 144, 146
Martens, FF, 62, 69
Mbaye, K, 185
Mbembe, A, 205
Médecins sans frontières, 120
middle power, 16, 39, 47, 49, 68, 74, 91, 97, 101, 121, 123, 177, 236–237, 240
middling capital, 17, 30–31, 39, 44, 48, 65, 68, 70–71, 177, 238
Mobutu Sese Seko, 106
Mobutu, J, 76
modernisation reforms, 72, 74, 96
moral imperialism, 94
multi-positionality, 62, 96, 215, 225
Mwangi, P, 72, 87

Ndadaye, M, 128, 130, 142–143, 152
neoliberal turn, 10, 12, 17, 19, 42–43, 101, 104–105, 108, 179, 181, 183, 235
New International Economic Order, 74, 108, 217, 229
NIEO *See New International Economic Order*
Niger, 79
Nigeria, 45, 53, 226, 234
Nkrumah, K, 38, 59, 74, 82, 87
Nkurunziza, P, 126, 129, 131, 134, 143–145, 150
nurture capitalism, 121

OECD, 3, 33–34, 83, 101–103, 146
Official Development Assistance, 7, 102
offshore capitalism, 11, 17–18, 43, 74, 89, 96, 101, 121, 157, 176–177, 236, 238
offshore justice, 3, 11–12, 18, 43, 74, 89, 91, 96, 100–101, 107, 120–121, 157, 176–177, 194, 199, 204, 213, 215, 223, 236, 238
Ogle, V, 48, 89–90, 96, 107–108
Oguamanam, C and Pue, W, 51–52, 54, 81
OHADA, 35, 185, 201, 203, 210
oil shocks, 105, 108
Onyema, CD, 227
Organisation for Economic Cooperation and Development *See OECD*
Organisation for the Harmonisation of Business Law in Africa *See OHADA*
Ouattara, A, 157–158, 165, 177
Ould-Abdallah, A., 103

Paulsson, J, 223
PCA *See Permanent Court of Arbitration*
PCIJ *See Permanent Court of International Justice*
Pellet, A, 221, 228
Permanent Court of Arbitration, 42, 63, 95, 116, 152, 218
Permanent Court of International Justice, xii, 42, 63, 95, 116, 210
Philippines, 94
Pistor, K, 9, 18, 101, 112, 115, 236, 239

political trials
  pre-independence, 63
  pre-independence British Empire, 65
  pre-independence French Empire, 64
Pritt, DN, 65–66
Privy Council, 1–4, 9–11, 17, 25, 38–39, 43, 48–49, 53–54, 58–59, 63, 65, 67–68, 70, 74, 86, 91–93, 118

Quatre Communes, 51, 95

Rainbow Rare Earths, 126, 145–146, 148
real post-colonial order, 40, 104, 240
regulatory state, 180, 183, 189
repeat players, 112, 208, 211, 216, 222, 230
re-regulation, 43, 100, 115, 241
resource curse, 12, 25
Riegels, M, 90–91
Rolin Jacquemyns, G, 62–63, 69
Rufyikiri, I, 151
rule of law reforms, 18, 42, 128, 133

Sankara, T, 232
Schmidhauser, JR, 45, 53
secrecy jurisdictions, 9, 14, 96, 178
sedimented imperialism, 44, 97, 120, 122, 236, 241
Segatwa, F, 142
Sizimwe, S, 152
Société Générale, 61
South Africa, 26, 45, 77
  Anglo–Boer War, 85
  Anglovaal, 147
  apartheid, 110
  corporate law, 195
  De Beers corporation, 86
  mining industry, 17, 74
  monopsonist contracts, 86
sovereign debt, 8, 187
sovereignty, 24, 32, 44, 48–49, 70, 93, 108, 148, 235, 238
  bifurcation, 128, 153, 176, 240
  flows and counterflows, 29–30, 236, 238
  layered, 17, 29, 48–49, 85, 92, 96, 240
Steinmetz, G, 16, 20, 24, 30, 39, 206
strategic litigation, 14, 25, 40, 155
structural adjustment programs, 6, 101, 105–106, 180, 187
structural banality, 30, 238
Subrahmanyam, S, 28
Swashbuckler capitalism, 18, 112, 236
symbolic capital, 70, 134, 184, 231, 238
  bank of symbolic credit, 184
  valuation, 13, 15, 25, 39, 213, 240

Tanganyika Gold, 144, 146
tax havens, 4, 9, 11, 13, 90, 101, 107, 178
  Delaware, 1, 3, 90
The Hague, 17, 41, 62, 74, 95, 115, 216, 225, 229, 238
Tilly, C, 13, 16, 22, 31–32
total, 189, 194–195
trafigura, 33–34, 108–109, 114, 122, 146, 154–155, 157, 168–171, 173–177
transnational corporations, 5–7, 9, 32, 35, 99, 107, 109, 114, 125, 147, 150, 172, 201, 218, 235
  Big 4, 129
  mining giants, 17, 23, 74, 84
  seven sisters, 23
transparency International, 188
Tunisia, 27, 38, 50–51, 79, 229
Twiss, T, 61

UN High Commissioner for Human Rights, 126–127, 133
UN High Commissioner for Refugees, 40, 142
United Nations, 8, 40, 73, 76, 103, 168
United States Agency for International Development, 103
US Foundations, 72
US Regulation Q, 89
US Supreme Court, 211, 231

Vauchez, A, 28, 30, 32, 36, 95–96, 179, 181, 183, 185, 189, 191–192, 221
vulture funds, 1, 7–8

Waldock, CHM, 228
Wall Street model of the corporate law firm, 18, 44, 70, 101, 121, 179, 181, 200–201, 236, 239

corporate lawyers, 34, 112, 122, 124, 179–180, 184–185, 195, 200, 203, 218
Willemez, L, 32
World Bank, 8, 35, 41, 102–103, 105–106, 123, 150, 158, 165, 185, 188, 197, 204, 217
Yuma, A, 10, 35, 107

Zaire *See Congo*
Zambia, 33, 83–84, 87, 99
copperbelt, 84, 86
Zimbabwe, 27, 171
Zola, E, 233

Printed by Integrated Books International,
United States of America